PHP and MySQL Manual

Springer

London
Berlin
Heidelberg
New York
Hong Kong
Milan
Paris
Tokyo

Simon Stobart and Mike Vassileiou

PHP and MySQL Manual

Simple, yet Powerful Web Programming

Springer

Simon Stobart, BA (Hons), PhD
School of Computing and Technology
University of Sunderland
Sunderland SR6 0DD
UK

Mike Vassileiou
iNET4U
Greece

British Library Cataloguing in Publication Data
Stobart, Simon
  PHP and MySQL manual : simple, yet powerful Web programming
  1. MySQL (Computer file) 2. PHP (Computer program language)
  3. Web sites - Design
  I. Title II. Vassileiou, Mike
  005.2'762
  ISBN 1852337478

Library of Congress Cataloging-in-Publication Data
A catalog record for this book is available from the Library of Congress

ISBN 1-85233-747-8 Springer-Verlag London Berlin Heidelberg
Springer-Verlag is part of Springer Science+Business Media
springeronline.com

Typeset by Sunrise Setting Ltd, Torquay, Devon, UK
Printed and bound at The Cromwell Press, Trowbridge, Wiltshire, UK
34/3830-543210 Printed on acid-free paper SPIN 10930007

Simon would like to dedicate this book to his parents, Ann and Ken Stobart

Mike would like to dedicate this book to Olga and his parents

Contents

Part 1

Getting Started

Introduction

1

Welcome

Welcome to the PHP manual, the book that will show you how to create dynamic Web sites that interact with people and make the development of sophisticated Web-based applications a possibility.

About PHP

PHP (PHP Hypertext Pre-processor) is a HyperText Markup Language (HTML) embedded scripting language. The goal of the language is to enable the construction of dynamic Web pages quickly and easily. PHP works in conjunction with a Web server and can be used with a variety of operating systems, including Microsoft Windows and UNIX.

PHP differs from other Common Gateway Interface (CGI) scripts, written in languages like Perl or C, as they require you to create separate programs, which output HTML. PHP is different because it is embedded within your HTML document with special start and end tags that allow you to enter and exit PHP. This provides quick page display time, high security and transparency to the end user. With PHP you can achieve all that can be accomplished by writing separate CGI applications, such as creating dynamic Web pages, form processing and file handling.

PHP syntax is similar to that of the C, C++ and Java programming languages. If you have some knowledge of these languages you will find the PHP language very familiar. If you have no experience of these languages don't worry, PHP is simple and easy to get to grips with.

One of the most important and strongest facilities of PHP is its ability to interface to a wide range of databases. Over 20 different databases are currently supported, allowing the PHP developer to create database-enabled Web pages easily. We will be using the MySQL database later.

Is this Book for You?

When creating this book we had in mind the type of individual we were expecting would want to read it. If you are:

(1) a practicing software engineer wishing to migrate your software development skills in order to be able to create Web-based applications;

(2) a professional Web site developer wishing to learning how to create more powerful dynamic Web applications using PHP;

(3) an intranet developer working for a company wishing to extend its networked applications using dynamic Web technology;

(4) a new graduate who has to learn how to program using PHP very quickly; or

(5) a student on a undergraduate or postgraduate degree that is required to develop a dynamic Web system as part of a project;

then we think this book is for you.

What We Assume about You …

We assume that you:

(1) know how to use a Microsoft Windows or UNIX computer reasonably well;

(2) know how to program Web pages using HTML;

(3) have some limited experience of scripting languages such as Javascript; and

(4) may have had some programming experience using languages such as C, Visual Basic, Java or COBOL.

If the above describes you then you will find that this book is targeted and written for you.

How to Use this Book

This book has been written for you to read from start to finish. Later chapters build upon the knowledge and ideas introduced in earlier ones. Once you have worked your way through the book you will be able to refer to individual chapters if you wish to refresh your knowledge of a particular aspect of the PHP language.

How this Book is Organized

This book is divided into chapters which cover specific aspects of the PHP language. The chapters themselves are grouped together into sections which address more general areas of the language.

Section One introduces the PHP language, explains how to set up a development environment and introduces you to your first PHP scripts.

Chapter 2 provides an introduction and overview to the PHP language.

Chapter 3 explains how to create a PHP development environment and where help and assistance can be sought.

Chapter 4 introduces Your First PHP Program.

Chapter 5 deals with PHP fundamentals.

Section Two introduces the basic PHP language constructs, variables and expressions.

Chapter 6 introduces PHP variables and types.

Chapter 7 examines Boolean, integer and floating point types.

Chapter 8 introduces the string type.

Chapter 9 explains the concept of predefined PHP variables and how to assess them.

Chapter 10 considers expressions, operands and operators.

Chapter 11 explains the if and switch constructs and illustrates how conditional and Boolean operators can be used within these constructs.

Chapter 12 describes the various loops which can be used with PHP.

Chapter 13 examines the concept of functional decomposition, function creation and include files.

Chapter 14 explains the concept of arrays.

Chapter 15 introduces dates, times and random numbers and how these can be accessed.

Section Three examines how the string and array types can be manipulated using various PHP standard functions.

Chapter 16 examines array manipulation.

Chapter 17 examines string manipulation.

Section Four introduces the concept of user interaction and explains how using forms users can interact with PHP applications.

Chapter 18 explains how your scripts can interact with the user.

Chapter 19 explains form data validation and adapt retention.

Chapter 20 examines form data security issues

Chapter 21 explains how you can use PHP to e-mail people.

Section Five explains two methods in which data can be retained from one Web page to another, i.e. cookies and sessions.

Chapter 22 introduces the concept of cookies.

Chapter 23 explains sessions and session management.

Section Six examines how errors can be handled by your scripts and how output to Web pages can be buffered and the contents of the buffer adjusted.

Chapter 24 examines error handling.

Chapter 25 explains how to buffer and modify Web page output.

Section Seven introduces the concept of file handling.

Chapter 26 explains how you can read and write data to files.

Chapter 27 looks in more detail into further things that can be done with files.

Chapter 28 explains how files can be uploaded to a server using forms.

Section Eight introduces the concept of graphical manipulation.

Chapter 29 examines simple graphic manipulation.

Chapter 30 introduces the GD library and explains how this can be used to create new graphical images dynamically.

Chapter 31 illustrates how the GD library can be used to create a useful graph application.

Section Nine looks into the concept of generating non-Web page documents through the PDF library extension.

Chapter 32 introduces PDF document generation.

Section Ten examines the concept of linking a database to a Web site using the MySQL database management system.

Chapter 33 introduces database table design.

Chapter 34 explains how the MySQL database and the PHPmyadmin can be installed.

Chapter 35 explains how you can configure the MySQL database.

Chapter 36 introduces how PHP can be used to interface with a MySQL database.

Section Eleven describes the object paradigm and describes how PHP can be used to create object-oriented applications.

Chapter 37 introduces the object-oriented concepts of classes and objects.

Chapter 38 continues the object-oriented theme, with an examination of class inheritance.

Finally, Section Twelve describes an e-commerce application which has been built, putting into practice all the knowledge described within the previous sections of this book.

Chapter 39 describes the front end e-commerce system.

Chapter 40 describes the e-commerce administration system.

PHP Scripts

This book includes many example scripts all of which have been tested with the latest version of the PHP environment. These scripts are available for download from the book Web site, www.phpmysql-manual.com, to save you the trouble of typing them in. However, it must be said that quite often more can be learnt from the activity of typing in your own examples and you may choose to do exactly that.

Off You Go . . .

Well, there is nothing more left to say than to turn the page and proceed to the next chapter. We hope you enjoy reading our book as much as we did writing it.

Introduction to PHP

2

Introduction

In this chapter we shall introduce you to PHP. We shall describe what PHP is, its history and its popularity. Let us begin by looking at exactly what PHP is.

What is PHP?

"PHP (a recursive acronym for: 'PHP Hypertext Preprocessor') is an open-source scripting language . . . for creating dynamic Web pages for e-commerce and other Web applications" (www.zend.com/zend/aboutphp.php). Dynamic Web pages are those which do not simply remain the same each time they are viewed, but instead interact with the user, enabling a richer, more interesting Web experience. Dynamic Web systems are used particularly in commercial e-commerce systems, which interact with databases enabling users to select and purchase products on-line.

PHP is freely available from www.php.net and is both a simple yet powerful solution for developing dynamic Web systems. PHP is actually embedded within HTML pages and thus enables the script instructions to be included in exactly the location where they are required.

PHP is widely supported by a large on-line community and its an open-source product. This community provides excellent support to developers and any bugs are quickly reported and fixed as the core PHP code is continuously improved and updated.

PHP has excellent database connectivity to a large number of databases (such as Oracle, MySQL) as well as integration with various external libraries which enable PHP to generate graphical images and PDF documents for example.

Finally, PHP is platform independent, in that it runs on UNIX and Windows platforms equally well.

The History of PHP

The history of PHP can be traced back to 1995. Since those early days PHP has undergone significant changes and improvement, resulting in the release of PHP version 5.0 in June 2003. Table 2.1 has been adapted from www.php.net/manual/en/history.php and describes the various major releases of the language since its original conception.

7

Table 2.1 PHP history.

Version	Description
PHP/FI Date: 1995	In 1995 Rasmus Lerdorf created a set of Perl scripts for tracking accesses to his Web system. These scripts where originally known as "Personal Home Page Tools". The original scripts were rewritten in the C programming language and were improved with greater functionality. This included database communication and enabled the development of simple Web applications. This version was known as Personal Home Page/Forms Interpreter and was released to the general public
PHP/FI 2.0 Date: 1997	In November 1997 PHP/FI 2.0 was officially released. At this time 50,000 domains reported that they had this software installed
PHP 3.0 Date: 1997	PHP 3.0 was the first version of PHP which looks similar to the version which we use today. It was created by Andi Gutmans and Zeev Suraki as a rewrite of PHP/FI 2.0 for a University e-commerce project. Andi Gutmans and Zeev Suraki decided to cooperate with Rasmus Lerdorf and announced PHP 3.0 as the official successor to PHP/FI 2.0
	Key features of PHP 3.0 were its strong extensibility, database connectivity and support for the object oriented paradigm
	The PHP 3.0 language was released under a new name – PHP, with the name being a recursive acronym – PHP Hypertext Preprocessor
	By the end of 1998 PHP 3.0 was installed on approximately 10% of the Web servers on the Internet
PHP 4 Date: 1999	In the winter of 1998 Andi Gutmans and Zeev Suraki had begun to rewrite the PHP core, in order to improve performance of complex applications. The new core engine was named "Zend Engine", the name being derived from their first names "Zeev and Andi"
PHP 5 Date: 2003	Released in beta version in mid-2003 PHP 5.0 is the latest release of the language and has at its core the new Zend Engine 2.0

But How Popular is PHP Really?

The popularity of PHP is huge and is growing. It is often difficult to determine a precise figure of how popular a programming language is as there are a number of different ways in which this can be measured. However, the Netcraft survey provides a measure of the amount of domains and Internet provider addresses which are using PHP. Figure 2.1 illustrates the latest Netcraft survey statistics (www.php.net/usage.php) which shows the growth of PHP usage since January 1999.

In another measure the TIOBE Programming Community Index (TPCI) gives an indication of the popularity of programming languages. As of July 2003 PHP was ranked the sixth most popular language currently used, as shown by the graph in Figure 2.2.

Web Servers and Common Gateway Interface

One of the main problems with HTML documents are that they are static as they can only display the same content each time they are accessed. Figure 2.3 illustrates a traditional Web server receiving a request for a specific Web page and serving this to the Web browser.

Dynamic Web pages on the other hand, are Web pages whose content is produced automatically by a program each time the page is accessed.

A standard for such programs emerged in the early days of the Web. The standard, known as the Common Gateway Interface (programs which comply with it are often known as CGI scripts) basically specifies how a Web server will pass data to a program when it

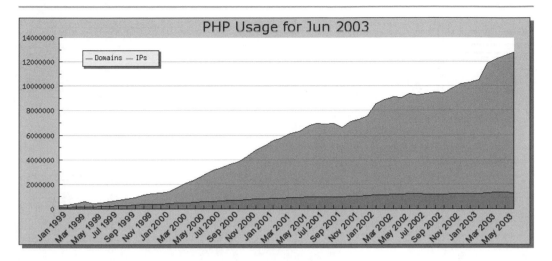

Figure 2.1 Netcraft survey.

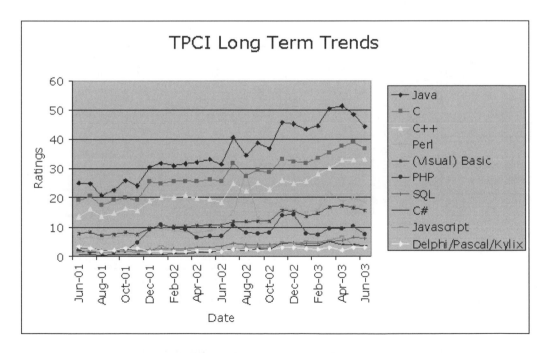

Figure 2.2 TPCI. Popularity of programming languages.

executes. CGI scripts can be written in a wide variety of languages including Perl, C, TCL etc.

But, how do CGI scripts work? Well, consider the diagram in Figure 2.4. Here CGI processing begins when a browser requests a document (which in this case is a CGI application) from a Web server. The browser doesn't care whether the requested page is a

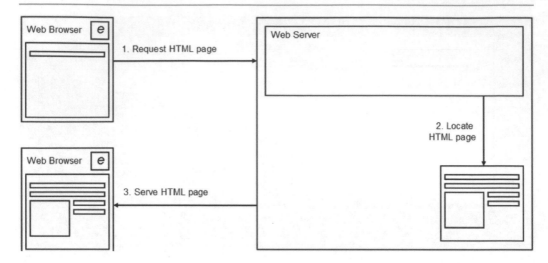

Figure 2.3 Serving a HTML page.

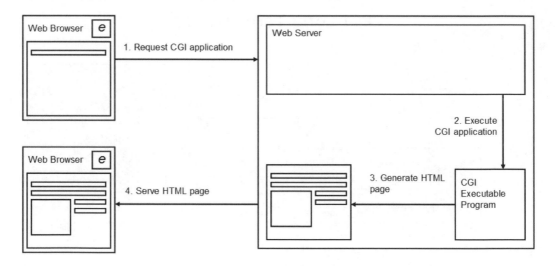

Figure 2.4 Dynamic Web page generation with CGI.

static HTML document or a CGI script, it just sends the request to the Web server. The Web server recognizes the request for a CGI script and executes the specific CGI application. The CGI script does whatever it has been programmed to do and outputs some standard HTML. This output is served to the browser for displaying as a Web page.

The main problem with CGI applications is that the HTML instructions which control the format of the dynamic information produced by the applications tend to get lost amid the program code. This effect makes it more difficult to produce attractive, easy to use dynamic Web pages which also has an impact on maintenance.

How Does PHP Work?

The PHP approach to dynamic Web pages is different in one major respect; instead of the HTML being embedded into program code, a PHP script has the program code embedded into the HTML. Figure 2.5 illustrates how a PHP script works.

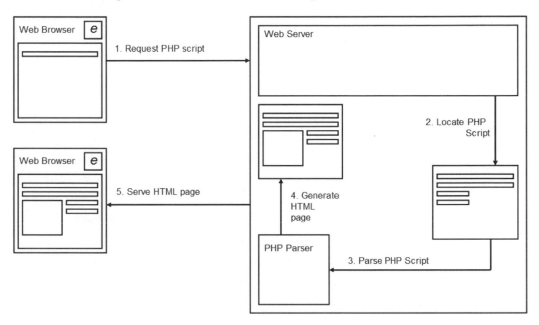

Figure 2.5 Dynamic Web page generation with PHP.

Figure 2.5 illustrates that when a browser requests a PHP script, the Web server runs the PHP parser and passes that interpreter any data supplied by the browser as well as the PHP script itself. The PHP script is processed by the parser. Any HTML in the script is passed straight back to the browser, but any program code therein is executed and any output fed back to the browser as well. The important thing to note here is that it is the responsibility of the PHP programmer to ensure that the PHP code outputs valid HTML syntax otherwise the browser will be unable to display it correctly.

Summary

In this chapter we have introduced the PHP language and described its development history. We have shown that PHP is widely used and that its use is still growing. In the next chapter we shall examine how and where you can obtain a copy of PHP and associated applications in order to create your own PHP development environment.

Environment Installation, Help and Assistance

3

Introduction

In this chapter we shall explain where you can obtain the software to create your own PHP development environment. If your service provider or Web administrator has already installed a Web server, PHP and associated applications you can ignore the first part of this chapter. What you should not ignore is the section where we shall explain where you can go for help if you run into any problems when you begin to create your own PHP applications. We shall explain where and how to access the PHP manual and introduce you to some other on-line resources which are very useful for the PHP developer to know about.

What Software Do I Need?

In order to begin PHP development you will need the following software:
- A Web browser
- A Web server
- PHP
- A text editor
- A database

Depending on your operating system, personal tastes and maybe organizational requirements there is a great deal of choice available for each of these applications. Let us examine each of these in turn.

Web Browser

The Web browser is the application, which is used to view the output from your HTML/PHP scripts. The two most common browsers are Microsoft Internet Explorer and Netscape. For Microsoft Windows users the easiest of these to obtain is Internet Explorer as it is included as part of the Windows operating system. Netscape is also a popular choice, especially for UNIX users. Both browsers are continually being updated and improved. You can obtain the latest version of Internet Explorer from www.microsoft.com/windows/ie/ and the latest version of Netscape from home.netscape.com/uk/download/.

Web Server

The second item of software that is required is a Web server. A Web server receives requests for Web documents from Web clients (the browsers), which it obtains and serves to the Web browser for display. While, it is possible to develop HTML scripts on a standalone computer without the need for a Web server, it is not possible if you wish to use PHP.

There are many different Web servers available across various different operating systems. Some are powerful and expensive commercial products and others while still being high quality, professionally developed products are free.

We would recommend the Apache Web server for UNIX system, available from: http://httpd.apache.org/download.cgi. For Windows platforms either Microsofts Internet Information Services server, which comes with Windows XP and Windows 2000, also available from www.microsoft.com/downloads/. In addition, we would recommend Appserv available from http://appserv.sourceforge.net/. As each Web server is different you will need to read and follow the installation guidelines for each product separately.

PHP

In order to view PHP scripts successfully you will need to download a copy of PHP. This is available for download from the PHP site at www.php.net. You will need to download the correct version of PHP for your operating system and configure both PHP and your Web server to work together. Most Web servers provide instructions on how to do this. But, don't worry, keep reading there is an easier solution which we shall get to shortly.

Text Editor

In order to begin creating HTML and PHP scripts you will need a text editor to edit your scripts. Any text editor will do and many people have their favourites. Emacs and vi are particular favourites with UNIX users and Windows comes with Notepad, a very simple but not very powerful text editor. We have used Notepad to create all the examples in this book, however, you may wish to use a text editor which you are more comfortable with but it really doesn't matter.

Database – MySQL

The final component you will require is a database. PHP works with a large number of different databases (see the PHP documentation for a full list), but we have selected to use the MySQL database because it is free and very powerful. MySQL is open source and can be downloaded from http://www.mysql.com/ for both Unix and Windows platforms.

MySQL doesn't come with a very friendly user interface. However, as we shall see later in the book help is at hand through the PHPMyAdmin tool which enables us to configure our MySQL databases quickly and easily. PHPMyAdmin is available from http://www.phpmyadmin.net/.

Software Bundles – All in One

Now one of the first things that people new to PHP say is "Wow, that's a lot of different software to get. How am I going to ensure that it all installs and works correctly?" Well, the good news is that you are not alone in thinking this and many others have struggled with the same problem. The solution that has been developed is the application bundle. To make things easier for the novice (and to a large extent the expert) the latest versions of all the software you require to begin PHP development have been bundled together in a single download and have been configured to work correctly with one another. There are a number of different bundles to choose from and many of these are listed on the hotscripts Web site: http://www.hotscripts.com/PHP/Software_and_Servers/Installation_Kits/

For Windows users we would recommend the Appserv Open project which comes with the latest version of AppServ server, PHP, MySQl and phpMyAdmin. This can be found at http://appserv.sourceforge.net/. It is very easy to download and install.

Getting Help and Assistance

No matter how much of a PHP expert you will become there will be some point in time where you will become stuck and may wish to obtain some help and assistance. You may obtain this assistance from the PHP manual or from other sources. In the remainder of this chapter we shall examine where the best places are to get help and guidance.

Read the PHP Manual!

The PHP manual is available on-line in a variety of languages. Point your browser to www.php.net/docs.php to select your language of choice and whether you wish to view a printer friendly or more graphically rich documentation. Figure 3.1 illustrates an example of what the on-line manual looks like.

For those of you who wish to have your own copy of the manual for reference off-line then you can download a variety of different language and manual formats. Table 3.1 lists the different document types that are available for download.

Table 3.1 Downloadable document formats.

Type	Description
Single HTML	A single very large HTML file containing the complete manual
Many HTML	A tar file (compressed) of many smaller HTML documents making up the complete manual
PDF	The manual in PDF format which can be viewed using Adobe Acrobat. This file can be installed on a pocket PC as long as a pocket PC version of Adobe Acrobat reader is installed
PalmPilot DOC	A DOC file standard for the PalmPilot
Palmilot iSilo	A iSilo file standard for the PalmPilot
Windows HTML Help	A .chm file format for windows

Note that not all formats listed in Table 3.1 are available in all languages.

Of the downloadable manuals available we find the .chm help file format for Windows very useful. The file provides a typical Windows help file which enables the user to

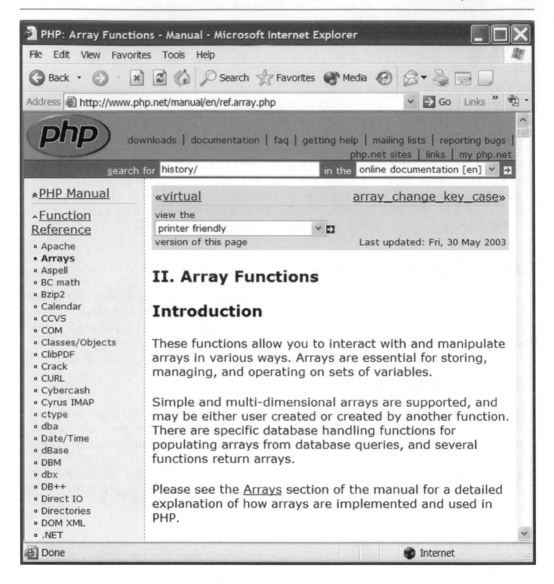

Figure 3.1 On-line PHP manual.

search for information quickly and easily and have this displayed in an easily to read and convenient way. Figure 3.2 illustrates what the Windows help file looks like when viewing its content on control structures.

MySQL Manual

The MySQL database which we shall be using later in this book to create dynamic database applications has a comprehensive set of documentation which can be downloaded. This documentation comes in a variety of formats, similar

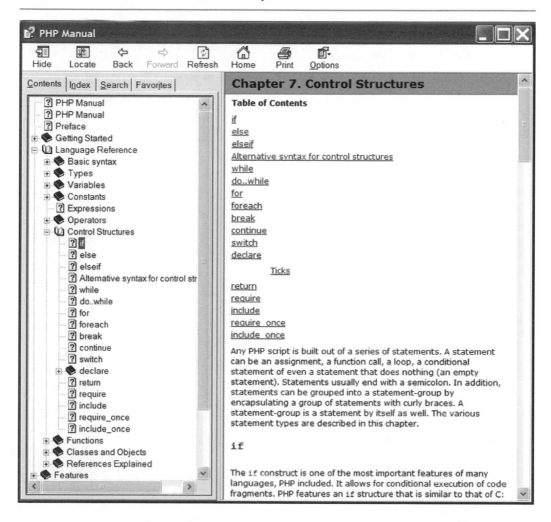

Figure 3.2 Windows help file.

to that of the PHP manual. The MySQL manual downloads are available from www.mysql.com/documentation/index.html and this page is illustrated in Figure 3.3.

GD Lib Manual

In Chapters 30 and 31 we illustrate that PHP can be used to create graphical image files dynamically. PHP is able to do this through use of the third party function library called the GD Library. We introduce many of the GD library functions in this book, and a fully comprehensive manual on the GD library is available for download from www.boutell.com/gd/.

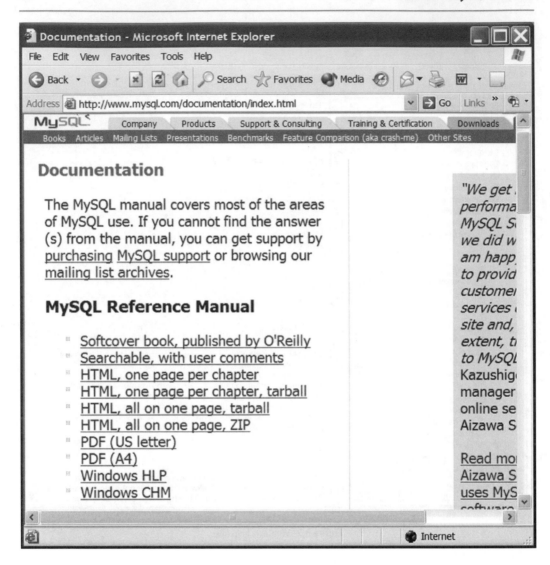

Figure 3.3 MySQL downloads page.

PDF Lib Manual

In Chapter 32 we will demonstrate how PHP can be used to create Adobe PDF documents dynamically. PHP does this by making use of a third party library of functions, known as PDFLib. This function library is very extensive and we only introduce some of the most commonly used functions. Full details of all the PDFLib functions available can be found at the PDFLib Web site (www.pdflib.com/products/pdflib/download/index.html) where full documentation can be downloaded, as shown in Figure 3.4.

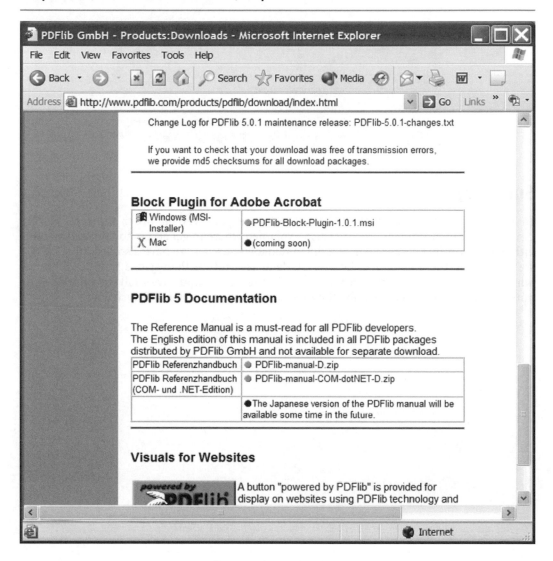

Figure 3.4 PDF Lib downloads.

PHP On-line Resources

In addition to the official PHP home site there are a large number of very useful on-line communities which have been created by PHP developers for developers. Table 3.2 provides a summary of some of these sites which we think are worth a visit.

Many of these Web sites have Web forums where you can post problems and await the replies (some good, others not so) from the PHP Web community.

Table 3.2 PHP on-line resources.

Name	URL
Name	URL
<?PHPBuilder?>	www.phpbuilder.com
DevShed	www.devshed.com
Webmonkey	hotwired.lycos.com/webmonkey/programming/php/
Hotscripts.com	www.hotscripts.com/PHP/Scripts_and_Programs/

Summary

In this chapter we have explained what software you need in order to create a PHP development environment. We have also explained where to get access to the PHP manual, either as an on-line resource or as a downloadable manual. We have also described where we can obtain the manual for the MySQL database and for the various function libraries which we shall be using later in this book. In the next chapter we shall introduce you to your first PHP script and describe the PHP software development lifecycle.

Your First PHP Program

4

Introduction

In this chapter we shall introduce you to your first PHP script. We shall explain how to create a PHP script, save it and execute it. We shall explain how errors in your scripts are reported and what to do if you encounter them.

Your First PHP Script

Let's get started by examining our first PHP script:

```
<?php

// First - Example 4-1
//---------------------

echo "Hello, Welcome to your first PHP script.";

?>
```

We have kept this as simple as possible as all we wish to accomplish is to show what a PHP script looks like. So, what do the lines in the above script mean? Well, firstly:

```
<?php
```

This line means that this is the start of some PHP instructions. The two lines beginning with "//" are comments:

```
// First - Example 4-1
//---------------------
```

You can miss these lines out if you wish as their only purpose is to provide the human reader with some instructions and information and are ignored by the computer. The next line begins with the statement echo:

```
echo "Hello, Welcome to your first PHP script.";
```

This instruction tells the PHP parser to output to the Web page the information within the inverted commas following the echo statement.

Finally, there is the line:

```
?>
```

This means that this is the end of the PHP instructions. The blank lines in the script don't mean anything and are simply included to make reading the script a little easier.

Editing Your PHP Scripts

The first thing you need to do when presented with a PHP script like the one previously is to type this in to the computer and save it. PHP scripts are stored as simple text files and as such require a text editor to enter, edit and save the scripts. You can use any text editor you like. We have used Notepad with Windows as this is a very simple text editor and is freely available with the Windows operating system. Figure 4.1 illustrates the above script entered into the Windows Notepad text editor.

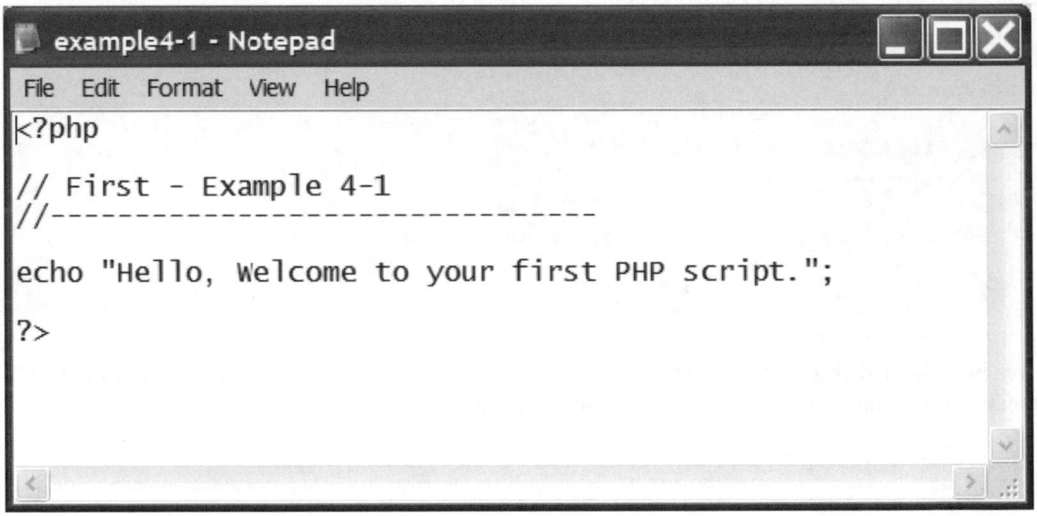

```
example4-1 - Notepad
File   Edit   Format   View   Help
<?php

// First - Example 4-1
//-------------------------------

echo "Hello, Welcome to your first PHP script.";

?>
```

Figure 4.1 Notepad window showing PHP script.

Saving Your PHP Scripts

Exactly where you save your PHP scripts will depend on the development environment you are using and in particular the Web server you have installed. On our computer we have used the Windows Internet Information Services Web server. As a default this Web server creates the following as a standard directory structure on the C:\ drive of the PC:

```
C:\
+ Inetpub
  + wwwroot
```

All HTML documents and PHP scripts must be saved in the directory wwwroot or within sub-directories of this directory. We have created the following directory structure below the wwwroot directory:

```
C:\
+ Inetpub
 + wwwroot
    + phpbook
       + files
       + graphics
       + pdf
       + uploads
```

We shall store all our PHP scripts in the phpbook directory. The other sub-directories below phpbook will be used in later chapters for storing generated files, images, PDF documents and any files which we upload. To save our PHP script in the phpbook directory using Notepad we select the File Save As option, navigate to the phpbook directory and enter a file name for our script, ending in .php. We have chosen to save the file as "example4-1.php". Note that with Notepad you must make sure that the Save As option type is set to "All Files". Failure to do this will result in Notepad appending the extension ".txt" to your saved files and they will not work correctly. This is illustrated in Figure 4.2.

Finally, clicking the Save button will save your file.

Viewing Your PHP Output

Having created and saved your script you are now in a position to view the output it produces. To do this we need:

1. To use a Web client (also known as a Web browser). We shall be using Microsoft Internet Explorer in all of our examples, however, as PHP generates HTML code all the examples in this book should work with any Web browser you choose to use.

2. You need to ensure that your Web server is running as this will be needed to serve your PHP script.

To view the output from the script we type the following address into the Web browser's address field:

```
http://localhost/phpbook/example4-1.php
```

This Web address is a "local address", used for development purposes only. This is used when you are using a Web server on the same computer as you are developing your scripts. Let us examine what this address means:

- http:// – This means that this is a HyperText Transfer Protocol Web address.
- localhost – This is the name of our Web server. As mentioned this is a development address.
- /phpbook – This is the directory in which our scripts are stored.
- /example4-1.php – This is the name of our script.

The resulting output from this script is illustrated in Figure 4.3.

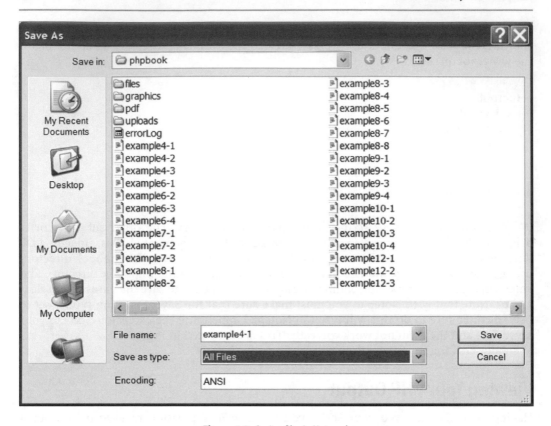

Figure 4.2 Saving files in Notepad.

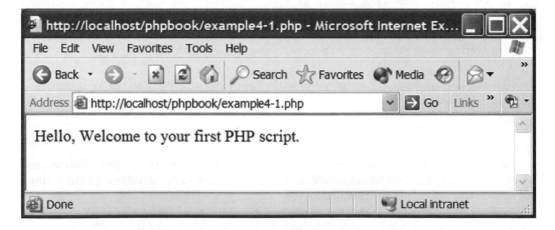

Figure 4.3 Our first PHP script.

Your Second PHP Script

Okay, let's try another script, something a little more complex:

```php
<?php

// First - Example 4-2
//--------------------


echo "Today is " . showDate();

function showDate() {
    $date = getthedate();
    return($date["year"] . '-'. $date["mon"] . '-'. $date["mday"]);
}
```

We are not going to explain how the script works at this point, but all parts of this script are introduced and discussed in later chapters. Instead the script has been designed to show how PHP can generate a simple dynamic Web page. Enter and save the above script into your Web server directory and view the resulting script in your chosen Web browser. The resulting output is illustrated in Figure 4.4.

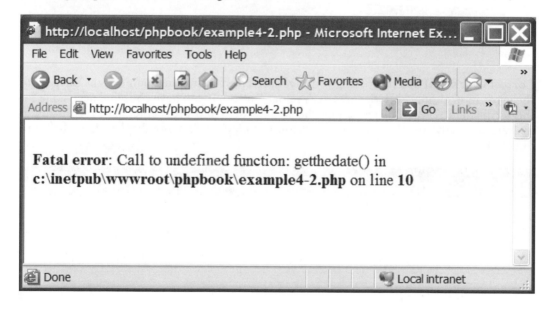

Figure 4.4 Our second PHP script – error.

Error Messages

Oh no! We have a problem, our second PHP script has produced an error message:

```
Fatal error: Call to undefined function: getthedate() in
c:\inetpub\wwwroot\phpbook\example4-2.php on line 10
```

In actual fact this was deliberate as we wanted to show what an error message looked like and what you need to do in order to correct it. The error message implies that there is a problem with the line:

```
$date = getthedate();
```

This is in fact the case, as the line should read:

```
$date = getdate();
```

The correct script should look like this:

```php
<?php
// First - Example 4-3
//---------------------
echo "Today is " . showDate();
function showDate() {
    $date = getdate();
    return($date["year"] . '-'. $date["mon"] . '-'. $date["mday"]);
}
```

Correct your script and resave it. If you have saved it with the same name as the script with the error in it, simply click the browser's reload button. If you have chosen a new name for the script then retype this name into the address field and press enter. The script should operate correctly this time and should result in today's date being displayed, as shown in Figure 4.5.

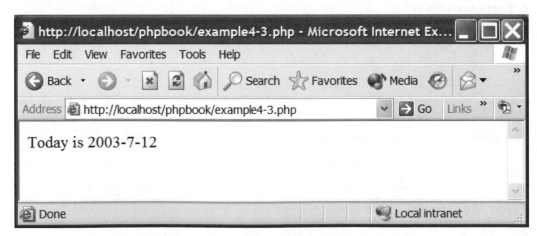

Figure 4.5 Our second PHP script.

The script is a dynamic script and it will display the correct date whenever you decide to view the script output.

Summary

In this chapter we have introduced you to your first PHP scripts and explained how you should enter and save these in your computer. We have explained how the output from the scripts can be viewed and what error messages look like when they occur. In the following chapter we shall continue our examination of PHP by taking a closer look at some fundamentals of the PHP language.

5

PHP Fundamentals

Introduction

In this chapter we shall take a closer look at some of the fundamental issues of developing using the PHP language. We shall consider how we are allowed to embed PHP scripts with HTML documents, how scripts can be formatted, the role of comments and the echo statement.

Jumping in and out of PHP

Previously we have shown that we must start a PHP script with the <?php statement and end it with the ?> statement. So, for example, we illustrated our first PHP script as follows:

```php
<?php

// Closer - Example 5-1
//---------------------

echo "Hello, Welcome to your first PHP script.";

?>
```

However, PHP can be embedded within HTML documents and you can have a mix of HTML and PHP, consider the following example:

```php
<body>
Hello, this is standard HTML

<?php

// Closer - Example 5-2
//---------------------

echo " and this is PHP generated.";

?>
</body>
```

In the above example we begin with a HTML <BODY> tag followed by some text "hello, this is standard HTML". We then have a PHP script which echos out the text "and this is PHP generated". After the closing PHP element ?> we return to HTML with a end body tag.

The great thing is that you can jump in and out of PHP within a HTML document whenever you like. Consider the following example:

```
<body>
Hello, this is standard HTML

<?php

// Closer - Example 5-3
//--------------------

echo " and this is produced using PHP. ";
?>

We are now back to HTML

<?php
echo "and once again with PHP. ";
?>

But we finish using HTML.

</body>
```

In this example, we illustrate that we are not simply limited to one <?php ?> script, but can include them multiple times. The output from the above script is illustrated in Figure 5.1.

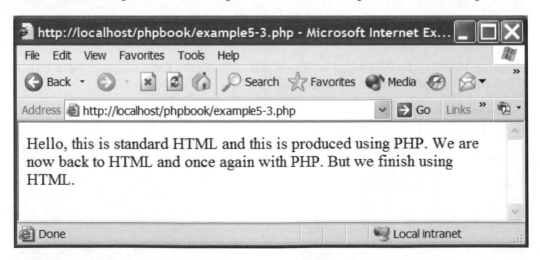

Figure 5.1 Jumping in and out of PHP.

Formatting PHP Instructions

The PHP scripting language is quite tolerant of how you lay out its instructions. For example, this:

```php
<?php
echo "Hello, World";
?>
```

is a perfectly acceptable way of including PHP instructions within a HTML document, however, the following is also equally valid:

```php
<?php echo "Hello, World" ?>
```

Note that in the second example the ; at the end of the echo statement is missing. The semicolon is used to terminate a PHP instruction as is the ?> tag. Therefore the semicolon can be omitted when there is a single line of PHP. However, the first example is generally easier to understand and thus all of the examples in this book will be presented in this style.

You can, if you wish, make your scripts totally unreadable by placing many separate instructions on the same line. For example:

```php
<?php

// Closer - Example 5-4
//---------------------
echo "Today is " . showDate(); function showDate()
  { $date = getdate();
return($date["year"] . '-'. $date["mon"] . '-'. $date["mday"]);}
?>
```

The above is a rewrite of the example 4-3.php date script in the previous chapter. It is not recommended that you make your scripts difficult to read, as you will find keeping them readable has many benefits when you are trying to correct problems, make changes or are simply trying to understand how a script works.

Echo and Print Statements

Echo is a PHP language construct and allows strings to be displayed on the Web page. We have already used echo to display some text in the previous example scripts, but here is an example of the statement again:

```php
echo "Hello";
```

This echo statement displays the text "Hello" on the Web page. The quotation marks (") indicate the start and end of the text to display. In this example the text "Hello" is very small, but if you had a much larger amount of text to display then you can span the output strings over multiple lines, for example:

```
echo "Hello, This string
spans a number
of lines";
```

This will display the text "Hello, This string spans a number of lines". This will be displayed on a single line, not split over multiple lines as you may think. Try this for yourself by viewing the following script:

```
<?php

// Closer - Example 5-5
//---------------------

echo "Hello, This string
spans a number
of lines";
?>
```

The output is shown in Figure 5.2

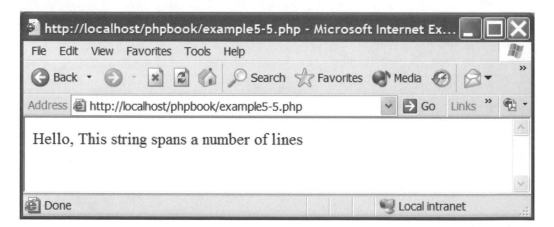

Figure 5.2 Multiple line echo statement.

Variables and multiple strings of characters can be output using echo and we shall introduce these in later chapters. PHP also supports another statement to facilitate output, print, which works in the same way as echo:

```
print "Hello, There";
```

This will display the text "Hello, There". You can either use echo or print in your scripts. All our examples use echo.

Comment Statements

PHP supports three forms of comments, which can be included to help the human reader understand what the PHP script is doing. The first type of comment spans multiple lines and is the same as that introduced in the C programming language:

```
/* This is a comment
which can be separated over
multiple lines */
```

The characters "/*" denote the start of the comment and the characters "*/" the end. The second form of comment is designed for a single line and is the same as those introduced in the C++ programming language:

```
// single comment line.
```

The characters "//" denote the start of a single line comment. Finally, the third form of comment is a UNIX shell type comment and also spans a single line:

```
# This is another single line comment.
```

Comments are ignored by the PHP parser and only help the human read to understand what is going on. All of our full scripts within this book have a two line comment near the top of the script, which looks something like this:

```
// Closer - Example 5-4
//---------------------
```

The comment is there to provide the name of the script as it should be saved. In the previous example since this is Example 5-4 it should be saved as example5-4.php. We know that by examining the script name that the script is Example 4 from Chapter 5.

We have avoided comments as much as possible in our examples and they have been made as short and simple as possible.

Summary

In this chapter we have examined PHP layout and the means by which it can be embedded within a HTML document. We have examined the echo statement and the role of comments within the language. In the next chapter we shall continue our examination of the PHP language and introduce the user to PHP variables.

Part 2

Basic Language Constructs

Introduction to Variables

6

Introduction

In this chapter we shall introduce the concept of variables. We shall examine how they are defined and used within PHP, the limitations of their use and why they are so important. We shall begin by explaining what variables are.

What is a Variable?

Variables are named containers, which can hold values. The value a variable holds can change during the execution of the script, hence its name "variable". Variables can hold numbers, characters or strings, which normally represent something, such as dates, surnames or salaries, for example.

Every variable has a unique name, which enables us to refer to it without any ambiguity.

Variables in PHP

Variables in PHP are defined by a dollar ($) symbol followed by the name of the variable. The name is case sensitive and therefore $SIMON is different to $simon. Variable names must start with either a letter or an underscore character, after which there can be any number of letters, numbers or underscore characters.

For example, the following are valid variable names:

```
$name;
$chapter45;
$_var;
```

However, the following is an illegal variable name, as it does not start with an underscore or letter character:

```
$1stName;
```

Assigning Variables by Value

Until the creation of PHP 4 assigning a variable by value was the one and only way that values could be assigned into a variable. Assigning a variable by value means that when a value is assigned to the variable the entire value of the original value is copied into the destination variable. Therefore, because a copy of the value is made changing the original value will have no effect on the copy. For example, if we have two variables named $tax and $net and these are assigned the values 17 and 200. Then if we declare a variable called $copyOfNet and assign it the value stored in variable $net, no matter what we do to variable $net, variable $copyOfNet will not be affected. This is illustrated in Figure 6.1.

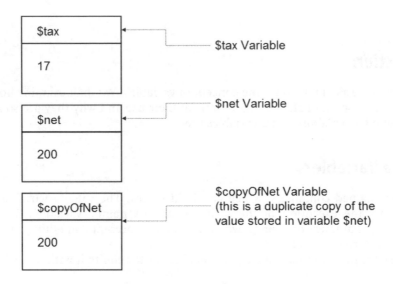

Figure 6.1 Assigning a variable by value.

To assign a value to a variable we use the equals (=) character. The following script illustrates assigning some variables by value:

```php
<?php

// Variables - Example 6-1
//---------------------

$tax = 17;
$net = 200;
$copyOfNet = $net;

?>
```

The example above illustrates the definition of three variables, $tax which is assigned the value of 17, $net the value of 200 and $copyOfNet which is assigned the value of variable

$net. This illustrates that not only can variables be assigned constants, but that they can be assigned the values of other variables.

Assigning Variables by Reference

With the introduction of PHP 4 came another way of assigning values to variables, assigning variables by reference. Assigning by reference means that the new variable simply becomes a reference also known as an alias and sometimes referred to as "pointing to" the original variable. This is illustrated in Figure 6.2.

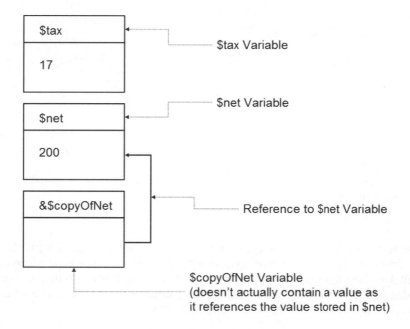

Figure 6.2 Assigning a variable by reference.

Changes to either the original or the new variable effect the other. No copying of values is performed and therefore this form of assignment can result in a performance increase, although you would be hard pressed to notice this. In addition, note that in assigning a variable by reference you cannot assign a constant in this way. To assign by reference, simply add an ampersand (&) to the beginning of the variable which is being assigned. The following example script illustrates assigning by reference:

```php
<?php

// Variables - Example 6-2
//----------------------
```

```
$tax = 17;
$net = 200;
$copyOfNet = &$net;
?>
```

Displaying Variables

Variables can be displayed using the echo statement, consider the following example:

```php
<?php

// Variables - Example 6-3
//---------------------

$tax = 17;
$net = 200;
$copyOfNet = &$net;
$anotherCopy = $net;

$net = 100;

echo $copyOfNet;
echo $anotherCopy;
?>
```

The above script defines four variables. $tax and $net are initialized with the constant values 17 and 200. Variable $net is assigned by reference to variable $copyOfNet and variable $net is then assigned by value to variable $anotherCopy. Finally, variable $net is set to a value of 100 and variables $copyOfNet and $anotherCopy are displayed using echo statements. The output of this script is shown in Figure 6.3.

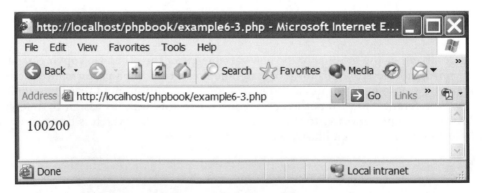

Figure 6.3 Variable output.

The resulting output of this script, although not well presented illustrates that the variable assigned by reference changes its value from 200 to 100 when the original copy

($nct) is altcrcd. Howcvcr, variablc $anthorCopy which was assigned by value keeps the original value of 200.

Declaring but Not Assigning Variable Values

It is not good practice to declare a variable and then use it before assigning a value to it. The reason being that you really have no idea what data is actually stored in the variable unless you expressly define it. Consider the following script:

```php
<?php

// Variables - Example 6-4
//--------------------

$tax;

echo $tax;
?>
```

The above example will cause an error notice to be created when the script is executed as the interpreter does not know what value the variable should be set to. This error is illustrated in Figure 6.4.

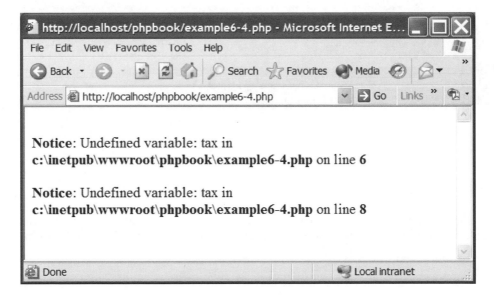

Figure 6.4 Undefined variable notice.

Variable Types

A type is a description of the format of which information is stored within a variable. PHP supports eight primitive types. These different types are listed in Table 6.1, along with a brief description and the chapter where they are first introduced and described.

Table 6.1 Variable types.

Type	Description	Chapter
Boolean	A Boolean expresses a truth value. It can be either TRUE or FALSE	7
Integer	An integer is a number of the set $Z = \{\ldots, -2, -1, 0, 1, 2, \ldots\}$	7
Floating-point number (float)	Floating point numbers (AKA "floats", "doubles" or "real numbers")	7
String	A string is a series of characters. In PHP a character is the same as a byte	8
Array	An indexed sequence of one or more variables	14
Object	A special "variable" defined by the user within the object oriented paradigm	37
Resource	A resource is a special variable holding a reference to an external resource such as a database	36
NULL	NULL represents that a variable has no value	7

The PHP manual also introduces some *pseudo-types* for readability reasons. These are listed in Table 6.2. These pseudo-types are used predominantly to help us describe function prototypes and we shall see them used later.

Table 6.2 Pseudo variable types.

Type	Description	Chapter
Mixed	Indicates that a parameter (to a function) may accept multiple (but not all) types	17
Number	Parameter can be either an integer or a float	–
Callback	Some functions accept user defined callback functions as a parameter	24

Type Casting

PHP allows you to cast (convert) from one variable type to another. To specify a cast you place the desired type in parentheses before the variable which is to be cast, for example:

```
$var = 4;
$bool = (Boolean) $var;
```

In the above example $var is an integer and is cast to $bool as a Boolean value. There are a number of different casts which are permitted and these are listed in Table 6.3.

Table 6.3 Casting.

Cast	Description
(int) (integer)	Cast to integer
(bool) (Boolean)	Cast to Boolean
(float) (double) (real)	Cast to floating point
(string)	Cast to string
(array)	Cast to array
(object)	Cast to object

Variable Scope

The scope of a variable is the context in which it is defined. Variable scope generally spans the whole of a PHP script, although there are exceptions. One specific exception are functions. Variables defined outside functions do not have any scope within the function and variables defined within the function have no scope outside of the function. A similar situation exists in the case of classes. Function scope within functions is discussed in Chapter 13 and Classes in Chapter 37.

Summary

This chapter has introduced the concept of variables. We illustrated how variables can be declared within PHP and how values can be assigned to them. We also briefly described the different types of variables which PHP supports. In the next chapter we shall take a more detailed look at Boolean, integer and floating point types.

Boolean, Integer and Floating Point Types

7

Introduction

In this chapter we shall examine three variable types in some detail. The three types that we shall examine are Boolean, integer and floating point. We shall, however, begin by explaining how PHP supports explicit type definitions.

Types

PHP doesn't actually support explicit type definitions unlike some other programming languages. In other words you don't specify what type a variable is when you create it. Instead a variables type is determined by the context in which that variable is used. So, for example, if you define a variable and assign an integer to it then that variable is an integer type. If a little later you then assign a floating point variable to it then the variable now becomes a floating point type.

Boolean Types

Booleans are the simplest type. A Boolean value expresses a truth value and can be either "TRUE" or "FALSE". The following illustrates the declaration of a variable and assigning it the value "TRUE":

```php
<?php

// Boolean, Integer and Floats - Example 7-1
//----------------------------

$weekday = TRUE;

echo $weekday;
?>
```

Note that the output from this example is "1" and not the text "TRUE". The reason for this is that PHP uses the value 1 to represent "TRUE" and 0 to represent "FALSE". Therefore, the contents of a Boolean variable are either 1 or 0 when displayed.

Converting to Boolean

As mentioned in the previous chapter, to convert to a Boolean we can use the (bool) or (Boolean) cast. In most cases we do not need to explicitly cast as the value will be automatically converted. However, when converting to a Boolean from other variable types you need to know what certain values will be converted as. These are shown in Table 7.1

Table 7.1 Boolean conversions.

Converted as	Conversion
FALSE	A Boolean FALSE
FALSE	A integer of value 0
FALSE	A float of value 0.0
FALSE	A empty string and a string "0"
FALSE	An array with zero elements
FALSE	An object with zero member variables
FALSE	The special NULL type
TRUE	All other values

Integers

An integer is a number of the set $\{\ldots, -2, -1, 0, 1, 2, \ldots\}$. The maximum size of an integer number is platform dependent, but is normally in the region of 2 billion.

Integer numbers can be specified in decimal notation as shown below:

```
$var = 123;
$var2 =-123;
```

Here, $var is defined as a positive integer of the value 123, while $var2 is defined as a negative integer of value −123. Like some other languages, PHP allows integers to be defined in other number bases, specifically octal and hexadecimal:

```
$var = 0123;
$var2 = 0x1a;
```

Here, $var is defined as an octal number 123 that is decimally equivalent to 83. Octal numbers are defined by having a 0 preceding the number. $var2 is defined as a hexadecimal number 1a, which is equivalent to 26 in decimal. Hexadecimal numbers are defined by having 0 × preceding the number. If you are unsure why 123 octal is equal to 83 in decimal or 1a hexadecimal is equivalent to 26 in decimal take a look at Figure 7.1.

Converting to an Integer

You can convert to an integer using the (int) or (integer) casts. Table 7.2 lists what values specific conversions will result in.

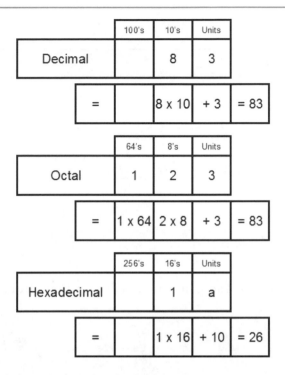

Figure 7.1 Working out decimal, octal and hexidecimal numbers.

Table 7.2 Integer conversions.

Converted as	Conversion
1	A Boolean TRUE
0	A Boolean FALSE
–	Converting from a floating point type will result in the number being rounded towards zero
–	String conversion is described in Chapter 8
–	Conversion from other types is undefined within the PHP language

Integer Overflow

If you specify an integer number beyond the bounds of the integer type then it will be automatically interpreted as a floating point value instead.

The Var_dump Function

We shall examine functions in more detail later, but it is useful for us to introduce a function at this point called var_dump. The function will display the type of a variable which is passed to it. The function format is as follows:

Function prototype:

```
Void var_dump(mixed variable);
```

Function arguments and return details:

Name	Type	Description
variable	Mixed	The variable we wish to examine
var_dump() returns	Void	Returns nothing

Function example:

```
var_dump($vab);
```

We can use this function to determine our variable type. Consider the following example:

```php
<?php

// Boolean, Integer and Floats - Example 7-2
//---------------------------

$smallInt = 1;

$bool = TRUE;
$largeInt = 12345678901234567890;

var_dump($smallInt);
var_dump($bool);
var_dump($largeInt);
?>
```

The output from this script is illustrated in Figure 7.2.

We can see from this example that $smallInt is an integer type, $bool is Boolean but $largeInt is actually stored as a floating point value.

Floating Point Types

Floating point numbers (also known as doubles, floats or real numbers) can be specified using any of the following syntaxes:

```
$var1 = 1.234;
$var2 = 1.2e3;
$var3 = 7E-10;
```

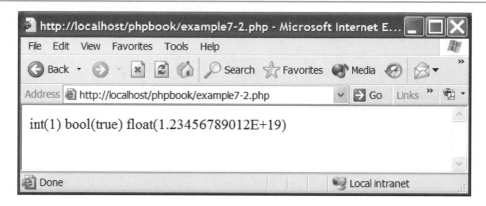

Figure 7.2 Var_dump function.

The size of a float is platform dependent, although you could expect a maximum of 1.8e308. There is an issue of precision with floats. Consider the following example:

```php
<?php

// Boolean, Integer and Floats - Example 7-3
//----------------------------

$one = 1;
$three = 3;
$third = $one/$three;

echo $third;
?>
```

In this example the value of $third is 0.333333333333. Programmers need to be aware of this loss of precision when performing floating point calculations.

Converting to Floating Point

You can convert to floats using the (float), (double) or (real) casts. String conversions to floats are described in the following chapter under the section on converting strings to numbers.

Summary

In this chapter we have examined the Boolean, integer and floating point types. We have illustrated how they can be defined and how one type can be converted into another. In the next chapter we shall take a more detailed look at string variable types.

Strings 8

Introduction

In this chapter we shall examine the string variable type. Strings are sequences of alphanumeric characters. We have used strings already in one or two of our previous PHP examples, specifically as part of the echo statement. We shall begin by examining how strings are defined in PHP, then examine the different types of strings which are available for us to use. We shall then consider how to join strings together, access individual characters within a string and convert strings to numbers.

String Types

There are two different ways that strings can be specified in PHP. We can use either using the ' or the " characters to denote the start and end of the string, for example:

```
$myString = 'First String';
$anotherString = "Another String";
```

Here, $myString is defined as a string containing the characters 'First String', while $anotherString is defined as a string containing the characters "Another String". So is there any difference between them? Well, the answer is yes and no depending on the context the string is being used, for example:

```
<?php

// Strings - Example 8-1
//--------------------

$myString = 'First String';
$anotherString = "Another String";

echo $myString;
echo "<br>";
echo $anotherString;

?>
```

In the above example the output is as follows:

```
First String
Another String
```

It would appear that both single-quoted strings and double-quoted ones are essentially the same. However, this is not entirely true as we shall see when we look more closely at the support these different string types have for escaped characters.

Single-quoted Strings

Single-quoted strings can only contain the escape characters listed in Table 8.1.

Table 8.1 Single-quoted string escape characters.

Sequence	Description
\\	Backslash character
\'	Single quote character

These escape sequences allow you to include the characters \ and ' in your strings. Consider the following example:

```php
<?php

// Strings - Example 8-2
//---------------------

$myString = 'This is a backslash: \\';
$anotherString = ' and this is a single quote \";

echo $myString;
echo $anotherString;

?>
```

The above script would display:

```
This is a backslash: \ and this is a single quote'
```

We need to escape these characters in this way because:
(1) If we wanted to display a single quote as part of the string then we need to tell the parser that this is a quote to display and not one which is denoting the end of the string.
(2) We use the backslash character to denote an escape character and so we need to escape this character when we want to display it.

Therefore, the following would cause an error if it were introduced into a script:

```
$var3 = 'but this quote ' would cause an error';
```

To display this correctly the line should read:

```
$var3 = 'but this quote \' would cause an error';
```

Double-quoted Strings

With double-quoted strings, things get a little more complicated. To begin with the number of escape characters that can be used, is far larger, consider Table 8.2.

Table 8.2 Double-quoted string escape sequences.

Sequence	Description
\n	Carriage return and line feed
\r	Carriage return
\t	Tab character
\\	Backslash
\$	Dollar sign
\"	Double quotation
\[0-7]	A character specified in octal notation with 1–3 digits. The first number of which is a 0
\x[0-9A-Fa-f]	A character specified in hexadecimal notation specified with 1 or 2 digits. Must have a x character before the number.

The \n sequence forces the cursor to jump to the start of a new line. The \r sequence forces the cursor to jump to the start of the current line. The \t sequence inserts a tab character. You will note from the examples in this book that these escape sequences are not used very much.

In addition, the \\ sequence inserts a backslash character. The \$ sequence inserts a dollar character. The \" sequence inserts a double quotes character. The final two escape sequences allow you to specify individual characters in either octal or hexadecimal numbers, in accordance with the ASCII (American Standard Code for Information Interchange). This is a code, which assigns a numeric value to each letter, number and character on the keyboard (and some characters which are not!).

Therefore, the following string:

```
$var = "Hello, \x4C\x69\x7A";
```

would produce the string:

```
Hello, Liz
```

Why? Well, 4C is a hexadecimal number equal to 76 decimal. Character 76 in the ASCII table is assigned to the 'L' character. 69 is equal to 105 in decimal and is assigned to the 'i' character. Finally, 7A is equal to 122 in decimal which is assigned to the 'z' character.

Heredoc Strings

Another way of defining strings is by using the heredoc syntax. This uses three less than characters (< < <) followed by an identifier. A closing identifier must be used to denote the end of the string. It must also use the same characters as the starting identifier and must begin in the first column of the line. It also requires a semicolon character straight after it. For example:

```php
<?php

// Strings - Example 8-3
//--------------------

$myString = <<<MST
This is an example of a string
spanning multiple lines
using the heredoc syntax
MST;

echo $myString;
?>
```

The heredoc string behaves in exactly the same way as the double-quoted string.

Variables in Strings

Double-quoted strings allow you to use more escape sequences than single-quoted strings. So why not just use double-quoted strings all of the time? Well, there is another difference between the two strings. That difference is that any variables included inside a double-quoted string will be expanded! What does this mean? Well, consider the following:

```php
$name = "Simon";
$message = "Hello, $name";
$message2 = 'Hello, $name';
```

In the above script fragment, the first line defines a string with the value "Simon". The second line, defines a string with the value "Hello, Simon" and the third line defines a string with the value 'Hello, $name'. The reason for this concerns the single- and double-quoted strings. With a single-quoted string the variable (in this case $name) is not recognized as a variable and the text '$name' is displayed. In the case of a string using double quotation marks the variable is recognized and replaced with the current value of the variable.

Strings can be assigned the value of another string using the equals (=) character or operator as it is referred, for example:

```
$name = "Simon";
$anotherName = $name;
```

Here, the value of variable $name is assigned (copied) into the variable $anotherName. The following script illustrates the use of variables in strings:

```
<?php

// Strings - Example 8-4
//---------------------

$firstname = 'Liz';
$surname = 'Hall';
$message = "Hello, $firstname";
$message2 = "Your fullname is $firstname $surname";

echo $message;
echo "<br />";
echo $message2;
echo "<br />";
echo "See you later, Ms. $surname";

?>
```

The above example produces the output illustrated in Figure 8.1.

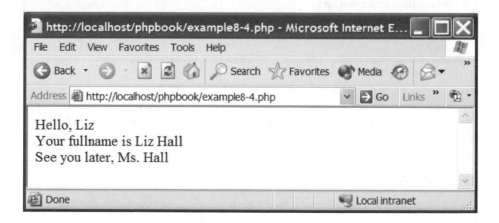

Figure 8.1 Variables in strings.

However, be warned things don't always work exactly how you would want them to. Consider the following script:

```php
<?php

// Strings - Example 8-5
//--------------------

$currency = "dollar";

echo "The currency is the $currency<br />";

echo "I would like some $currencys <br />";

echo "I would like some ${currency}s <br />";
?>
```

The above script causes an error, as shown in Figure 8.2.

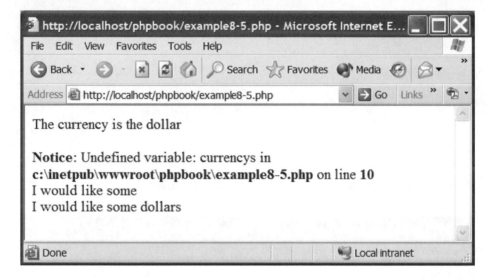

Figure 8.2 Problems with variables in strings.

The reason for the error is that the computer parses the variable name on the second echo statement as being $currencys and not $currency. To overcome this problem you can enclose the variable name in curly braces { } as shown in the third echo statement.

Joining Strings

Strings can be joined or concatenated easily using the " . " dot operator, for example:

```php
$title = "Ms ";
$firstName = "Liz ";
$surName = "Hall";
$fullName = $firstName . $surName;
$titleName = $title . $firstName . $surName;
```

In the above code fragment a string $fullName is created with the value "Liz Hall". Note, that the space between the first name and surname would not be included if there was not a space character at the end of the string "Liz ". $titleName is created with the value "Ms. Liz Hall".

We can also use this operator in our echo statement to display variables more neatly. Consider the following example:

```php
<?php

// Strings - Example 8-6
//---------------------

$tax = 17;
$net = 200;
$copyOfNet = &$net;
$anotherCopy = $net;

$net = 100;

echo "$copyOfNet $anotherCopy";
echo "<br>";
echo $copyOfNet . " " . $anotherCopy;
?>
```

The above example illustrates how we can employ the dot operator to join strings together within an echo statement.

String Character Access

Characters in a string may be accessed by specifying the zero based offset of the desired character after the string in curly braces, for example:

```php
$name = "Liz Hall";
$second = $name{1};
```

Figure 8.3 illustrates how this string is stored and referenced. The variable $second has the value "i".

0	1	2	3	4	5	6	7
L	i	z		H	a	l	l

Figure 8.3 String characters.

Note that in earlier versions of PHP the characters [] could be used instead of the { } characters, but this is now depreciated. The following script illustrates the use of string concatenation and character referencing:

```php
<?php

// Strings - Example 8-7
//--------------------

$firstName = 'Liz ';
$surName = 'Hall';
$fullName = $firstName . $surName;

$first = $fullName{0};
$second = $fullName{1};
$third = $fullName{2};
$fourth = $fullName{3};
$fifth = $fullName{4};
$sixth = $fullName{5};
$seventh = $fullName{6};
$eighth = $fullName{7};

echo "The full name is : " . $fullName . "<p>";
echo "The 1st character in $fullName is $first<br>";
echo "The 2nd character in $fullName is $second<br>";
echo "The 3rd character in $fullName is $third<br>";
echo "The 4th character in $fullName is $fourth<br>";
echo "The 5th character in $fullName is $fifth<br>";
echo "The 6th character in $fullName is $sixth<br>";
echo "The 7th character in $fullName is $seventh<br>";
echo "The 8th character in $fullName is $eighth<br>";
?>
```

The output from the above script is illustrated in Figure 8.4.

Converting Strings to Numbers

Strings can be evaluated as numeric values in certain circumstances. The value and type of the numeric are determined as follows:

(1) The string will be evaluated as a float if it contains any of the following characters " . ", "e" or "E". Otherwise it will be evaluated as an integer.

(2) The numeric value will be determined from the initial part of the string. If this is a valid numeric then this value will be used, otherwise the string will be evaluated as 0.

The following script illustrates this conversion:

```php
<?php

// Strings - Example 8-8
//--------------------

$num = 23;
```

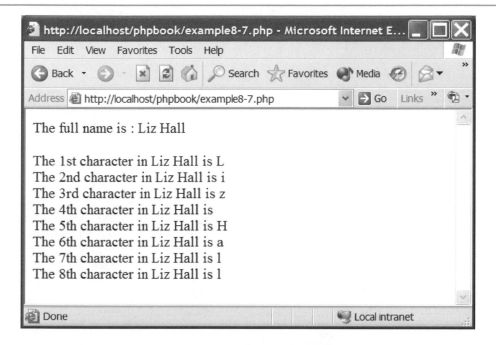

Figure 8.4 Referencing single characters within a string.

```
$string = "45";
$add = $num + $string;
$males = "3.45 males";
$females = 2 + $males;

echo "23 + '45' is equal to $add<br />";
echo "2 + '3.45' is equal to $females<br />";

?>
```

The output from the script is:

```
23 + '45' is equal to 68
2 + '3.45' is equal to 5.45
```

Summary

This chapter has introduced the string type. We have explored the different ways that a string can be defined within PHP and how these different string types effect the way the string can be used. We have considered how to join multiple strings together, how to access individual characters within a string and how to convert strings to numbers. In the next chapter we shall introduce the concept of variables from outside PHP.

Predefined PHP Variables

Introduction

In this chapter we shall introduce some variables which are produced outside of PHP and are known as predefined variables. We shall see that the Web server, system environment and HTML forms generate variables which we can (and in many cases need) to access. Predefined variables are made available to any script, but as many of them are platform and Web server dependent it is difficult to fully document them all. We shall begin by explaining a fundamental change which occurred in PHP from version 4.2 which greatly effects the way in which we access these predefined variables.

Register Globals

With the release of PHP 4.2.0 onwards PHP has been released with the register_globals directive (located in the php.ini file) set to off. This means that form, server and cookie etc variables are no longer registered as global variables. This is a major change to PHP and vastly increases script security. It does mean, however, the PHP scripts written before version 4.2.0 will not work correctly unless the new form of accessing predefined variables is followed (this is the way we do things in this book) or (not to be recommended) that the register_globals directive is set to on within the php.ini file.

Phpinfo() Function

PHP include a very useful function called phpinfo(). This function displays a whole host of useful information about the current state of PHP. This information includes which compilation options are turned on, which extensions have been activated and which predefined variables are available. For us this is particularly helpful as it will display all of the predefined variables which the system has defined. The format of the function is:

Function prototype:

```
Int phpinfo(int option);
```

Function arguments and return details are:

Name	Type	Description
option	Int	Configuration options, values (1,2,4,8,16,32,64 and -1): 1 – General info 2 – PHP credits 4 – Configuration (php directives set in the php.ini file) 8 – Loaded modules 16 – Environment variables 32 – Predefined variables 64 – License information -1 – All of the above – this is the default if no value is included
phpinfo returns	Int	Returns "TRUE" if successful or "FALSE" if an error occurred

Function example:

```
phpinfo(32);
```

The following script illustrates the use of this function:

```
<?php

// Predefined Variables - Example 9-1
//------------------------

phpinfo(32);

?>
```

The output from this script is illustrated in Figure 9.1.

Server Variables

Server variables are those variables which are set by the Web server. As each manufacturer's Web server is essentially a different product there is no guarantee that all Web servers will provide any of these variables, although most will provide at least some. Table 9.1 lists the most common server variables and a description of their content.

Server variables (as are all predefined variables described in this chapter) are stored in a predefined array. You will be introduced to how to create your own arrays in Chapter 14, but for now all you need to be able to understand is how to access the predefined variables stored in an array. To access the server variables the array name $_SERVER is used followed by square brackets with the name of the predefined variable included within them inside single quotation marks, for example:

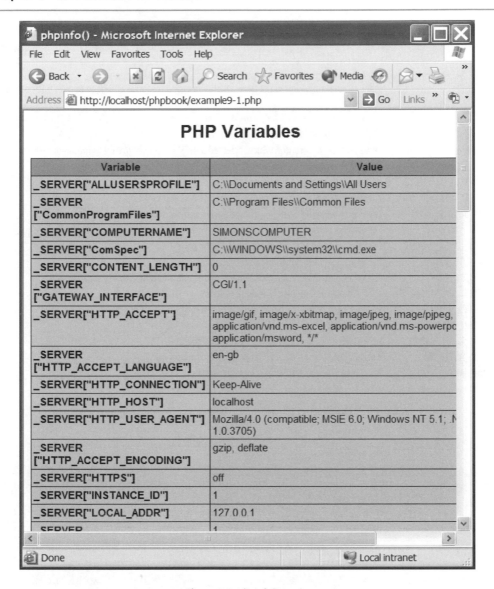

Figure 9.1 phpinfo() output.

```
$script = $_SERVER['PHP_SELF'];
```

The above will store the script name in the variable $script. The following script illustrates the contents of some of these variables:

Table 9.1 Server variables.

Variable	Description
'PHP_SELF'	The filename of the current script, relative to the root document directory. This is used on many of our scripts later in the book where we introduce forms and need to refer back to the script itself
'GATEWAY_INTERFACE'	What version of the CGI is being used
'SERVER_NAME'	The name of the host server
'SERVER_SOFTWARE'	Server identification string which is passed in HTML headers when responding to requests
'SERVER_PROTOCOL'	Name and version of the information protocol with which the page was requested
'REQUEST_METHOD'	Which request method was used to access the page i.e. 'POST'
'QUERY_STRING'	The query string (if any) with which the page was accessed
'DOCUMENT_ROOT'	The document root file, defined in the server's configuration file
'HTTP_REFERER'	The address of the Web page which referred the user agent (Web page) to the current page
'HTTP_USER_AGENT'	The user agent header which is accessing the page
'REMOTE_ADDR'	The IP address from which the user is viewing the page
'REMOTE_PORT'	The post being used on the user's machine to communicate with the Web server
'SCRIPT_FILENAME'	The absolute path name of the current script
'SERVER_PORT'	The port being used by the server for communication
'SCRIPT_NAME'	The current script's path
'PHP_AUTH_USER'	Apache Web server – username provided by the user
'PHP_AUTH_PW'	Apache Web server – password provided by the user
'PHP_AUTH_TYPE'	Apache Web server – HTTP authentication type

```php
<?php

// Predefined Variables - Example 9-2
//------------------------

echo "PHP_SELF: " . $_SERVER['PHP_SELF'];
echo "<br />SERVER_NAME: " . $_SERVER['SERVER_NAME'];
echo "<br />SERVER_SOFTWARE: " . $_SERVER['SERVER_SOFTWARE'];
echo "<br />SERVER_PROTOCOL: " . $_SERVER['SERVER_PROTOCOL'];
echo "<br />HTTP_USER_AGENT: " . $_SERVER['HTTP_USER_AGENT'];
echo "<br />REMOTE_ADDR: " . $_SERVER['REMOTE_ADDR'];
echo "<br />SERVER_PORT: " . $_SERVER['SERVER_PORT'];
echo "<br />SCRIPT_NAME: " . $_SERVER['SCRIPT_NAME'];

?>
```

The output from the above script is illustrated in Figure 9.2.

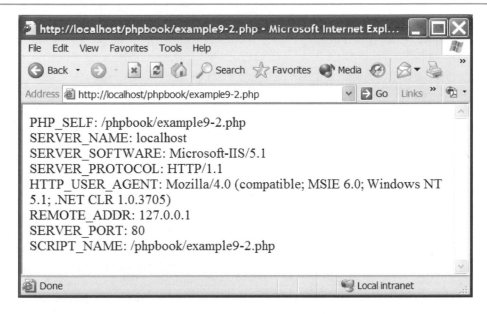

Figure 9.2 Predefined SERVER variables.

Environment Variables

Environment variables are made available to PHP from the operating system under which PHP is running. As such a definitive list would be very difficult to produce since there are many different operating systems and shells under which PHP operates. Using the phpinfo() function will provide a useful list of these functions which are available for your PHP installation. Table 9.2 provides some descriptions of a few of these variables available within a Windows XP PHP installation.

Table 9.2 Environment variables.

Variable	Description
'COMPUTERNAME'	The computer's name
'HTTP_HOST'	The Web server's address (localhost is common for development environments)
'HTTP_USER_AGENT'	The Web browser's identification string
'LOCAL_ADDR'	The URL of the local computer
'NUMBER_OF_PROCESSORS'	The number of processors
'OS'	The operating system
'Path'	The operating system path
'PATH_INFO'	The path of the current script from the root script directory
'PATH_TRANSLATED'	The full path of the current script
'PROCESSOR_IDENTIFIER'	The processor identification string
'SERVER_SOFTWARE'	The identification string of the Web server

To access the server variables the array name $_ENV is used followed by square brackets with the name of the predefined variable included within them inside single quotation marks, for example:

```php
$os = $_ENV['OS'];
```

This will store the operating system in the variable $os. The following script illustrates the contents of some of these variables:

```php
<?php

// Predefined Variables - Example 9-3
//-----------------------

echo "COMPUTERNAME: " . $_ENV['COMPUTERNAME'];
echo "<br />HTTP_HOST: " . $_ENV['HTTP_HOST'];
echo "<br />HTTP_USER_AGENT: " . $_ENV['HTTP_USER_AGENT'];
echo "<br />LOCAL_ADDR: " . $_ENV['LOCAL_ADDR'];
echo "<br />NUMBER_OF_PROCESSORS: " . $_ENV['NUMBER_OF_PROCESSORS'];
echo "<br />OS: " . $_ENV['OS'];
echo "<br />Path: " . $_ENV['Path'];
echo "<br />PATH_INFO: " . $_ENV['PATH_INFO'];
echo "<br />PATH_TRANSLATED: " . $_ENV['PATH_TRANSLATED'];
echo "<br />PROCESSOR_IDENTIFIER: " . $_ENV['PROCESSOR_IDENTIFIER'];
echo "<br />SERVER_SOFTWARE: " . $_ENV['SERVER_SOFTWARE'];

?>
```

The output from the above script is illustrated in Figure 9.3.

Form Variables

In Chapter 18 we will introduce the concept of interacting with the user using forms. You will see that the user is able to enter data via a form which in turn is stored in variables which can be accessed by the PHP script. Form data which is passed to the script via the POST method is stored in an array called $_POST and can be accessed in the same way as server variables, for example:

```php
$formField = $_POST['formField'];
```

In addition to the POST method of passing data is the GET method. Form data passed via the GET method can be used by accessing the $_GET array, for example:

```php
$dataField = $_GET['dataField'];
```

We shall be only using the POST method in our examples.

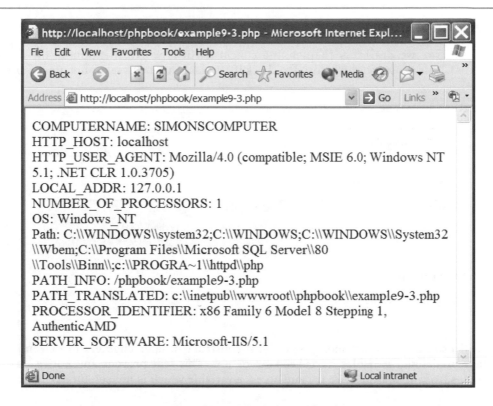

Figure 9.3 Predefined ENV variables.

Session Variables

In Chapter 23 we will introduce sessions and explain how they can be used to provide an individually customized Web page for each Web user. Variables stored for each user are held in session files and can be accessed through the $_SESSION array, for example:

```
$sessData = $_SESSION['sessData'];
```

Cookie Variables

In Chapter 22 we will introduce cookies and explain how they can be used to store data for a specific user, locally on the client's computer. Cookie variables can be accessed through the $_COOKIE array, for example:

```
$cookieData = $_COOKIE['cookieData'];
```

Isset() Construct

Finally, before we draw this chapter to a conclusion it is worth mentioning the isset() construct. This construct can be used to check if a variable has been set or not, its prototype is:

Function prototype:

```
bool isset(mixed var)
```

Function arguments and return details are:

Name	Type	Description
var	Mixed	The variable you wish to check is set
isset() returns	Bool	"TRUE" if variable is set and "FALSE" if it is not

Function example:

```
isset($_ENV['OS']);
```

We will use this construct along with the if construct in later chapters to determine if certain predefined variables have been set or not. This will prevent any notice "error" messages from appearing if we try and access a variable which is not set, for example:

```php
<?php

// Predefined Variables - Example 9-4
//-----------------------

echo "<br />QUERY_STRING: " . $_SERVER['QUERY_STRING'];

?>
```

The above script should return a notice as follows:

```
Notice: Undefined index: QUERY_STRING in
c:\inetpub\wwwroot\phpbook\example9-4.php on line 6

QUERY_STRING:
```

We shall see later how isset() can be used to prevent this.

Summary

In this chapter we have introduced the variable different predefined variable types, which are available within PHP. Not all have been examined in any great detail as they will be introduced in later chapters where appropriate. However, it is important to note that we have only used the secure form of predefined variable access introduced in PHP version 4.2.0 where global variables are not registered for global access. In the next chapter we shall examine the subject of expressions, operands and operators.

Expressions, Operands and Operators 10

Introduction

In the previous three chapters we have examined various types of variables and now in this chapter we turn to ways of manipulating the information they hold. We shall introduce the concepts of expressions, operands and operators. Expressions are used to calculate a result involving a number of operands (either variables or constants). Operators allow us to manipulate the variables and constants in the expressions. Operands are the constants or variables which the operators operate upon.

Expressions

In programming terms, an expression is something, which *expresses* a value. It is either a simple value – a single operand to express a single value:

```
5
"Some Text"
$place
```

or a set of operands which are combined together using operators:

```
20 + 7 + 15,
"the meaning of" . "life"
"Welcome to " . $place
```

The operands of an expression may be variables, constants or other sub-expressions. Figure 10.1 illustrates the difference between operands, operators and expressions in two simple examples.

A simple expression is:

```
$var = 5;
```

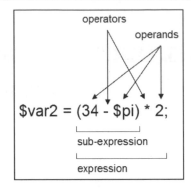

Figure 10.1 Operands, operators and expressions.

Here, the variable $var is assigned the constant value 5. In this example, 5 is the expression. Another example is:

```
$var = $var2;
```

Here, $var is assigned the value of $var2. In this example $var2 is the expression.
    Consider now the following expression:

```
$var = 5 + 3 + 2;
```

The expression 5+3+2 consists of two operators and three operands. This expression is simple to work out as the variables 5, 3 and 2 are added together and the result of 10 is stored in $var. However, what happens if we used a – (minus) operator instead of the + operator:

```
$var = 5 - 3 - 2;
```

Does this expression mean subtract 3 from 5, giving 2 and then subtract 2 from this giving 0? Or does it mean that 2 will be subtracted from 3, giving 1 and then 1 is subtracted from 5 making 4? Fortunately, the use of parentheses can be used to make the intended expressions clear:

```
$var = (5 - 3) - 2;
$var = 5 - (3 - 2);
```

We shall examine the order in which expressions are evaluated later in this chapter.

Operators

Operators allow you to manipulate or "operate upon" variables and constants and although you are probably already familiar with them, you may not have heard them referred to as operators before. Familiar operators are the mathematical operations of add (+), subtract (−), divide (/) and multiply (.). Operators are described as being unary, binary or ternary depending on whether they take, one, two or three operands (arguments). The plus, minus, multiplication and division operators are all binary operators.

Operands

An operand is simply something that an operator works on. In an expression like 34 − $pi, one operand is a constant (34) the other a variable ($pi).

Arithmetic Operators

PHP supports five different arithmetic operators which are listed in Table 10.1

Table 10.1 Arithmetic operators.

Name	Operator	Example	Description
Addition	+	$a + $b	Add $a and $b
Subtraction	−	$a − $b	Subtract $b from $a
Multiplication	*	$a * $b	Multiply $a and $b
Division	/	$a/$b	Divide $a by $b
Modulus	%	$a % $b	Remainder of dividing $a by $b

The following script provides an example of the use of arithmetic operators:

```php
<?php

// Expressions - Example 10-1
//-----------------------

$a = 5;
$b = 3;

echo 'a + b = ' . ($a + $b) . '<br>';
echo 'a - b = ' . ($a - $b) . '<br>';
echo 'a * b = ' . ($a * $b) . '<br>';
echo 'a/b = ' . ($a/$b) . '<br>';
echo 'a % b = ' . ($a % $b);

?>
```

Figure 10.2 illustrates the output produced by this script.

Notice that in the example the % operator returns the remainder of dividing 3 into 5, which is 2.

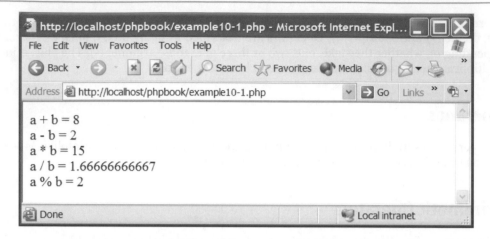

Figure 10.2 Using arithmetic operators.

Assignment Operators

The description of expressions given previously is oversimplified. The equals sign (=) in PHP is itself an operator – the assignment operator. It operates by setting the operand on its left to the value of the operand on its right. This means that the whole of $a = 5 + 3, for example (not just the bit to the right of the "="), is an expression. This is illustrated in Figure 10.3.

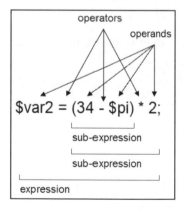

Figure 10.3 A complete expression.

Don't consider "=" to be an "equal to" character, it should be read as an "assign to" character. The simplest use of the assignment operator is:

```
$var = 56;
```

This reads "the value 56 is assigned into the variable $var". A more complex example could be:

```
$var = $a = $b;
```

This reads that the value in $b is assigned into $a which in turn is assigned into $var. PHP also supports the following "combined operators":

```
$a = 3;
$a += 4;
$b = "Hello ";
$b .= "There!";
```

The first line assigns the value 3 to the variable $a.

```
$a = 3;
```

The second line assigns the value of 7 to $a, in exactly the same way if we had written:

```
$a = $a + 4;
```

The third and fourth lines result in the value of "Hello There!" being assigned to $b. This is the same as writing:

```
$b = "Hello ";
$b = $b . "There!";
```

It doesn't matter which form of assignment operator you use. Pick one that you feel the most comfortable using.

Bit Manipulation Operators

Bit manipulation operators, also known as bitwise operators allow you to switch the individual bits within an integer from 0 to 1 and 1 to 0. For example, consider the expressions:

```
$a = 31;
$b = 12;
$c = $a & $b;
```

These expressions will result in the value of 12 being assigned into variable $c. This is because the & operator ANDs the bits in the first integer with those of the second. In order to see how this works we need to understand how integers are stored as binary numbers inside a computer. Consider Figure 10.4.

Figure 10.4 illustrates how the two numbers 31 and 12 are represented in 8 bit binary notation. When we AND these two numbers together only the bits which are currently 1 in both cases are left as 1 and all the others are set to 0. This is illustrated in Figure 10.5.

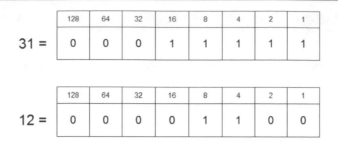

Figure 10.4 Binary storage of integers.

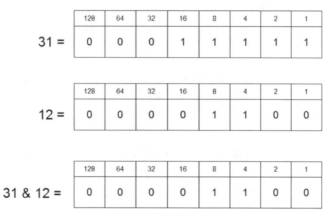

Figure 10.5 ANDing numbers.

Table 10.2 Bit manipulation operators.

Operator	Example	Description
&	$a & $b;	Set bits to 1 where the bits in both operands are set to 1
|	$a | $b;	Set bits to 1 where either bit in both operands is set to 1
^	$a ^ $b;	Set bits to 1 where either bit in both operands is set to 1, but not both
Shift left	$a << $b;	Shift bits left
Shift right	$a >> $b;	Shift bits right
AND	$a AND $b;	Set bits to 1 where the bits in both operands are set to 1
OR	$a OR $b;	Set bits to 1 where either bit in both operands is set to 1
XOR	$a XOR $b;	Set bits to 1 where either bit in both operands is set to 1, but not both

When we AND the integers 31 and 12 we end up with the value 12. Table 10.2 lists the bit manipulation operators available in PHP.

The shift left < < operator will move the bits in the operand to the left and set all vacated bits to zero. Each shift left has the same effect as multiplying the operand by two. Shift right > > will move the bits in the operand to the right and set vacated bits to zero. Each shift right is the same as dividing by 2. The following script demonstrates the use of the bit manipulation operators:

```php
<?php

// Expressions - Example 10-2
//-----------------------

echo "(7 & 2) = " . (7 & 2) . '<br>';
echo "(7 | 2) = " . (7 | 2) . '<br>';
echo "(7 ^ 2) = " . (7 ^ 2) . '<br>';
echo "(2 << 2) = " . (2 << 2) . '<br>';
echo "2 >> 1 = " . (2 >> 1);
?>
```

Figure 10.6 illustrates the output from the above script.

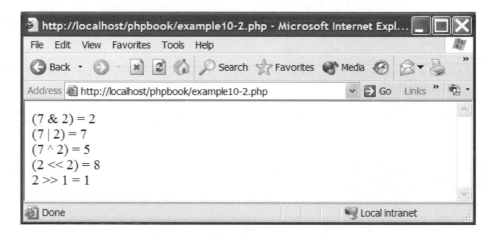

Figure 10.6 Using bit manipulation operators.

Comparison Operators

Comparison operators are used to compare expressions both logically and arithmetically. They are most often used in flow of control statements, which we covered in Chapter 8. Table 10.3 illustrates the comparison operators supported by PHP.

The difference between equal and identical operators is that the equal and not equal operators check whether the values of the two operands are the same or not. With the identical operators, the value and the type of the operands are also checked to see if they are identical or not.

Table 10.3 Comparison operators.

Operator	Example	Description
==	$a == $b	Equal
===	$a === $b	Identical
!=	$a != $b	Not equal
!==	$a !== $b	Not identical
<	$a < $b	Less than
>	$a > $b	Greater than
>=	$a >= $b	Greater than or equal to
<=	$a <= $b	Less than or equal to

Conditional Operator

PHP supports a "conditional operator". This is a ternary operator as it requires three operands. Its syntax is:

```
(expr1) ? (expr2) : (expr3);
```

This operator expresses the value of expr2 if expr1 is true, otherwise it expresses the value of expr3. For example:

```
$stockString = ($stock >0 )? "In stock" : "Out of stock."
```

Here, if $stock is greater than 0, the value "In stock" is assigned to $stockString, otherwise the value "Out of stock" is assigned.

Increment and Decrement Operators

PHP supports pre- and post-increment and decrement operators and these are listed in Table 10.4.

Table 10.4 Increment and decrement operators.

Name	Example	Description
Pre-increment	++$I	Increments $i by 1, then returns $I
Post-increment	$i++	Returns $i and then increments $i by 1
Pre-decrement	--$I	Decrements $i by 1, then returns $I
Post-decrement	$i--	Returns $i and then decrements $i by 1

The following script fragment illustrates the use of these operators:

```
$i = 3; // assign 3 to i
$i++; // i is incremented to 4
++$i; // i is incremented to 5
$i--; // i is decremented to 4
--$i; // i is decremented to 3
```

In the script fragment above, there does not seem to be any difference between the post- and pre-forms of the operators. The difference becomes clearer when the increment/decrement operator is used in an assignment expression. Consider the following script fragment:

```
$a = 5; // a is assigned the value 5
$b = ++$a; // a is incremented and then assigned to b
$b = $a++; // a is assigned to b and then incremented
```

Here, the result of these assignments is that b = 6 and a = 7. The following script illustrates the use of these operators:

```
<?php

// Expressions - Example 10-3
//-----------------------

$i = 3;
$j = 0;
$i++;
echo $i . '<br />';
++$i;
echo $i . '<br />';
$i--;
echo $i . '<br />';
--$i;
echo $i . '<br />';
$j = ++$i;
echo '$i = ' . $i . ' and j = ' . $j . '<br />';
$j = $i++;
echo 'i = ' . $i . ' and j = ' . $j ;

?>
```

Figure 10.7 illustrates the output from this script. Note that the values of $I and $j are different when the post- and pre-forms of the operator are used.

Logical Operators

PHP supports a number of logical operators, which are listed in Table 10.5. Be careful not to confuse them with the bitwise operators of the same name, they are unrelated.

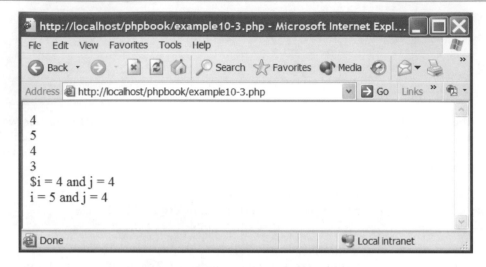

Figure 10.7 Using increment and decrement operators.

Table 10.5 Logical operators.

Operator	Example	Description
And	$a and $b	True if both $a and $b are true
Or	$a or $b	True if either $a or $b are true
Xor	$a xor $b	True if either $a or $b is true, but false if they are both true
Not	!$a	True if $a is not true
And	$a && $b	True if both $a and $b are true
Or	$a || $b	True if either $a or $b are true

The logical operators are used to combine the results of comparison operators according to the laws of Boolean algebra. In PHP a value of 0 is used to represent a logical false condition and a value of 1 for a logical true condition.

The reason why there are two And and two Or operators (AND, &&, OR, ||) listed in the table concerns operator precedence which is covered next. The following script illustrates the use of these logical operators:

```php
<?php

// Expressions - Example 10-4
//-----------------------

$i = 3;
$j = 4;

echo (($i < $j) || ($j > 5)) . '<br>';
echo (($i < $j) && ($j > 5)) . '<br>';
```

```
echo ($i < $j) xor ($j > 5);

?>
```

Operator Precedence

When there is more than one operator in an expression and the order of processing of the expression has not been made clear using parentheses, then the parser decides how the expression will be evaluated based on the operator precedence table. This is illustrated in Table 10.6, which lists all of the operators from the highest precedence (those operators processed first) to the lowest. Some operators have the same order of precedence and are shown on the same line of the table. In these cases the associativity of these operators is shown as either being from right to left or from left to right. In other words they are processed from the left- or right-hand side of the expression.

Table 10.6 Operator precedence.

Associativity	Operator
Right to left	[
Right to left	! ~ ++ --
Left to right	* / %
Left to right	+ - .
Non-associative	< <= > >=
Non-associative	== != === !==
Left to right	&
Left to right	^
Left to right	|
Left to right	&&
Left to right	||
Left to right	?:
Left to right	= += -= *= /= .= &= |= ^= ~=
Right to left	print
Left to right	and
Left to right	xor
Left to right	or
Left to right	,

Let us consider an expression such as:

```
$a * $b + $c
```

This would be evaluated as:

```
($a * $b) + $c
```

because the * operator is higher in the precedence table. Whereas:

```
$a/$b * $c
```

although they have the same order of precedence, would be evaluated as:

```
($a/$b) * $c
```

This is because they have left to right associativity.

Summary

In this chapter expressions, operands and operators have been examined in some detail. In the next chapter we will introduce the if statement and its role in controlling the flow of the script and thus deciding which statements within our scripts to execute.

If and Switch Constructs   11

Introduction

In this chapter we will introduce the "if" construct. All programming languages use a form of the if statement to create logical conditions. PHP supports a variety of forms of the if statement and we shall examine each of these. In addition we shall introduce the switch statement which is equivalent to a complex if structure.

Basic If Statement

A basic if statement has a simple structure, as shown below:

```
if ( condition )
{
        statements to be executed if condition is true
}
```

The word "if" is followed by parentheses which contain the conditional expression which will be evaluated when the if construct is reached. If the condition is true then the statements within the braces will be processed, otherwise they will not.

Let's see an example of a real if construct. Assume that you have four different colours and you ask a user to choose which of them they think is our favourite. If the red colour is the correct answer, then a simple if statement structure for this example will look like this:

```php
<?php

//If Statements - Example 11-1
//----------------------

$colour = "red";

if ($colour == "red")
    {
    echo "The colour is red";
    }

?>
```

Note, that in order to get the example above to work we have set the variable $colour = "red" so that the if condition will always be true. If you only have one statement which you wish to be performed when the if statement is true then you can omit the braces, for example:

```php
<?php

//If Statements - Example 11-2
//----------------------

$colour = "red";

if ($colour == "red")
        echo "The colour is red";

?>
```

We can also modify the script again to display the value of $colour. We can simply change the echo statement so that the value of $colour is displayed. We can only modify the if expression to:

```php
If($colour)
```

This now translates as "if $colour contains a value other than zero". In our case the value of "red" will mean that the condition will evaluate to true as a non-null string evaluates to the value of 1. Here is the complete script:

```php
<?php

//If Statements - Example 11-3
//----------------------

$colour = "red";

if ($colour)
        echo "The colour is $colour";

?>
```

Operators

We introduced you to the various comparison and logical operators in Chapter 12. With the introduction of the if statement we now have the means to use these in a meaningful way.

The following script fragment illustrates an if statement with the logical equal operator (==):

```
if ($a == 1)
{
        echo "TRUE";
}
```

The above script fragment evaluates if variable $a is set to 1, then the word "TRUE" will be displayed. If variable $a is set to any other value nothing will be displayed.

The following script fragment illustrates the use of the not equal (!=) operator:

```
If($a != 1)
{
        echo "FALSE";
}
```

In this example if variable $a is set to 1 nothing will be displayed but if variable $a is set to any value other than 1 the text "FALSE" will be displayed.

A combination of comparison and logical operators can be used to create complex statements. A few examples are shown in Table 11.1.

Table 11.1 Comparison and logical operators in if statements.

```
if ($a == 1 or $a == 2){ statement }
if ($a == $b and $c == d){ statement }
if ($a == $b and $c == d){ statement }
if($a != $b and $c < 5){ statement }
if(($a == $b and $c == $d) or ($e < $f)){ statement }
if(($a == $b and $c == $d) or ($e < $f or $e === $g)){ statement }
if (function()){ statement }
```

If ... Else Statement

Sometimes you may wish to have one or many statements executed if an expression is true and another set of statements if the expression is false. The "else" statement is used in conjunction with the if statement to achieve this. The syntax for using the else statement is:

```
if ( condition ) { statement }else { statement }
```

Consider the following:

```php
<?php

//If Statements - Example 11-4
//----------------------

$number = 2;

if ($number%2) {
        echo "Number $number is odd";
}
else {
        echo "Number $number is even";
}

?>
```

The above example will display "Number 2 is even" because the variable $number is an even number. If the number was changed to 1 it would display "Number 1 is odd". The if condition works by using the modulo operator which in this case returns the remainder of dividing $number by 2.

Elseif Statement

The elseif statement is a combination of if and else. In operates in a similar way to the else statement, in that it allows a statement to be executed when the if expression is false. However, unlike else, elseif will only execute the expression if the elseif expression is true. Consider the example script below:

```php
<?php

//If Statements - Example 11-5
//----------------------

$number1 = 100;
$number2 = 80;

if ($number1 > $number2) {
        echo "$number1 is larger than $number2";
}

elseif ($score == $number2) {
        echo "$number1 is equal to $number2";
}

else {
        echo "$number1 is smaller than $number2";
}
?>
```

This example checks if the value of $score is greater than $score2 and if true displays a message to this effect. If this is not true then the values are compared to see if they are equal and if true the message stating this is displayed. Finally, if either of the above is false a further message is displayed indicating that $score is smaller.

Complex Statements

If statements can be combined together to create very complex applications. We can use any combination of logical or comparison operators to control the if statement. We can use ifelse(){..} or else{..} to produce more complex if statements and we can use nested if statements. The following example illustrates how to check a username and password using if statements:

```php
<?php

//If Statements - Example 11-6
//-----------------------

$user = "admin";
$pass = "12345";

$username = "admin";
$password = "123456";

//Check username

if($user == "") {
        echo "Empty username!";
}
elseif($user == "$username") {
        echo "Username OK!";
}
else {
        echo "Not valid username";
}

echo "<br />";

//Check password

if($pass == "") {
        echo "Empty password!";
}
elseif($pass == "$password") {
        echo "Password OK!";
}
```

```
else {
        echo "Not valid password";
}

?>
```

The above example uses two if statements: one for checking if a username is correct and one to check that the password is correct. We assume that the stored username is "admin" and its password "123456".

The script begins by declaring variables $user and $pass which represent the username and password supplied by the user. Variables $username and $password are also declared and contain the values that $user and $pass will be compared against:

```
$user = "admin";
$pass = "12345";

$username = "admin";
$password = "123456";
```

The next part of the script checks if a username has been supplied and if so checks that the value supplied is equal to the value stored in $username:

```
//Check username

if($user == "") {
        echo "Empty username!";
}
elseif($user == "$username") {
        echo "Username OK!";
}
else {
        echo "Not valid username";
}

echo "<br />";
```

The last part of the script performs the same operations on the password which were done above on the username:

```
//Check password

if($pass == "") {
        echo "Empty password!";
}
elseif($pass == "$password") {
        echo "Password OK!";
}
else {
        echo "Not valid password";
}
```

The output from the above script is illustrated in Figure 11.1.

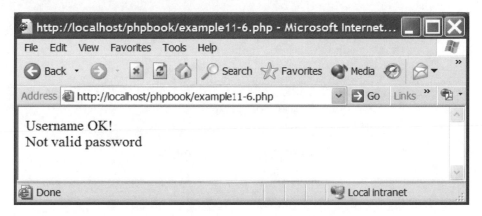

Figure 11.1 A simple login script with if statements.

Switch Statement

The switch statement is similar to a collection of if statements. The switch statement is used when you wish to compare a variable against a number of different values and execute different code depending on its value. You can implement this using a number of if statements, but the code can become complex and difficult to understand. The syntax of the switch statement is:

```
switch (expression)
{
        case constant expression : statement
        case constant expression : statement
        ...
        default : statement
}
```

The following script uses a switch statement to check the local time and show a greeting. The current hour is stored in variable $time. If this is 8 then the message "Time to get up" is displayed. If it is 16 then the message "Time for tea" is displayed. Finally, if it is 23 then the message "Time for bed" is displayed. Any other hour will result in the text "Time to do anything" being displayed.

```php
<?php

//If Statements - Example 11-7
//-----------------------

$time = date("G");

echo "Time is $time - ";

switch ($time) {

        case 8 : echo "Time to get up<br />";
            break;
        case 16 : echo "Time for tea<br />";
            break;
        case 23 : echo "Time for bed<br />";
            break;

        default: echo "Time to do anything<br />";
}

?>
```

The break statements in this example are used to break out of the switch statement. If these were omitted, all statements in all cases after the first one, which was deemed to be true are executed. This is illustrated below:

```php
<?php

//If Statements - Example 11-8
//-----------------------

$time = date("G");

echo "Time is $time - ";

switch ($time) {

        case 8 : echo "Good morning! <br />";
```

```
        case 16 : echo "Good afternoon! <br />";

        case 21 : echo "Good night! <br />";
}

?>
```

In this example if the hour is 16 then the output produced is illustrated in Figure 11.2.

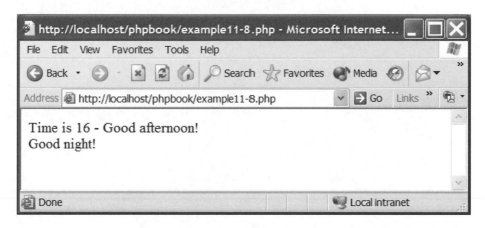

Figure 11.2 Switch statements with no breaks.

Summary

In this chapter we have introduced the if and switch statements and illustrated how they can be used to control which statements are executed. We have shown how the operational and comparison operators introduced in the previous chapter are used with these statements. In the next chapter we shall introduce some further control structures – loops.

Loops 12

Introduction

As in any programming language, loops are an essential part of the language. Loops are used to enable the repeated execution of a block of code. There are four types of loops: for; while; do while; and for each. Each of them has their specific uses. All loop types are controlled by expressions and conditions. In this chapter we will examine the first three types of loops. The for each loop construct will be explained in Chapter 14 as this type of loop is only used to access the contents of an array. We shall begin by examining the while loop.

While Loop

While loops have a simple structure and are commonly used in PHP. The meaning of a while statement is simple. It tells PHP to execute the statement(s) nested within the loop repeatedly, as long as the while expression evaluates to TRUE. The format of the while loop is:

```
while (expression) {statement}
```

For each iteration, the value of the expression is checked at the beginning of the loop. If the while expression evaluates to FALSE from the start, the nested statement(s) won't even be executed once. Braces can be used with the while loop to surround a number of statements to be executed within the loop. The following script illustrates a simple while loop:

```php
<?php

//Loops - Example 12-1
//---------------------

$a = 1;

while ($a<=10)

{
        echo "This is number $a<br>";
        $a++;
}
?>
```

In this example the variable $a is set to 1. The loop expression checks to see if the value of $a is less than or equal to 10. If so the contents of the loop are processed. In this case an echo statement is used to display the value of variable $a. In addition the value of variable $a is incremented by 1 each time the contents of the loop are executed. Eventually the value of $a will be equal to 11 and then the script will terminate. The output from the script is shown in Figure 12.1.

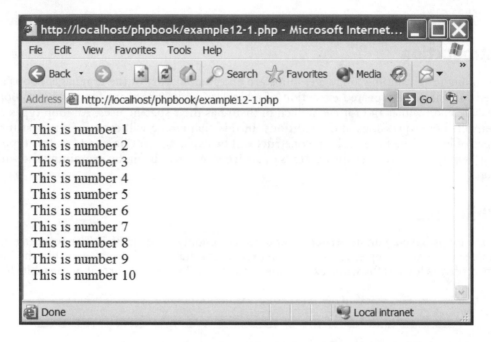

Figure 12.1 Simple while loop.

While loops are most often used with an integer variable which is either incremented or decremented with each iteration though the loop. The loop expression is checked each time to determine if the loop should be executed once more or whether control should jump to the instruction after the loop (in this case the end of the script). If a variable is not incremented or decremented within the loop then the loop will never terminate and neither will your PHP script. For example:

```php
<?php

//Loops - Example 12-2
//---------------------

$a = 1;
while ($a<=10)
        echo "This is number $a<br>";
?>
```

We would recommend that you do not try running this script in your browser as it could cause your Web server to stop responding. However, the script does illustrate a useful feature which happens with all loops – if you only have one instruction within the loop then you can omit the start and end braces.

Do While Loop

The do while loop is similar to the while loop. The difference is where and when the loop expression is checked for true or false. In a while loop we have shown that the loop expression is checked at the start of the loop. Therefore, if the expression is false then none of the statements within the loop will be executed. In the case of a do while loop the expression is evaluated at the end of the loop, after the statements within the loop have been executed at least once. Because of this, a do while loop is known as a one or many iterative loop, as the statements within it are executed at least once, and perhaps many times. A while loop on the other hand is known as a zero, one or many loop as the statements may not be executed at all. The format of the while loop is as follows:

```
do {statement} while (expression);
```

The following script illustrates a simple do while loop:

```php
<?php

//Loops - Example 12-3
//---------------------

$num = 0;
do {
echo"this is a do-while loop";
} while ($num > 0);

?>
```

The above example illustrates a loop, which would not display anything if it were implemented using a while loop, as the expression evaluates to false straightaway. However, as a do while loop always processes the contents of the loop at least once (since the expression is checked at the end rather than the start) then the message "this is a do-while loop" is displayed.

For Loop

For loops are another commonly used loop, although at first glance they would appear to be far more complex than the while and do while loops as they have three expressions incorporated into the for construct. The first expression is used to set a start point for the loop, the second one is the main expression to control how many times the loop will be repeated and the third one is normally used to increment the variable which is used to control the number of iterations around the loop. The format for the for loop is as follows:

```
for (expression1; expression2; expression3) {statement}
```

Braces can be used with the for loop to surround a number of statements to be executed within the loop, in the same way as those used in the while and do while loops. The following example illustrates a short for loop used to create ten numbers:

```php
<?php

//Loops - Example 12-4
//---------------------

for($count=0;$count<=10;$count++)
{
        echo "$count ";
}
?>
```

In this example the starting value of variable $count is defined as 0 by the first expression in the loop. This tells the loop to begin from 0. The second expression is the loop termination test and checks to see if $count is less than or equal to 10. If so the loop is finished. The last expression increments variable $count by 1 on each iteration of the loop. The output from this script is illustrated in Figure 12.2.

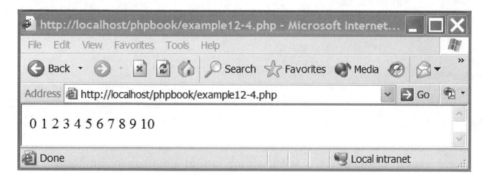

Figure 12.2 Using a for loop to create ten numbers.

Loops very often can be used to create lots of HTML code and especially tables. In the following example we will see how a for loop can create a table with six rows and two columns:

```php
<?php

//Loops - Example 12-5
//---------------------

?>
```

```
<html>
<body>
<table width="40%" border="1">

<?
for($c=0;$c<6;$c++)
{

        echo "<tr>";
        echo "<td>Cell 1 Row $c</td>";
        echo "<td>Cell 2 Row $c</td>";
        echo "</tr>";

}
?>
</table>
</body>
</html>
```

The output from the above script is shown in Figure 12.3.

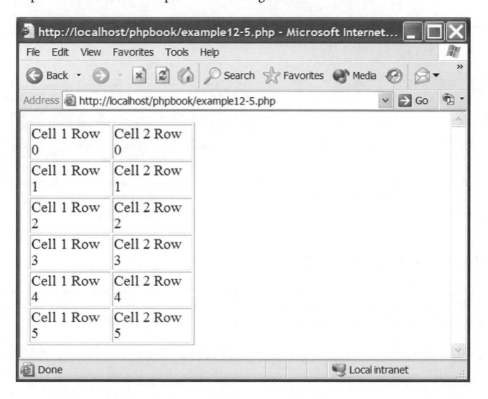

Figure 12.3 Using a for loop to create a table with usernames and passwords.

Nested Loops

A nested loop is a loop within another loop. With nested loops the outer loop begins its first iteration and then processes the inner loop until the inner loop is completed. Then the second iteration of the outer loop begins, processing the inner loop once again and so on. Nested loops are a very powerful programming facility and can produce complex output from relatively few statements.

Any combination of loops of different types can be nested, the following fragment illustrates a nested while loop within a for loop:

```php
<?php

//Loops - Example 12-6
//---------------------

for($y=4;$y<6;$y++){

echo "<br><b> Timestable $y </b><br>";

        $x=1;
        while($x<13){

                $result = $x*$y;
                echo "$y * $x = $result <br>";
                $x++;
        }

}

?>
```

The above example creates the fourth and fifth times tables. The outer for loop is used to create each times table and the inner while loop is used to create the contents and calculations of each table. The output produced is shown in Figure 12.4.

Break or Continue a Loop

The break command can also be used to end the execution of a loop, whether it be a while, do while or for loop. Break can also accept a numerical argument which tells it how many nested loops are to be broken out from. Consider the following example:

```php
<?php

//Loops - Example 12-7
//---------------------
```

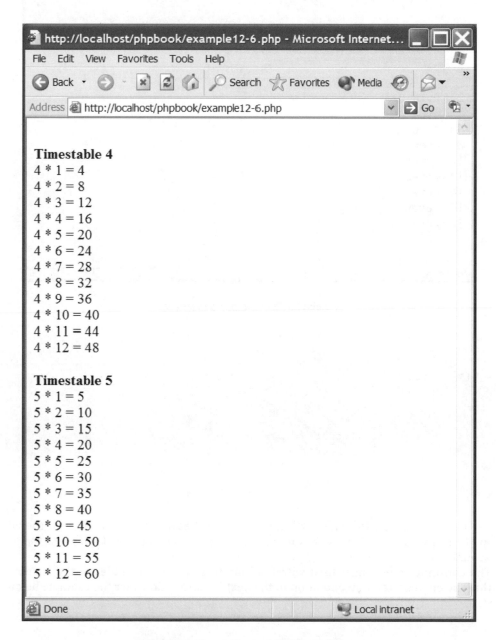

Figure 12.4 Times tables created with nested loops.

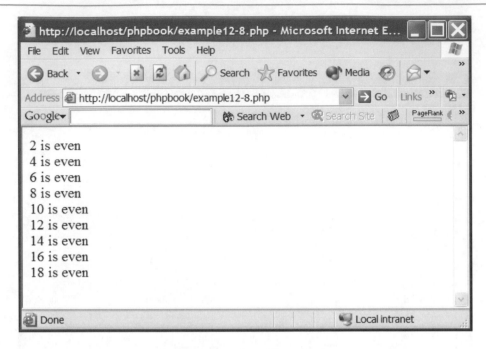

Figure 12.5 Using the continue statement.

```
$count = 0;

while (1){

        echo "Iteration $count<br>";

        if ($count == 10){ break;}
        else{ $count++; }
}
?>
```

Here, a while loop is used which will iterate forever because the expression in the while loop (1) is always true. The break command is used to terminate the loop when the value of $count reaches 10.

The continue statement is used within a loop to skip the remainder of the statements within the current iteration and jump to the next iteration. Consider the example below:

```
<?php

//Loops - Example 12-8
//--------------------
```

```
for($count=1; $count<20; $count++){

        if ($count % 2){ continue; }

        echo "$count is even <br>";

}
?>
```

This script loops through from 1 to 19 and displays only the odd numbers from the loop. Why? Well, because if the value of $count is even the continue statement is executed and the echo statement is missed. The output from this script is shown in Figure 12.5.

Summary

In this chapter we have introduced the concept of flow of control using loops. We have shown that loops can be used to repeat a section of code many times and are thus extremely useful to the programmer as they can reduce the amount of coding required. We have shown that loops can contain a varying number of PHP statements within them and can also include other loops. In the next chapter we shall examine how you can begin to divide up and structure your code using functions and include files.

Functions and Includes 13

Introduction

This chapter introduces you to the concept of functions. PHP comes with a function library of many hundreds of functions already written for you to use. Functions make your life as a programmer much easier by expanding the core of the language and providing you with advanced features. However, no matter how good a function library is, it will never contain every function that you will want. In such cases you will need to create your own. Furthermore you may wish to divide your code into separate PHP files and include these together to form a large single PHP script. This chapter explains how.

What is a Function?

Functions are blocks of code, which are processed only when the function is invoked. If the function is not invoked the code inside the function is never executed. A function can be invoked (also known as being "called") from anywhere inside the script. When the function has executed the flow of control of the program returns to point in the script immediately after where it was called.

User Defined Functions

User defined functions are blocks of script which you may wish to invoke time and time again. Functions remove the need to duplicate the same block of script as the function can be invoked from within a simple loop. This results in the overall size of the script being smaller and makes the programmer more productive. Functions make scripts more readable and thus make maintenance to the script easier.

A function may be defined using the following syntax:

```
function name (arg_1, arg_2, ..., arg_n)

{
 script
 .

 .
 return value;
}
```

Functions always have a unique name (so we can identify which function we wish to use). They also have some script enclosed in braces which denotes the start and end of the function. Some functions have arguments, these are variables that are passed to the function and determine what the function will do. Some functions also return a single variable value.

Creating and Calling a Function

The following example will illustrate a simple function that creates a HTML table. No arguments are defined and no returning value is given after the execution of the function but a table will be created. This is the simplest structure of a user-defined function and is rarely used:

```php
<?php

//Functions and includes - Example 13-1
//-----------------------------

function create_table ()
{
 echo" <table border='1' bgcolor='#DBDBDB' width='394'
        height='121'> ";
 echo"  <tr> ";
 echo"    <td>cell 1</td> ";
 echo"    <td>cell 2 </td> ";
 echo"  </tr> ";
 echo" </table> ";
 echo"<br />";
}

//Call the function
create_table();

?>
```

The above script defines a function with the name of "create_table". The script within the function is that between the {} braces and consists of a series of echo statements:

```php
function create_table ()
{
 echo" <table border='1' bgcolor='#DBDBDB' width='394'
        height='121'> ";
```

```
    echo" <tr> ";
    echo"   <td>cell 1</td> ";
    echo"   <td>cell 2 </td> ";
    echo" </tr> ";
    echo" </table> ";
    echo"<br />";
}
```

In order to "execute" the function we need to invoke this and we do this with the line:

```
create_table();
```

This statement invokes the function passing it no arguments. The output from this function is shown in Figure 13.1.

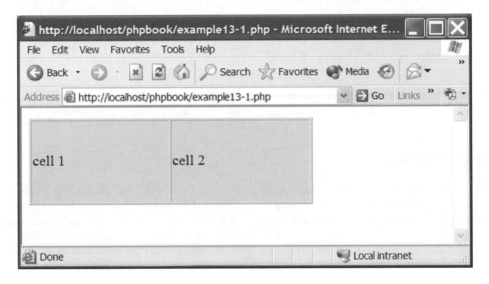

Figure 13.1 Simple function output.

Creating a Function with Arguments

Arguments are used to control the output of the function and what the function will do. In the previous example we have created a static HTML table and nothing more. But what if we want to modify the size of the table according to our needs? This can be done by using arguments to control the width and height of the table. On the following example argument "$w" will define the width of table and "$h" the height of the table. Arguments are separated by commas (,) and there is no limit on how many of them can be used within a function. In the case of a single argument no comma is required. Here is an example script using a function with arguments:

```php
<?php

//Functions and includes - Example 13-2
//-------------------------------

 function create_table ($w, $h)
{
 echo" <table border='1' bgcolor='#DBDBDB' width='$w' height='$h'>
";
 echo" <tr> ";
 echo" <td>cell 1</td> ";
 echo" <td>cell 2 </td> ";
 echo" </tr> ";
 echo" </table> ";
 echo"<br>";
}
//Call the function with values
create_table(500,100);

?>
```

The output from the above script is similar to that of the previous example, except that now the table width is much larger. Try calling the function with different argument values.

Default Arguments

Sometimes, when we are using functions in different parts of our script, we would like arguments to have default values, which will be used if we invoke the function without any arguments. For example, suppose that most of the time we would like our table function to default to providing tables of width and height of 100×100 pixels, respectively. However, we would like to be able to override this if required. We can do this with default arguments. Default values can be set with a "=" after each argument in the function definition, for example, $w=100.

Note that some or all arguments can have default values and these must be separated by commas (,). Here is an example script:

```php
<?php

//Functions and includes - Example 13-3
//-------------------------------

function create_table ($w=100, $h=100)
{
 echo" <table border='1' bgcolor='#DBDBDB' width='$w'
        height='$h'>";
```

```
   echo"   <tr> ";
   echo"     <td>cell 1</td> ";
   echo"     <td>cell 2 </td> ";
   echo"   </tr> ";
   echo" </table> ";
   echo"<br>";
}

//Call the function without values
create_table();

//Call the function with values
create_table(300,100);


?>
```

In this example the same function create_table() is used but the arguments $w and $h have been given a default value of 100 each:

```
function create_table ($w=100, $h=100)
```

We can now call the function without any arguments:

```
create_table();
```

But we can overwrite the default arguments by setting a new value while calling the function:

```
create_table(300,100);
```

The output from this script is illustrated in Figure 13.2.

Returning Values

Functions will stop executing the code within them if the keyword "return" is encountered:

```
<?php

//Functions and includes - Example 13-4
//--------------------------------
```

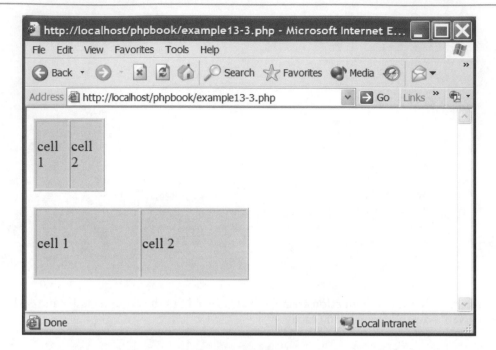

Figure 13.2 Default arguments.

```
function test ()
{
 echo "This is a test";
 return;
 echo "This another test";
}



test();
?>
```

With this example the output produced is "This is a test" because the return statement is encountered before the second echo statement is reached.

This keyword is not very useful when used in this way, but it does have another use. The return command can be used to return a value. In PHP functions can be defined which return a single value:

```
<?php

//Functions and includes - Example 13-5
//-------------------------------
```

```
function addition ($first, $second)
{
 $sum = $first + $second;
 return $sum;
}
//Call the function
$check = addition(2,5);

echo $check;

?>
```

In the above example we have a simple function that uses two arguments. The function simple adds these two variable values together and returns the result:

```
function addition ($first, $second)
{
 $sum = $first + $second;
 return $sum;
}
```

As this function returns a value we need to "catch it" or it will be lost. To catch it we can store this in a variable which we have called $check:

```
$check = addition(2,5);
```

Whatever the function returns is stored in the variable $check. Using an echo statement we can observe what the function has returned, which in this case should be the value 7.

The following example shows a more useful case of a returned value:

```
<?php

//Functions and includes - Example 13-6
//-------------------------------

 function checktotal ($a, $b, $c)
{
 $sum = $a + $b + $c;
 return $sum;
}
```

```
//Call the function
$total = checktotal(10,52,26);
$total_vat = $total * 1.175;

echo "Total without VAT: <b>$total</b>";
echo "<br>";
echo "Total with VAT 18%: <b>$total_vat</b>";

?>
```

The above function receives three values which it totals and the total is returned. Assume that we have an e-commerce system and we want to check the total price of three products. These products cost 10, 52 and 26, respectively, and we want to show the total cost and total cost with VAT. Function checktotal() is used to add three prices together and return this result into variable $total. Assuming that VAT is 17.5% we multiply the returned value (in $total) by 1.175 to get the actual price with VAT:

```
$total = checktotal(10,52,26);
$total_vat = $total * 1.175;
```

Finally we use two echo statements to display the total price with and without VAT, the output of which is shown in Figure 13.3.

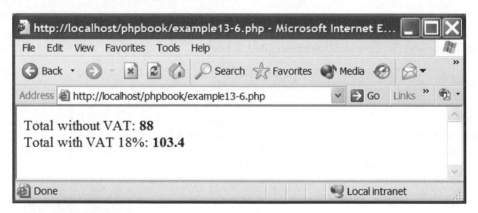

Figure 13.3 Making use of returned values.

Returning More Values

We mentioned previously that functions within PHP cannot return more than one value. What is more correct is that they can only return a single type. Arrays can be used to "get around" the issue of functions being only able to return single values. You will see in the following chapter how to define and use arrays but for now here is a simple example of a function returning an array. Don't worry if you don't understand the array syntax just yet; it is explained shortly:

```php
<?php

//Functions and includes - Example 13-7
//--------------------------------

function three_names()
{

$names = array("Simon", "Mike", "Liz");

return $names;
}

//Call the function
$myNames = three_names();

echo "First name : " . $myNames[0];
echo "<br />Second name : " . $myNames[1];
echo "<br />Third name : " . $myNames[2];
?>
```

Arguments Passed by Value

When an argument is passed to a function its value is automatically "passed by value". This means that only a copy of the variable is passed. If that value is changed in the function the value of the variable outside the function remains unchanged. Consider the example below:

```php
<?php

//Functions and includes - Example 13-8
//--------------------------------

$number = 2;

function simple($number)
{
        $number = $number + 2;
}

simple($number);
echo $number;

?>
```

This example declares a variable $number and assigns the value 2 to it. The value is passed to function simple(), the value is then changed to 4. After the function invocation the value of $number is displayed. The value displayed is 2, it is almost like the function had no effect on the variable's value and in a way that is true.

The reason why the variable appears to "revert back" to its original value is because only a copy of the variable was passed to the function. The function changed the copy but not the original. When the function had completed execution the original variable outside the function was still in existence and unchanged.

Arguments Passed by Reference

You may wish to pass a variable to a function "by reference". Using variables by reference was introduced in Chapter 6. To pass a variable by reference to a function we simply include the character "&" before the variable name. The use of variables by reference permits the function to modify the original variable value. Consider the example below:

```php
<?php

//Functions and includes - Example 13-9
//-------------------------------

$variable = 2;

function simple(&$variable)
{
        $variable = $variable + 2;
}
simple($variable);
echo $variable;

?>
```

This example declares a variable $number and assigns the value 2 to it. The value is passed to function simple() by reference, the value is then changed to 4. After the function invocation the value of $number is displayed. The script outputs the value 4.

Passing variables by reference is considered dangerous practice by many software professionals as it extends the scope of the variable and you may alter a variable's value by mistake. You are advised to use caution when passing variables by reference.

Functions Within Functions

Functions can invoke functions within themselves. Consider the following example:

```php
<?php

//Functions and includes - Example 13-10
//-------------------------------
```

```
function decimal($num)
{
        $num = round($num, 2);
        return $num;
}

function multiply(&$number)
{
        $number = $number * 3.14;
        echo $number . "<br />;
        $number = decimal($number);
        echo $number;
}

$value = 5.2234;
        multiply($number);
?>
```

In this script a floating point number is defined and passed to function multiply():

```
$value = 5.2234;
multiply($number);
```

The function multiplies the number by 3.14 and then displays its current value:

```
        $number = $number * 3.14;
        echo $number . "<br />;
```

It then invokes function decimal() passing it the value of $number and assuming that the value will be returned and finally displayed:

```
        $number = decimal($number);
        echo $number;
```

Function decimal() receives the variable and using a predefined function round() rounds the value to two decimal places and returns this value:

```
function decimal($num)
{
        $num = round($num, 2);
        return $num;
}
```

The output from the above script is:

```
16.401476
16.4
```

Recursive Functions

A recursive function is one which calls itself. This is a complicated scenario which you are unlikely to meet frequently. Recursive functions are useful in evaluating certain types of mathematical functions. You may also encounter certain dynamic data structures such as linked lists or binary trees. Recursion is a very useful way of creating and accessing these structures. The following example is a recursive function used to calculate if a number is a power of 2:

```
<?

//Functions and includes - Example 13-11
//-------------------------------

function is_power_of_two($n)
{
if ($n == 1) {
    echo "yes";
    }

elseif ($n%2 == 1) {
    return "no";
    }
else {
    $n /= 2;
        return is_power_of_two($n);
    }
}

echo is_power_of_two(256) ;
?>
```

In this example the number 256 is checked to see if this is a power of 2 or not by passing it to function is_power_of_two():

```
echo is_power_of_two(256) ;
```

When the function is invoked an if statement checks to see if the number is equal to 1. If so the value "yes" is displayed. If not then another if statement is used to check if dividing the current value of $n by 2 is equal to 1. If this is true then the value "no" is displayed:

```
if ($n == 1) {
    echo "yes";
    }

elseif ($n%2 == 1) {
    return "no";
```

If the number does not satisfy either of these statements then it is divided by 2 and the function calls itself (by return function()) and the process is repeated:

```
}
else{
    $n /= 2;
    return is_power_of_two($n);
}
```

Include, Include_once

So far in this chapter we have shown how we can create functions to perform specific operations. Functions allow us to divide up our code into manageable "chunks". Another way of dividing up code is to separate a large PHP script into several smaller ones. This allows you to share and reuse parts of your scripts more easily. Consider the following script:

```
<?php

//Functions and includes - Example 13-12
//-------------------------------

$firstname = "Simon";
$surname = "Stobart";

?>
```

Yes, we know it is not very exciting as all it does is define two variables. But we can include this file inside another script by using the include statement:

```
Include ( filename );
```

For example:

```
<?php

//Functions and includes - Example 13-13
//-------------------------------
```

```
echo $firstname;

include ("example13-12.php");

echo "<br />" . $surname;

?>
```

The above script uses the include statement to "copy in" the script in file example13-12.php at the point in the script where the include statement is placed. This results in the following being displayed:

```
Notice: Undefined variable: firstname in
  c:\inetpub\wwwroot\phpbook\example13-13.php on line 6

Stobart
```

The notice is generated because the value of variable $firstname is not known when the first echo statement is reached. If the include statement were moved before the first echo statement then the notice message would be removed.

If an included file cannot be found a warning message is generated, but the processing of the script continues.

The include_once() statement operates the same as the include() statement except that the script from a file is only ever included once in the execution of a script. The format of the statement is:

```
Include_once ( filename );
```

Require, Require_once

These statements operate in exactly the same way as the include and include_once statements. The only difference is in how they handle failure. In the case of a file not being located a fatal error is generated and execution of the script is terminated.

Summary

This chapter has introduced the concept of functions. It has shown how these can be created and how variables can be passed to them by both value and reference. We have also shown how we can include separate PHP scripts within an executing script. In the following chapter we shall consider the data structure known as an array.

Arrays **14**

Introduction

In this chapter we shall introduce the concept of an array. Arrays are essential for the manipulation of sets of related variables. PHP supports both single and multi-dimensional arrays. Arrays are used to collect together data, such as people's names and perform operations on this data as easily as possible. We shall begin by examining what a single dimensional array is and how to create one.

Single Dimensional Arrays

Single dimensional arrays are containers, which can store a single sequence of indexed elements. Arrays are similar to variables, but whereas a variable can store only a single value, arrays can store multiple values. Figure 14.1 illustrates a single dimensional array containing a list of garden vegetables. The array consists of a name, $veg and a number of elements each of which contains a value, which in this example is a vegetable. Each element has an index. By default the index is automatically created, beginning with the number 0 and incrementing by 1 for each element in the array.

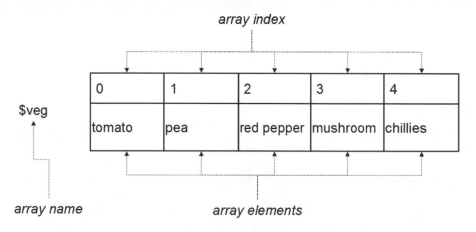

Figure 14.1 Single dimensional array.

The Array Construct

Arrays are created in PHP using the language construct array, the form of which is as follows:

```
array = array([ mixed ...])
```

To create the array illustrated in Figure 14.1 we can declare our array as follows:

```
$veg = array("tomato", "peas", "redPepper", "mushrooms",
"chillies");
```

This creates an array called $veg which contains five elements storing our garden vegetables. We can refer to the elements within the array by using a subscript to the array name. Because the index defaults to numbering the array index from 0 to in this case to 4 then we can access the first element of the array by the following statement:

```
echo($veg[0]);
```

and the last element of the array by:

```
echo($veg[4]);
```

The following script declares the vegetable array and displays the contents of the array using a for loop:

```php
<?php

//Array - Example 14-1
//---------------------

$veg = array("tomato", "peas", "redPepper", "mushrooms", "chillies");

for($a=0;$a<5;$a++)
      echo($veg[$a] . "<br>");
?>
```

The output from this script is illustrated in Figure 14.2.

While Figure 14.2 shows us that we can access our array contents it is not very spectacular. Let's make the output a little more interesting. In the following script we have modified the output so that we generate a simple table:

```php
<table border='1'><tr>

<?php
//Array - Example 14-2
//--------------------
```

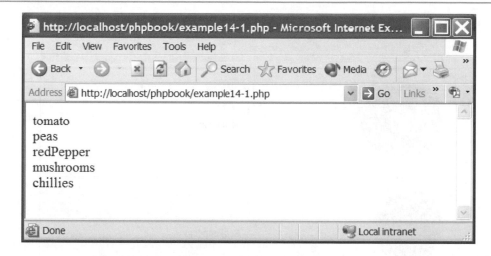

Figure 14.2 Displaying an array.

```
$veg = array("tomato", "peas", "redPepper", "mushrooms", "chillies");

for($a=0;$a<5;$a++)
        echo("<td><img src='graphics/" . $veg[$a] . ".jpg'></td>");
echo("</tr>");
?>
</table>
```

The above script displays a table and within the table cells we output the values of the array. However, to make the display more interesting we have created some simple graphics, which we use to represent the vegetables within the array. These have been created and saved with the same name as that stored in the array, but with a .jpg extension. The graphics and their filename are listed in Table 14.1. We have saved these in a sub-directory called "graphics" below our root directory.

Figure 14.3 illustrates the output from the previous script.

Specifying a Numerical Index

In our previous example we created an array with an automatic index. We can, however, specify the index to the array manually, consider the following:

```
$veg = array(0=>"tomato", 1=>"peas", 2=>"redPepper", 3=>"mush-
rooms", 4=>"chillies");
```

An index can be specified using the operator =>. In the above example the index has been specified exactly as the default index would, a numerical index starting from 0 and incremented by 1 each time. But what if we put the index items in a different order and even missed out an index number, for example:

Table 14.1 Vegetable image graphics.

Image	Filename
	Tomato.jpg
	RedPepper.jpg
	Peas.jpg
	Mushrooms.jpg
	Chillies.jpg

```
$veg = array(0=>"tomato", 2=>"peas", 1=>"redPepper", 3=>"",
4=>"mushrooms",
5=>"chillies");
```

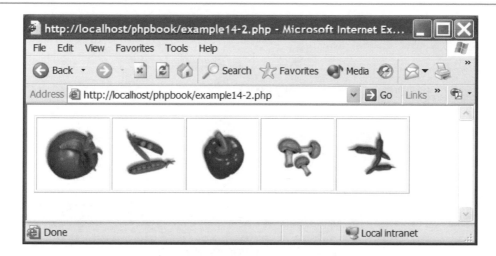

Figure 14.3 More interesting array output.

In the above example, the index is not given in numerical order. To illustrate what happens in this case, the array has been included in the following script:

```
<table border='1'><tr>

<?php

//Array - Example 14-3
//---------------------

$veg = array(0=>"tomato", 2=>"peas", 1=>"redPepper", 3=>"",
4=>"mushrooms", 5=>"chillies");
for($a=0;$a<6;$a++) {
        if($veg[$a] == "")
                echo("<td><img src='graphics/question.jpg'></td>");
        else
                echo("<td><img src='graphics/" . $veg[$a] .
                ".jpg'></td>");
}
echo("</tr>");
?>
</table>
```

The output from the above script is shown in Figure 14.4.

Figure 14.4 illustrates that while we declared the index elements in a non-numerical order this did not make any difference. The peas were placed at index 2 and the red pepper at index 1 and this is how they appear. In the case of index element 3, which was specified as blank, there is no vegetable to be output so a question mark graphic has been displayed

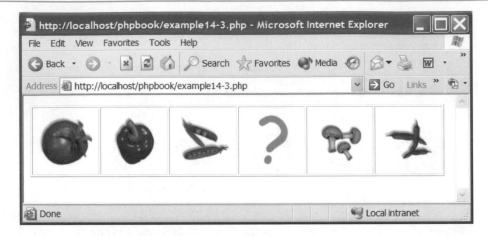

Figure 14.4 Specifying our own index output.

which we called question.jpg. This is accomplished through the use of an if statement within the script, to check whether the index is blank:

```
if($veg[$a] == "")
        echo("<td><img src='question.jpg'></td>");
```

Foreach Loop

PHP includes a loop construct specifically designed for iterating through arrays. This loop construct is known as the foreach loop and there are two syntaxes. The first form is:

```
Foreach ($array as $value) statement
```

Here, the loop will iterate through the array provided by $array. The value in the current index is assigned to $value. The array index is then incremented by one so the next iteration of the loop will access the next element of the array. An example of this loop has been included in the following script that is a rewrite of the previous one:

```
<table border='1'><tr>

<?php

//Array - Example 14-4
//---------------------
```

```
$veg = array(0=>"tomato", 2=>"peas", 1=>"redPepper",
4=>"mushrooms", 5=>"chillies");

foreach($veg as $vegItem)
        echo("<td><img src='graphics/$vegItem.jpg'></td>");
echo("</tr>");
?>
</table>
```

Note that the script is a little less complex than the previous example. Also, note that the need to check for blank index positions is removed as the foreach loop automatically moves to the next indexed element. This is shown with the output illustrated in Figure 14.5. Note that the output of the vegetables is also in the order in which they were declared, not in the numerical index order, as with the for loop.

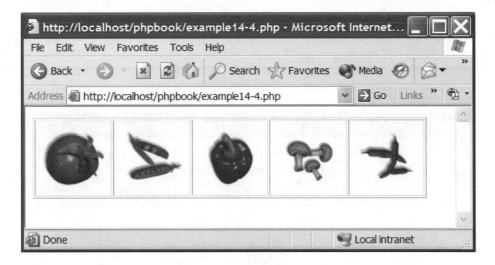

Figure 14.5 Foreach loop output.

The second form of the foreach loop is:

```
Foreach ($array as $key => $value) statement
```

This foreach statement does much the same thing as the previous example but in addition assigns the value of the current element's index to the variable $key. This is shown in the following script:

```
<table border='1'><tr>

<?php

//Array - Example 14-5
//--------------------

$veg = array(0=>"tomato", 2=>"peas", 1=>"redPepper", 4=>"mushrooms",
5=>"chillies");

foreach($veg as $vegItem)
        echo("<td><img src='graphics/$vegItem.jpg'></td>");
echo("</tr><tr>");
foreach($veg as $key=>$vegItem)
        echo("<td align='center'>$key</td>");

?>
</tr></table>
```

The above script uses two foreach loops, the first outputs the images representing the vegetable contents of the $veg array. The second foreach loop accesses the index key for each element of the array and outputs that value in a second table row below the vegetable images. The output from this script is illustrated in Figure 14.6.

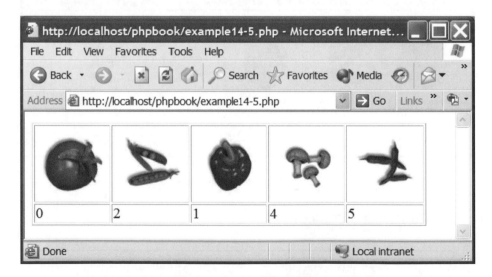

Figure 14.6 Foreach index output.

But why would we want to access the index values? We have already been able to calculate these using the for next loop examples earlier in the chapter. Well, the reason is that index values don't need to be numeric, let's see what this means in practice by specifying some non-numerical indexes.

Specifying a Non-numerical Index

Instead of specifying an array with a numerical index we can specify an array with a string index. For example:

```
$veg = array("Tomato"=>"tomato", "Peas"=>"peas",
"Red Pepper"=>"redPepper", "Mushrooms"=>"mushrooms",
"Chillies"=>"chillies");
```

The above declares an array consisting of our vegetables once again, but instead of using a numerical index it specifies an index of strings representing the values stored in the array element. The following script illustrates the use of such an array:

```
<table border='1'><tr>

<?php

//Array - Example 14-6
//--------------------

$veg = array("Tomato"=>"tomato", "Peas"=>"peas",
"Red Pepper"=>"redPepper", "Mushrooms"=>"mushrooms",
"Chillies"=>"chillies");

foreach($veg as $vegItem)
        echo("<td><img src='graphics/$vegItem.jpg'></td>");
echo("</tr><tr>");
foreach($veg as $key=>$vegItem)
        echo("<td align='center'>$key</td>");

?>
</tr></table>
```

The output from the above script is illustrated in Figure 14.7.

Notice in Figure 14.7 that we can now see both the names of the vegetables, obtained from the indexes and the images representing the vegetables.

Using Single Dimensional Arrays

We now know enough about single dimensional arrays to begin using them to help us. Consider the following script:

```
<table border='1'><tr>

<?php
```

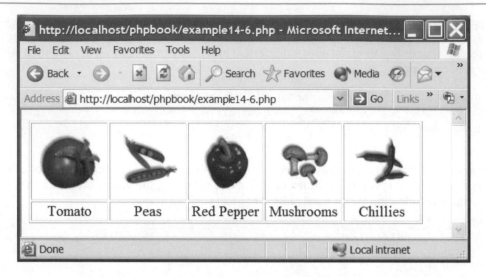

Figure 14.7 String index array output.

```
//Array - Example 14-7
//---------------------

$veg = array("tomato"=>23, "peas"=>78, "redPepper"=>34,
"mushrooms"=>56, "chillies"=>97);

$cost=0;
foreach($veg as $key=>$vegCost)
            echo("<td><img src='graphics/$key.jpg'></td>");
echo("</tr><tr>");
foreach($veg as $vegCost) {
            echo("<td align='center'>$vegCost p</td>");
            $cost=$cost+$vegCost;
}
echo("</tr>");

$cost=$cost/100;
echo("<tr><td align='center' colspan='5'>Total cost of the
Vegetables is £$cost</td></tr>");

echo("<tr><td colspan='5' align='center'><img src='graphics/
 peas.jpg'> + <img src='graphics/mushrooms.jpg'>");
echo(" is £" . ($veg['peas'] + $veg['mushrooms'])/100);
?>
</tr></table>
```

An array is created with indexes consisting of strings. The index values happen to be the names of our images and will enable us to access them. The elements of the array contain integer values, which represent the cost of our vegetables:

```
<table border='1'><tr>
<?php
$veg = array("tomato"=>23, "peas"=>78, "redPepper"=>34, "mush-
rooms"=>56,
"chillies"=>97);
```

Two foreach loops are used to output the vegetable images and to display the costs of the vegetables. Note that the variable $cost is used to store the total count of all vegetables:

```
$cost=0;
foreach($veg as $key=>$vegCost)
        echo("<td><img src='graphics/$key.jpg'></td>");
echo("</tr><tr>");
foreach($veg as $vegCost) {
        echo("<td align='center'>$vegCost p</td>");
        $cost=$cost+$vegCost;
}
echo("</tr>");
```

The total cost of the vegetables is displayed in pounds:

```
$cost=$cost/100;
echo("<tr><td align='center' colspan='5'>Total cost of the
Vegetables is
£$cost</td></tr>");
```

The final part of the script illustrates how powerful arrays with string indexes are. In this example the value of peas and mushrooms is added together and displayed. Note that the code is far more readable as the index values of "peas" and "mushrooms" are used as opposed to using integer values:

```
echo("<tr><td colspan='5' align='center'><img
src='graphics/peas.jpg'> + <img
src='graphics/mushrooms.jpg'>");
echo(" is £" . ($veg['peas'] + $veg['mushrooms'])/100);
?>
</tr></table>
```

Figure 14.8 illustrates the output from the above script.

Multi-dimensional Arrays

PHP supports multi-dimensional arrays in addition to single dimensional ones. Multi-dimensional arrays are in fact arrays of single dimensional arrays. Instead of being able to

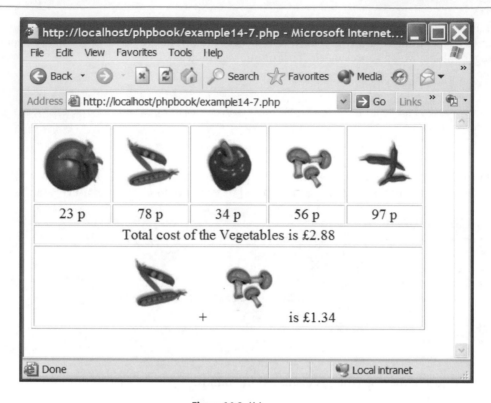

Figure 14.8 Using arrays.

store a single row of elements multi-dimensional arrays can store many rows of elements. Figure 14.9 illustrates a multi-dimensional array. The array consists of rows storing the name of the shape, the size of the shape and the number of shapes.

Creating a Multi-dimensional Array

Multi-dimensional arrays are created using the array construct. To create the array illustrated in Figure 14.9 we use the following syntax:

```
$shapes = array(
        array("star","sun","wheel","flower","inkBlot"),
        array(50,100,25,125,150),
        array(8,4,14,3,2)
);
```

The construct consists of the overall array called $shapes and within this are three single dimensional arrays, which have no names. Each of these single dimensional arrays holds separately the shape's name, size and the quantity of these shapes.

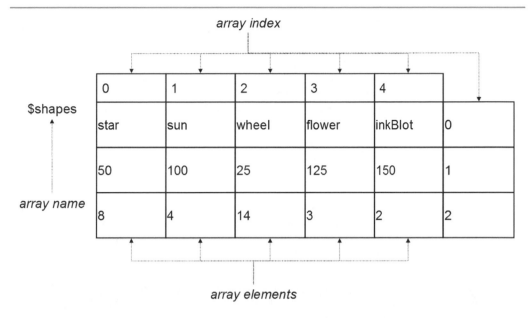

Figure 14.9 Multi-dimensional array.

The different arrays can be accessed using a subscripted value as we did with the single dimensional array. As this array has two dimensions then we need to use two subscripts. For example:

```
$var = $shapes[0][2];
```

The above statement will access the data at array 0 (the first array), element 2, which in this example is "wheel". The following script illustrates accessing the contents of the array data using a for loop:

```
<table border='1'>
<tr><th width=150>Shape</th><th width=100>Size</th><th
width=100>Quantity</th></tr>

<?php

//Array - Example 14-8
//----------------------

$shapes = array(
                array("star","sun","wheel","flower","inkBlot"),
                array(50,100,25,125,150),
                array(8,4,14,3,2)
);
```

```
for($a=0;$a<5;$a++) {
        $name=$shapes[0][$a];
        $size=$shapes[1][$a];
        $quantity=$shapes[2][$a];
        echo("<tr><td>$name</td><td>$size</td>
         <td>$quantity</td></tr>");
}
?>
</table>
```

The above program uses a single for loop to access the contents of the array. Note that because the $shapes array consists of three other arrays we have used the subscripts [0], [1] and [2] to access all of the elements of each of the three arrays. The output from the above script is illustrated in Figure 14.10.

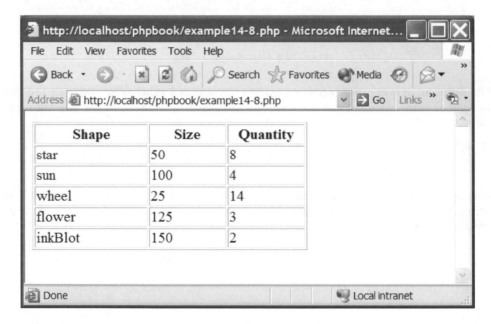

Figure 14.10 Multi-dimensional array output.

Using Foreach with a Multi-dimensional Array

As with single dimensional arrays we can use the foreach loop to access the array contents. Let us revise the script in our previous example and produce some more interesting output. The following script uses the same array as before, however, the data is accessed using a foreach loop:

```
<table border='1'>
<tr>

<?php

//Array - Example 14-9
//--------------------

$shapes = array(
          array("star","sun","wheel","flower","inkBlot"),
          array(50,100,25,125,150),
          array(8,4,14,3,2)
);

foreach($shapes[0] as $key=>$shape){
       $size=$shapes[1][$key];
       $quantity=$shapes[2][$key];
       echo("<td valign='top'>");
       for($count=0;$count<$quantity;$count++)
            echo("<img src='graphics/$shape.jpg' width='$size'
height='$size'><br>");
       echo("</td>");
}
?>
</tr></table>
```

In addition to the foreach loop the data extracted from the array is used to alter the output produced by the script. For each shape in the array a corresponding image is displayed. The size (width and height) of the image are controlled by the data in the second array element and the number of these images which are output is controlled by the data in the third array. For example the star image is displayed as a 50×50 pixel image and there are eight of them to be output. While, the wheel image is displayed as 25×25 pixels in size and there are 14 of them. The output from the above script is illustrated in Figure 14.11.

Using a Non-numerical Index with Multi-dimensional Arrays

In our previous multi-dimensional array examples we have not specified any indexes and so the array defaulted to a numerical integer index. We can, however, specify our own numerical index or even use strings. For example:

```
$shapes = array(
          'image'=>                  array("star","sun","wheel",
                                     "flower","inkBlot"),
          'size'=>                   array(50,100,25,125,150),
          'quantity'=>   array(8,4,14,3,2)
);
```

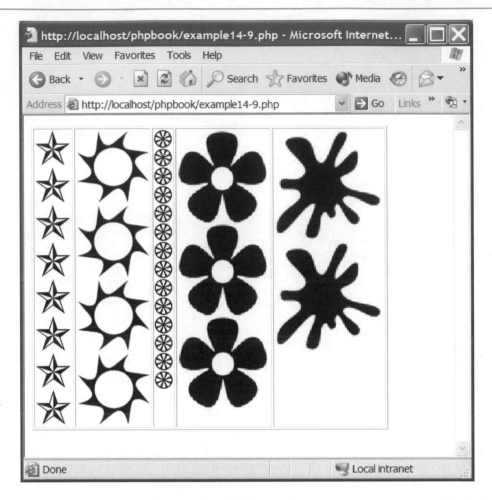

Figure 14.11 Multi-dimensional array output.

In the above example we have given each of our three arrays an index value: image; size; and quantity. The following is a rewrite of the previous script to illustrate how we would use these indexes:

```
<table border='1'>
<tr>

<?php

//Array - Example 14-10
//--------------------
```

```
$shapes = array(
        'image'=>                    array("star","sun","wheel",
                                     "flower","inkBlot"),
        'size'=>                     array(50,100,25,125,150),
        'quantity'=>  array(8,4,14,3,2)
);

foreach($shapes['image'] as $key=>$shape){
        $size=$shapes['size'][$key];
        $quantity=$shapes['quantity'][$key];
        echo("<td valign='top'>");
        for($count=0;$count<$quantity;$count++)
             echo("<img src='graphics/$shape.jpg' width='$size'
height='$size'><br>");
        echo("</td>");
}
?>
</tr></table>
```

The output from this script is the same as that shown in Figure 14.11. We can also specify the index values for each element of the array as we showed for the single dimensional array. The following is an example of this:

```
$shapes = array(
        'image'=>
        array(1=>"star",2=>"sun",3=>"wheel",4=>"flower",5=>"inkBlot"),
        'size'=>          array(1=>50,2=>100,3=>25,4=>125,5=>150),
        'quantity'=>   array(1=>8,2=>4,3=>14,4=>3,5=>2)
);
```

All the above does is specify that the index elements of the arrays start at the numerical value of 1 and not 0.

Summary

This chapter has introduced the concept of arrays. We have shown how we are create both single and multi-dimensional arrays and display their content. In the following chapter we are going to examine how to access system dates and times.

Dates, Times and Random Numbers

15

Introduction

Being able to access the system time and date is a very useful ability. Dates and times can be used for a variety of tasks, from the simple activity of being able to display the correct date and time on your Web page to creating a time stamp of when a database record was created. In addition we shall see that being able to obtain the time is essential in enabling us to create random numbers. This chapter will introduce some of the key functions involved in accessing the date and time and illustrate how random numbers can be created.

Getting the Date and Time

Both the date and time can be accessed through a single function called getdate().

Function prototype:

```
array getdate();
```

The getdate() function returns an array containing the current date and time. The array is a string indexed array and the index values and contents that it contains are illustrated in Table 15.1.

Function example:

```
$date = getdate();
```

The following script illustrates accessing the getdate() function array elements:

```php
<?php

// Dates Times and Random numbers - Example 15-1
//--------------------------------
```

Table 15.1 The getdate() array.

Name	Description
seconds	The seconds part of the current time
minutes	The minutes part of the current time
hours	The hours part of the current time
mday	Day of the month
wday	Numerical day of the week (Sunday $= 0$)
mon	Numerical month
year	Numerical year
yday	Numerical day of the year, i.e. 312
weekday	Textual day of the week, i.e. "Monday"
month	Textual month of the year, i.e. "May"

```
$date = getdate();

$seconds = $date['seconds'];
$minutes = $date['minutes'];
$hours = $date['hours'];
$mday = $date['mday'];
$wday = $date['wday'];
$mon = $date['mon'];
$year = $date['year'];
$yday = $date['yday'];
$weekday = $date['weekday'];
$month = $date['month'];

echo("The time is $hours:$minutes:$seconds<br>");
echo("The date is $mday/$mon/$year<br>");
echo("The month is $month and the day of the week is $week-
day<br>");
echo("It is day $wday out of 6 this week (with Sunday being
0)<br>");
echo("There have been $yday days so far this year.");
?>
```

The script invokes the getdate() function and then assigns each of the returned array
elements into separate variables for the sake of clarity. These are then displayed on the
Web page, as illustrated in Figure 15.1.

Obviously, the time and dates displayed on your computer will be different from those
above, depending on when you run the script. At the moment we are not doing anything
useful with this data (apart from displaying it), however, we shall see a useful example of
their use later in this chapter as well as in subsequent chapters of this book.

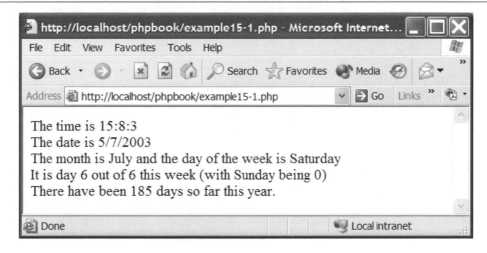

Figure 15.1 Date and time values.

Microtime

The getdate() function returns the current time to the nearest second. While this is useful, you may need to get a more accurate time stamp and this can be achieved through the microtime() function.

Function prototype:

```
String microtime(void)
```

Function arguments and return details:

Name	Type	Description
microtime() returns	String	This function returns a string consisting of two parts: "msec sec"
		The value of sec is the number of seconds, which have passed since midnight on the 1st January 1970. The msec part of the string is the microseconds fraction of the current non-whole second

Function example:

```
$secs = microtime();
```

The following script illustrates an example of the use of the function:

```
<?php

// Dates Times and Random numbers - Example 15-2
//-------------------------------

$secs = microtime();
echo($secs);
?>
```

The above script invokes function microtime() and displays its contents. While we realize that the microtime() function does not seem very impressive it is actually very useful. We shall return to this function later in this chapter when we come to generate random numbers.

Checking a Date

Sometimes we may wish a user to enter a date. Unfortunately, some dates are valid and others are not, consider these dates:

31st September 1402
30th April 1999
29th February 1400

Only some of these dates are valid, but how would we check which ones are valid within a script. Luckily, the checkdate() function exists which returns TRUE value if the date passed to it is valid and a value of FALSE if it is not. The format of this function is:

Function prototype:

Int checkdate(int month, int day, int year);

Function arguments and return details:

Name	Type	Description
month	Int	The month
day	Int	The day
year	Int	The year
checkdate() returns	Int	TRUE if the date is valid or FALSE if it is not

Function example:

```
$date = checkdate(2,29,1402);
```

The function receives three integer parameters, which represent the month, day and year of the date. An example of this function in use is shown in the following script:

```php
<?php
// Dates Times and Random numbers - Example 15-3
//--------------------------------

$date = checkdate(2,29,1402);
if($date)
        echo("This is a valid date!");
else
        echo("This is an invalid date");
?>
```

The script passes a date of 29th February 1402 to the checkdate() function and then displays a message indicating whether the date is valid or not. You can try changing the date passed to function checkdate() to see which of the dates above are valid or not.

Generating a Random Number

Being able to generate a random number is a useful facility in any programming language. Without random numbers games programs, for example, would become very predictable. In PHP there are two steps to generating a random number. The first concerns the seeding of the random number generator using the srand() function, the format of which is:

Function prototype:

Void srand(int seed);

Function arguments and return details:

Name	Type	Description
seed	Int	Random seed to the random number generator
srand() returns	Void	Returns nothing

Function example:

```
srand(1);
```

The srand() function is used to set the random number generator to a random position before we start obtaining our random numbers. Failure to do this will result in a predictable set of random numbers To seed the random number generator we need a large random number to begin with! One way of achieving this is to use the microtime() function to obtain the microseconds part of its output and multiply this to a large number (we told you that we would return to this function). We can do this with the statement:

```
srand((double) microtime() * 1000000);
```

The above randomly seeds the random number generator with a random number produced from when the current time was obtained from the microtime() function. We are now ready to obtain random numbers and the function rand() enables us to do this. The format of this function is:

Function prototype:

```
int rand ([int start, int end]);
```

Function arguments and return details:

Name	Type	Description
start	Int	Optional minimum value of the random number to be generated
end	Int	Optional maximum value of the random number to be generated
rand() returns	Int	Random number

Function example:

```
$rand = (10,1000);
```

The rand() function can be invoked without any parameters and this returns a random number, the maximum and minimum values of which are outside your control. However, you can limit the range of random numbers produced by including start and end parameters, for example:

```
rand (10,1000);
```

This will produce random numbers between 10 and 1000. A use of the random number generating facility is shown in the following script:

```php
<?php

// Dates Times and Random numbers - Example 15-4
//--------------------------------

srand((double) microtime() * 1000000);
$randVal = rand(1,6);
echo("Random Number: $randVal");
?>
```

The above example simply produces a random number between 1 and 6, not very exciting we admit, but random numbers produced between 1 and 6 are commonly produced in the real world when you throw a six-sided dice. Let's see if we can spice up this example a little.

Dice Example

We are going to create a Web page, which displays the output from six, six-sided dice. The first thing we need to do is to create six dice images, shown in Figure 15.2.

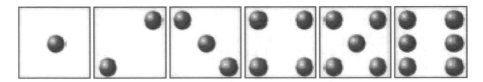

Figure 15.2 Dice images.

Each of these images is stored in your graphics sub-directory directory, with the names 1.jpg, 2.jpg etc. Now consider a script that we have created to use them:

```php
<?php

// Dates Times and Random numbers - Example 15-5
//-------------------------------

srand((double) microtime() * 1000000);
$randVal = rand(1,6);
echo("<img src='graphics/$randVal.jpg'>");
$randVal = rand(1,6);
echo("<img src='graphics/$randVal.jpg'>");
$randVal = rand(1,6);
echo("<img src='graphics/$randVal.jpg'>");
$randVal = rand(1,6);
echo("<img src='graphics/$randVal.jpg'>");
$randVal = rand(1,6);
echo("<img src='graphics/$randVal.jpg'>");
$randVal = rand(1,6);
echo("<img src='graphics/$randVal.jpg'>");
?>
```

The above script seeds the random number generator, and then obtains a random number between 1 and 6 which is stored in variable $randVal. This value is output within a <img> tag to display the relevant die image. This is repeated six times. The output from the above program is shown in Figure 15.3. If you click on the reload icon of the browser then the dice displayed will randomly change.

While, Figure 15.3 illustrates that we can jazz up our random number generator script it still isn't doing anything really useful. So, let's return to our date functions and create a script, which will output a useful calendar.

Implementing a Calendar

Figure 15.4 illustrates a simple calendar for the month of November

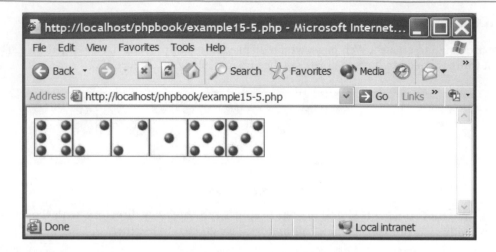

Figure 15.3 Random dice example.

April						
Sun	Mon	Tue	Wed	Thu	Fri	Sat
					1	2
3	4	5	6	7	8	9
10	11	12	13	14	15	16
17	18	19	20	21	22	23
24	25	26	27	28	29	30

Figure 15.4 A simple calendar.

While, this calendar may appear to be quite simple it is in fact quite complex. For example, the days of the week, from Sunday to Saturday appear in fixed columns, however, the day that the month begins will vary between any of these. In the November example, the 1st day of the month is Friday, and thus we have a number of blank cells to output until a 1 is placed in the Friday column.

To create the calendar we will need to employ many of the functions that have been introduced in this chapter:

```php
<table border='1'>
<?php

// Dates Times and Random numbers - Example 15-6
//---------------------------------

$date = getdate();
```

```
$mday = $date['mday'];
$mon = $date['mon'];
$wday = $date['wday'];
$month = $date['month'];
$year = $date['year'];

$dayCount = $wday;
$day = $mday;
while($day > 0) {
        $days[$day--] = $dayCount--;
        if($dayCount < 0)
                $dayCount = 6;
}
$dayCount = $wday;
$day = $mday;

if(checkdate($mon,31,$year))
        $lastDay = 31;
elseif(checkdate($mon,30,$year))
        $lastDay = 30;
elseif(checkdate($mon,29,$year))
        $lastDay = 29;
elseif(checkdate($mon,28,$year))
        $lastDay = 28;

while($day <= $lastDay) {
        $days[$day++] = $dayCount++;
        if($dayCount > 6)
                $dayCount = 0;
}

echo("<tr><td colspan='7' align='center'>$month</td></tr>");
echo("<tr><td>Sun</td><td>Mon</td><td>Tue</td><td>Wed</td><td>
Thu</td><td>Fri</td><td>Sat</td></tr>");

$startDay = 0;
$d = $days[1];
echo("<tr>");
while($startDay < $d) {
        echo("<td></td>");
        $startDay++;
}

for ($d=1;$d<=$lastDay;$d++) {
        if($d == $mday)
                echo("<td bgcolor='lightblue'>$d</td>");
        else
                echo("<td>$d</td>");
```

```
        $startDay++;
        if($startDay > 6 && $d < $lastDay){
                $startDay = 0;
                echo("</tr><tr>");
        }
}
echo("</tr>");
?>
</table>
```

Our script will begin by outputting a table tag and invoking the getdate() function to obtain the day, month and year and the numeric day of the week:

```
<table border='1'>
<?php
$date = getdate();

$mday = $date['mday'];
$mon = $date['mon'];
$wday = $date['wday'];
$month = $date['month'];
$year = $date['year'];
```

Next a while loop is used to begin to populate the $days array. The $days array contains the numerical day of the week for each day in the month. This while loop calculates the day of the week for all of the dates from the current date to the beginning of the month:

```
$dayCount = $wday;
$day = $mday;
while($day > 0) {
        $days[$day--] = $dayCount--;
        if($dayCount < 0)
                $dayCount = 6;
}
$dayCount = $wday;
$day = $mday;
```

In our example the $days array currently looks like this, with the current day of the month being the 3rd, which is a Sunday and the dates of the 2nd and 1st also being included:

0	1	2	3	4	5	6	7	8	9	10	11	12	13	14	15	16	17	18	19	20	21	22	23	24	25	26	27	28	29	30
	5	6	0																											

Next, the checkdate() function is used to determine what the last date of the current month is. It could be 31, 30, 29 or even 28:

```
if(checkdate($mon,31,$year))
        $lastDay = 31;
elseif(checkdate($mon,30,$year))
        $lastDay = 30;
elseif(checkdate($mon,29,$year))
        $lastDay = 29;
elseif(checkdate($mon,28,$year))
        $lastDay = 28;
```

Next, a while loop is used to store in the $days array the day of the week for all of the dates from the current date to the end of the month:

```
while($day <= $lastDay) {
        $days[$day++] = $dayCount++;
        if($dayCount > 6)
                $dayCount = 0;
}
```

In our example the $days array currently looks like this:

0	1	2	3	4	5	6	7	8	9	10	11	12	13	14	15	16	17	18	19	20	21	22	23	24	25	26	27	28	29	30
	5	6	0	1	2	3	4	5	6	0	1	2	3	4	5	6	0	1	2	3	4	5	6	0	1	2	3	4	5	6

The above array tells us that while the first day of the month is a Friday, the last day of the month is a Saturday. We now have a complete array of numerical days of the week, which we can use to create the remainder of our calendar table. We begin by outputting the month and days of the week headings:

```
echo("<tr><td colspan='7' align='center'>$month</td></tr>");
echo("<tr><td>Sun</td><td>Mon</td><td>Tue</td><td>Wed</td><td>
Thu</td><td>Fri</td><td>Sat</td></tr>");
```

Next, we obtain the first day of the week date from the $days array and store this in the variable $d. A while loop is used to output blank table cells until the correct day of the week column is arrived at:

```
$startDay = 0;
$d = $days[1];
echo("<tr>");
while($startDay < $d) {
        echo("<td></td>");
        $startDay++;
}
```

We are now ready to output all of the days of the month. This is done using a for loop. When the current day of the month is reached the background colour of the table cell is displayed is "lightblue" to highlight it:

```
for ($d=1;$d<=$lastDay;$d++) {
        if($d == $mday)
                echo("<td bgcolor='lightblue'>$d</td>");
        else
                echo("<td>$d</td>");
```

Within the loop an if condition checks when the end of a week is reached (i.e. when a Saturday is encountered) and outputs an end of row element to ensure that the table is formatted correctly:

```
        $startDay++;
        if($startDay > 6 && $d < $lastDay){
                $startDay = 0;
                echo("</tr><tr>");
        }
}
echo("</tr>");
?>
</table>
```

The output from this script is illustrated in Figure 15.5. This script could be modified to allow a user to click on a date as part of some form input, for example.

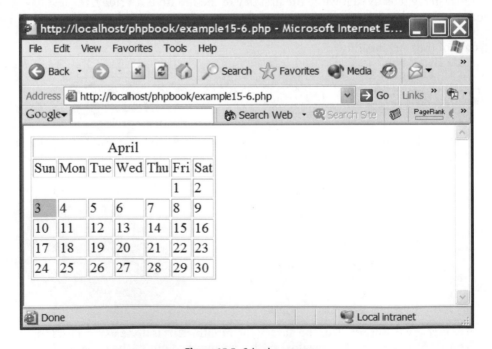

Figure 15.5 Calendar output.

Summary

In this chapter we have introduced the functions which enable us to access the system date and time. We have shown how accessing the time is very important in being able to generate random numbers. We concluded the chapter by examining how to create a useful calendar. The date and time functions within this chapter have used arrays to return their values. Arrays were introduced in the previous chapter, but we shall now return to arrays and consider some of the functions that are available to manipulate them.

Part 3

Manipulating Arrays and Strings

Array Manipulation

16

Introduction

In Chapter 14 we introduced the concept of arrays and provided some examples of their use. We showed that PHP supports both single and multi-dimensional array types. But that is not the end of the story. You can see that the PHP function library contains a large number of functions to help you manipulate your arrays easily. In this chapter we shall introduce some of these functions and illustrate how they can be used to assist you in your programming.

Counting Array Elements

You may wish to be able to count the number of elements in an array. The functions sizeof() and count() both provide you with a means of accomplishing this. The format for these functions is:

Function prototypes:

```
Int count(array theArray);
Int sizeof (array theArray);
```

Function arguments and return details:

Name	Type	Description
theArray	Array	The array to use
count() returns	Int	The size of the array
sizeof() returns	Int	The size of the array

Function examples:

```
$count = count($array);
$count = sizeof($array);
```

The following script illustrates the use of the count() function. The script obtains the size of the array using the count() function. The size of the array is used to control the termination of the for loop:

```
<table border='1'><tr>
<?php

// Array Manipulation - Example 16-1
//------------------------

$veg = array(0=>"tomato", 1=>"peas", 2=>"redPepper", 3=>"mushrooms",
4=>"chillies");

for($item=0;$item<count($veg);$item++)
      echo("<td><img src='graphics/" . $veg[$item] . ".jpg'></td>");
echo("</tr><tr><td align='center' colspan='" . count($veg) . "'>
The array contains " . count($veg) . " items.</td></tr>");
?>
</table>
```

The script also displays a message indicating the number of elements in the array. It uses this value to determine the number of columns that the rowspan attribute of the <TD> element should be set to in order to ensure that the first cell of the second table row, spans the entire width of the table. This enables the "The array contains ... " message to be centred across the table. The output from the above script is shown in Figure 16.1.

Figure 16.1 Counting array elements.

Random Array Elements

Having created an array of elements you may wish to be able to randomize the array contents, placing each element in the array in a random position. The shuffle() function enables you to accomplish this easily. The format of this function is:

Function prototype:

```
Void shuffle(array theArray);
```

Function arguments and return details:

Name	Type	Description
theArray	Array	The array to shuffle
shuffle() returns	Void	Returns nothing

Function example:

```
shuffle($array);
```

In order for the shuffle() function to format correctly the random number generator has to be seeded using the srand() function, described in Chapter 15. The following script illustrates the use of this function:

```
<table border='1'>
<?php

// Array Manipulation - Example 16-2
//-----------------------


srand((double)microtime()*1000000);

$veg = array(0=>"tomato", 1=>"peas", 2=>"redPepper", 3=>"mushrooms",
4=>"chillies");


for($count=0;$count<3;$count++) {
        echo("<tr>");
        foreach($veg as $vegItem)
                echo("<td><img src='graphics/$vegItem.jpg'></td>");
        echo("</tr>");
        shuffle($veg);
}
?>
</table>
```

The script begins by seeding the random number generator and then creating the array. A for loop with a nested foreach loop is used to output the contents of the array three times. After each iteration of the outer for loop a shuffle() function is used to randomize the contents of the loop. The output from this script displays the contents of the array as it was created and then displays the contents of the array twice more after they have been randomized. A typical output from the script is illustrated in Figure 16.2.

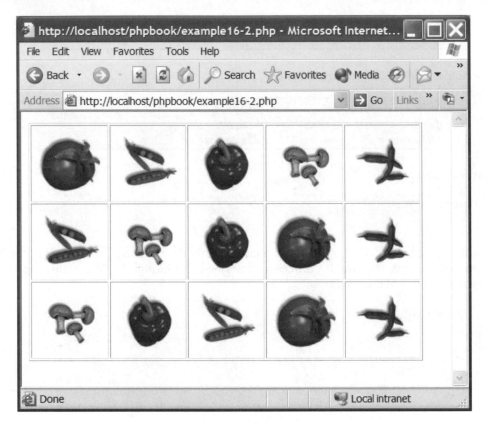

Figure 16.2 Randomizing an array.

Picking Random Elements

Instead of randomizing an entire array you may wish to keep the array as it was created but simply extract a random element from the array. To do this we can use the array_rand() function, which has the following format:

Function prototype:

```
Mixed array_rand(array theArray);
```

Function arguments and return details:

Name	Type	Description
theArray	Array	The array for obtaining a random element
array_rand() returns	Mixed	Random array element

Function example:

```
$pos = array_rand($veg);
```

The array_rand() function is passed an array as a parameter and it returns a random array element index. The array_rand() function also requires that the random number generated be seeded. The following script illustrates the use of the function:

```
<table border='1'>
<?php

// Array Manipulation - Example 16-3
//-----------------------

srand((double)microtime()*1000000);

$veg = array(0=>"tomato", 1=>"peas", 2=>"redPepper", 3=>"mushrooms",
4=>"chillies");

for($rows=0;$rows<3;$rows++) {
    echo("<tr>");
for($cols=0;$cols<5;$cols++) {
        $pos = array_rand($veg);
        echo("<td><img src='graphics/" . $veg[$pos] . ".jpg'></td>");
    }
    echo("</tr>");
}
?>
</table>
```

The script begins by firstly seeding the random number generator and creating an array. Next, two nested for loops are used to output three rows of five random array elements. Figure 16.3 illustrates the output from the above script. Note that while our previous example, as shown in Figure 16.2 outputs all elements of the array in a random order, the example in Figure 16.3 outputs random elements and in a number of cases the same vegetable is displayed more than once.

Adding Elements to the End of an Array

Once an array has been created you may wish to add new elements to the end of the array. One method of accomplishing this is as follows:

```
$array[] = $newItem;
```

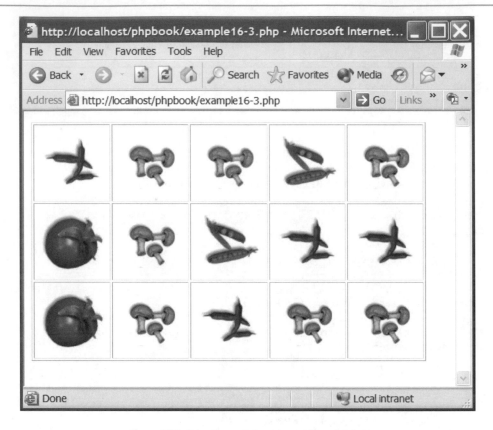

Figure 16.3 Extracting a random element from an array.

The above assignment statement assigns the value of $newItem to the array $array. By not specifying the index of the array into which the value is to be placed the value is automatically stored in a new element at the end of the array. The following script illustrates an example of doing this:

```
<table border='1'>
<?php

// Array Manipulation - Example 16-4
//-----------------------

$veg = array(0=>"tomato", 1=>"peas", 2=>"redPepper", 3=>"mushrooms");

echo("<tr>");
for($rows=0;$rows<count($veg);$rows++) {
    echo("<td><img src='graphics/" . $veg[$rows] . ".jpg'></td>");
    }
```

```
echo("</tr><tr>");
$veg[]="chillies";
for($rows=0;$rows<count($veg);$rows++) {
      echo("<td><img src='graphics/" . $veg[$rows] . ".jpg'></td>");
      }
echo("</tr>");
?>
</table>
```

The script first creates an array and displays its contents using a for loop. Next a new element "chillies" is added to the end of the array. The array contents are then displayed once again. Figure 16.4 illustrates the output from the script. Note that the additional array element is displayed by the second loop.

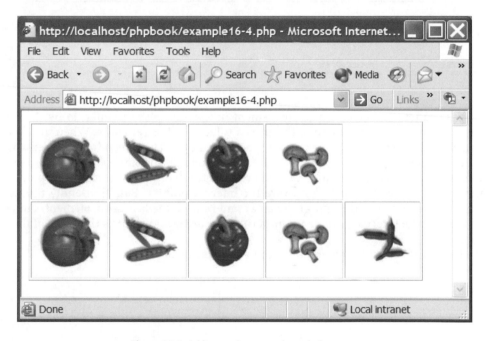

Figure 16.4 Adding an element to the end of an array.

Walking the Array

PHP supports five functions, which are useful for "walking an array". Walking an array is a term used to describe a programming requirement where each element of the array is accessed and used in some way. The foreach loop is an example of a construct, which allows us to walk an array. However, the loop only enables us to walk the array in a single direction, from start to end. The reset(), next(), prev(), current() and end() functions allow us to move from element to element easily. The format of these functions is as follows:

Function prototypes:

```
mixed next (array theArray)
mixed prev (array theArray)
mixed current (array theArray)
mixed end (array theArray)
mixed reset (array theArray)
```

Function arguments and return details:

Name	Type	Description
theArray	Array	The array to walk
functions returns	Mixed	Various array element values

Function example:

```
$element = end($array);
```

The next() function returns the array element in the next place pointed to by the arrays internal array pointer. At the end of the array a value of null is returned. When the element is returned, the value of the array pointer is advanced by 1. The prev() function returns the previous element pointed to by the array internal pointer. If the start of the array is reached a value of 0 is returned. Function current() returns the array element currently pointed to by the array pointer and does not move the internal pointer. Function end() moves the internal array pointer to the end of the array and returns the last array element. Function reset() moves the internal pointer to the start of the array and returns the value of the first element.

The following script illustrates an example of walking an array:

```
<table border='1'>
<?php

// Array Manipulation - Example 16-5
//------------------------

$veg = array(0=>"tomato", 1=>"peas", 2=>"redPepper", 3=>"mushrooms",
4=>"chillies");

echo("<tr>");
reset($veg);
$vegt = current($veg);
while($vegt) {
```

```
            echo("<td><img src='graphics/$vegt.jpg'></td>");
            $vegt = next($veg);
    }
    echo("</tr><tr>");
    $vegt = end($veg);
    while($vegt) {
            echo("<td><img src='graphics/$vegt.jpg'></td>");
            $vegt = prev($veg);
    }
    echo("</tr>");
    ?>
    </table>
```

In the script an array is declared and the array pointer reset. The current array element (i.e. the first) is obtained. Using a while loop the array elements are output and the next array element obtained. At the end of the array the array pointer is set to the end of the array using the end() function. A second while loop displays the array elements and invokes the prev() function to walk back through each the array. Figure 16.5 illustrates the output from the above script. Note that the result of the script is the ability to output the contents of the array normally or in reverse.

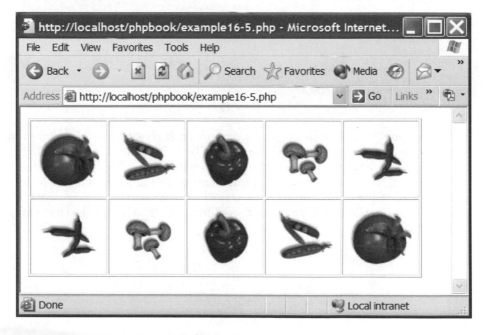

Figure 16.5 Traversing an array.

Pushing and Popping – Creating a Stack

Arrays are used to store information and quite often the amount of information will increase and decrease. What we often need to be able to do is to implement an array, which will allow us to add and remove data to and from the end of the array. This is known as implementing a stack. Adding data to the end of the stack is known as pushing and removing data is known as popping. PHP has two functions which enable you to push and pop data, the format of these are:

Function prototypes:

```
mixed array_pop(array theArray)
int array_push(array theArray, mixed ArrayElement)
```

Function arguments and return details:

Name	Type	Description
theArray	Array	The array to pop/push
arrayElement	Mixed	Individual array element
array_pop() returns	Mixed	Value stored in the last element of the array
array_push() returns	Mixed	The number of elements stored in the array

Function example:

```
$pop = array_pop($veg);
array_push($veg,$push);
```

Function array_pop() requires an array as a parameter. It returns the value stored in the last element in the array and reduces the array size by 1. Function array_push() requires an array and the data you wish to add to the array as parameters. The array is increased in size by one element and the data is stored in this element. The function returns the number of elements stored in the array.

The following script illustrates the use of these functions. It begins by declaring an array of four elements:

```
<table border='1'>
<?php

// Array Manipulation - Example 16-6
//-----------------------
```

```
$veg = array(0=>"tomato", 1=>"peas", 2=>"redPepper", 3=>"mushrooms");
$push = "chillies";

echo("<tr>");
foreach($veg as $vegItem)
        echo("<td><img src='graphics/$vegItem.jpg'></td>");
echo("</tr>");
$pop = array_pop($veg);
echo("<tr>");
foreach($veg as $vegItem)
        echo("<td><img src='graphics/$vegItem.jpg'></td>");
echo("</tr>");
array_push($veg,$push);
echo("<tr>");
foreach($veg as $vegItem)
        echo("<td><img src='graphics/$vegItem.jpg'></td>");
echo("</tr>");
?>
</table>
```

In the script a new data item is created called $push to hold the string "chillies" which will be added to the array later. Using a foreach loop the array contents are displayed. The array_pop() function is invoked removing the last item from the array. The array contents are again displayed illustrating that the last element has been removed. Finally, the array_push() function is invoked to add the $push variable to the end of the array. The array contents are finally displayed illustrating the new contents of the last element. The output generated from the above script is illustrated in Figure 16.6.

Counting Occurrences

Sometimes arrays contain a number of identical elements. For example, we may have asked 100 people for their favourite vegetable and stored the answers in the array. Having obtained this data we now require to process it in order to determine what the results of our survey were. The array_count_values() function is a useful facility to determine the number of identical items held within an array. The format of the function is as follows:

Function prototype:

Array array_count_values(array theArray)

Function arguments and return details:

Name	Type	Description
theArray	Array	The array to count identical elements
array_count_values() returns	Array	Returns an array of values indicating the number of occurrences of a particular item within the array

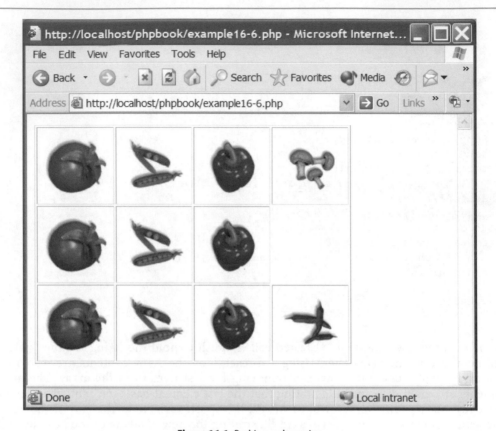

Figure 16.6 Pushing and popping.

Function example:

```
$count = array_count_values($array);
```

The function requires an array as a parameter and returns an array of the results. If, for example, an array was created consisting of the following elements:

```
$array = array("tomato","peas","redPepper","peas","peas");
```

then invoking the array_count_values() function, like so:

```
$count = array_count_values($array);
```

would create an array $count with the contents shown below:

```
("tomato"=>1,"peas"=>3,"redPepper"=1)
```

The following script illustrates the array_count_values() function in operation:

```
<table border='1'>
<?php

// Array Manipulation - Example 16-7
//------------------------

$veg = array("tomato","peas","redPepper","mushrooms","chillies",
             "tomato","peas","redPepper","mushrooms",
             "tomato","redPepper","mushrooms","chillies",
             "mushrooms","chillies","tomato","tomato","tomato",
             "tomato","peas","redPepper","mushrooms",
             "tomato","redPepper","mushrooms","tomato","peas",
             "tomato","peas","tomato","peas");
$count = array_count_values($veg);
echo("<tr>");
foreach($count as $vegItem=>$vegCount)
        echo("<td align='center'><img
src='graphics/$vegItem.jpg'><br>$vegCount</td>");
echo("</tr>");
?>
</table>
```

The script declares an array $veg consisting of vegetables. The array_count_values() function is invoked creating an array called $count which contains the corresponding number of each different vegetable stored in array $veg. The contents of array $count are then displayed using a foreach loop. Note that the array $count uses the vegetable names from array $veg as an index. The output generated by the above script is illustrated in Figure 16.7.

Sorting

The functions sort() and rsort() are used to sort an array. The function sort() is used to sort an array in numerical or alphabetical order from lowest to highest. The function rsort() will sort the array from highest to lowest, the format of these functions is:

Function prototypes:

```
Void sort(array theArray)
Void rsort(array theArray)
```

Function arguments and return details:

Name	Type	Description
theArray	Array	The array to sort
sort() returns	Void	Returns nothing
rsort() returns	Void	Returns nothing

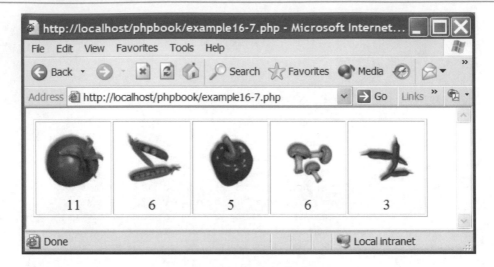

Figure 16.7 Counting occurrences in an array.

Function examples:

```
sort($letters);
rsort($letters);
```

Both functions require an array as a parameter. The following script illustrates the use of both of these functions:

```
<table border='1'>
<?php

// Array Manipulation - Example 16-8
//------------------------

$letters = array("b","d","c","a","i","f","e","h","g");

echo("<tr>");
foreach($letters as $letter)
    echo("<td align='center'><img src='graphics/$letter.jpg'></td>");
echo("</tr>");
sort($letters);
echo("<tr>");
foreach($letters as $letter)
    echo("<td align='center'><img src='graphics/$letter.jpg'></td>");
echo("</tr>");
```

```
rsort($letters);
echo("<tr>");
foreach($letters as $letter)
    echo("<td align='center'><img src='graphics/$letter.jpg'></td>");
echo("</tr>");
?>
</table>
```

The script declares an array called $letters which consists of randomly ordered letters. The contents of the array is displayed, then sorted and redisplayed. Next, the array is reverse sorted and finally displayed. In order to make the output from the script more interesting a variety of graphics were created to represent the letters in the array. Table 16.1 illustrates these images and their filenames.

Table 16.1 Letter graphics.

A	B	C	D	E	F	G	H	I
a.jpg	b.jpg	c.jpg	d.jpg	e.jpg	f.jpg	g.jpg	h.jpg	i.jpg

Figure 16.8 illustrates the output created by the above script.

Figure 16.8 Sorted arrays.

Multisorting

The function array_multisort() can be used to sort several arrays at once or a single multi-dimensional array. The format of the function is:

Function prototype:

> Bool array_multisort (array theArray, mixed flags)

Function arguments and return details:

Name	Type	Description
theArray	Array	The array to sort
flags	Array	SORT_ASC – sort in ascending order
		SORT_DESC – sort in descending order
		SORT_REGULAR – compare items normally
		SORT_NUMERIC – compare items numerically
		SORT_STRING – compare items as strings
array_multisort() returns	Bool	Returns TRUE if the sort was successful or FALSE if an error occurred

Function example:

```
array_multisort($veg[0],SORT_ASC, SORT_STRING,
                       $veg[1],SORT_NUMERIC);
```

The array_multisort() function returns TRUE or FALSE depending on whether the sort was accomplished successfully or not. Let's examine an example of the use of this function:

```
<table border='1'>
<?php

// Array Manipulation - Example 16-9
//------------------------

$veg = array(
          array("tomato","peas","redPepper","mushrooms","chillies",
          "tomato","peas","redPepper","mushrooms",
          "mushrooms","chillies","tomato","tomato","tomato",
          "tomato","peas","tomato","peas"),
          array(10,20,30,10,20,25,35,40,35,45,50,20,25,30,
          25,30,20,30)
          );

echo("<tr>");
foreach($veg[0] as $vegItem)
       echo("<td align='center'><img src='graphics/$vegItem.jpg'
```

```
width='25' height='25'></td>");
echo("</tr>");
echo("<tr>");
foreach($veg[1] as $vegPrice)
        echo("<td align='center'>$vegPrice</td>");
echo("</tr>");
array_multisort($veg[0],SORT_ASC, SORT_STRING,
                $veg[1],SORT_NUMERIC);
echo("<tr>");
foreach($veg[0] as $vegItem)
        echo("<td align='center'><img src='graphics/$vegItem.jpg'
width='25' height='25'></td>");
echo("</tr>");
echo("<tr>");
foreach($veg[1] as $vegPrice)
        echo("<td align='center'>$vegPrice</td>");
echo("</tr>");
?>
</table>
```

The script begins by declaring a multi-dimensional array called $veg which consists of two arrays. These store the name of the vegetable and the price of the vegetable. Two foreach loops are used to display the contents of the array in a table. Next a array_multisort() function is invoked:

```
array_multisort($veg[0],SORT_ASC, SORT_STRING,
                        $veg[1],SORT_NUMERIC);
```

The function is passed the first array $veg[0] which is to be sorted in ascending order and by string value. The second array $veg[1] is to be sorted numerically. The result of the sort is then displayed using two foreach loops. The output from the above script is illustrated in Figure 16.9. It is important to note that the function array_multisort() does not sort the first array and then the second array independently and thus result in vegetables with incorrect prices. In fact the relationships between the data in each array is maintained. The sorting of the second array just enables all the vegetables of a single type to be output in price order.

Explode and Implode

The final two functions we shall introduce in this chapter are the explode() and implode() functions. These allow the user to convert an array into a delimited string and also to convert the string back into an array. Why would you want to do this? Well, you may wish to store the array in a database or file and this is a convenient method of extracting and storing the data as a string. In addition we shall learn in a later chapter that there is a problem in passing arrays within forms and one way of overcoming this problem is to pass the array as a string. The two functions are:

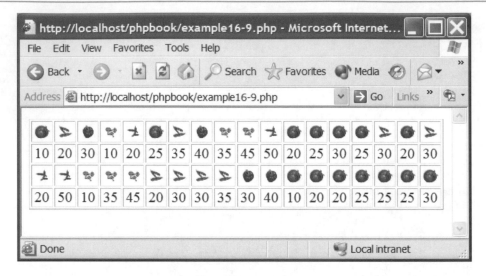

Figure 16.9 Multisort output.

Function prototypes:

Array explode(string separator, string theString)
String implode(string separator, array theArray)

Function arguments and return details:

Name	Type	Description
theArray	Array	The array to implode
theString	String	The string to explode
separator	String	The character to use in order to separate the array contents
explode() returns	Array	An array of exploded items
implode() returns	String	A string of the array items

Function example:

```
$string = implode("|",$veg);
$newVeg = explode("|",$string);
```

The following script illustrates the imploding of an array into a string that is then displayed. The string is then exploded back into a new array that is also displayed:

```
<table border='1'>
<?php

// Array Manipulation - Example 16-10
//-------------------------
```

```
$veg = array(0=>"tomato", 1=>"peas", 2=>"redPepper", 3=>"mushrooms",
 4=>"chillies");

$string = implode("|",$veg);
echo("<tr><td align='center' colspan='5'>$string</td></tr><tr>");
$newVeg = explode("|",$string);

foreach($newVeg as $vegItem)
            echo("<td><img src='graphics/$vegItem.jpg'></td>");
echo("</tr>");
?>
</table>
```

The output from the above script is illustrated in Figure 16.10.

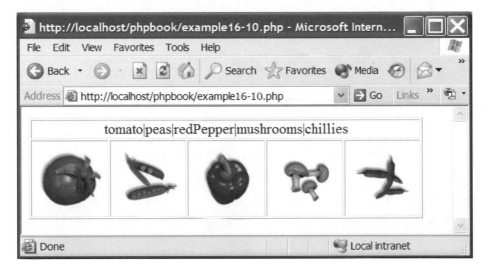

Figure 16.10 Exploding and imploding arrays.

Summary

This chapter has revisited the concept of arrays. We have explored a number of functions with which we can manipulate the data held within our arrays in different ways. In the following chapter we shall return to the string data type introduced in Chapter 8 and consider what functions are available to manipulate strings.

String Manipulation

17

Introduction

In Chapter 8 we introduced the concept of strings and illustrated how to declare and use them. Strings are used all the time in PHP and there are a vast number of functions which have been created to help manipulate them. In this chapter we introduce some of these functions and illustrate their use.

Calculating String Length

Probably the most common string function is strlen(). Using this function we can count the number of characters within a string. The function looks like this:

Function prototype:

```
int strlen ( string inputString );
```

Function arguments and return details:

Name	Type	Description
inputString	String	String that we are going to count the number of characters
strlen() returns	Int	The number of characters in the string

Function example:

```
$size = strlen($title);
```

In the following example we use strlen() to check a title message which has been posted on a forum. The post message title should not exceed 60 characters and we need to prevent users from posting titles on their topics which are longer than this.

```php
<?php

// String Manipulation - Example 17-1
//--------------------------------
$title = "This is my post";

$size = strlen($title);

if($size <= 60) {
        echo "Title length is $size. Accepted";
}
else {
        echo "Title length is $size. Not accepted";
}


?>
```

The above script firstly checks the strlen() of the title variable:

```php
$title = "This is my post";

$size = strlen($title);
```

The size of the string is then checked and an appropriate message displayed:

```php
if($size <= 60) {
        echo "Title length is $size. Accepted";
}
else {
        echo "Title length is $size. Not accepted";
}
```

The output from the above script is displayed in Figure 17.1.

Explode/Implode String Parts and Elements

Function explode() is used to create an array of elements from the parts of a string divided by a separator character. The separator can be an individual character/number or a string. Function implode() is the opposite of function explode() and is used to create a string from array elements with each one separated by a separator. The full details of these functions can be found in Chapter 16, but here are the function prototypes as a reminder:

```
Array explode(string separator, string theString);

String implode(string separator, array theArray);
```

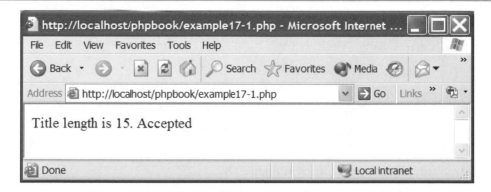

Figure 17.1 Checking string length.

In the following example we have a string consisting of first names and we would like to create a small table with these names each on a different row:

```php
<?php

// String Manipulation - Example 17-2
//--------------------------------

        $names = "mike simon david mary";
        $list = explode(" ",$names);
        $rows = count($list);

            echo "<table border=1 width=220><tr>";
            echo "<td bgcolor='#999999'> Names</td></tr>";

        for($i=0;$i<$rows;$i++){
            echo "</tr><td> $list[$i] </td></tr>";
        }
            echo "</table>";
?>
```

Firstly, the script defines a string and explodes this into an array:

```php
$names = "mike simon david mary";
$list = explode(" ",$names);
```

Next, the number of rows in the array is counted:

```php
$rows = count($list);
```

Finally, a for loop is used to construct the table displaying the items of each array on each row:

```
            echo "<table border=1 width=220><tr>";
            echo "<td bgcolor='#999999'> Names</td></tr>";

        for($i=0;$i<$rows;$i++){
            echo "</tr><td> $list[$i] </td></tr>";
        }
            echo "</table>";
    ?>
```

The output from the script is shown in Figure 17.2.

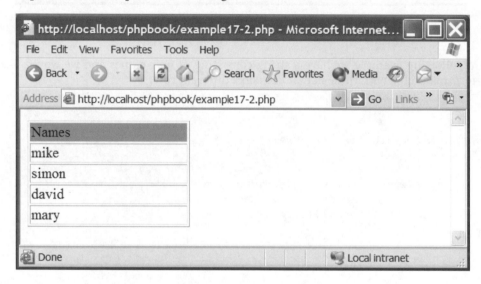

Figure 17.2 Explode example.

Finding a String Within a String

The strstr() function can be used to find a specific part of a string (even a single character) inside another string. Using a string identifier "needle" the function will return the part of the string "inputString" from the first occurrence of "needle" to the end of input string. The function looks like this:

Function prototype:

string strstr (string inputString, string needle)

Function arguments and return details:

Name	Type	Description
inputString	String	The string to use
needle	String	String identifier
strstr() returns	String	Part of a string

Function example:

```
$email = 'user@example.com';
$domain = strstr($email, '@');
```

The following PHP script illustrates the use of this function:

```
<?php

// String Manipulation - Example 17-3
//-------------------------------

        $email = 'user@example.com';
        $domain = strstr($email, '@');
        echo "$email<br>$domain";

?>
```

The output from the script is:

```
user@example.com
@example.com
```

Replace Part of a String

The str_replace() function is commonly used in order to change parts of a string to another string. The format of the function is as follows:

Function prototype:

String str_replace (String searchPart, string replacePart, string start)

Function arguments and return details:

Name	Type	Description
searchPart	String	String to search for
replacePart	String	String to replace searchPart
start	String	String to perform operation upon
str_replace() returns	String	Modified string

Function example:

```
$text = "Hi, this is a [b]bold text[/b]";
$text = str_replace("[b]","<h>",$text);
```

Consider the following example script using this function:

```php
<?php

// String Manipulation - Example 17-4
//--------------------------------

        $text = "Hi, this is a [b]bold text[/b]";
        echo "$text";

        $text = str_replace("[b]","<b>",$text);
        $text = str_replace("[/b]","</b>",$text);

        echo "<br><br>";
        echo "$text";

?>
```

In the above script the code "[b]word[/b]" needs to be converted to <b>word</b> so that the "word" text can appear in bold within a Web browser. The script searches for the [b] part of the string first and replaces it with a <b> tag. Then the [/b] string is replaced with </b>. Figure 17.3 illustrates the output produced by this script.

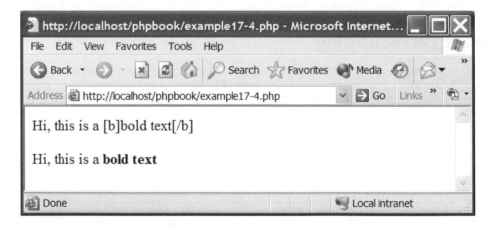

Figure 17.3 Replace part of a string.

Repeat and Reverse a String

You may wish to be able to repeat a string without repeating the same string many times manually or be able to reverse a string. For these two situations the following functions are available:

Function prototypes:

```
string str_repeat ( string inputString, int multiplier);

string strrev ( string inputString);
```

Function arguments and return details:

Name	Type	Description
inputString	String	The string to use
multiplier	Int	Number of times to repeat
str_repeat() returns	String	Returns input string repeated X times defined by multiplier
strrev() returns	String	Returns input string in reverse order

Function examples:

```php
$repeated = str_repeat ( $inputString, 5 );

$reverse = strrev ( $inputString );
```

In the following example we wish to have a table with 10 columns. This can be done by repeating the string "<td>space</td>" ten times as illustrated below:

```php
<?php

// String Manipulation - Example 17-5
//------------------------------

        echo "<table border='1' height=10>";
        echo "<tr>";

        echo str_repeat("<td width=50> </td>",10);

        echo "</tr>";
        echo "</table>";

?>
```

The example output is illustrated in Figure 17.4.

Change String Case

Sometimes we want to change the case of some strings we use in our scripts. The following functions are very useful as they help us change the case of the words in our strings or alter the first character of each word in the string:

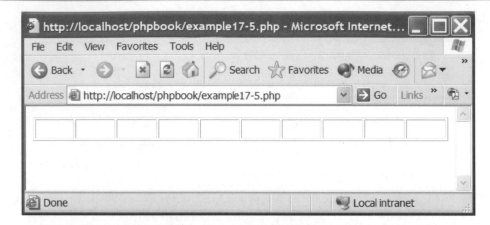

Figure 17.4 Repeating part of a string (<td>space</td>).

Function prototype:

```
string strtoupper ( inputString );

string strtolower ( inputString );

string ucfirst ( inputString );

string ucwords ( inputString );
```

Function arguments and return details:

Name	Type	Description
inputString	String	The string to use
strtoupper () output	String	Convert input string to uppercase
strtolower () output	String	Convert input string to lowercase
ucfirst () output	String	Convert input string's first character to uppercase
ucwords () output	String	Uppercase the first character of each word in the input string

Function examples:

```
$text_upper = strtoupper($text);
$text_lower = strtolower($text);
$text_ufirst = ucfirst($text);
$text_uwords = ucwords($text);
```

In the following example we have a simple string (a sentence of five words) and we will use these functions to transform the string in different ways:

```php
<?php

// String Manipulation - Example 17-6
//-------------------------------

        $text = "hello this is a STRING";

        $text_upper = strtoupper($text);
        $text_lower = strtolower($text);
        $text_ufirst = ucfirst($text);
        $text_uwords = ucwords($text);

        echo "Original text: $text <br><br>";
        echo "Uppercase: $text_upper <br>";
        echo "Lowercase: $text_lower <br>";
        echo "First character upper: $text_ufirst <br>";
        echo "Capitalised: $text_uwords";

?>
```

The output from the above script is illustrated in Figure 17.5.

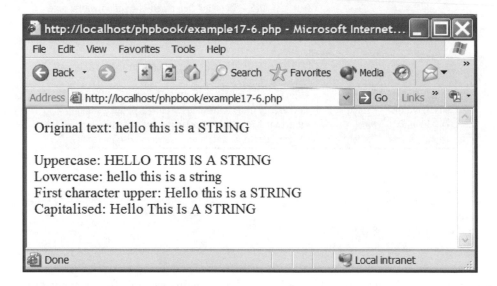

Figure 17.5 Changing string letter cases.

Encrypting Strings

There are more that 10 methods of encrypting strings. Encryption can be one-way (there is no decryption) and two-way (the encrypted word can be decrypted using a dictionary or other methods). We will present the four most common encryption methods. Some of them are often used for checking file and data integrity. MD5() is mostly used to encrypt passwords on Web applications and Crypt() to encrypt Linux system passwords. Functions md5() and crypt() are also examined in Chapter 20 which looks at the issue of data security. The functions are as follows:

Function prototypes:

```
string md5 ( string inputString );

string sha1 ( string inputString );

int crc32 ( string inputString );

string crypt ( string inputString , string option);
```

Function arguments and return details:

Name	Type	Description
inputString	String	The string to use
option	String	CRYPT_STD_DES – Standard DES-based encryption with a two character salt
		CRYPT_EXT_DES – Extended DES-based encryption with a nine character salt
		CRYPT_MD5 – MD5 encryption with a 12 character salt starting with 1
		CRYPT_BLOWFISH – Blowfish encryption with a sixteen character salt starting with 2
md5() returns	String	A 32-bit length string containing the encrypted input string
sha1() returns	String	A 40-character string containing the encrypted input string
crc32() returns	Int	A string containing the crc32 polynomial of input string
crypt() returns	String	A 40-character string containing the encrypted input string

Function example:

```
$encrypt = md5 ( $inputString );
$encrypt = sha1 ( $inputString );
$crc = crc32 ( $inputString );
$encrypt = crypt ( $inputString);
```

Using an example input string "test" will give the following results after encryption:

MD5:   098f6bcd4621d373cade4e832627b4f6
SHA1:   a94a8fe5ccb19ba61c4c0873d391e987982fbbd3
Crc32:   -662733300
Crypt: 1LD1.2H2.$9kNYlkYWiNiWbomSR73kR.

The following script illustrates a simple password check example, using the MD5 encryption method:

```php
<?php

// String Manipulation - Example 17-7
//--------------------------------

$my_pass = "377729";
$md5_pass = md5($my_pass);


$spass = md5("377728");

if($spass == $md5_pass) {
        echo "Password ok!";
}
else {
        echo "Password failed!";
}

?>
```

In this script we have encrypted a password "377729" with the MD5 method:

```php
$my_pass = "377729";
$md5_pass = md5($my_pass);
```

The script encrypts the submitted password (377728) and compares it to the previous encrypted one. If the encrypted (32 bit) strings are the same a successful login can be given:

```php
$spass = md5("377728");

if($spass == $md5_pass) {
        echo "Password ok!";
}
else {
        echo "Password failed!";
}
```

The output from the above script is shown in Figure 17.6.

Word Count

The str_word_count() function can be used to count the number of words inside a string. The function is as follows:

Function prototype:

```
mixed str word_count ( string inputString , int mode )
```

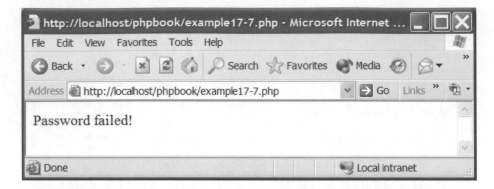

Figure 17.6 Simple password check example.

Function arguments and return details:

Name	Type	Description
inputString	String	The string to use
mode	Int	1 – returns an array containing all the words found inside the string
		2 – returns an associative array, where the key is the numeric position of the word inside the string and the value is the actual word itself
str_word_count() returns	Mixed	If the mode is not specified outputs the total number of words in the input string

Function example:

```
$count = str_word_count($string,1);
```

If a mode is not specified, then the result will be a number indicating the number of words found inside the string. If mode is set to "1" the result will be an array containing all the words found inside the string and if mode is set to "2" the result will be an associative array, where the key is the numeric position of the word inside the string and the value is the actual word itself.

Add and Remove Slashes

Sometimes when we are using a database there is a need to escape certain characters. These characters are single quote ('), double quote ("), backslash (\) and NULL (the NULL byte). The function that is used to escape these characters is the addslashes() function. If we want to remove the slashes we can used the stripslashes() function as follows:

Function prototypes:

```
string addslashes ( string inputString );
string stripslashes ( string inputString );
```

Function arguments and return details:

Name	Type	Description
inputString	String	String to perform slashes operation upon
addslashes() returns	String	String with escapes characters
stripslashes() returns	String	String with slashes removed

Function examples:

```
$escapedString = addslashes ( $inputString );
$normalString = stripslashes ( $inputString );
```

Convert Special Characters to HTML Entities

Certain characters have special significance in HTML, and should be represented by HTML entities if they are to preserve their meanings. The htmlspecialchars() function returns a string with these characters converted into their HTML codes:

Function prototype:

```
string htmlspecialchars ( string inputString );
```

Function arguments and return details:

Name	Type	Description
inputString	String	String to perform operation upon
htmlspecialcharacters() returns	String	HTML encoded string

Function example:

```
$htmlEncoded = htmlspecialchars ( $inputString );
```

The translations performed are:

  & (ampersand) becomes '&'.
  " (double quote) becomes '"' when ENT_NOQUOTES is not set.
  ' (single quote) becomes ''' only when ENT_QUOTES is set.
  < (less than) becomes '<'.
  > (greater than) becomes '>'.

The following script illustrates the use of this function:

```php
<?php

// String Manipulation - Example 17-8
//-------------------------------

$originalString = "& < > \" \'";

$htmlEncoded = htmlspecialchars ( $originalString );

echo "Original: $originalString <br> Encoded: $htmlEncoded";

$len = strlen($originalString);
$len2 = strlen($htmlEncoded);

echo "<br>Original Length: $len <br> Encoded Length: $len2";
?>
```

The output from this script is illustrated in Figure 17.7.

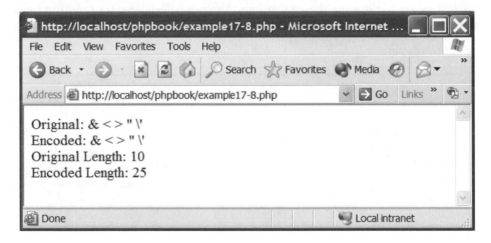

Figure 17.7 HTML special characters example.

Note that in the example shown in Figure 17.7 the text output is the same in both cases. This is because a Web browser will display a "&" and a "&amp" as a "&". However, you can tell that the conversion has taken place because the length of the two strings is different.

Comparing Strings with Different Cases

Sometimes we need to be able to compare strings to see if they contain the same words, but we are not bothered if the case of the string is different. For example, we want to be able to tell that the string "Simon" is the same as "sIMON". We can use the function strncasecmp() to do this:

Function prototype:

```
string strncasecmp( string String1, string String2, int len );
```

Function arguments and return details:

Name	Type	Description
string1	String	First string to compare
string2	String	Second string to compare
len	Int	Number of characters in each string to be used in the comparison
strncasecamp() returns	Int	Returns 0 if strings are equal

Function example:

```
$equal = strncasecmp("Simon", "sIMON", 5);
```

Summary

This chapter has revisited the concept of strings. We have explored a number of functions with which we can manipulate the data held within our strings in different ways. Those illustrated are the most common programmers use from day to day, but there are still more that 20 different string functions that can be used for more specific applications and scripts.

In the following chapter we shall introduce the concept of user interaction. We shall explain how PHP applications can interact with end users and what operations are available.

Part 4

User Interaction

Interacting with the User

18

Introduction

Unless programs are able to interact with users their use is very limited. PHP is able to interact with a user via a Web page by using forms. Forms allow data to be entered and submitted to the server for processing by PHP. Forms manifest themselves in all sorts of shapes and sizes. Some forms are easy to identify as being forms whereas others are less obvious. In this chapter we shall introduce the basic form elements and illustrate how they can be combined to enable quite complex interactions.

PHP and Forms

Forms are part of HTML and not part of PHP. While PHP can output forms in the same way that it can output all other HTML elements it is not adding anything new to the functionality offered by standard HTML. PHP can, however, be used to control forms and process the data which the user provides by interacting with the form, which is something that HTML cannot do. As PHP is a server-side scripting language form data must be transmitted back to the server for processing and then the output generated be transmitted back to the user. This is different from the way that JavaScript can be used, where the processing can be done on the client's machine within the browser.

A Simple Form

We shall begin by creating a standard HTML form and illustrating some of the data entry elements. Consider the following script:

```
<html>

<!- Interacting with the user - Example 18-1 ->
<!- ----------------------------------- ->
```

```
<body>
        <h2>Please enter your personal details:</h2>
        <form action='example18-2.php' method='post'>
        Firstname: <input type='text' name='firstname'>
        <br>
        Surname: <input type='text' name='surname'>
        <br>
        Username: <input type='text' name='username'>
        <br>
        Password: <input type='password' name='password'>
        <br>
        <input type='submit'>
        </form>
</body>
</html>
```

Note that this script is a HTML document and not a PHP script and thus it should be saved with a .html extension. The script illustrates the basic elements of a HTML form. Firstly, the form begins with a <form> element, which has two key attributes: action and method. Attribute action specifies where the form data is to be sent for processing. This can be a CGI application written in any programming language or it could be a PHP script. The method attribute specifies how the data from the form will be sent to the application. There are two main methods, POST and GET. PHP supports POST so we have to use this. In our example the form element specifies that the script to process the form data is called example18-2.php, but we haven't written this yet:

```
<form action='example18-2.php' method='post'>
..
</form>
```

The rest of the form consists of four data entry fields, three of which are type text and one is of type password:

```
        Firstname: <input type='text' name='firstname'>
        <br>
        Surname: <input type='text' name='surname'>
        <br>
        Username: <input type='text' name='username'>
        <br>
        Password: <input type='password' name='password'>
        <br>
```

These are essentially the same type of data entry fields, accept that password fields hide the data that is typed into them and display "*" characters instead. Note that each data input field has a separate field name, which has been chosen to represent the data that each element represents. These form field names are important, as we shall need them to access the form data later in our PHP script. The form concludes with a input field of type submit:

```
<input type='submit'>
```

This field is required in order for the user to submit the form data once they have completed the form. The output from the above HTML script is shown in Figure 18.1. Essentially, this is as far as HTML goes with forms. While, we shall see later in this chapter that there are a few other HTML form field types, if we want to do anything with the form data then we will need to begin to create a PHP script to handle the data entered on the form.

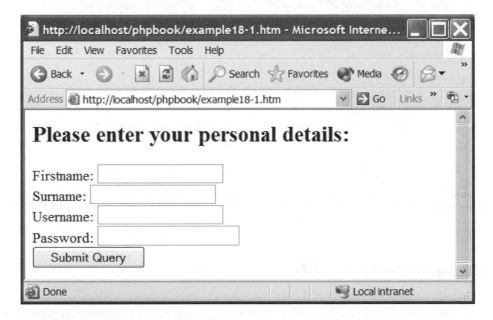

Figure 18.1 A simple form.

We shall now create a PHP script to handle the form data passed to it. The script is very simple as all it does is echo out the data it receives, as shown in Figure 18.2:

```php
<?php

// Interacting with the user - Example 18-2
//---------------------------------


$firstname = $_POST["firstname"];
$surname = $_POST["surname"];
$username = $_POST["username"];
$password = $_POST["password"];

echo("Hello $firstname $surname<br>");
echo("Your username is $username and your password is $password");
?>
```

Accessing form data is essentially very easy. When a form is created an associated array of variables is created. This array is called $_POST. Each HTML form element that has a unique name is stored in the array and can be accessed by the PHP script. To access, for example, the form element "firstname" we use the syntax:

```
$firstname = $_POST["firstname"];
```

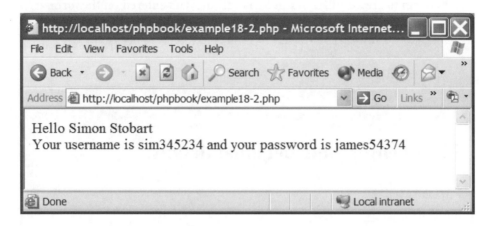

Figure 18.2 Form data output.

Combining Forms and PHP

In our previous example the HTML form and the PHP script were written as two separate files. The first one contained the HTML form and the second the PHP script to process the data. This is not the best way of implementing this as it is difficult to refer back to the form if we need the user to re-enter some new data. The best method is to combine the form and the PHP processing together in the same script, as shown below:

```html
<html>
<body>
    <h2>Please enter your personal details:</h2>
    <form action='example18-3.php' method='post'>
    Firstname: <input type='text' name='firstname'>
    <br>
    Surname: <input type='text' name='surname'>
    <br>
    Username: <input type='text' name='username'>
    <br>
    Password: <input type='password' name='password'>
    <br>
    <input type='submit'>
    </form>
```

```
</body>
</html>
<?php

// Interacting with the user - Example 18-3
//-------------------------------

$firstname = $_POST["firstname"];
$surname = $_POST["surname"];
$username = $_POST["username"];
$password = $_POST["password"];

echo("Hello $firstname $surname<br>");
echo("Your username is $username and your password is $password");
?>
```

The above script combines the HTML form and the PHP script together into one single place. However, there is a problem as illustrated in Figure 18.3.

The problem is that when the script is processed the form is output first then the PHP echo statements are processed. This is not a problem after the first time the form is submitted but the first time the page is loaded the form variables contain no data and this results in the display of an incomplete message. What we need is a means of determining if the form data was submitted or not. Consider the following script:

```
<html>
<body>
   <h2>Please enter your personal details:</h2>
   <form action='<?php echo $_SERVER["PHP_SELF"]; ?>' method='post'>
   Firstname: <input type='text' name='firstname'>
   <br>
   Surname: <input type='text' name='surname'>
   <br>
   Username: <input type='text' name='username'>
   <br>
   Password: <input type='password' name='password'>
   <br>
   <input type='submit' name='submit'>
   </form>
</body>
</html>
<?php

// Interacting with the user - Example 18-4
//-------------------------------
```

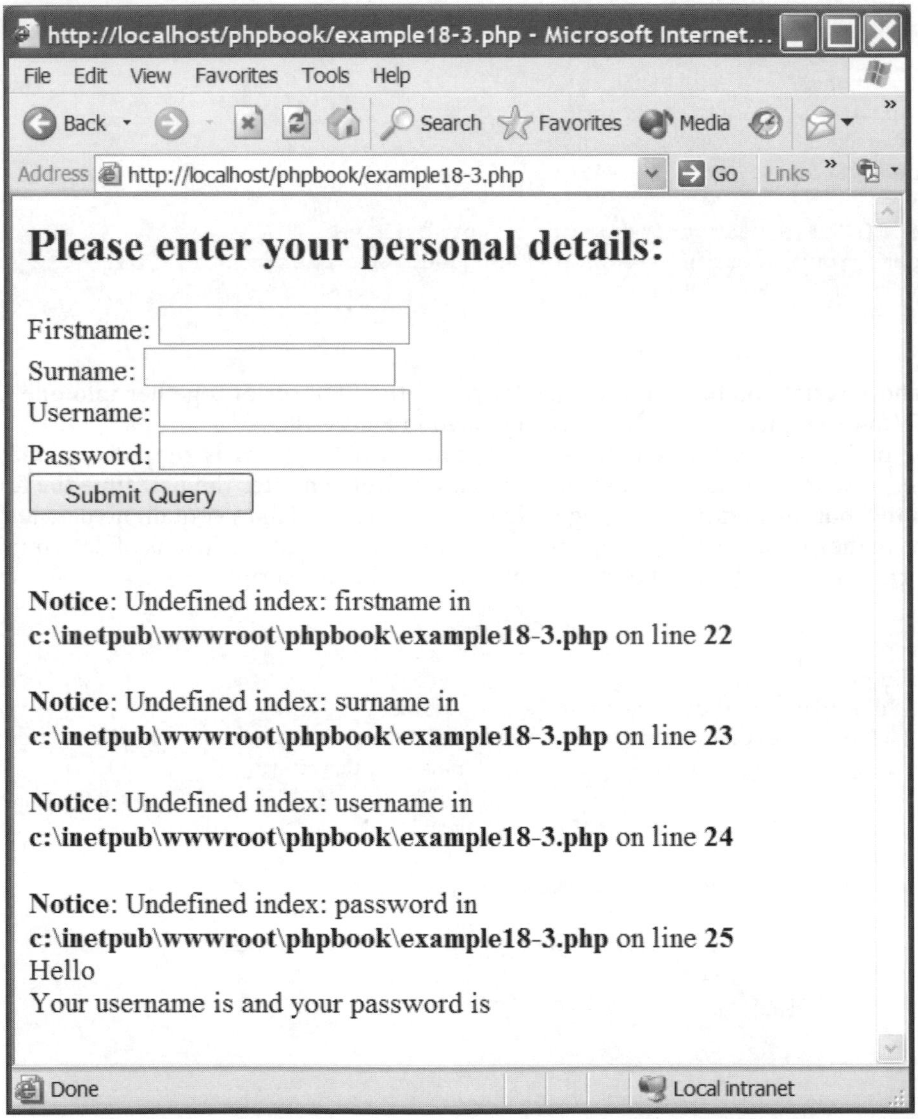

Figure 18.3 The form problem.

```
if(isset($_POST["submit"])){
    $firstname = $_POST["firstname"];
    $surname = $_POST["surname"];
    $username = $_POST["username"];
    $password = $_POST["password"];

    echo("Hello $firstname $surname<br>");
    echo("Your username is $username and your password is $password");
}
?>
```

This is a rewrite of the previous script and solves the issue of displaying blank variable values when the form has not been submitted. The first change in the program has nothing to do with this problem, but makes life far easier for the developer. The change replaces the name of the program which is invoked with the variable PHP_SELF:

```
<?php echo $_SERVER["PHP_SELF"]; ?>
```

This is a server variable (introduced in Chapter 9) and contains the name of the current script and by including this ensures that the script will always call itself, no matter what name it has been saved as. The next change involves providing the submit button with a name:

```
<input type='submit' name='submit'>
```

Here, the name has been set to "submit". Finally, an if statement has been included to check the result of invoking the function isset(), which was first mentioned in Chapter 9. Function isset() has the format:

Function prototype:

Int isset(mixed value);

Function arguments and return details:

Name	Type	Description
value	Mixed	Variable to check if exists or not
isset() returns	Int	TRUE if the variable exists and FALSE if not

Function example:

```
$set = isset($_POST["submit"]);
```

The function requires a variable to be passed to it, which it then determines if this has been set or not. If the variable is set it returns a TRUE value, otherwise it returns a FALSE value. The program checks that the value of variable $submit is set. This is only true if the form has been submitted, thus solving our problem, as illustrated in Figure 18.4.

```
http://localhost/phpbook/example18-4.php - Microsoft Internet...
File   Edit   View   Favorites   Tools   Help
Back  ·            ·  ✗  🔁  🏠    🔍 Search  ⭐ Favorites  📀 Media  🕒  ✉ ▾
Address  🔲 http://localhost/phpbook/example18-4.php        ✔  ➔ Go    Links  ▾  🔲 ▾
```

Please enter your personal details:

Firstname: [   ]
Surname: [   ]
Username: [   ]
Password: [   ]
[Submit Query]

```
🔲 Done                                                        🔲 Local intranet
```

Figure 18.4 The form problem solved.

Minimum Coin Calculator

So far our form examples have been very basic. Let's see if we can create something that is a little more interesting. The following script illustrates a very simple form combined with a "useful" function. The script allows a user to enter a value via a form field and submit this. The value represents a price. For example 134 represents 1 pound and 34 pence and 56 represents 56 pence. The script calculates the minimum number of coins that would be required to present the amount entered via the form. The program uses the images (saved in the graphics directory) illustrated in Table 18.1.

Table 18.1 Coin images and filenames.

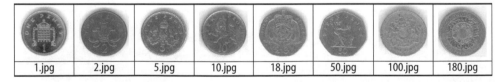

| 1.jpg | 2.jpg | 5.jpg | 10.jpg | 18.jpg | 50.jpg | 100.jpg | 180.jpg |

Take a look at the script which accomplishes this:

```
<h2>Minimum Coin Calculator</h2>
<form action='<?php echo $_SERVER["PHP_SELF"]; ?>' method='post'>
Enter Amount: <input type='text' name='amount'>
```

```php
<input type='submit'>
</form>

<?php

// Interacting with the user - Example 18-5
//--------------------------------


if(isset($_POST["amount"]))
        coins($_POST["amount"]);


function coins($amount) {
        while($amount >= 200){
                $amount=$amount-200;
                echo("<img src='graphics/200p.jpg'>");
        } // while
        while($amount >= 100){
                $amount=$amount-100;
                echo("<img src='graphics/100p.jpg'>");
        } // while
        while($amount >= 50){
                $amount=$amount-50;
                echo("<img src='graphics/50p.jpg'>");
        } // while
        while($amount >= 20){
                $amount=$amount-20;
                echo("<img src='graphics/20p.jpg'>");
        } // while
        while($amount >= 10){
                $amount=$amount-10;
                echo("<img src='graphics/10p.jpg'>");
        } // while
        while($amount >= 5){
                $amount=$amount-5;
                echo("<img src='graphics/5p.jpg'>");
        } // while
        while($amount >= 2){
                $amount=$amount-2;
                echo("<img src='graphics/2p.jpg'>");
        } // while
        if($amount > 0){
                echo("<img src='graphics/1p.jpg'>");
        }
}
?>
```

The script begins by outputting a simple form which consists of a text input field and a submit button:

```
<h2>Minimum Coin Calculator</h2>
<form action='<?php echo $_SERVER["PHP_SELF"]; ?>' method='post'>
Enter Amount: <input type='text' name='amount'>
<input type='submit'>
</form>
```

The PHP script begins by determining if an amount has been entered via the form, by checking the $amount variable. If this is set then function coins() is invoked passing it the amount entered on the form:

```
<?php

if(isset($_POST["amount"]))
        coins($_POST["amount"]);
```

The function coins() calculates which coin images to display. It consists of a number of while loops, which subtracts the value of the current coin being processed from the total amount. The function is designed to subtract the higher coin values first and thus calculate the minimum number of coins required to equal the value entered:

```
function coins($amount) {
        while($amount >= 200){
                $amount=$amount-200;
                echo("<img src='graphics/200p.jpg'>");
        } // while
        while($amount >= 100){
                $amount=$amount-100;
                echo("<img src='graphics/100p.jpg'>");
        } // while
        while($amount >= 50){
                $amount=$amount-50;
                echo("<img src='graphics/50p.jpg'>");
        } // while
        while($amount >= 20){
                $amount=$amount-20;
                echo("<img src='graphics/20p.jpg'>");
        } // while
        while($amount >= 10){
                $amount=$amount-10;
                echo("<img src='graphics/10p.jpg'>");
        } // while
```

```
          while($amount >= 5){
                $amount=$amount-5;
                echo("<img src='graphics/5p.jpg'>");
          } // while
          while($amount >= 2){
                $amount=$amount-2;
                echo("<img src='graphics/2p.jpg'>");
          } // while
          if($amount > 0){
                echo("<img src='graphics/1p.jpg'>");
          }
   }
   ?>
```

When first run, the output from the above program is as illustrated in Figure 18.5. If the user enters a value in the form field and clicks the "submit" button the program calculates the minimum number of coins, which would be required to make up that amount. For example, typing 99 (representing 99p) results in the output shown in Figure 18.6.

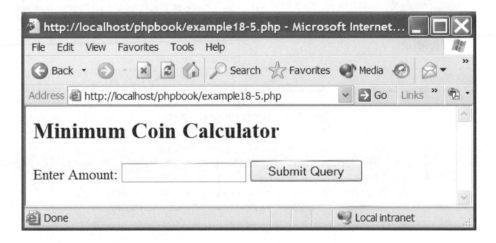

Figure 18.5 The coin calculator user input.

Radio Buttons

In addition to the text, password and submit form fields we have introduced thus far there are a number of other types. The first of these is the radio type. The radio entry type does not allow the user to enter any text but provides a series of "radio buttons" from which the user can make a selection. Only one of the buttons grouped together can be selected. In order to ensure that the form knows which buttons form a group all grouped buttons must share the same name. An example of the radio type is shown in the script below:

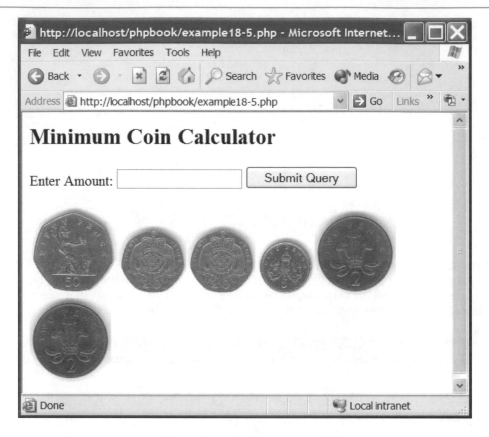

Figure 18.6 The coin calculator output.

```
<form action='<?php echo $_SERVER["PHP_SELF"]; ?>' method='post'>
<h2>Please select your favorite color:</h2>
Blue <input type='radio' name='col' value='blue'>
Green <input type='radio' name='col' value='green'>
Yellow <input type='radio' name='col' value='yellow'>
Red <input type='radio' name='col' value='red'>
<br>
<h2>Please select your favorite type of music:</h2>
Pop <input type='radio' name='mus' value='Pop'>
Rock <input type='radio' name='mus' value='rock'>
Classical <input type='radio' name='mus' value='classical'>
<br><br>
<input type='submit' name='submit'>
</form>

<?php
```

```
// Interacting with the user - Example 18-6
//---------------------------------

if(isset($_POST["submit"])){
    $col = $_POST["col"];
    $mus = $_POST["mus"];
    echo("Your favorite color is $col<br>");
    echo("Your favorite type of music is $mus");
}
?>
```

The script displays two sets of radio buttons, one given the name "col" and the other "mus". A check is made to determine if the submit button has been pressed and if so the values stored in variables $col and $mus are displayed. The output from running the above script is shown in Figure 18.7.

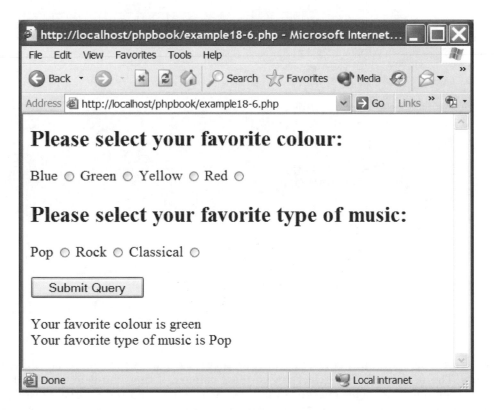

Figure 18.7 Radio buttons.

Checkbox Fields

Checkbox fields enable the user to select as many options as they like from the form. Each checkbox is given a unique name. An example of the use of the form field is shown in the script below:

```php
<form action='<?php echo($_SERVER["PHP_SELF"]) ?>' method='post'>
<h2>Please select all the colors you like:</h2>
Blue <input type='checkbox' name='cb1' value='blue'>
Green <input type='checkbox' name='cb2' value='green'>
Yellow <input type='checkbox' name='cb3' value='yellow'>
Red <input type='checkbox' name='cb4' value='red'>
<br><br>
<input type='submit' name='submit'>
</form>

<?php

// Interacting with the user - Example 18-7
//---------------------------------

if(isset($_POST["submit"])){
    if (isset($_POST["cb1"]))
        $cb1 = $_POST["cb1"];
    else
        $cb1 = "";
    if (isset($_POST["cb2"]))
        $cb2 = $_POST["cb2"];
    else
        $cb2 = "";
    if (isset($_POST["cb3"]))
        $cb3 = $_POST["cb3"];
    else
        $cb3 = "";
    if (isset($_POST["cb4"]))
        $cb4 = $_POST["cb4"];
    else
        $cb4 = "";
    echo("Colors you like are $cb1 $cb2 $cb3 $cb4");
}
?>
```

The script displays a form consisting of four checkbox fields which represent different colours. The user is asked to select any of these colours. If the submit button has been clicked then the values of the checkbox variables ($cb1, $cb2, $cb3 and $cb4) are displayed. If a checkbox was not selected the corresponding variable will contain no value and thus nothing will be displayed. The output from running the above script is shown in Figure 18.8.

Figure 18.8 Checkbox fields.

Selection Fields

The form selection field uses a different format from the other form fields, which we have come across before. The field uses two HTML elements: select and option. The select element surrounds all of the option elements making up the menu. For each item you wish to appear on the pull down selection menu you need to include an option element. Because each option element surrounds the data there is no need to include any value attributes. An example of the use of this element is shown in the following script:

```
<form action='<?php echo($_SERVER["PHP_SELF"]) ?>' method='post'>
Please select your title: <select name='title'>
      <option>Mr</option>
      <option>Miss</option>
      <option>Ms</option>
      <option>Mrs</option>
      <option>Dr</option>
</select>
<br><br>
<input type='submit' name='submit'>
</form>


<?php

// Interacting with the user - Example 18-8
//--------------------------------
```

```
if(isset($_POST["submit"])){
    $title = $_POST["title"];
    echo("Your title is $title");
}
?>
```

The script displays a form consisting of a single selection menu called title. The menu is made up of a selection of titles. The script checks to see if the submit button has been clicked and if so displays the value of $title. The output from running the above script is shown in Figure 18.9.

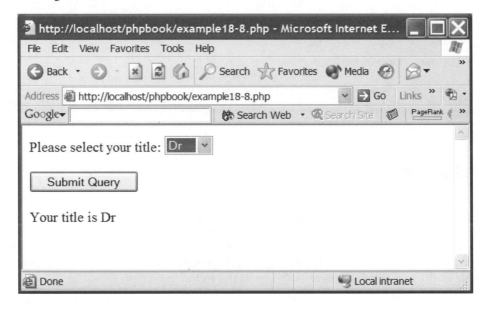

Figure 18.9 Selection fields.

Textarea Fields

The textarea form element allows a text box to be created with a certain number of rows and columns. The user can enter any text in this box. Consider the following script:

```
<?php

// Interacting with the user - Example 18-9
//--------------------------------

if(isset($_POST["submit"])){
    if($_POST["address"] == "")
        $addressErr = 1;
```

```
}
?>
    <form action='<?php echo($_SERVER["PHP_SELF"]) ?>' method='post'>
    <h2>Please enter your personal details:</h2>
    Address: <textarea name='address' rows='5'></textarea><?php
if(isset($addressErr)) echo("<font color='red' size='2'>
Please enter an Address</font>");?>
    <br><br>
    <input type='submit' name='submit'>
    </form>
```

The script displays a form consisting of a textarea field. The user is asked to enter their address within the field. If the submit button has been pressed, but no text entered in the textarea then a message is displayed prompting the user to enter an address. Figure 18.10 illustrates the output from the above script.

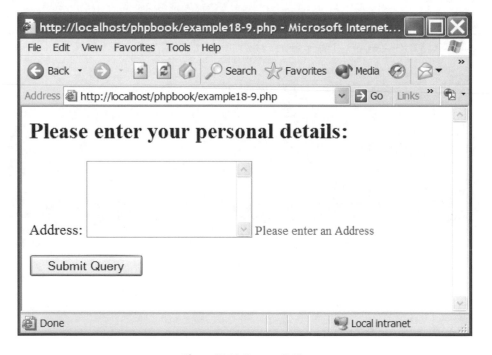

Figure 18.10 Textarea fields.

Image Fields

Forms can process images as input fields. While, this may at first seem strange consider the image illustrated in Figure 18.11. This image consists of three button shapes.

The image form field is illustrated in the following script. The program does not include a submit button because when the user clicks on the image the x and y coordinates of where

Figure 18.11 Button image.

the user clicked on the image are transmitted to the script. These values are stored in two variables, which take the name button_x and button_y because the field has been given the name "button":

```
    <form action='<?php echo($_SERVER["PHP_SELF"]) ?>' method='post'>
    Please click on the image:<br>
    <input type='image' src='graphics/buttons.jpg' name='button'>
    </form>

<?php

// Interacting with the user - Example 18-10
//---------------------------------


if(isset($_POST["button_x"])){
    if($_POST["button_x"] > 22 && $_POST["button_x"] < 210 &&
$_POST["button_y"] < 155 && $_POST["button_y"] > 100)
        echo("You clicked the blue button.");
    else
        echo("You clicked the image.");

}
?>
```

The above script displays the image as a form image. As there is no submit button the only action that will submit the form is when the user clicks on the image. When this happens the script checks the X and Y values passed as the variables button_x and button_y to determine if the user has clicked on the blue button (the middle one) and displays a message to that effect, as illustrated in Figure 18.12. We can determine if the user has clicked the middle button because we know that the top left-hand corner of the button is at position 22×100 and the bottom right-hand corner is at position 210×155 of the image. If the values stored in button_x and button_y are within these ranges then the button has been clicked.

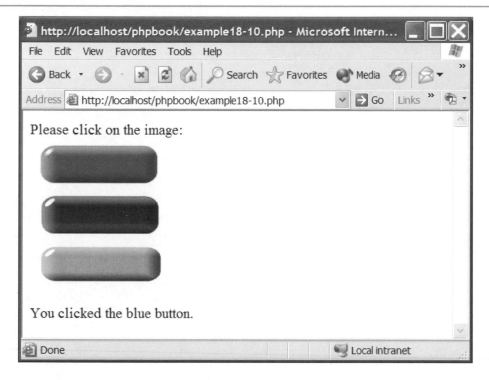

Figure 18.12 File field output.

File Uploads

Forms can employ an element that allows the user to select a file from the local computer and upload this to the server for access by the PHP script. This is a complex process and is covered in some detail in Chapter 28.

Summary

This chapter has shown how PHP can be used to interact with the user via HTML forms. Each of the different form elements has been presented and the method in which the data it contains can be extracted has been shown. However, there is more to user interaction than simply displaying a form and accessing the data that it contains. In the following chapter we shall examine the role of form data validation and form data redisplay.

Form Validation and Data Retention 19

Introduction

When interacting with the user it is important to ensure that the data that you think the user has entered is in fact what you want. Users are notorious in not typing what you expect and thus form data validation is very important. Consider if an error in the data entered on the form is detected then the form should be redisplayed to the user for correction. However, it would be very annoying if the user had to reenter all of the form data, even that which was correct in the first instance. Therefore, a means of retaining and redisplaying form data is required. This chapter describes how form data validation and the redisplaying of form data can be accomplished.

Present or Absent Validation

One of the simplest forms of validation is to determine if the user has entered anything in the form field or not. Checking that a text or password field contains any data is a simple case of checking that the variable created from the form field is of zero length. This can be done by using an if statement such as:

```
if ($variable == "")
```

In the case of a select form field things are a little different as by default the first item on the menu is automatically selected, fine if this is what the user wants, not so if it is not and they have forgotten to enter it. One way around this problem is to include a "false" menu item at the top of the menu list. You can then check the value of the variable for this value and thus reject the entry if this is found.

The following script illustrates the validation of a form select element:

```php
<?php

// Form Validation and Data Retention - Example 19-1
//---------------------------------
```

```
if(isset($_POST["submit"])){
   if($_POST["title"] == "Select...")
      $titErr = 1;
   else
      $titErr = 0;
   if($_POST["firstname"] == "")
      $firstErr = 1;
   else
      $firstErr = 0;
   if($_POST["surname"] == "")
      $surErr = 1;
   else
      $surErr = 0;
   if (isset($_POST["mus"])) {
      if ($_POST["mus"] == "")
      $musErr = 1;
   else
      $musErr = 0;
   }
   else
      $musErr = 1;
}
else {
   $titErr = 0;
   $firstErr = 0;
   $surErr = 0;
   $musErr = 0;
}
?>
   <form action='<?php echo($_SERVER["PHP_SELF"]) ?>' method='post'>
   <h2>Please enter your personal details:</h2>
   Title: <select name='title'>
   <option>Select...</option>
   <option>Mr</option>
   <option>Miss</option>
   <option>Ms</option>
   <option>Mrs</option>
   <option>Dr</option>
</select><?php if($titErr) echo("<font color='red' size='2'> Please
Select a Title</font>");?>
   <br>

   Firstname: <input type='text' name='firstname'><?php if($firstErr)
echo("<font color='red' size='2'> Please enter
a Firstname</font>");?>
   <br>
   Surname: <input type='text' name='surname'><?php if($surErr)
echo("<font color='red' size='2'> Please enter a Surname</font>");?>
```

```
   <br>
   <h2>Please select your favorite type of music:</h2>
   Pop <input type='radio' name='mus' value='Pop'>
   Rock <input type='radio' name='mus' value='rock'>
   Classical <input type='radio' name='mus' value='classical'>
<?php if($musErr) echo("<font color='red' size='2'>
Please select your favorite Music</font>");?>
   <br><br>
   <input type='submit' name='submit'>
   </form>
```

The script begins with determining if the form has been submitted. If so the value of title, a select form item is checked to see if it is equivalent to the value "Select...". This is the first menu option and is not a valid input. The next three if statements check that the values of firstname, surname and mus are blank. If any of the form variables are blank then the corresponding error variables are set to the value 1:

```php
<?php

// Form Validation and Data Retention - Example 19-1
//--------------------------------

if(isset($_POST["submit"])){
        if($_POST["title"] == "Select...")
             $titErr = 1;
        else
             $titErr = 0;
        if($_POST["firstname"] == "")
             $firstErr = 1;
        else
             $firstErr = 0;
        if($_POST["surname"] == "")
             $surErr = 1;
        else
             $surErr = 0;
        if (isset($_POST["mus"])) {
             if ($_POST["mus"] == "")
             $musErr = 1;
        else
             $musErr = 0;
        }
        else
             $musErr = 1;
}
```

```
else {
        $titErr = 0;
        $firstErr = 0;
        $surErr = 0;
        $musErr = 0;
}
?>
```

The next part of the script outputs the form and the first form element; the select element:

```
<form action='<?php echo($_SERVER["PHP_SELF"]) ?>' method='post'>
<h2>Please enter your personal details:</h2>
Title: <select name='title'>
<option>Select...</option>
<option>Mr</option>
<option>Miss</option>
<option>Ms</option>
<option>Mrs</option>
<option>Dr</option>
```

The next part checks the value of variable $titErr (the variable set if an error was detected) and if equal to 1 outputs an error message:

```
</select><?php if($titErr) echo("<font color='red' size='2'>
Please Select a Title</font>");?>
        <br>
```

The final part of the script outputs the three other form fields and checks the corresponding error variables ($firstErr, $surErr and $musErr) in order to determine whether to display any error messages or not:

```
Firstname: <input type='text' name='firstname'><?php if($firstErr)
echo("<font color='red' size='2'>
Please enter a Firstname</font>");?>
    <br>
    Surname: <input type='text' name='surname'><?php if($surErr)
    echo("<font color='red' size='2'>
    Please enter a Surname</font>");?>
    <br>
    <h2>Please select your favorite type of music:</h2>
    Pop <input type='radio' name='mus' value='Pop'>
    Rock <input type='radio' name='mus' value='rock'>
    Classical <input type='radio' name='mus' value='classical'><?php
    if($musErr)
```

```
echo("<font color='red' size='2'>
Please select your favorite Music</font>");?>
   <br><br>
   <input type='submit' name='submit'>
   </form>
```

Figure 19.1 illustrates the output produced from this script, where a user has failed to enter any data into the form.

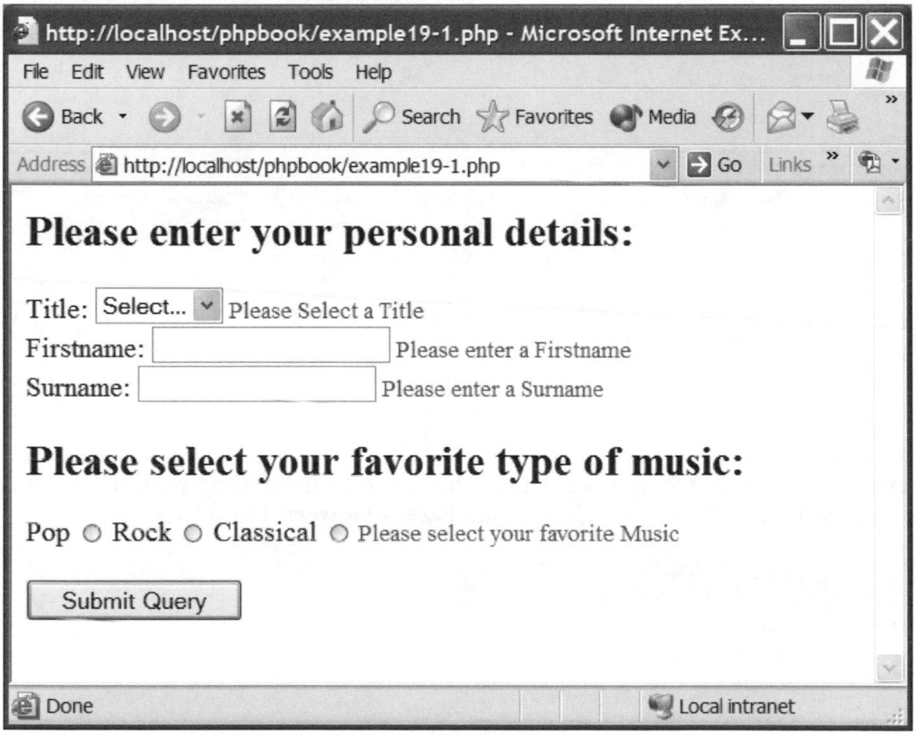

Figure 19.1 Present or absent form data error messages.

Range Validation

Range validation is also quite easy to perform. Suppose you want the user to enter a value between two numbers, say for example the number of products which they would like to purchase. This can be performed using a simple if statement. The following script illustrates a simple example:

```php
<?php

// Form Validation and Data Retention - Example 19-2
//---------------------------------

if(isset($_POST["submit"])){
    $purchase = $_POST["purchase"];
    $purErr=0;
    if( $purchase < 1 || $purchase > 100)
            $purErr=1;
    else
            echo("You wish to purchase $purchase products.");
}
else
    $purErr=0;
?>

    <form action='<?php echo($_SERVER["PHP_SELF"]) ?>' method='post'>
    <h2>Please enter a number between 1 and 100</h2>
    Number to purchase <input type='text' name='purchase'><?php
if($purErr) echo("<font color='red' size='2'>
Invalid Range</font>");?>
    <br><br>
    <input type='submit' name='submit'>
</form>
```

The script begins by checking if a form has been submitted and determining if the range of the value stored in the form variable $purchase is between 1 and 100:

```php
if(isset($_POST["submit"])){
    $purchase = $_POST["purchase"];
    $purErr=0;
    if( $purchase < 1 || $purchase > 100)
            $purErr=1;
    else
            echo("You wish to purchase $purchase products.");
}
else
    $purErr=0;
?>
```

If the value is between the valid range a message is output indicating the number of products to purchase, otherwise a variable $purErr is set to the value 1. Next, the form is output with a single text field requesting the user to enter a value between 1 and 100. Note that an error message is displayed if the value of $purErr is set to 1:

```
<form action='<?php echo($_SERVER["PHP_SELF"]) ?>' method='post'>
    <h2>Please enter a number between 1 and 100</h2>
    Number to purchase <input type='text' name='purchase'><?php
    if($purErr)
echo("<font color='red' size='2'> Invalid Range</font>");?>
    <br><br>
    <input type='submit' name='submit'>
    </form>
```

If an invalid range was detected then the error message is displayed, as illustrated in Figure 19.2.

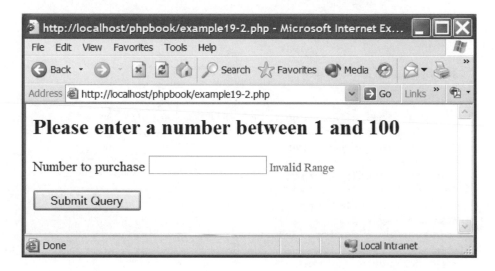

Figure 19.2 Range validation error message.

String Validation

It is easy to mistype text at anytime and form fields are no exception. One way to solve this problem is to minimize the amount of typing that the user has to do. This can be accomplished by providing as many form entries as possible via select menus and thus mistyping is eliminated. Sometimes this is not possible, however. The following script illustrates two methods of obtaining and validating a string input which represents a month of the year. The form contains a select menu from which the user selects a month (the easy way) and the second a text entry field that the user has to enter the month string. It is this field that we need to validate:

```php
<?php

// Form Validation and Data Retention - Example 19-3
//---------------------------------

$months = array("January", "February",
"March","April","May","June","July","August","September","October",
"November","December");

if(isset($_POST["submit"])){
    $month = $_POST["month"];
    $monErr=-1;
    for($c=0;$c<12;$c++)
            if(!strncasecmp($months[$c],$_POST["month2"],3))
                $monErr=$c;
    if($monErr != -1)
            echo("You selected $month and typed " . $months[$monErr]);
}
else
    $monErr=-1;
?>

    <form action='<?php echo($_SERVER["PHP_SELF"]) ?>' method='post'>
    <h2>Please select the month you were born</h2>
    Month <select name='month'>
    <option>January</option>
    <option>February</option>
    <option>March</option>
    <option>April</option>
    <option>May</option>
    <option>June</option>
    <option>July</option>
    <option>August</option>
    <option>September</option>
    <option>October</option>
    <option>November</option>
    <option>December</option>
    </select>
    <br>

    Month <input type='text' name='month2'><?php if($monErr == -1)
echo("<font color='red' size='2'> Unrecognised Month</font>");?>
    <br><br>
    <input type='submit' name='submit'>
    </form>
```

The script begins by declaring an array $months and populating it with the months of the year. An if statement then checks if the form has been submitted:

```
$months = array("January", "February", "March","April","May","June",
"July","August","September","October","November","December");

if(isset($_POST["submit"])){
```

Next, a variable $monErr is declared and set to –1. This variable will be used to store the array location of the month if it is found successfully. A for loop iterates 12 times comparing each month in the array with the data entered on the form. The function strncasecmp() is used to do this, which was introduced in Chapter 17. The function checks the first three characters of the entered data against the first three of the current array item. The function is case independent so it doesn't matter if the user typed the month in upper or lower case. If a match is found variable $monErr is set to the current array count. If after all 12 items in the array are compared and a match is found a message is displayed:

```
    $month = $_POST["month"];
    $monErr=-1;
    for($c=0;$c<12;$c++)
        if(!strncasecmp($months[$c],$_POST["month2"],3))
            $monErr=$c;
    if($monErr != -1)
        echo("You selected $month and typed " . $months[$monErr]);
}
else
    $monErr=-1;
```

The next part of the script outputs the selection menu element:

```
<form action='<?php echo($_SERVER["PHP_SELF"]) ?>' method='post'>
<h2>Please select the month you were born</h2>
Month <select name='month'>
<option>January</option>
<option>February</option>
<option>March</option>
<option>April</option>
<option>May</option>
<option>June</option>
<option>July</option>
<option>August</option>
<option>September</option>
<option>October</option>
<option>November</option>
<option>December</option>
</select>
<br>
```

Finally, the text form field is displayed along with an error message if the $monErr flag has been set:

```
Month <input type='text' name='month2'><?php if($monErr == -1)
echo("<font color='red' size='2'> Unrecognised Month</font>");?>
<br><br>
<input type='submit' name='submit'>
</form>
```

Figure 19.3 illustrates the error message output from the above script.

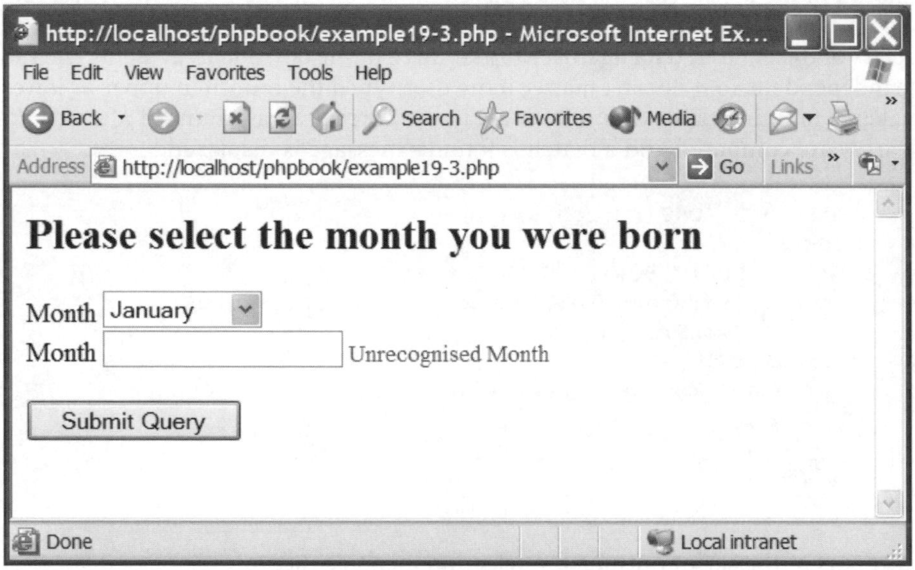

Figure 19.3 Unrecognized month error.

Retaining Text and Password Form Field Data

In the examples of form validation illustrated thus far any data the user entered on the form is lost when the form is redisplayed along with the corresponding error messages. While it may be considered good practice not to redisplay any data which was deemed incorrect, not including fields which did pass the validation tests is annoying to the user as they have to retype the information; a hindrance at best and could result in the user making mistakes in the data entry which were not made the first time around. What would be better is if any data was entered correctly then this is redisplayed in the relevant form fields when the form is represented to the user.

The following script illustrates an example of redisplaying form data within the text form field:

```php
<?php

// Form Validation and Data Retention - Example 19-4
//----------------------------------------------
```

```php
if(isset($_POST["submit"])){
   $surname = $_POST["surname"];
   $firstname = $_POST["firstname"];

   if($firstname == "")
      $firstErr = 1;
   else
      $firstErr = 0;
   if($surname == "")
      $surErr = 1;
   else
      $surErr = 0;
}
else {
   $firstErr = 0;
   $surErr = 0;
   $surname = "";
   $firstname = "";
}
?>


<form action='<?php echo($_SERVER["PHP_SELF"]) ?>' method='post'>
   <h2>Please enter your personal details:</h2>
   Firstname: <input type='text' name='firstname' value='<?php
echo($firstname)?>'><?php if($firstErr) echo("<font color='red'
size='2'>
   Please enter a Firstname</font>");?>
   <br />
   Surname: <input type='text' name='surname'value='<?php
echo($surname)?>'><?php if($surErr) echo("<font color='red'
   size='2'>Please enter a Surname</font>");?>
   <br /><br />
   <input type='submit' name='submit'>
   </form>
```

The script begins by checking if the form has been submitted and if so checks to see if there has been any data entered in the firstname and surname fields:

```php
if(isset($_POST["submit"])){
      $surname = $_POST["surname"];
      $firstname = $_POST["firstname"];

      if($firstname == "")
            $firstErr = 1;
      else
            $firstErr = 0;
```

```
            if ($surname == "")
                    $surErr = 1;
            else
                    $surErr = 0;
    }
    else {
            $firstErr = 0;
            $surErr = 0;
            $surname = "";
            $firstname = "";
    }
    ?>
```

The next part of the script outputs the start of the form:

```
<form action='<?php echo($_SERVER["PHP_SELF"]) ?>' method='post'>
        <h2>Please enter your personal details:</h2>
```

The clever bit of code that enables us to retain the data on the form is shown below. Note that the firstname and surname text fields now have a value attribute. Also, note that PHP script has been included to echo out the value of the $firstname and $surname variables into the value attribute. This ensures that the values contained within these variables are displayed in the text field when the form is displayed, thus retaining the data:

```
    Firstname: <input type='text' name='firstname' value='<?php
echo($firstname) ?>'><?php if ($firstErr) echo("<font
color='red'size='2'>
Please enter a Firstname</font>");?>
    <br />
    Surname: <input type='text' name='surname' value='<?php
    echo($surname)
?>'><?php if ($surErr) echo("<font color='red' size='2'> Please
enter a Surname</font>");?>
    <br /><br />
    <input type='submit' name='submit'>
    </form>
```

Figure 19.4 illustrates a form which has been submitted. While the firstname has been entered the surname has not and thus an error message is displayed. Note that the firstname data is redisplayed on the form.

Retaining Textarea Form Data

Retaining data entered in a textarea form field is easy. Consider the following script:

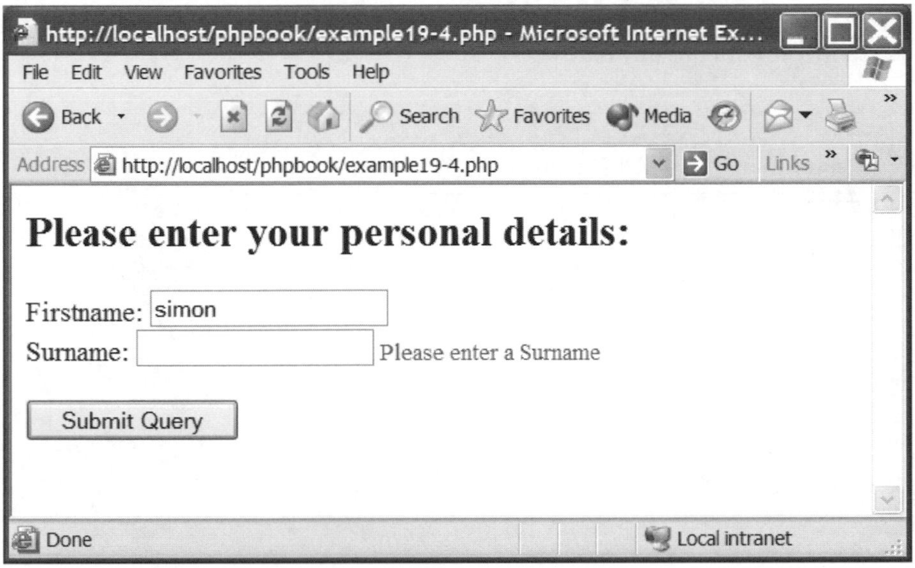

Figure 19.4 Retaining text field data.

```php
<?php

// Form Validation and Data Retention - Example 19-5
//---------------------------------

if(isset($_POST["submit"])){
    $address = $_POST["address"];
    if($address == "")
        $addressErr = 1;
    else
        $addressErr = 0;
}
else {
    $addressErr = 1;
    $address = "";
}
?>


<form action='<?php echo($_SERVER["PHP_SELF"]) ?>' method='post'>
    <h2>Please enter your personal details:</h2>
    Address: <textarea name='address' rows='5'><?php echo($address)
?></textarea><?php if($addressErr) echo("<font color='red' size='2'>
Please enter an address</font>");?>
    <br><br>
    <input type='submit' name='submit'>
    </form>
```

This script begins by checking that the form has been submitted and if so checks that the variable $address contains any data:

```
if(isset($_POST["submit"])){
    $address = $_POST["address"];
    if($address == "")
        $addressErr = 1;
    else
        $addressErr = 0;
}
else {
    $addressErr = 1;
    $address = "";
}
?>
```

The next part of the script outputs the form:

```
<form action='<?php echo($_SERVER["PHP_SELF"]) ?>' method='post'>
    <h2>Please enter your personal details:</h2>
```

To retain the textarea form field data the value of the variable $address is output between the start and end tags of the textarea element:

```
    Address: <textarea name='address' rows='5'><?php echo($address)
?></textarea><?php if($addressErr) echo("<font color='red' size='2'>
Please enter an address</font>");?>
    <br><br>
    <input type='submit' name='submit'>
    </form>
```

The output from the above script is illustrated in Figure 19.5.

Retaining Checkbox and Radio Button Form Field Data

Checkbox and radio button form elements can retain their selection in much the same way as text and password fields. The following script illustrates how the user's selection is maintained:

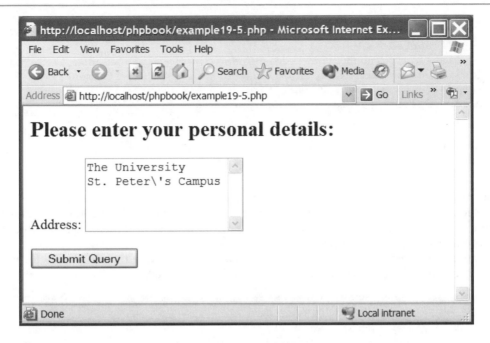

Figure 19.5 Retaining textarea data.

```php
<?php

// Form Validation and Data Retention - Example 19-6
//---------------------------------

if(isset($_POST["submit"])){
    $mus = $_POST["mus"];
    if($mus == "")
        $musErr = 1;
    else
        $musErr = 0;
}
else {
    $musErr = 1;
    $mus = "";
}
?>

<form action='<?php echo($_SERVER["PHP_SELF"]) ?>' method='post'>
    <h2>Please select your favorite type of music:</h2>
    Pop <input type='radio' name='mus' value='pop' <?php
    if($mus == 'pop')
echo('checked'); ?>>
    Rock <input type='radio' name='mus' value='rock' <?php
```

```
    if($mus == 'rock')
echo('checked'); ?>>
    Classical <input type='radio' name='mus' value='classical' <?php
if($mus == 'classical') echo('checked'); ?>><?php if($musErr)
echo("<font color='red' size='2'>
Please select your favorite Music</font>");?>
    <br><br>
    <input type='submit' name='submit'>
    </form>
```

The important part of this script is the checked attributed which can be included in a radio or checkbox form type. The following script checks to see if the value of $mus which is the name of the form data element is equal to the current button. If so then the text "checked" is output as part of the form element.

Figure 19.6 illustrates the output from the above script. Note that while this form has been submitted the user selection of "Rock" has been retained.

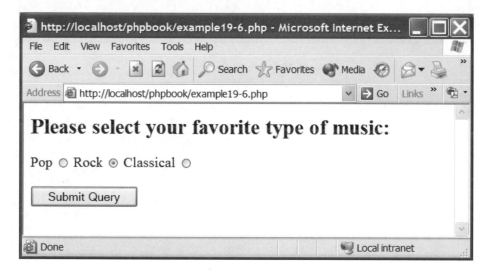

Figure 19.6 Retained radio button selection.

Retaining Select Menu Form Field Data

Selection menus can also retain their menu selection, consider the following script:

```
<?php

// Form Validation and Data Retention - Example 19-7
//----------------------------------
```

```
if(isset($_POST["submit"])){
 $title = $_POST["title"];
 if($title == "Select...")
    $titErr = 1;
 else
    $titErr = 0;
}
else {
 $titErr = 1;
 $title = "";
}
?>

<form action='<?php echo($_SERVER["PHP_SELF"]) ?>' method='post'>
 <h2>Please enter your personal details:</h2>
 Title: <select name='title'>
 <option>Select...</option>
 <option <?php if($title == "Mr") echo("Selected") ?>>Mr</option>
 <option <?php if($title == "Miss") echo("Selected") ?>>Miss</option>
 <option <?php if($title == "Ms") echo("Selected") ?>>Ms</option>
 <option <?php if($title == "Mrs") echo("Selected") ?>>Mrs</option>
 <option <?php if($title == "Dr") echo("Selected") ?>>Dr</option>
 </select><?php if($titErr) echo("<font color='red' size='2'> Please
Select a Title</font>");?>
 <br><br>
 <input type='submit' name='submit'>
 </form>
</body>
</html>
```

The script outputs the menu selection options and checks that the value of variable title, which stores the value of the selected option, is equal to the current option. If so, the attribute "selected" is output as part of the option element. Figure 19.7 illustrates that a submitted selection element option of "Mrs" was retained.

Hidden Data

Forms can be used to pass data each time the form is displayed but you don't want the user to see this data. This is achieved through the use of the hidden form element type. Why would we want to do this? Well, you might want to pass some information from one script to another or back to the same script via a form but you don't want the user to see what this data is and thus not be able to interfere with it. Let's create an example script to illustrate what we mean:

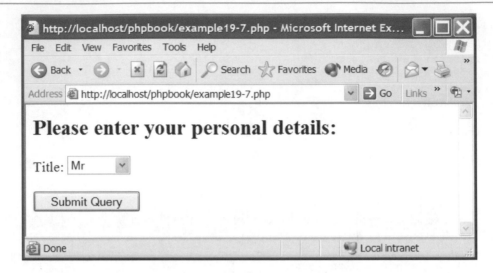

Figure 19.7 Retaining a selection elements chosen option.

```php
<?php

// Form Validation and Data Retention - Example 19-8
//--------------------------------

if(isset($_POST["submit"])){
      $count = $_POST["count"];
      $count++;
}
else
      $count = 1;
?>


<form action='<?php echo($_SERVER["PHP_SELF"]) ?>' method='post'>
      <h2>The number of times this form has been submitted is:
      <?php echo($count)?></h2>
      <input type='hidden' name='count' value='<?php
      echo($count) ?>'>
      <input type='submit' name='submit'>
      </form>
```

The script is very simple and begins by checking if the form was submitted and if so incrementing variable $count. If the form has not been submitted then the value of variable $count is set to 1:

```
if(isset($_POST["submit"])){
     $count = $_POST["count"];
     $count++;
}
else
     $count = 1;
?>
```

The next part of the script outputs the form and a heading. The heading outputs the value of variable $count:

```
<form action='<?php echo($_SERVER["PHP_SELF"]) ?>' method='post'>
     <h2>The number of times this form has been submitted is: <?php
     echo($count)
?></h2>
```

Hidden within the form is a new type of form element known as "hidden". Hidden form elements can take many of the same attributes as other elements, such as name and value. In this case the name of the element is count (the name of the variable) and the value is the current value of the variable $count:

```
<input type='hidden' name='count' value='<?php echo($count) ?>'>
<input type='submit' name='submit'>
</form>
```

Essentially, what happens is that when the user clicks the submit button the value of count is passed back to the script (although the user doesn't see this happen) and the value is incremented and then redisplayed. The output from this script is shown in Figure 19.8.

Arrays and Forms

In the previous part of this chapter we illustrated how form data can be retained and/or hidden within the form. One area, which we did not discuss was that of passing arrays through forms. The main reason for this is because we need to treat arrays in a slightly different way to other variables. You see you might think that you can include an array as a hidden data entry in a form, however, as we shall see below this doesn't work. The following script checks to see if the form has been submitted. If so the contents of an array which we have hidden within the form are displayed:

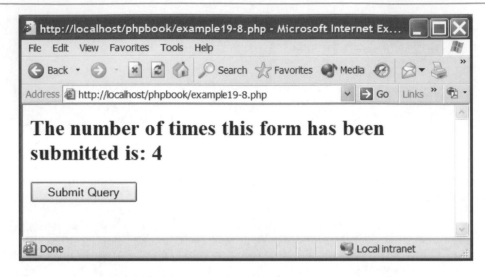

Figure 19.8 Hidden form data enabling us to count the number of form submissions.

```php
<?php

// Form Validation and Data Retention - Example 19-9
//---------------------------------

if(isset($_POST["submit"])){
        echo("The array contains:<br>");
        $names = $_POST['names'];
        for($a=0;$a<4;$a++)
            echo($names[$a] . "<br>");
}
else
        $names = array("Simon","Liz","Gemma","Hayley");
?>

<form action='<?php echo($_SERVER["PHP_SELF"]) ?>' method='post'>
        <h2>This form contains a hidden array.</h2>
        <input type='hidden' name='names' value='<?php
        echo($names) ?>'>
        <input type='submit' name='submit'>
        </form>
```

A for loop is then used to display the contents of the array:

```
if(isset($_POST["submit"])){
        echo("The array contains:<br>");
        $names = $_POST['names'];
        for($a=0;$a<4;$a++)
                echo($names[$a] . "<br>");
}
```

if the form hasn't been submitted then the array is created for the first time:

```
else
        $names = array("Simon","Liz","Gemma","Hayley");
?>
```

The form is output and as illustrated earlier a hidden form element is included to contain the values of the names array:

```
<form action='<?php echo($_SERVER["PHP_SELF"]) ?>' method='post'>
        <h2>This form contains a hidden array.</h2>
        <input type='hidden' name='names' value='<?php
        echo($names) ?>'>
        <input type='submit' name='submit'>
        </form>
```

All this looks well, until we submit the form and we get the output illustrated in Figure 19.9. What has happened to your array data? Well, unfortunately, you cannot pass arrays between forms in this way and the data is lost.

There is, however, a couple of methods that we can use to get around this problem. Remember that an array is an indexed sequence of variables. If we were to split the array apart and output each array element as a separate form variable then we could pass them using the form. We will need to recombine the data together after the form submission, but at least the array contents will be retained.

Consider the following script, which is a modified version of the previous one. The first part determines if the form has been submitted. If so, the array names is created from the separate variables which we shall see created later:

```
<?php

// Form Validation and Data Retention - Example 19-10
//----------------------------------
```

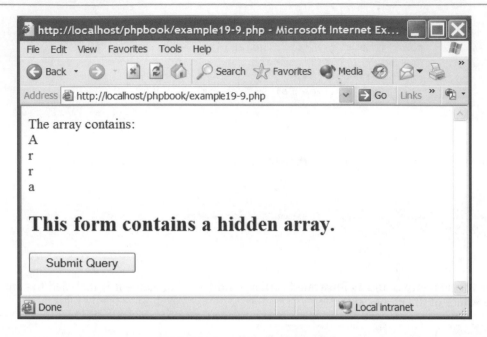

Figure 19.9 Incorrect passing of an array.

```php
if(isset($_POST["submit"])){
        echo("The array contains:<br>");
        $names =
array($_POST['name0'],$_POST['name1'],
        $_POST['name2'],$_POST['name3']);
        for($a=0;$a<4;$a++)
            echo($names[$a] . "<br>");
}
else
        $names = array("Simon","Liz","Gemma","Hayley");
?>

<form action='<?php echo($_SERVER["PHP_SELF"]) ?>' method='post'>
        <h2>This form contains a hidden array.</h2>

        <?php
        for($a=0;$a<4;$a++)
            echo("<input type='hidden' name='name$a' value='" .
            $names[$a] ."'>");
        ?>
        <input type='submit' name='submit'>
        </form>
```

A for loop is then used to display the contents of the array:

```
if(isset($_POST["submit"])){
        echo("The array contains:<br>");
        $names =
array($_POST['name0'],$_POST['name1'],$_POST['name2'],
$_POST['name3']);
        for($a=0;$a<4;$a++)
              echo($names[$a] . "<br>");
}
else
        $names = array("Simon","Liz","Gemma","Hayley");

?>
```

As in the previous example the next part of the script outputs the form:

```
<form action='<?php echo($_SERVER["PHP_SELF"]) ?>' method='post'>
        <h2>This form contains a hidden array.</h2>
```

The following part of the script uses a for loop to output the values of the array as hidden form elements. Note that each element is given a different name starting at name0 then name1 and so on:

```
<?php
        for($a=0;$a<4;$a++)
            echo("<input type='hidden' name='name$a' value='" .
            $names[$a] ."'>");
        ?>
        <input type='submit' name='submit'>
        </form>
```

While the above example works there is another way that we can accomplish the same thing, but in a more elegant way. Consider the following script, which does exactly the same thing as the previous one, but using a different technique:

```
<?php

// Form Validation and Data Retention - Example 19-11
//---------------------------------
```

```
if(isset($_POST["submit"])){
        echo("The array contains:<br>");
        $name = $_POST['name'];
        $names = explode("|",$name);
        for($a=0;$a<4;$a++)
                echo($names[$a] . "<br>");
}
else {
        $names = array("Simon","Liz","Gemma","Hayley");
        $name = implode("|",$names);
}
?>

<form action='<?php echo($_SERVER["PHP_SELF"]) ?>' method='post'>
        <h2>This form contains a hidden array.</h2>

        <?php
        echo("<input type='hidden' name='name' value='$name'>");
        ?>
        <input type='submit' name='submit'>
        </form>
```

The script checks that the form has been submitted and if so uses the explode() function (introduced in Chapter 16) to extract a single string of name separated by "|" characters into an array, which is then displayed using a for loop:

```
if(isset($_POST["submit"])){
        echo("The array contains:<br>");
        $name = $_POST['name'];
        $names = explode("|",$name);
        for($a=0;$a<4;$a++)
                echo($names[$a] . "<br>");
}
```

If the form has not been submitted then the array is created and the implode() function used to create a single string of the array contents, separated with the "|"character:

```
else {
        $names = array("Simon","Liz","Gemma","Hayley");
        $name = implode("|",$names);
}
```

The form is output as before:

```
<form action='<?php echo($_SERVER["PHP_SELF"]) ?>' method-'post'>
      <h2>This form contains a hidden array.</h2>
```

However, instead of having to output a number of hidden variables only the single imploded string has to be included:

```
<?php
echo("<input type='hidden' name='name' value='$name'>");
?>
<input type='submit' name='submit'>
</form>
```

Figure 19.10 illustrates the output from the two previous scripts.

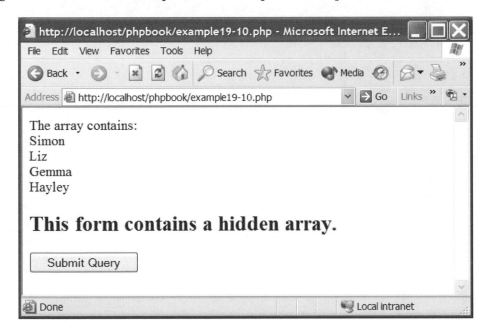

Figure 19.10 The correct way of passing an array.

Summary

This chapter has illustrated how form validation can be performed and why it is an important aspect of user interaction. We have seen how form data can be maintained between each redisplay of the form and thus remove the need for the user to retype and select the form data when not required. In the following chapter we examine some of the security aspects of using forms and the potential dangers that they can create.

Security Issues 20

Introduction

Many Web applications use common authentication/login methods. These grant access to the system to specific users and prevent unauthorized access to those who do not have access rights. However, simply using a password to login into a system is not the only way to secure a Web-based system. Encryption methods should be used for storing passwords in database or text files. In addition referral pages can be checked to determine that the data being passed to a Web page is in fact coming from an expected source and not an unknown one. In this chapter we examine how to make your on-line Web systems more secure.

Encryption Methods

Encryption increases security in all network systems. With encryption we can be reasonably sure that no one will be able to steal our passwords and gain unauthorized access to the system. PHP supports two encryption methods that are commonly used to protect data – the MD5 and CRYPT methods. These are supported through the two functions md5() and crypt(), the formats of which are:

Function prototypes:

```
string md5 ( string word );
```

```
string crypt ( string word , string option);
```

Function arguments and return details:

Name	Type	Description
word	String	String to be encrypted
option	String	CRYPT_STD_DES – Standard DES-based encryption with a 2-character salt
		CRYPT_EXT_DES – Extended DES-based encryption with a 9-character salt
		CRYPT_MD5 - MD5 encryption with a 12-character salt starting with 1
		CRYPT_BLOWFISH - Blowfish encryption with a 16-character salt starting with 2
md5()/crypt() returns	String	Encrypted string

Function examples:

```
$encrypt = md5($text);
$encrypt2 = crypt($text, CRYPT_STD_DES);
```

The following example script illustrates the use of these functions:

```php
<?php

// Security Issues - Example 20-1
//---------------------

define("TEST","test");

$encrypt = md5(TEST);
$encrypt2 = crypt(TEST, CRYPT_STD_DES);

echo "$encrypt<p>$encrypt2";
?>
```

The output of the text "test" after encryption is:

MD5:   098f6bcd4621d373cade4e832627b4f6
Crypt: 1$MDgPcadkr82

Of the two, MD5 is the faster and most common encryption method. The encrypted sting is 32-characters long and cannot be decrypted easily. When we use CRYPT the output encrypted string is random and cannot be easily used for Web authentication methods.

Login and Authentication

Using secure forms along with encrypted passwords we can ensure that our scripts will have the maximum security and only permit the right access to those who have permission to access these systems. There are two types of authentication: the simple login form and HTTP authentication. The second method uses the authentication module from Apache and is more secure and very difficult to break. Passwords should be encrypted and stored encrypted. In this case if someone reads the password file it is impossible for him to use them as they cannot be decrypted.

Simple Form Login System Using a Password File with Single User

The following script illustrates checking of passwords using the username "john" and encrypted password "test":

```php
<?php

// Security Issues - Example 20-2
//-------------------------------

if(isset($_POST["submit"])) {

    $userpass = array("john", "098f6bcd4621d373cade4e832627b4f6");

    if(($_POST["username"] == "$userpass[0]") AND
(md5($_POST["password"]) == $userpass[1]))
{
        echo "Login Successful!";
    }
}
?>

<html>
<body bgcolor="#FFFFFF" text="#000000">
<form name="form1" method="post" action="">
Username:<input type="text" name="username">
<br>
Password:<input type="password" name="password">
<br>
<input type="submit" name="submit" value="Login">
<input type="reset" name="Submit2" value="Reset">
</form>
</body>
</html>
```

The above script checks if the form has been submitted:

```php
if(isset($_POST["submit"])) {
```

If so then the password array is initiated:

```php
$userpass = array("john", "098f6bcd4621d373cade4e832627b4f6");
```

If the username and passwords match a message is output to this effect:

```php
        if(($_POST["username"] == "$userpass[0]") AND
(md5($_POST["password"]) == $userpass[1]))
{
```

```
                echo "Login Successful!";
        }
}
?>
```

The final part of the script creates the user form:

```html
<html>
<body bgcolor="#FFFFFF" text="#000000">
<form name="form1" method="post" action="">
Username:<input type="text" name="username">
<br>
Password:<input type="password" name="password">
<br>
<input type="submit" name="submit" value="Login">
<input type="reset" name="Submit2" value="Reset">
</form>
</body>
</html>
```

Secure HTTP Authentication Using Apache

When you are using an Apache server there is another form of authentication which can be used. This uses the function header() to send a HTTP header to the browser:

Function prototype:

```
void header ( string httpHeader);
```

Function arguments and return details:

Name	Type	Description
httpHeader	String	HTTP header
header() returns	Void	Returns nothing

Function example:

```
header("WWW-Authenticate: Basic realm=\"Secure Login\"");
```

The following script illustrates an example of using this function:

```php
<?php

// Security Issues - Example 20-3
//--------------------------------

$userpass = array("john", "098f6bcd4621d373cade4e832627b4f6");

if((isset($_SERVER["PHP_AUTH_USER"]))
        OR (empty($_SERVER["PHP_AUTH_PW"]))
        OR ($_SERVER["PHP_AUTH_USER"] != $userpass[0])
        OR (md5($_SERVER["PHP_AUTH_PW"]) != $userpass[1])) {

 Header("WWW-Authenticate: Basic realm=\"Secure Login\"");
 Header("HTTP/1.0 401 Unauthorized");

 echo"Login Failed. Try again";

}
else
 echo "Login Successful!";
?>
```

In this example we use the HTTP authentication method to secure any access on our system. We use the header() function to send an "Authentication Required" message to the client browser causing it to pop up a Username/Password input window. Once the user has filled in a username and a password, the URL containing the PHP script will be invoked with the predefined variables PHP_AUTH_USER and PHP_AUTH_PW, containing the username and password. The popup window generated is illustrated in Figure 20.1.

Checking Referral Pages

When a registration script is being developed maximum security must be taken in order to protect the system from unwelcome, massive or automatic registrations that might harm our system and our database where all usernames/passwords are kept. It is very easy for someone to create a simple script to generate e.g. 100,000 random usernames in order to "flood" your application with logins.

For example, imagine that you have a Web form for on-line registration. This form consists of two textboxes (one for the username and the other one for a password) and a submit button. Assume that the first textbox is named "user", the second textbox is named "pass" and submit button's name is "submit". When a HTTP Post is made (when you press the Submit button) these three variables ($user, $pass, $submit) are passed to the script and this registers the user.

Well, this is what is supposed to happen. But, what if someone (on another site) creates a Web script which passes the same three variables to your registration script? What will happen if this script is run a million times? Well, it may allow someone to break into your application through automatically generated random username and passwords. The solution is to ensure that your script checks the "referrer" of the page. In others words the

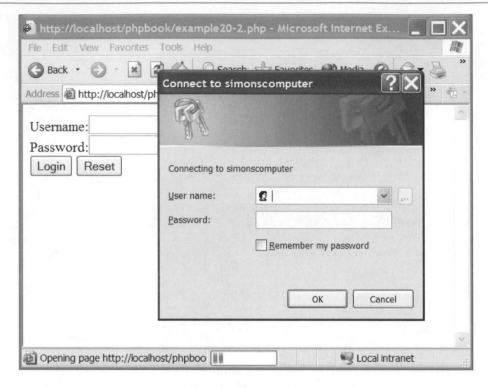

Figure 20.1 Standard HTTP authorization type.

name of the Web page/script which passed the data to your script. If it is not the name you were expecting then you can ignore the data.

Consider the following example:

```php
<?php

// Security Issues - Example 20-4
//--------------------------------

if(isset($_SERVER["HTTP_REFERER"])) {
   if ($_SERVER["HTTP_REFERER"] ==
"http://localhost/phpbook/example20-4.php") {

      if($_POST["submit"])
         echo "Registration Successful!";
      else
         echo "Wrong referral page. Registration failed";
   }
```

```
    }

    ?>

    <html>
    <body bgcolor="#FFFFFF" text="#000000">
    <form name="form1" method="post" action="">
    Username:
    <input type="text" name="user">
    <br>
    Password:
    <input type="text" name="pass">
    <br>
    Email:
    <input type="text" name="email">
    <br>
    <br>
    <input type="submit" name="submit" value="Register">
    <input type="reset" name="Submit2" value="Reset">
    </form>
    </body>
    </html>
```

In this example the referral page is http://localhost/phpbook/example20-4.php. You will need to alter this depending on the name and location of where you store your scripts on your PHP server. The script is divided into two main parts, the first checks if the referrer page and the second displays the form which the user would normally complete in order to "register" with the application. Figure 20.2 illustrates the output from this script.

Redirecting the User

In many cases (often concerning security) you may wish to direct the user to a new Web page automatically to stop them using the current page. We can accomplish this with the header() function introduced previously in this chapter, but with now using the "Location: " string, for example:

```
    header ("Location: example20-5.php");
```

To see an example of this working first create the following script:

```
    <?php

    // Security Issues - Example 20-5
    //-------------------------------

    echo "This is a different page";

    ?>
```

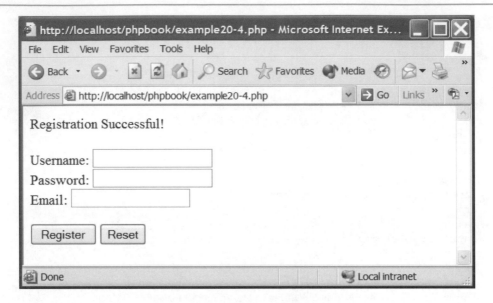

Figure 20.2 Correct referral page.

Next, create the following script which is a modification of example20-2.php:

```php
<?php

// Security Issues - Example 20-6
//--------------------------------

if(isset($_POST["submit"])) {

    $userpass = array("john", "098f6bcd4621d373cade4e832627b4f6");

    if(($_POST["username"] == "$userpass[0]") AND
(md5($_POST["password"]) == $userpass[1]))
{
        echo "Login Successful!";
    }
    else {
        header("location: example20-5.php");
    }
}
?>

<html>
<body bgcolor="#FFFFFF" text="#000000">
<form name="form1" method="post" action="">
Username:<input type="text" name="username">
<br>
```

```
Password:<input type="password" name="password">
<br>
<input type="submit" name="submit" value="Login">
<input type="reset" name="Submit2" value="Reset">
</form>
</body>
</html>
```

The only difference between the above script and the previous example is that now if the password and username do not match then the user is redirected to page example20-5.php

Summary

This chapter has introduced the concept of Web applications security using login and register systems. We have also illustrated the most common methods for encrypting strings and passwords and how these can be implemented to secure our authentication scripts. Finally the "referral page check" solution has been introduced to prevent unwanted or automated registrations. In the next chapter we shall examine how we can e-mail users and how we can create plain or HTML style e-mail messages.

Summary

E-mailing Users

Introduction

E-mail has become one of the key means of electronic communication. PHP includes function support for e-mail creation and interactivity. In this chapter we introduce the mail() function which is widely used within PHP scripts in order to send raw text, HTML and MIME-type messages to one or more recipients at the same time. In addition to demonstrating how to use this function in its basic form, we shall also examine some of the mail() function's more advanced features. These include the means to enable extra headers to be defined, change the type of the e-mail being sent, define reply addresses and other useful attributes.

The Mail() Function

Sending e-mail with PHP is very simple. In order to do this we use the mail() function. This allows us to transmit the message from a source mail server to a target e-mail account on the same or another mail server. In order to use this function successfully, you must have access to a mail server. The appropriate mail client that is to be used is defined within the php.ini file. By default the section of the php.ini file appropriate to mail is as follows:

```
[mail function]
; For Win32 only.
SMTP = localhost ; for Win32 only

; For Win32 only.
sendmail_from = me@localhost.com ; for Win32 only

; For Unix only. You may supply arguments as well (default:
"sendmail -t -i").
;sendmail_path =
```

Whether your PHP server is running on a UNIX or a Windows environment will depend on how you should configure this file. In the case of a Windows user you must configure the location of your SMTP mail server and your e-mail address. UNIX users need to enter the location of their sendmail application which is normally "/usr/bin/sendmail" by default.

The format of the mail() function is as follows:

Function prototype:

```
bool mail ( string to, string subject, string message, string headers );
```

Function arguments and return details:

Name	Type	Description
to	String	Message recipient
subject	String	Subject of message
message	String	The message body
headers	String	Additional headers on the message
mail() returns	Boolean	"TRUE" if the mail was successfully accepted for delivery, "FALSE" otherwise

Function example:

```
mail ("someone@example.com", "My Subject", "Line 1\n Line 2\n Line
3");
```

The mail() function consists of four attributes. The first attribute is used to specify the destination mail account where the message should be sent. The second attribute is the text which will appear in the subject line of the message. The third attribute is the text which will appear in the body of the message. Finally, the fourth attribute can be used to specify additional parameters and headers. We shall consider these later in this chapter but for now let us look at how we can send a simple mail message.

Sending Mail

You can use the following simple format of the mail() function to send a fast plain message to an e-mail account. In this example the e-mail account is: stobbie1966@yahoo.co.uk. Note that this example does not use the fourth attribute of the mail() function:

```
<?php

//Email - Example 21-1
//--------------------

mail("stobbie1966@yahoo.co.uk", "Hello", "Hello Stobbie, how are
you?");

?>
```

When you execute this script using your Web browser you will get no message displayed indicating that the message has been sent. In fact you will get nothing displayed in the

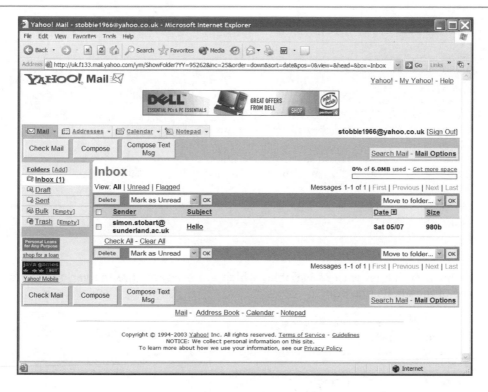

Figure 21.1 Receiving a small e-mail.

Web browser window at all. However, an examination of Stobbie's inbox will reveal that the e-mail message sent by the PHP script has been sent. This is illustrated in Figure 21.1.

Note that the sender is simon@mailserver.com. PHP uses a common mail account gateway for all messages, as defined within the php.ini file. On many servers the mail gateway for PHP is the main e-mail account of the host server (e.g. root@mailserver.com). In order to use a personal e-mail account we would either have to modify the php.ini file each time or, more sensibly, we can add some extra header information to the mail() function.

Sending Mail with Headers

The fourth argument of the mail() function enables us to provide additional header information about the e-mail we wish to send. Multiple extra headers are separated with carriage returns and new-line characters (\r\n). The header "From:" specifies the real e-mail address of the message we wish to send. The header "Reply-To:" specifies the reply address shown when the recipient clicks on the e-mail message to send a reply. The following script illustrates the use of these headers:

```php
<?php

//Email - Example 21-2
//--------------------

$e-mail = "stobbie1966@yahoo.co.uk";
$subject = "Hello";
$message = "Hello Stobbie, how are you?";

$headers = "From: simon@domain.net\r\n";
$headers .= "Reply-To: simon@domain.net";

mail($e-mail, $subject, $message, $headers);

?>
```

This script first defines various variables which are used to store the various attributes required of the mail() function:

```php
$e-mail = "stobbie1966@yahoo.co.uk";
$subject = "Hello";
$message = "Hello Stobbie, how are you?";

$headers = "From: simon@domain.net\r\n";
$headers .= "Reply-To: simon@domain.net";
```

These are then passed as arguments in the function call:

```php
mail($e-mail, $subject, $message, $headers);
```

Once again nothing is displayed in the browser window. However, an examination of the user's inbox will reveal that the message has been received and now has a different sender. This is shown in Figure 21.2.

Sending a Complex/HTML E-mail

Sometimes there is a need to create more colourful messages instead of simple raw text ones. More sophisticated HTML-based e-mails can be composed by inserting HTML code into the message attribute of the mail() function. However, simply doing this is not enough to enable the e-mail message to include and display the HTML. In addition some additional headers are required in order to define the content type of the message. These headers are:

```php
$headers = "MIME-Version: 1.0\r\n";
$headers .= "Content-type: text/html; charset=iso-8859-1\r\n";
```

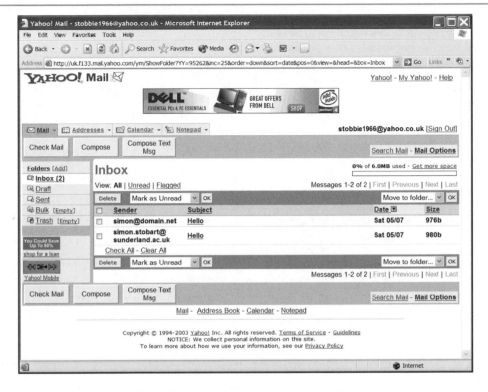

Figure 21.2 Receiving an e-mail with extra headers.

MIME stands for Multipurpose Internet Mail Extensions. MIME extends the format of Internet mail to allow more sophisticated non-textual-based e-mail messages. The e-mail client needs to know what version of MIME we are using so the MIME header defines the MIME version. The Content-type header is a mandatory header which specifies the format of the message body (in this case text and HTML) and the character set being used. The following example illustrates sending an HTML-style e-mail message to three users simultaneously:

```php
<?php

//Email - Example 21-3
//--------------------

// Send To
$to = "stobbie1966@yahoo.co.uk, ";
$to .= "kelly@domain.com, ";
$to .= "mary@domain.com";
```

```
//Subject of message
$subject = "Happy Christmas!";

//HTML Message
$message = '
<html>
<body bgcolor="#FFFFCC" text="#000000">
<div align="center">
<h1>HAPPY NEW YEAR!</h1>
<br>
<table width="385" border="0" cellspacing="2" cellpadding="2"
 height="74">
  <tr bgcolor="#CC9900">
   <td bgcolor="#CC0000">Company Meeting:</td>
   <td>20:00</td>
  </tr>
  <tr bgcolor="#CC9900">
   <td bgcolor="#CC0000">New year's Eve Party:</td>
   <td>22:00</td>
  </tr>
 </table>
</div>
</body>
</html>
';

// To send HTML mail we must define the Content-type header
$headers = "MIME-Version: 1.0\r\n";
$headers .= "Content-type: text/html; charset=iso-8859-1\r\n";

// From Header
$headers .= "From: Company Name <info@company.com>\r\n";

mail($to, $subject, $message, $headers);

?>
```

The script first defines the variable $to, which is used to store the list of e-mail recipients, and the variable $subject containing the text which will appear in the message subject:

```
// Send To
$to = "stobbie1966@yahoo.co.uk, ";
$to .= "kelly@domain.com, ";
$to .= "mary@domain.com";

//Subject of message
$subject = "Happy Christmas!";
```

The next block of code defines the HTML message body which is stored in variable $message:

```
//HTML Message
$message = '
<html>
<body bgcolor="#FFFFCC" text="#000000">
<div align="center">
<h1>HAPPY NEW YEAR!</h1>
<br>
<table width="385" border="0" cellspacing="2" cellpadding="2"
height="74">
  <tr bgcolor="#CC9900">
   <td bgcolor="#CC0000">Company Meeting:</td>
   <td>20:00</td>
  </tr>
  <tr bgcolor="#CC9900">
   <td bgcolor="#CC0000">New year's Eve Party:</td>
   <td>22:00</td>
  </tr>
 </table>
</div>
</body>
</html>
';
```

Finally, the message headers are defined and the mail function invoked:

```
// To send HTML mail we must define the Content-type header
$headers = "MIME-Version: 1.0\r\n";
$headers .= "Content-type: text/html; charset=iso-8859-1\r\n";

// From Header
$headers .= "From: Company Name <info@company.com>\r\n";

mail($to, $subject, $message, $headers);

?>
```

Each recipient will receive an e-mail message which, when viewed using the mail tool, will look like the example shown in Figure 21.3.

Creating an E-mail Form

More and more often these days, Web sites provide e-mail forms giving users the ability to send messages directly to the site manager or individual within an organization. This is usually known as a "feedback form" or "e-mail form". In order to create a typical

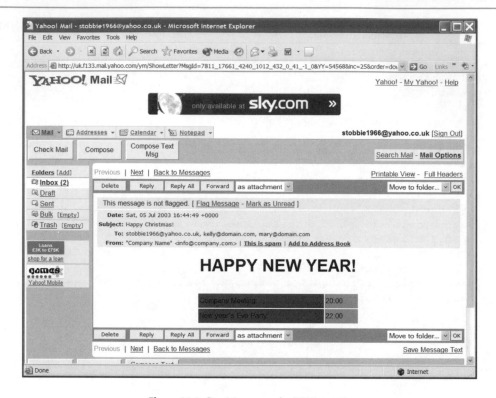

Figure 21.3 Receiving a complex/HTML e-mail.

feedback form a simple HTML form is required with three or more textboxes and one submit button (sometimes a reset button is also used to reset all data in the fields). The first textbox contains the name of the user who is actually sending the e-mail. The second textbox contains the user's e-mail so that the site can reply back to the user and the third textbox contains the actual message of the mail. Here is an example of such a form:

```php
<?php

//Email - Example 21-4
//---------------------

//If button is pressed send message

if(isset($_POST["submit"])) {

    $name = $_POST["name"];
    $message = $_POST["message"];
    $e-mail = $_POST["e-mail"];

    $comments = "$name wrote: /n/n $message";
```

```
        $sendmail = mail("stobbie1966@yahoo.co.uk", $comments, $message,
"From: $e-mail");

        if($sendmail)
              echo "Message sent successfully!";
        else
              echo "Message could not be sent";
}

?>

<html>
<body bgcolor="#FFFFFF" text="#000000">
<form name="form1" method="post" action="<?php echo
$_SERVER["PHP_SELF"]; ?>">
 <b>Send us a message:</b><br>
 <table width="75%" border="0" cellspacing="0" cellpadding="0"
 height="182">
   <tr>
    <td>Name:</td>
    <td><input type="text" name="name"></td>
   </tr>
   <tr>
    <td>E-mail:</td>
    <td><input type="text" name="e-mail"></td>
   </tr>
   <tr>
    <td>Message:</td>
    <td><textarea name="message" cols="40" rows="4"></textarea></td>
   </tr>
   </table>
   <input type="submit" name="submit" value="Send Message">
   <input type="reset" name="reset" value="Reset">
</form>
</body>
</html>
```

The first part of this script checks that the form has been submitted:

```
if($_POST["submit"]) {
```

If so, the data from the form are extracted and the mail() function is used to send an e-mail:

```
        $name = $_POST["name"];
        $message = $_POST["message"];
        $e-mail = $_POST["e-mail"];
```

```
    $comments = "$name wrote: /n/n $message";
    $sendmail = mail("stobbie1966@yahoo.co.uk", $comments, $message,
"From: $e-mail");
```

A message is then displayed indicating whether the message was sent successfully:

```
    if($sendmail)
            echo "Message sent successfully!";
    else
            echo "Message could not be sent";
}
```

The final part of the script outputs the HTML form:

```
<html>
<body bgcolor="#FFFFFF" text="#000000">
<form name="form1" method="post" action="<?php echo
$_SERVER["PHP_SELF"]; ?>">
 <b>Send us a message:</b><br>
 <table width="75%" border="0" cellspacing="0" cellpadding="0"
 height="182">
  <tr>
   <td>Name:</td>
   <td><input type="text" name="name"></td>
  </tr>
  <tr>
   <td>E-mail:</td>
   <td><input type="text" name="e-mail"></td>
  </tr>
  <tr>
   <td>Message:</td>
   <td><textarea name="message" cols="40" rows="4"></textarea></td>
  </tr>
 </table>
 <input type="submit" name="submit" value="Send Message">
 <input type="reset" name="reset" value="Reset">
</form>
</body>
</html>
```

Figure 21.4 illustrates the form with which the user interacts to send an e-mail message.

Summary

This chapter has shown how PHP can be used to send an e-mail to a user entirely automatically or with user interaction via a Web mail form. Two different styles of e-mails

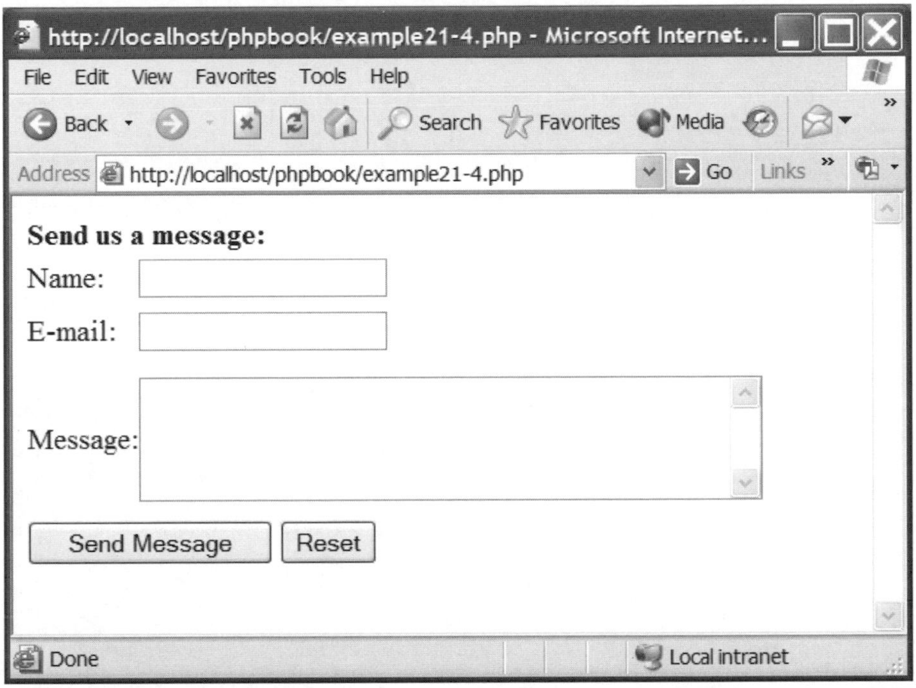

Figure 21.4 A simple Web mail form.

have been introduced, enabling the user to send either simple or more complex messages. In the following chapter we shall introduce the concept of cookies and illustrate how these can be used to interact with the user.

Part 5

Retaining Data Across Pages

Cookies 22

Introduction

This chapter introduces the concept of cookies. Cookies are a means of storing variable data locally on the user's computer. Cookies can be stored on every user's computer and the data stored in each of these cookies can be different. Therefore, by using cookies we are able to store user preferences and thus provide a customized dynamic experience for each user accessing a Web site. Common examples of this are e-commerce sites which allow every user to select the different products they wish to purchase.

Create a Cookie

To create a cookie we need to use the setcookie function.

Function prototype:

```
bool setcookie ( string name , string value , int expire , string path , string domain, int secure )
```

With the setcookie() function all the arguments except the name argument are optional. If only the name argument is present, a cookie by that name will be deleted from the remote client. You may also replace any argument with an empty string ("") in order to skip that argument.

Function arguments and return details:

Name	Type	Description
name	String	Name of the cookie file
value	String	Data to be stored in cookie file
expire	Integer	Date string that defines the valid life time of that cookie
path	String	Subset of URLs in a domain for which the cookie is valid
domain	String	Domain attributes of the cookie made with the Internet domain name of the host from which the URL will be fetched
secure	Boolean	If set to "1" it will only be transmitted if the communications channel with the host is secure
setcookie() returns	Boolean	"TRUE" on success, "FALSE" on failure

Function examples:

```
setcookie ("TestCookie", $value);
setcookie ("TestCookie", $value,time()+3600);
setcookie ("TestCookie", $value,time()+3600, "/username/",
"domain.com", 1);
```

When using the cookie function you will need to know the following:

✔ Cookies will not become visible until the next loading of a page for which the cookie should be visible. To test whether a cookie was successfully set, check for the cookie on the next loading page before the cookie expires. The expire time is set via the expire parameter.

✔ Cookies must be deleted with the same parameters with which they were set.

✔ Cookies' names can be set as array names and will be available to your PHP scripts as arrays but separate cookies are stored on the user's system. You may wish to consider using the explode() or serialize() functions to set one cookie with multiple names and values.

Consider the following example which illustrates the setcookie() function:

```php
<?php

// Cookie - Example 22-1
//---------------------

$value = "Hello, this is a text into cookie";
setcookie ("TestCookie", $value,time()+3600);

?>
```

The output from this script is not very exciting. In fact, nothing is outputted and the browser screen remains blank. In order to see that we have successfully set our cookie, we need to know how to read them.

Reading a Cookie

Viewing and accessing cookies is easy – you simply treat them as a predefined variable. We mentioned in Chapter 9 that cookie variables could be accessed using the array $_COOKIE and this is exactly how we shall access them. Remember that cookies will not become visible until the page from which the cookie should be visible is loaded. To test whether a cookie has been successfully set, check for the cookie on the next loading page before the cookie expires. The following script illustrates that we can access the cookies we have created and display them:

```php
<?php

// Cookie - Example 22-2
//---------------------

$value = "Hello, this is a text into cookie";
setcookie ("TestCookie", $value,time()+3600);

?>

<html>
    <body>

    <b>TestCookie contains:</b>

    <?php echo($_COOKIE["TestCookie"]); ?>

    </body>
</html>
```

The output from this script is illustrated in Figure 22.1.

Figure 22.1 Cookie variable displayed.

Another way to check if a cookie is set correctly and to read its data is to use the phpinfo() function:

```php
<?php

// Cookie - Example 22-3
//---------------------
```

```
$value = "Hello, this is a text into cookie";
setcookie ("TestCookie", $value,time()+3600);

?>

   <html>
     <body>
        <?php
        phpinfo();
        ?>
        </body>
</html>
```

This script invokes the phpinfo() function which displays the information about the PHP environment. When displayed, if you scroll down the browser display window you come to the PHP variables section. Note that the second and third lines in the PHP variables table contain the following entries: _COOKIE["TestCookie"]. This is illustrated in Figure 22.2.

Delete a Cookie

We have already shown that cookies can be created with in-built expiry times; but what if you wished to delete a cookie that you had created that did not contain such an expiry time or wished to delete a cookie sooner than you had planned? To force the expiry of a cookie, set a negative expiry time. The syntax should be the same as with the creation of a cookie.

```
setcookie ("TestCookie", "",time()-3600);
setcookie ("TestCookie", "",time()-3600, "/username/",
"domain.com", 1);
```

or

```
setcookie ("TestCookie");
```

Array Cookies

It is possible to store an array in a cookie. However, we need to store each element of the array separately within the cookie, like this:

```
setcookie ("cookie[0]", "cookiethree");
setcookie ("cookie[1]", "cookietwo");
setcookie ("cookie[2]", "cookieone");
```

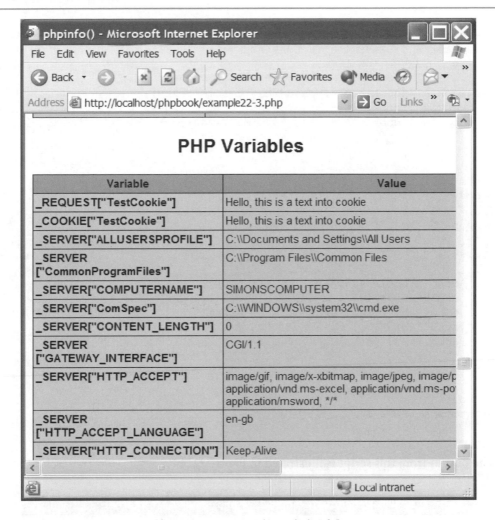

Figure 22.2 Viewing cookies with phpinfo().

Although the array elements have to be stored separately, when we come to read the array it will be returned as an array which we can access:

```php
$list = $_COOKIE["cookie"];
```

The following script illustrates setting and accessing an array using cookies:

```php
<?php

// Cookie - Example 22-4
//---------------------
```

```
$address = $_SERVER['REMOTE_ADDR'];
$browser = $_SERVER['HTTP_USER_AGENT'];
$os = $_SERVER['OS'];

setcookie ("cookie[0]", "$address", time()+200);
setcookie ("cookie[1]", "$browser", time()+200);
setcookie ("cookie[2]", "$os", time()+200);

?>

<html>
<body>

<?php

$list = $_COOKIE["cookie"];

    echo "<b> IP Address:</b> $list[0]";
    echo "<br>";
    echo "<b> Client Browser:</b> $list[1]";
    echo "<br>";
    echo "<b> Operating System:</b> $list[2]";

?>

</body>
</html>
```

The output from this script is illustrated in Figure 22.3.

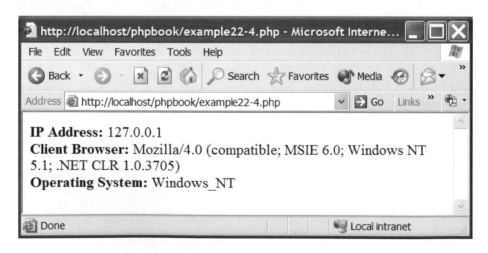

Figure 22.3 Arrays and cookies.

Multi-data Cookies

Another way of storing multiple variable data within a cookie is to create a string with all preferred information stored within it and pass it as a single value to the cookie. We can then use the explode() function to extract all the information from the cookie. This technique does require a more complex structure for the data to be inserted into the cookie but does not require an array of cookies.

Consider the following example, which is a rewrite of the previous script but uses the multi-data method:

```php
<?php

// Cookie - Example 22-5
//----------------------

$address = $_SERVER['REMOTE_ADDR'];
$browser = $_SERVER['HTTP_USER_AGENT'];
$os = $_SERVER['OS'];

$info = "$address::$browser::$os";

setcookie ("data", "$info", time()+200);


?>

<html>
<body>

<?php

$readcookie = $_COOKIE["data"];
$list = explode ("::", $readcookie);

    echo "<b> IP Address:</b> $list[0]";
    echo "<br>";
    echo "<b> Client Browser:</b> $list[1]";
    echo "<br>";
    echo "<b> Operating System:</b> $list[2]";

?>

</body>
</html>
```

Creating a Members System

We can use cookies to create a members system. We shall use a form to get an appropriate username and password. On successful entry, the supplied username is added by a cookie on the client's computer. The system checks if the cookie exists: if yes a "Hello user" message is printed; if not, a message "Not a valid username or password" is shown:

```php
<?php

// Cookie - Example 22-6
//--------------------

$username = "simon";
$password = "12345";

if(isset($_POST['login'])){

  if($_POST['user'] == "$username" && $_POST['pass'] == "$password"){

      setcookie("member", "$username", time()+600);
  }else{
      echo "Not a valid username or password";
  }
}
?>
<html>
<head>
  <title>Members</title>
</head>
<body bgcolor="#FFFFFF" text="#000000">

<?php
  if(isset($_COOKIE['member'])){
      echo "Hello <b> $_COOKIE[member] </b>";
  }else{
      echo "<b>Not logged in </b>";
      echo "<form name='form1' method='post' action=''>";
      echo "Username: <input type='text' name='user'><br>";
      echo "Password: <input type='password' name='pass'><br>";
      echo "<input type='submit' name='login' value='Login to
      members area'>";
      echo "</form>";
  }
?>

</body>
</html>
```

The output from this script is illustrated in Figure 22.4.

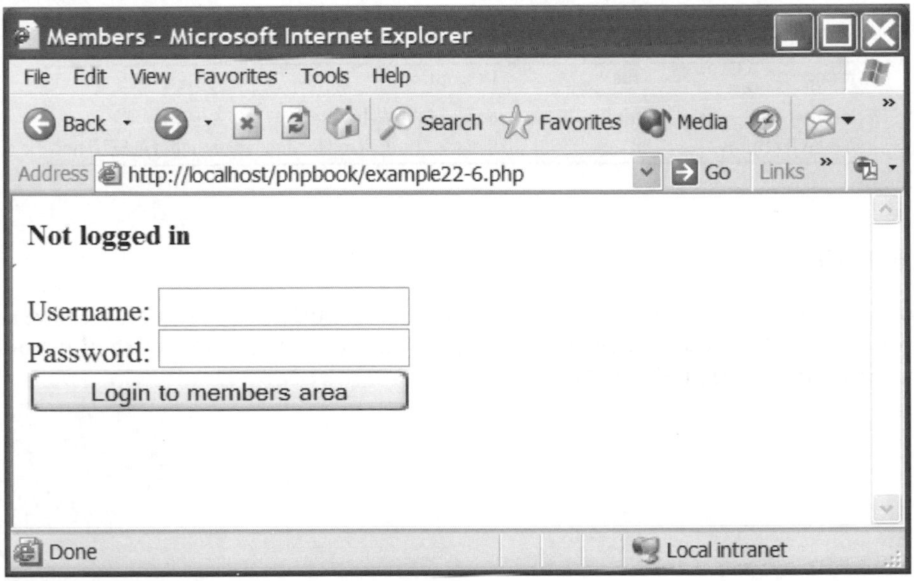

Figure 22.4 Members system.

In our previous script we have shown how to login members into our system. The following script can be used to verify a logged-in member on any page under the member's site and redirect non-authorized members to a login page. If the cookie exists, the script "resets" the cookie's expire time to 10 minutes. This script needs to be placed on every page within the members system. Remember this file should be included at the beginning of every page.

```php
<?php

// Cookie - Example 22-7
//--------------------

if(isset($_COOKIE['member'])){
        setcookie("member", "$_COOKIE[member]", time()+600);
    }else{
        HEADER("location: example22-6.php");
    }

?>
```

Note that this script uses the HEADER() function to redirect the user automatically to a new Web page.

Function prototype:

```
Int header(string location);
```

Function arguments and return details:

Name	Type	Description
location	String	Name of the Web page
header() returns	Int	Returns "TRUE" if redirection is okay and "FALSE" if not

Summary

This chapter has introduced the concept of cookies and illustrated their use. We have shown how cookies can be set and removed if required. In the next chapter we shall introduce a similar technology – that of sessions.

Session Management **23**

Introduction

We have seen in the previous chapter that cookies can be useful for maintaining user-specific information. However, cookies can be disabled and/or deleted. What we really need is a means by which user-specific information can be created, preserved across multiple Web accesses and all this performed as automatically as possible. Session support in PHP provides this facility and, as we shall show, it will enable you to build more interesting Web sites that enable more user-specific customization.

What Are Sessions?

Sessions are a mechanism for storing different information for each user who accesses your Web system. Essentially, sessions allow variables and their values to be stored for each and every user. The values of these variables can differ for every user and, thus, enable different users to be assigned different preferences.

How Do Sessions Work?

Sessions work by assigning a visitor a unique id, known as a session id. This is stored in a cookie by the user or is embedded as part of the URL. A session id looks something like this:

```
sess_f231be97d46fb1ca96c1323e88f4523f
```

On the server a session file is created with the same name. This file is used to store the values of the variables assigned to the session. The contents of a session file may look like this:

```
count|i:18;name|s:5:"Simon";
```

In this example, count is a variable which has been stored in the session. The variable count is of type integer and contains the value 18. name is a variable of type string and contains the value "Simon".

So how do we create a session? Well, the first thing that we need to do is to invoke the session_start() function:

Function prototype:

```
Bool session_start(void)
```

Function arguments and return details:

Name	Type	Description
session_start() returns	Bool	Returns "TRUE"

Function example:

```
session_start();
```

The session_start() function checks whether a session has been created for this user and if not creates one. If a session exists then, all variables and their values are retrieved and are available for use. The function always returns true.

Session variables are registered using the $_SESSION associative array. For example:

```
$_SESSION['count'] = 0;
```

This line of code registers a variable called count with the session. Each user will have their own separate session file and variable values. Let's consider a simple example of this.

Counting the Number of Accesses

Using what we have learnt so far we can use sessions to enable us to determine the number of accesses to a page that a specific user has made. Consider the following script:

```php
<?php
// Sessions - Example 23-1
//------------------

session_start();
if (!isset($_SESSION['count']))
  $_SESSION['count'] = 0;
else
  $_SESSION['count']++;
echo "Hello, you have accessed this page " . $_SESSION["count"] .
" times.";
?>
```

This script invokes the session_start() function either to create a new session or to access an existing one. The variable count is registered with the session and set to zero if it has not been previously registered:

```
if (!isset($_SESSION['count']))
$_SESSION['count'] = 0;
```

Otherwise the variable count is then incremented and an echo statement used to output the value of count:

```
else
  $_SESSION['count']++;
echo "Hello, you have accessed this page " . $_SESSION["count"] .
" times.";
```

Each time the user accesses the page the value of $count is incremented and stored in the session file. The effect is to create a user-specific counter that records the number of accesses to the page that a particular user has made. The output from the script is illustrated in Figure 23.1.

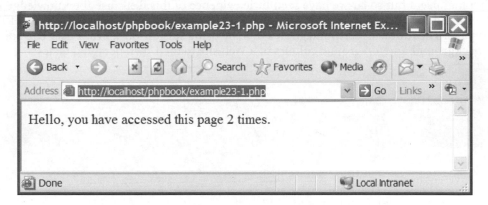

Figure 23.1 User page counter.

Of course, Figure 23.1 doesn't prove that the session is actually working. What we need to do is to encourage another user to access the same page and see if the script is able to track the accesses for that user separately from yours. One way of emulating this is to open a new browser window and point this at the same script. The two browser windows should maintain the page accesses for each "user" separately.

Obtaining a Session Id

You can obtain the value of the current session id using the function session_id() – the format of this function is:

Function prototype:

```
string session_id([string id]);
```

Function arguments and return details:

Name	Type	Description
id	String	Replacement session id
session_id() returns	String	Session id

Function example:

```
$id = session_id();
```

Allowing a User to Choose the Page Colours

We started this chapter by explaining that sessions allow us to customize a Web page for individual users but so far we have seen little evidence of this. Let's use the knowledge we have gained to create a script that allows a user to change the background colour of the Web page. The following script illustrates that, by using session variables, a user can adjust the background and foreground colours of a Web site to their own personal tastes:

```php
<?php
// Sessions - Example 23-2
//-----------------

session_start();

if (!isset($_SESSION['bgCol']))
    $_SESSION['bgCol'] = 0;
if (!isset($_SESSION['textCol']))
    $_SESSION['textCol'] = 0;

if (isset($_POST["submit"])) {
    $bgCol = $_POST["nbgCol"];
    $textCol = $_POST["ntextCol"];
    $_SESSION['bgCol'] = $bgCol;
    $_SESSION['textCol'] = $textCol;
    echo("<body bgcolor='$bgCol' text='$textCol'>");
}

?>
```

```
<h2>What Colours would you like?</h2>
<form action='<?php echo($_SERVER["PHP_SELF"]) ?>' method='post'>
Background Colour: <select name='nbgCol'>
    <option>red</option>
    <option>green</option>
    <option>blue</option>
    <option>cyan</option>
    <option>yellow</option>
</select>
<br>
Text Colour: <select name='ntextCol'>
    <option>red</option>
    <option>green</option>
    <option>blue</option>
    <option>cyan</option>
    <option>yellow</option>
</select>
<br><br>
<input type='submit' name='submit'>
```

The script begins by declaring a session and registering two variables:

```
session_start();

if (!isset($_SESSION['bgCol']))
    $_SESSION['bgCol'] = 0;
if (!isset($_SESSION['textCol']))
    $_SESSION['textCol'] = 0;
```

The values of the form variables $nbgCol and $ntextCol are checked to see if they have been received. If so, then the session variables are set to these new values:

```
if (isset($_POST["submit"])) {
    $bgCol = $_POST["nbgCol"];
    $textCol = $_POST["ntextCol"];
    $_SESSION['bgCol'] = $bgCol;
    $_SESSION['textCol'] = $textCol;
    echo("<body bgcolor='$bgCol' text='$textCol'>");
}
```

The remainder of the script outputs the body element with the attributes bgcolor and text to allow us to alter the background and foreground text colour. The form is also displayed enabling us to choose the background colour from a selection menu:

```
<h2>What Colours would you like?</h2>
<form action='<?php echo($_SERVER["PHP_SELF"]) ?>' method='post'>
Background Colour: <select name='nbgCol'>
    <option>red</option>
    <option>green</option>
    <option>blue</option>
    <option>cyan</option>
<option>yellow</option>
</select>
<br>
Text Colour: <select name='ntextCol'>
    <option>red</option>
    <option>green</option>
    <option>blue</option>
    <option>cyan</option>
    <option>yellow</option>
</select>
<br><br>
<input type='submit' name='submit'>
```

The output from this script is shown in Figure 23.2.

Figure 23.2 Changing colours.

Once again you will need to open a second browser window to prove that the session aspect of the Web page is working correctly.

Unregistering Variables

Session variables can be unregistered. You may wish to *do* this to ensure that the session you have created is completely clear of any variable values. The unset() function will clear a variable currently registered with the session and has the following format:

Function prototype:

```
void unset(mixed variable);
```

Function arguments and return details:

Name	Type	Description
variable	Mixed	Variable to unregister
unset() returns	Void	Returns nothing

Function example:

```
unset($_SESSION['bgCol']);
```

Making Pages More Accessible

Making Web pages accessible to as many people as possible is an important aspect of Web page design. In the following example we show how the text size of a Web page can be adjusted by the user. The example uses two separate Web pages in order to demonstrate that session values are accessible across multiple pages within a Web site. The first script should be saved as example23-3.php and this opens a session:

```php
<?php
// Sessions - Example 23-3
//-----------------

session_start();
if (isset($_SESSION['size']))
    $size = $_SESSION['size'];
else
    $size = 3;
echo("<basefont size=$size>");
?>

Welcome to the main page. Note that the text is displayed in a font
size which you can adjust by clicking
<a href=example23-4.php>here</a>.
```

The value of size is used to change the page basefont:

```
echo("<basefont size=$size>");
?>
```

Users can elect to change the base font by clicking on the hyperlink:

```
Welcome to the main page. Note that the text is displayed in a
font size which you can adjust by clicking <a href=changesize.php>
here</a>.
```

The output from this script is illustrated in Figure 23.3.

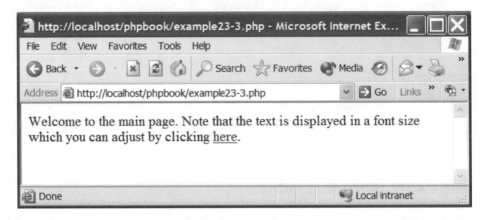

Figure 23.3 Starting font size.

Clicking on the hyperlink in this script invokes the following script:

```php
<?php
// Sessions - Example 23-4
//------------------

session_start();
if (isset($_POST['submit'])) {
    $size = $_POST['size'];
        $_SESSION['size'] = $size;
}
else {
    if (isset($_SESSION['size']))
        $size = $_SESSION['size'];
    else
        $size = 3;
}
echo("<basefont size=$size>");
?>
```

```
A form is output with a selection menu allowing the user to change
the current text size:
Adjust the Text Size<br>
<form action='<?php echo $_SERVER['PHP_SELF'] ?>' method='post'>
Text Size: <select name='size'>
    <option>1</option>
    <option>2</option>
    <option>3</option>
    <option>4</option>
    <option>5</option>
</select>
<br><br>
<input type='submit' name='submit'>
</form>
Go <a href="example23-3.php">back</a> to main page.
```

This script must be saved as "example23-4.php". The script begins by accessing the session, checking that the form variable size has been received and outputting the basefont using the value of variable $size:

```
session_start();
if (isset($_POST['submit'])) {
    $size = $_POST['size'];
        $_SESSION['size'] = $size;
}
else {
    if (isset($_SESSION['size']))
        $size = $_SESSION['size'];
    else
        $size = 3;
}
echo("<basefont size=$size>");
?>
```

A form is output with a selection menu allowing the user to change the current text size:

```
<form action='<?php echo $_SERVER['PHP_SELF'] ?>' method='post'>
Text Size: <select name='size'>
    <option>1</option>
    <option>2</option>
    <option>3</option>
```

```
        <option>4</option>
        <option>5</option>
    </select>
    <br><br>
    <input type='submit' name='submit'>
    </form>
    Go <a href="example23-3.php">back</a> to main page.
```

Figure 23.4 illustrates the output from this script after the user has selected a font size of 5.

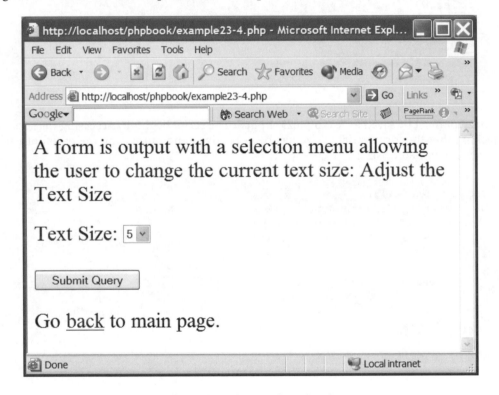

Figure 23.4 A font size of 5 is selected.

If you then click the back hyperlink on this page you will return to the original session23-3.php page. You will notice that the text on this page is now also size 5. The text size will be maintained between both pages until you change it.

Summary

This chapter has introduced the concept of sessions and shown how you can create and store variable values that can be changed independently from user to user. In the following chapter we shall examine the concept of error handling and explain how it can make our Web applications appear more professional.

Part **6**

Handling Errors and Buffering

Error Handling 24

Introduction

Developing code that is error free is the Holy Grail of software engineering but, unfortunately, the quest for methods and tools to enable us to accomplish this successfully is still on going. In the mean time, we need to put up with errors within our programs. However, many programming languages provide the developer with the ability to "catch" errors as they occur and perform some action in response. This action may be something as simple as displaying an error message warning the user that something has happened but the program is still allowed to continue executing. In more fatal cases, the program may have to be halted immediately.

In this chapter we shall introduce the error-handling capabilities of PHP, which not only enables you to determine which errors get displayed to users but also enables you to write your own error-handling functions. In addition, we shall examine how to trigger our own error messages when required and log errors for future examination.

Error Types

Normally, when an error is encountered in a PHP script, an error message is displayed indicating what the error was, in which script it occurred and on what line of that script the error was detected. Depending on the severity of the error the execution of the script may be halted at this point or allowed to continue. While error messages may be tolerated in a development environment, standard error messages would look unprofessional to users in a live working environment.

Error trapping allows us to intercept errors as they occur, hiding their display from the user. If the error can be corrected, it usually is (without the user knowing) and the script allowed to continue execution. If the error is more serious and cannot be corrected, then a message can be outputted to the browser explaining what has happened and the script execution stopped. PHP supports three different types of errors that differ in their level of severity. Table 24.1 lists these three types and provides examples of what would cause them to be generated.

Each of these three error types can be generated at different times by different components of the PHP development engine. They can be generated as the PHP engine is

Table 24.1 Error types.

Error type	Description
Notices	Notices are generated when a script is run. They are generally trivial (i.e. the PHP interpreter is able to make a guess at what the programmer meant and thus keep executing the script). An example of such a notice would be generated if you used a variable without first initializing it.
Warnings	Warnings are more serious as the interpreter is unable to compensate for the problem; however, script execution is still able to continue. An example of a warning would occur if you tried to include() a file which did not exist.
Fatal errors	Fatal errors are the most serious problem. On detection the interpreter is unable to continue execution and so the script is terminated. An example of such an error would occur if you tried to invoke a function that was not declared.

started, during parse time, during compile time or during the running of a script. The core PHP engine, the function library surrounding the core engine or your application script can generate them. All of these combinations result in the definition of 11 different error types. Each of these is defined by both a numerical value and a named constant and these are listed in Table 24.2.

Table 24.2 Error values, constants and descriptions.

Value	Constant	Description
1	E_ERROR	Fatal run-time error
2	E_WARNING	Non-fatal run-time warnings
4	E_PARSE	Compile-time parse errors
8	E_NOTICE	Run-time notices (not as serious as warnings)
16	E_CORE_ERROR	Fatal startup errors
32	E_CORE_WARNING	Non-fatal startup warnings
64	E_COMPILE_ERROR	Fatal compile-time errors
128	E_COMPILE_WARNING	Non-fatal compile-time warnings
256	E_USER_ERROR	User-generated error message
512	E_USER_WARNING	User-generated warning message
1024	E_USER_NOTICE	User-generated notice message
2047	E_ALL	All these

Don't worry about these error types, constants and values just yet – we shall be returning to them later in the chapter. First, we want to create some scripts which will generate the different error messages in order to see what they look like.

Examples of Notices, Warnings and Errors

The following script will cause a notice error to appear on the Web page:

```php
<?php

// Error Handling - Example 24-1
//---------------------

$var;
echo("Still running.<br>")
?>
```

The script declares a variable $var but does not assign it a value. The script will generate the following message in the browser:

```
Notice: Undefined variable: var in
c:\inetpub\wwwroot\phpbook\example24-1.php on line 6
Still running.
```

Note that the notice informs us of the type of error, the name of the script in which the error occurred and the line on which the notice error was detected. We can see that the script continues to execute, as the text "Still running." is displayed and this was output by the script after the error was detected.

Next, let's consider a script which will generate a more serious warning message:

```php
<?php

// Error Handling - Example 24-2
//---------------------

include("doesnotexist.php");
echo("Still running.<br>");
?>
```

The script attempts to include a file "doesnotexist.php" which (hopefully in this instance) does not exist. This will cause the script to generate the following warning message:

```
Warning: main(doesnotexist.php): failed to open stream: No such
file or directory in c:\inetpub\wwwroot\phpbook\example24-2.php on
line 6

Warning: main(): Failed opening 'doesnotexist.php' for inclusion
(include_path='.;c:\php\includes') in
c:\inetpub\wwwroot\phpbook\example24-2.php on line 6
Still running.
```

Once again note that the warning error informs us of the error, the name of the script where the warning error occurred and on which line this was detected. Once again, the "Still running." text demonstrates that the script continues to execute.

The final script in this section produces the most serious form of error – a fatal error message:

```php
<?php

// Error Handling - Example 24-3
//---------------------

ball();
echo("Still running.<br>");
?>
```

The script causes a fatal error by trying to invoke a function which has not been defined within the script. The script generates the following output message:

```
Fatal error: Call to undefined function: ball() in
c:\inetpub\wwwroot\phpbook\example24-3.php on line 6
```

While the message type, script and line number are output as before, note that the script terminates on detection of the fatal error as no "Still running." text is displayed.

Adjusting Your Error Reporting

So far we have seen the standard error-reporting output generated by PHP automatically when different errors are detected. However, PHP allows you to decide which of the three levels of errors are reported and which are simply ignored. The function error_reporting() allows you to set the current "level" of error reporting:

Function prototype:

```
Int Error_reporting(int level);
```

Function arguments and return details:

Name	Type	Description
level	Int	Level of error reporting
error_reporting() returns	Int	Returns the level of reporting

Function example:

```
error_reporting()
```

The function accepts a single integer or constant value. Knowing what value to pass as a parameter to this function requires us to consult Table 24.2 where the different types of errors have all been given a unique integer and constant value. Table 24.3 illustrates some example combinations of integer values and constants that can be passed to the error_reporting() function. A description of what level of error reporting the example parameter will achieve is also included.

Table 24.3 Error_reporting examples.

Example	Description
Error_reporting(0);	No errors will be reported
Error_reporting(2047);	All errors will be reported
Error_reporting(E_ALL);	All errors will be reported (same as previous example)
Error_reporting(3);	Only report E_ERROR and E_WARNING errors
Error_reporting(E_ERROR|E_WARNING);	Only report E_ERROR and E_WARNING errors (same as previous example)

The function error_reporting() returns a integer value, which is the current level at which error reporting has been set. You can check the current level by invoking the function with no parameter, for example:

```php
<?php

// Error Handling - Example 24-4
//----------------------

echo ("The current value of error reporting is " . error_reporting());
?>
```

The output from this script is illustrated in Figure 24.1.

Figure 24.1 Error-reporting level.

The value of 2047 means that this script will display all errors, no matter how inconsequential they may be. It is recommended that when developing your scripts that you keep your error reporting at the highest level as it will help you create scripts with the minimum number of errors within them.

@ Operator – Selectively Turn Off Expression Error Display

It is worth mentioning at this point that PHP supports the @ operator. The @ operator can be used to selectively "turn off" error messages generated from function calls, for example:

```php
<?php

// Error Handling - Example 24-5
//---------------------

@ball();
echo("Still running.<br>");
?>
```

The output from this script will generate no error message whatsoever. However, the error is still detected (calling a function which has not been defined) and because the error generated was a Fatal Error, execution of the script will terminate and the message "Still running." will not be displayed. Removing the @ operator will display the fatal error once again. Why would you wish to hide the error message generated from invoking a function? Well, often functions are written by other developers and not by your self. Reusing such functions with permission is good programming practice. However, you may not have access to the core code within the function and if an error occurs your only way of hiding the error message is by using the @ operator.

Creating Your Own Error Handler

So far we have seen that PHP has an in-built error handler and that we can adjust the level at which different errors are reported. However, this is not the end of the story as we can also create our own custom error handler. This allows us to decide how different errors are displayed (if at all). Custom error handlers are created using the set_error_handler() function:

Function prototype:

```
String Set_Error_handler(string errorHandler);
```

Function arguments and return details:

Name	Type	Description
errorHandler	String	The function name to be invoked when an error occurs
set_error_handler() returns	String	"TRUE" if function executed correctly or "FALSE" if there was a problem

The Set_error_handler() function is supplied a value which is the name of a function which will be invoked when an error occurs. This function should be written to accept the following parameters:

Name	Type	Description
code	String	The error code
message	String	A description of the error
filename	String	The script in which the error has occurred
lineNumber	Int	Line number in the script in which the error occurred
context	Array	An array pointing to the active symbol table at the point at which the error occurred

In addition, the set_error_handler() function returns a string, which is the currently defined error handler function (if any has been defined). The following script illustrates an example of using this function:

```php
<?php

// Error Handling - Example 24-6
//----------------------

set_error_handler("errorHandler");

include("doesnotexist.php");

function errorHandler($code, $message, $filename, $lineNumber){
echo("<h2>Unfortunately an Error has occurred</h2>");
echo("The error information is as follows:<br><br>");
echo("Error code: $code<br>");
echo("Error message: $message<br>");
echo("Error occurred in file: $filename<br>");
echo("Error occurred on line: $lineNumber<br>");
}
?>
```

The script invokes the set_error_handler() function passing it the value "errorHandler". The function errorHandler() defined at the end of the script simply displays the values passed to the function from the internal error handler on separate lines. In the middle of the script an include() function attempts to include a file which does not exist, thus generating a warning error. The output generated from this script is illustrated in Figure 24.2.

While the ability to create our own custom error handler functions may seem like an excuse to display the error in different format from that of the standard error handler, there are other reasons to create one. One example is to decide to terminate the script on detection of certain errors.

Die and Exit

Two functions exist which enable you to terminate a script at a given point. These functions are often used when a warning or notice error is detected and the programmer does not want the script to continue, even if the interpreter is able to do so. The functions are:

Figure 24.2 Custom error handler output.

Function prototypes:

```
Void exit(void);
Void die(string message);
```

Function arguments and return details:

Name	Type	Description
message	String	Message to display before termination
exit() and die() return	Void	Return nothing

Function example:

```
die("Terminating the script");
```

Both functions terminate a script but the die() function will output a message to the browser first. The following script illustrates the use of the die() function. The script is the same as our previous one except that now after the error message is displayed the script is terminated:

```php
<?php

// Error Handling - Example 24-7
//----------------------

set_error_handler("errorHandler");

include("doesnotexist.php");

function errorHandler($code, $message, $filename, $lineNumber){
echo("<h2>Unfortunately an Error has occurred</h2>");
echo("The error information is as follows:<br><br>");
echo("Error code: $code<br>");
echo("Error message: $message<br>");
echo("Error occurred in file: $filename<br>");
echo("Error occurred on line: $lineNumber<br>");
die("Terminating the script");
}
?>
```

Of course this script will display the same style output for all error message types. It will also terminate the script on detection of any error type. However, custom error handlers allow us to have more control over what will occur depending on the type of error which is detected.

Different Custom Messages for Different Errors

It is common practice to create error handler functions that output different types and styles of error messages depending on the type of error. The error handler can also be written to terminate a script but only on detection of certain error types. The following example script modifies our errorHandler() function to display different error messages for E_NOTICE and E_WARNING error types:

```php
<?php

// Error Handling - Example 24-8
//----------------------

set_error_handler("errorHandler");

$a;
include("doesnotexist.php");

function errorHandler($code, $message, $filename, $lineNumber){

switch($code) {
```

```
case E_NOTICE:
    echo("<br><br>NOTICE: an error was detected on line $lineNumber
    of file $filename");
    echo("<br>The error message was $message");
    break;

case E_WARNING:
    echo("<br><br>WARNING: an error was detected on line $lineNumber
    of file $filename");
    echo("<br>The error message was $message");
    break;
}
}
?>
```

The script uses a switch statement to test variable $code for the constant values of E_WARNING and E_NOTICE – depending on which is detected a different error message is displayed. The script generates both notice and warning error message types and the output generated is illustrated in Figure 24.3.

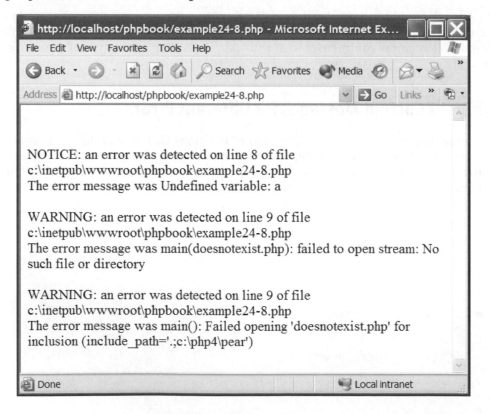

Figure 24.3 Custom error messages.

Catching E_PARSE and E_ERROR error types

In the previous example we illustrated that our custom error handler function could trap E_NOTICE and E_WARNING errors. Don't you find it interesting that we didn't try and trap an E_ERROR message as well? Well, let's give this a go now. The following script is a modification of the previous one but now the error handling function has been adapted to display an error message when an E_ERROR message is encountered:

```php
<?php

// Error Handling - Example 24-9
//---------------------

set_error_handler("errorHandler");

$a;
include("doesnotexist.php");
funt();

function errorHandler($code, $message, $filename, $lineNumber){

switch($code) {

case E_NOTICE:
    echo("<br><br>NOTICE: an error was detected on line $lineNumber
    of file $filename");
    echo("<br>The error message was $message");
    break;

case E_WARNING:
    echo("<br><br>WARNING: an error was detected on line $lineNumber
    of file $filename");
    echo("<br>The error message was $message");
    break;

case E_ERROR:
    die("<br><br>FATAL ERROR: on line $lineNumber of file $filename");
}
}
?>
```

The output from this script is illustrated in Figure 24.4.

The important thing to note here is that the fatal error message was detected, but the error message defined in our error handler function was not what was displayed. The reason for this is that E_ERROR and E_PARSE error types are always handled by the inbuilt error handler and not the custom error handler. This is true whether you write code in your own error handler function to process these error types or not. In other words, the

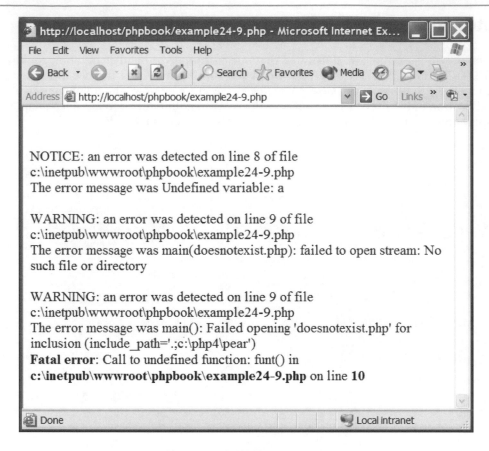

Figure 24.4 E_ERROR error message.

modification we made to the error handler function in the previous script was a waste of time.

Triggering Errors

In addition to creating your own error handling function, PHP allows you to trigger errors in your script when you so wish. To do this we can use one of two functions – the user_error() function and the trigger_error() function – which are simply aliases of each other:

Function prototypes:

```
void trigger_error(string message, [int errorLevel]);
void user_error(string message, [int errorLevel]);
```

Function arguments and return details:

Name	Type	Description
message	String	Message to display when error is triggered
errorLevel	Int	Error value
trigger_error() and user_error() returns	Void	Return nothing

Function example:

```
trigger_error("A Notice error has occurred.<br>");
```

Either function allows you to raise any of the E_USER errors, namely E_USER_NOTICE, E_USER_WARNING and E_USER_ERROR, and the corresponding integer values can be found in Table 24.2. The following script illustrates the triggering of each of these different error types:

```php
<?php

// Error Handling - Example 24-10
//----------------------

trigger_error("A Notice error has occurred.<br>");

trigger_error("<br>A Warning error has occurred.<br>",
E_USER_WARNING);

trigger_error("<br>A Fatal error has occurred.<br>", E_USER_ERROR);

echo("End of Program.");
?>
```

The script illustrates that we can create E_USER_NOTICE errors in one of two ways: we could have supplied the trigger_error() function with an error message along with an E_USER_NOTICE constant. The alternative, illustrated in the script, is to supply the trigger_error() function with just an error message. This will automatically result in the creation of an E_USER_NOTICE level message. To create E_USER_WARNING and E_USER_ERROR messages, we must specify the error level as the second parameter to the trigger_error() function. The output from this script is illustrated in Figure 24.5.

In the previous example the in-built error handler handled our triggered errors. As you would expect, it is possible to combine error triggering with the error_trigger() function with custom error handling using the errorHandler() function. The following script illustrates an error handler function that is able to process E_USER_NOTICE and E_USER_WARNING error types:

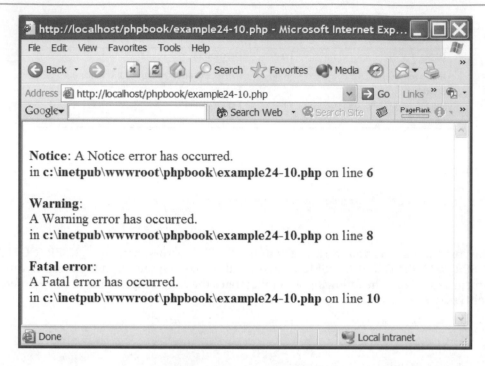

Figure 24.5 Triggering E_USER errors.

```php
<?php

// Error Handling - Example 24-11
//-----------------------

set_error_handler("errorHandler");

trigger_error("A Notice error has occurred.");

trigger_error("A Warning error has occurred.", E_USER_WARNING);

trigger_error("A Fatal error has occurred.", E_USER_ERROR);

echo("End of Program.");


function errorHandler($code, $message, $filename, $lineNumber){

switch($code) {

case E_USER_NOTICE:
   echo("<br><br>NOTICE: an error was detected on line $lineNumber
   of file $filename");
```

```
    echo("<br>The error message was $message");
    break;

case E_USER_WARNING:
    echo("<br><br>WARNING: an error was detected on line $lineNumber
    of file $filename");
    echo("<br>The error message was $message");
    break;


case E_USER_ERROR:
    die("<br><br>FATAL ERROR: on line $lineNumber of file $filename");
}
}
?>
```

The output from this script is illustrated in Figure 24.6

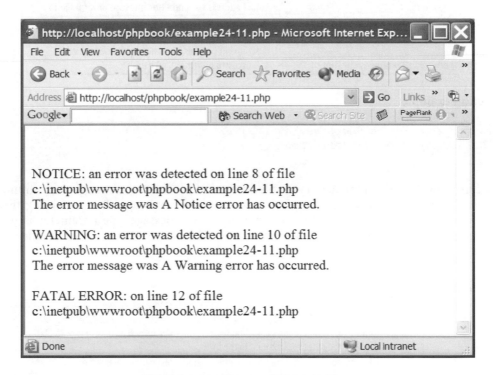

Figure 24.6 Triggering errors with error handling.

It is worth noting that just like our previous error handling example that dealt with system-generated errors, any triggered fatal errors are also handled by the internal error handler and not by your own custom error handler function.

Recording Errors

Instead of simply displaying the message you may wish to record somewhere that an error has occurred. Recording errors in what are termed error log files is common practice. The error log provides a permanent record of the errors that have occurred each and every time the script is run. PHP allows you to record error information in either a default error log file or a file of your choosing or it can even e-mail the error to an e-mail address. All of this is achieved through the use of the error_log() function:

Function prototype:

```
Int error_log(string message, int messageType [, string destination [, string headers]]);
```

Function arguments and return details:

Name	Type	Description
message	String	Message to record in the error log
messageType	Int	Where to record the error message
destination	String	E-mail address to send error message or local file to append error message
headers	String	Optional. The e-mail headers which can be used were described in Chapter 23 in the mail function
error_log() returns	Int	1 if successfully written or 0 if error

Function example:

```
error_log("$code:$message:\n$filename,
$lineNumber\n\n",3,"errorLog");
```

The error_log() function can take a variable number of parameters, although the minimum is two. The first parameter "message" specifies the error message. The remaining three specify where to store or send the error message. The messageType parameter is used to specify what type of storage we wish to use. The values that can be specified for messageType are listed in Table 24.4.

Table 24.4 Error_log() types.

Message type	Description
0	The message is sent to the system logger. This has to be turned on in your PHP.INI file, otherwise the output will be sent to the browser
1	The message is sent by e-mail to the address in the destination parameter
3	The message is appended to the file specified in destination

The following script illustrates the use of the error_log() function to store any errors in a file called errorLog:

```php
<?php

// Error Handling - Example 24-12
//---------------------

set_error_handler("errorHandler");

$a;
include("doesnotexist.php");

function errorHandler($code, $message, $filename, $lineNumber){

error_log("$code: $message:\n$filename, $lineNum-
ber\n\n",3,"errorLog");
}
?>
```

The errorLog file will be saved in the same default file directory as your scripts or, more exactly, the directory where the script is run. Figure 24.7 illustrates what the contents of the errorLog file look like the first time this script is run.

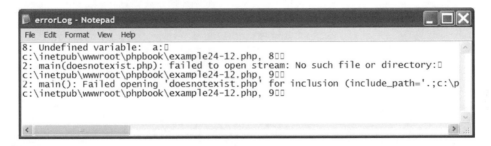

Figure 24.7 ErrorLog file.

If you have access to an e-mail server then you can send your error messages via e-mail. This is illustrated in the following script:

```php
<?php

// Error Handling - Example 24-13
//---------------------

set_error_handler("errorHandler");

$a;
include("doesnotexist.php");

error_log("$code: $message:\n$filename,
```

```
function errorHandler($code, $message, $filename, $lineNumber){
$lineNumber\n\n",1,"simon.stobart@sunderland.ac.uk");
}
?>
```

Being able to e-mail error messages requires access to an e-mail server and some editing of your PHP.INI file. How to do this is explained in Chapter 23 – 'E-mailing Users'.

Summary

In this chapter we have explained the concept of error handling. We have shown how PHP's in-built error handler can trap errors and how to create our own custom error handler functions. We have also illustrated how an error log can be created to store errors that occur permanently. In the next chapter we shall examine the concept of output buffering and consider how this can be used to help us improve our error handling.

Output Buffering 25

Introduction

Normally PHP scripts send their output directly to the standard output device, which is normally a Web browser. However, this is not always an ideal thing to do. For example, if your script has output part of a Web page and then encounters an error, while we have seen in the previous chapter that such errors can be caught, your error message may appear unprofessional, as part of your output has already been sent to the browser. In this chapter we introduce the concept of buffering, which allows you to store all output generated by the script and manipulate it if you want to.

Everything is Fine Until we Encounter an Error

We shall begin with a simple script which outputs a heading and text to a Web page. An error handling function has been defined to catch any errors which occur:

```php
<?php

// Output Buffering - Example 25-1
//----------------------

set_error_handler("catchError");
echo("<h1>Hello, welcome to the world of buffering.</h1>");
echo("Buffering is useful in preventing partial web page output if
an error occurs.");

function catchError() {
    echo("<br>Unfortunately an error has occurred!.");
}
?>
```

Of course, there are no errors in this script so, in order to illustrate what happens when one is encountered then, we need to introduce one:

```php
<?php

// Output Buffering - Example 25-2
//----------------------

set_error_handler("catchError");
echo("<h1>Hello, welcome to the world of buffering.</h1>");
echo("Buffering is useful in preventing partial web page output if
an error occurs.");
echo($doesnotexist);

function catchError() {

    echo("<br>Unfortunately an error has occurred!.");
}
?>
```

In the script an echo statement attempts to display a variable which does not exist, thus generating an error. Of course you would be unlikely to encounter an error in this form in your own scripts – it is simply a convenient way of us generating an error. When the error is encountered the catchError() function is invoked which displays the error message. The output from this script is illustrated in Figure 25.1.

Figure 25.1 Error message displayed with other texts.

Figure 25.1 illustrates that we have trapped the error and displayed an error message. The output sent to the browser before the error was encountered is also displayed. Ideally we may not wish for this to appear. Luckily, PHP allows us to control our output through buffering and thus gain control of what information is eventually sent to the user.

Let's Buffer our Output

The function ob_start() is used to turn the output buffering on. When the buffer has been activated then no output is sent from the script to the browser – instead it is held in an internal buffer. The format of function ob_start() is:

Function prototype:

```
Void ob_start([string funct])
```

Function arguments and return details:

Name	Type	Description
funct	String	Optional function invocation
ob_start() returns	Void	Returns nothing

The ob_start() function can accept an optional function name to invoke the start of buffering. We shall explain how this is used later in this chapter.

Any output is stored in the buffer and nothing will be displayed until the ob_end_flush() function is invoked which will send the contents of the buffer to the browser. The format of this function is:

Function prototype:

```
Void ob_end_flush(void);
```

The function requires no parameters and returns nothing. After the contents have been sent to the browser, output buffering is switched off. Finally, before considering an example of using these functions, there is one more function we need to introduce – ob_end_clean():

Function prototype:

```
Void ob_clean(void);
```

This function deletes all data in the output buffer. It also requires no parameters and returns nothing. Let's consider an example of using buffering. In the following script, the buffer is switched on and an error handling function registered:

```php
<?php

// Output Buffering - Example 25-3
//----------------------

ob_start();
set_error_handler("catchError");
echo("<h1>Hello, welcome to the world of buffering.</h1>");
echo("Buffering is useful in preventing partial web page output if
an error occurs.");

echo($doesnotexist);
ob_end_flush();

function catchError() {
    ob_clean();
    echo("<br>Unfortunately an error has occurred!.");
}
?>
```

The output from the script is stored in the buffer. However, the buffer ob_end_flush()
function is never reached as an error is encountered in the previous line, causing the
function catchError() to be invoked. This function cleans the contents of the buffer and
then displays an error message. The output generated from this script is illustrated in
Figure 25.2.

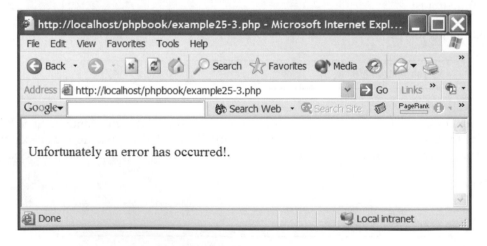

Figure 25.2 Error message only.

Note that Figure 25.2 shows us that while our script had generated some output, we were
able to intercept this, delete it and output something different to the browser.

Accessing the Buffer's Contents

You may wish to be able to access and view the contents of your buffer. Function ob_get_contents() returns the contents of the buffer:

Function prototype:

```
String ob_get_contents(void);
```

Function arguments and return details:

Name	Type	Description
ob_get_contents() returns	String	The function returns the contents of the buffer as a string

Function example:

```
$out = ob_get_contents();
```

The following script is a modification of the previous one and illustrates that the contents of the buffer can be accessed and displayed before they are deleted:

```php
<?php

// Output Buffering - Example 25-4
//----------------------

ob_start();
set_error_handler("catchError");
echo("<h1>Hello, welcome to the world of buffering.</h1>");
echo("Buffering is useful in preventing partial web page output if
an error occurs.");

echo($doesnotexist);
ob_end_flush();

function catchError() {
    $out = ob_get_contents();
    ob_clean();
    echo("<br>Unfortunately an error has occurred!<br>");
    echo("The following was output '$out'");

}
?>
```

Within the catchError() function the ob_get_contents() function is invoked, storing the contents of the buffer in the variable $out. This is then displayed. The output from this script is illustrated in Figure 25.3.

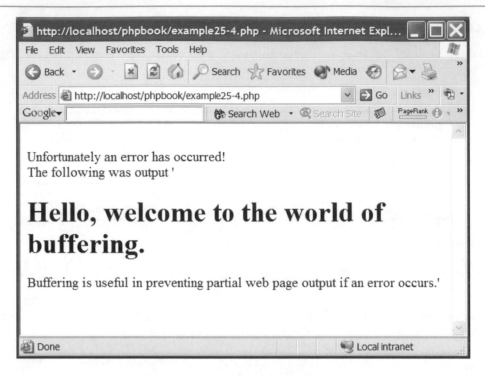

Figure 25.3 Displaying the output of the buffer.

Note that Figure 25.3 illustrates that the output from the buffer is now displayed after the error message. Of course this may not be of much use but if you can access the contents of the buffer then you can edit them.

Editing the Output

The following script illustrates that by using the function ob_get_contents() we can access the contents of the buffer and change them:

```php
<?php

// Output Buffering - Example 25-5
//-----------------------

ob_start();
set_error_handler("catchError");
echo("<h1>Hello, welcome to the world of buffering.</h1>");
echo("Buffering is useful in preventing partial web page output
if an error occurs.");

echo($doesnotexist);
ob_end_flush();
```

```
function catchError() {
    $out = ob_get_contents();
    ob_clean();
    $out = str_replace("Hello", "Hi", $out);
    echo("$out");
}
?>
```

This time function catchError() invokes function ob_get_contents() to obtain the contents of the buffer, which is stored in variable $out. The buffer is then wiped clean and the function str_replace() is used to replace any occurrences of "Hello" with "Hi" in variable $out. This is then displayed. The output from the script is illustrated in Figure 25.4.

Figure 25.4 Modifying the buffer contents.

While this example shows us that we can modify the contents of the buffer, we did this through an error handling function. There is, however, a method of intercepting the contents of the buffer before it is output even though no error is encountered.

Callback Functions

The ob_start() function can take a parameter which is a name of a function which will be invoked just before function ob_end_flush() is invoked. The function which is invoked is often known as a callback function. The following script illustrates an example of such a function:

```php
<?php

// Output Buffering - Example 25-6
//----------------------

ob_start("callBack");
?>
<h1>The £X Deal</h1>
We are happy to introduce our latest product. For only
£X a month you can have ....

<?php
ob_end_flush();

function callBack($buffer) {
    return str_replace("£X", "£15.99", $buffer);
}
?>
```

Note that the function, which has been given the name callBack() has to be able to receive a string, which will contain the contents of the buffer. It must also return this string in order for the contents of the buffer to be output to the browser. Within the function you can modify the contents of the string as we have done in this example. The output from this script is illustrated in Figure 25.5.

Figure 25.5 Modifying a buffer's contents.

Compressing Buffer Output

While you may have read through this chapter and thought 'Okay I understand what the buffer is and how it can be used, but I don't really see that I can make much use of it', consider the ob_gzhandler() function:

Function prototype:

String ob_gzhandler(string buffer)

Name	Type	Description
buffer	String	Buffer contents
ob_gzhandler() returns	String	Returns the output

This function is designed to be a callback function for function ob_start(). It receives the contents of the buffer and if the Web browser is able to accept gz_encoded pages, i.e. compressed Web pages, then the buffer contents are compressed and sent to the browser. What advantages are gained by doing this? Well, the transmission speeds of your Web site will be faster resulting in faster Web-page display speeds. An example of using this in a script follows.

```php
<?php

// Output Buffering - Example 25-7
//----------------------

ob_start("ob_gzhandler");
?>
<h1>A Fast Web Page</h1>
This page will be compressed and sent to the browser if the
browser supports compression.
<?php
ob_end_flush();
?>
```

Summary

This chapter has introduced the concept of buffering and demonstrated how output from scripts can be buffered before being sent for display. We have shown how the contents of the buffer can be accessed, modified if required or even deleted. We concluded by introducing the concept of callback functions and, in particular, the ob_gzhandler() function which can speed up Web page access. In the next chapter we shall examine the role of files within PHP and look at how to create and manipulate them.

Part **7**

File Handling

Reading and Writing to Files 26

Introduction

In this chapter we will examine how to read and write data to files. In physical terms a file is a sequential collection of characters which can be manipulated. In logical terms a file might be viewed as a collection of data records or a computer program. Many computer systems use files for storing information for later access. PHP has facilities to use and manipulate files.

Opening a File

PHP can open a file using a very basic function named fopen():

Function prototype:

```
int fopen (string filename, string mode);
```

Function arguments and return details:

Name	Type	Description
filename	String	The name of the file and its full system path
mode	String	"r" – Open for reading only; place the file pointer at the beginning of the file
		"r+" – Open for reading and writing; place the file pointer at the beginning of the file
		"w" – Open for writing only; place the file pointer at the beginning of the file and truncate the file to zero length. If the file does not exist, attempt to create it
		"w+" – Open for reading and writing; place the file pointer at the beginning of the file and truncate the file to zero length. If the file does not exist, attempt to create it
		"a" – Open for writing only; place the file pointer at the end of the file. If the file does not exist, attempt to create it
		"a+" – Open for reading and writing; place the file pointer at the end of the file. If the file does not exist, attempt to create it
fopen() returns	Integer	A stream connection to the specified file

The previous table illustrates the different modes in which a file can be opened. Function examples:

```
$fp = fopen ("/home/book/file.txt", "r");
$fp = fopen ("/home/book/file.gif", "wb");
$fp = fopen ("http://www.example.com/file.txt", "r+");
$fp = fopen ("ftp://user:password@example.com/file.txt", "w");
```

PHP allows you to open a file on the local machine as well as on a remote machine (if security permissions allow). Remote files can be accessed via an HTTP or an FTP connection. If the filename begins with http:// then an HTTP connection is opened to the specified server and a pointer returned to the requested file. If the filename begins with ftp://, then an ftp connection to the specified server is opened and a file pointer is returned to the requested file. If the filename begins with anything else, the file will be opened from the local file system and a file pointer returned to the requested file. If the function fails, then FALSE is returned. Files can be opened in a number of different modes depending on what you wish to do with them.

Closing a File

Once you have finished accessing a file you should close the file to free up memory and inform the operating system that you have finished with the file. In PHP the function fclose() is used to close a file. The file pointer must be valid and must point to a file successfully opened by fopen():

Function prototype:

```
bool fclose (int filePointer);
```

Function arguments and return details:

Name	Type	Description
filePointer	Integer	File pointer produced by fopen()
fclose() returns	Boolean	"TRUE" on success and "FALSE" on failure

Function example:

```
$fp = fopen ("/home/book/file.txt", "r"); fclose($fp);
```

Getting the Size of a File

The size of a file in bytes can be easily found by using the filesize() function:

Function prototype:

```
int filesize (string filename);
```

Function arguments and return details:

Name	Type	Description
filename	String	File to be used and its full system path
filesize() returns	Int	Returns file size in bytes

Function example:

```
$bytes = filesize ($filename);
```

This function will not work on remote files and the file to be examined must be accessible via the server's file system.

Reading an Entire File

After opening a file we can read its contents or a part of it. In order to read the whole file (from the start to the end), we can use the fread() function:

Function prototype:

```
string fread (int filePointer, int length);
```

Function arguments and return details:

Name	Type	Description
filePointer	Integer	The file pointer produced by fopen()
length	Integer	Total size of the file
fread() returns	String	Entire file as text into a string

Function examples:

```
$fp = fopen ($filename, "r");
$contents = fread ($fp, filesize ($filename));
```

Note that we need to use the filesize() function to determine the size of the file.

Reading an Entire File into a String

Another function that can be used to read the entire file is file_get_contents():

Function prototype:

```
string file_get_contents ( string filename );
```

Function arguments and return details:

Name	Type	Description
filename	String	File name
file_get_contents() returns	String	File contents

Function examples:

```
$contents = file_get_contents ("test.txt");
$contents = file_get_contents ("http://www.yahoo.com");
```

With this function the contents of the file are placed into a string. You can use a URL as a file name with this function if the fopen() wrappers have been enabled. Note that if a file is too big, this is not the correct function for opening it.

Reading an Entire File into an Array

There is a function called file() which is used to read an entire file into an array. Each element of the array corresponds to a line in the file, with the new line still attached. If the file consists of 12 lines, this will produce an array with 12 elements:

Function prototype:

```
array file ( string filename );
```

Function arguments and return details:

Name	Type	Description
filename	String	File name to use
file() returns	Array	Outputs the file into an array

Function arguments and return details:

```
$content = file("test.txt");
$line1 = $content[0];
$line2 = $content[1];
```

Reading a Character from a File

Characters can be read from a file using the fgetc() function. This function has the following syntax:

Function prototype:

```
string fgetc(int filePointer);
```

Function arguments and return details:

Name	Type	Description
filePointer	Integer	File pointer from fopen()
fgetc() output	String	String containing a single character read from the file

Function examples:

```php
$fp = fopen ($filename, "r");
$character = fgetc($fp);
```

The function requires a single parameter, which is the file pointer, supplied from the fopen function. The function returns a string which contains a single character read from the file. The following script displays the first character from the test.txt file. The test.txt file is a simple text file stored in the file's subdirectory containing the following text:

```
1. The quick brown fox jumped over the lazy dog.
2. The quick brown fox jumped over the lazy dog.
3. The quick brown fox jumped over the lazy dog.
4. The quick brown fox jumped over the lazy dog.
```

This script example can be used with any file to detect the first character.

```php
<?php

// Reading And Writing to files - Example 26-1
//----------------------------

$fp1 = fopen("files/test.txt", "r");
$c = fgetc($fp1);

echo("First character is $c");

fclose($fp1);
?>
```

Reading a File a Line at a Time

In addition to reading single characters from a file, PHP also supports reading an entire line of characters from a file. The function which enables you to do this is called fgets() and its syntax is as follows:

Function prototype:

```php
string fgets (int filePointer, in length);
```

Function arguments and return details:

Name	Type	Description
filePointer	Integer	File pointer produced by fopen()
length	Integer	Total size of the reading file
fgets() returns	String	Returns a string of up to length -1 bytes read from the file pointed to by filePointer

Function examples:

```
$s = fgets($fp1, 4096);
```

The function will read a number of characters into a string until the size of length is reached, a new-line character is read or the end of the file marker is encountered. To detect the end of the file marker we need to use the feof() function:

Function prototype:

```
int feof (int filePointer);
```

Function arguments and return details:

Name	Type	Description
filePointer	Integer	File pointer produced by fopen()
feof() returns	Int	Return "TRUE" if at end of file, otherwise "FALSE"

Function examples:

```
$s = feof($fp1);
```

The following script illustrates an example of reading a file line by line:

```php
<?php

// Reading And Writing to files - Example 26-2
//-----------------------------

$fp1 = fopen("files/test.txt", "r");

echo("The content of file test.txt is:<p>");
echo("<form>");
echo("<textarea cols=70 rows=15>");
$c=1;
$s = fgets($fp1, 4096);
```

```
while(!feof($fp1)) {
      echo("$c: $s");
      $c++;
      $s = fgets($fp1, 4096);
}
echo("</textarea></form>");
fclose($fp1);
?>
```

Reading a Remote File

A remote file can be easily opened (like a local file) as soon as permission is granted. The following script allows you to specify the name of a Web page (which, of course, is stored as a file) which is then read and displayed in a textarea field:

```php
<?php

// Reading And Writing to files - Example 26-3
//--------------------------------

if (isset($_POST['webpage']))
      $webpage = $_POST['webpage'];
else
      $webpage = "";

echo "Enter Web page address http://";
echo "<form action='" . $_SERVER['PHP_SELF'] ."' method='post'>";
echo "<input type='text' size='30' name='webpage' value='$webpage'>";
echo "<input type = 'submit' value='Display'>";
echo "</form>";

if ($webpage) {
      $fp1 = fopen("http://" . $_POST['webpage'],"r");
      echo "The content of the web page is:<p>";
      echo "<form>";
      echo "<textarea cols=70 rows=15>";
      $c=1;
      $s = fgets($fp1, 4096);
      while(!feof($fp1)) {
          echo "$s";
          $s = fgets($fp1, 4096);
      }
      echo "</textarea></form>";
```

```
        fclose($fp1);
}

?>
```

The output from this script is illustrated in Figure 26.1.

Figure 26.1 Reading a remote file.

If a Web page address is given the Web page contents are placed into a textarea, see Figure 26.2.

Writing to Files

So far the examples have shown that files can be read and displayed. However, using PHP file handling facilities, you can also write data to files. The function fwrite() allows strings to be written to a file and its syntax is as follows.

Function prototype:

```
int fwrite(int fp, string str, int length);
```

Function arguments and return details:

Name	Type	Description
filePointer	Integer	File pointer produced by fopen()
length	Integer	Total size of the reading file
fwrite() returns	Int	Number of bytes written to the file

Function examples:

```
$fp = fopen ($filename, "w");
$fw = fwrite ($fp, $content );
```

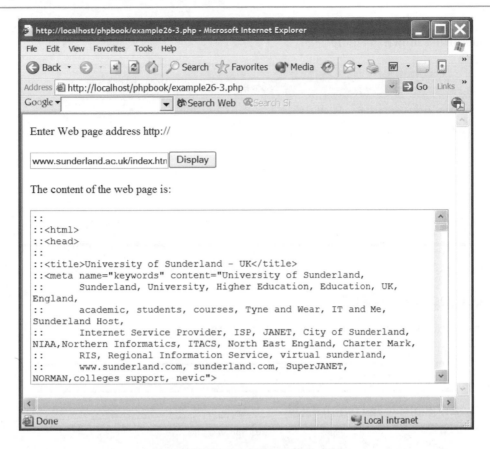

Figure 26.2 Results of a remote file reading.

In the following example we use the fopen() function to create (using the "w" option) a file "test2.txt" and fwrite() to write a small string in it. Note that the new file will be created in the "file" directory and must have the correct permissions so that PHP can write to it.

```php
<?php

// Reading And Writing to files - Example 26-4
//-------------------------------

$filename = "files/test2.txt";
$content = "Hello this is my file.";

$fp = fopen($filename, "w");

$fw = fwrite($fp, $content);

fclose($fp);

?>
```

Examining the contents of the "files" directory and viewing the content of file test2.txt we reveal the file shown in Figure 26.3.

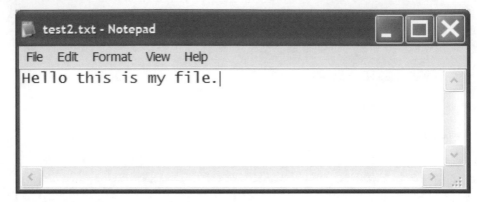

Figure 26.3 Created file.

Checking a File Exists

To check that a file exists, we use the file_exists() function:

Function prototype:

```
Bool file_exists(string filename);
```

Function arguments and return details:

Name	Type	Description
filename	String	File name
file_exists() returns	Bool	Returns "TRUE" if the file exists or "FALSE" if it does not

Function example:

```
$file = file_exists($fielname);
```

Building a Guestbook using File Handling

A very common and simple application that can make use of file functions is the guestbook. Using read-and-write file functions, we can read stored messages and write new ones respectively. In the following example we shall introduce a quick way of implementing such an application:

```php
<?php

// Reading And Writing to files - Example 26-5
//-------------------------------
```

```php
$datafile = "files/data.txt";

if(isset($_POST['submit'])){

        $name = $_POST['name'];
        $comments = $_POST['comments'];

        $new_content = "$name::$comments\n";

        $fp = fopen($datafile, "a");
        $fw = fwrite($fp, $new_content);
        $fc = fclose($fp);
}

?>
<html>
<body bgcolor="#FFFFFF" text="#000000">
<b>GUESTBOOK </b>
<form name="form1" method="post" action="<?php echo
$_SERVER['PHP_SELF'];
?>">
 <table width="30%" border="0" cellspacing="0" cellpadding="0"
height="50">
  <tr>
   <td width="31%">Name:</td>
   <td width="69%"><input type="text" name="name"></td>
  </tr>
  <tr>
   <td width="31%">Comments:</td>
   <td width="69%"><textarea name="comments" rows="3"></textarea>
 </td>
  </tr>
 </table>
 <input type="submit" name="submit" value="Submit Comment">
 <input type="reset" name="Reset" value="Reset">
 <br>
</form>
<hr>

<?php

//Read data from file and create a loop to output them

if (file_exists($datafile)) {
        $read_data = file($datafile);
        $num_comments = count($read_data);

        for($c=0;$c<$num_comments-1;$c++){
```

```
            $content = explode("::", $read_data[$c]);

            echo "<b>Name:</b> $content[0]";
            echo "<br>";
            echo "<b>Comment:</b> $content[1]";
            echo "<br><br>";
        }


}
?>
<hr>
</body>
</html>
```

The first part of the script processes the form data and opens the file:

```
$datafile = "files/data.txt";

if(isset($_POST['submit'])){

    $name = $_POST['name'];
    $comments = $_POST['comments'];

    $new_content = "$name::$comments\n";

    $fp = fopen($datafile, "a");
    $fw = fwrite($fp, $new_content);
    $fc = fclose($fp);
}
```

The next part displays the form:

```
<html>
<body bgcolor="#FFFFFF" text="#000000">
<b>GUESTBOOK </b>
<form name="form1" method="post" action="<?php echo
$_SERVER['PHP_SELF'];
?> ">
 <table width="30%" border="0" cellspacing="0" cellpadding="0"
 height="50">
  <tr>
   <td width="31%">Name:</td>
   <td width="69%"><input type="text" name="name"></td>
  </tr>
```

```
  <tr>
   <td width="31%">Comments:</td>
   <td width="69%"><textarea name="comments" rows="3"></textarea>
   </td>
  </tr>
 </table>
 <input type="submit" name="submit" value="Submit Comment">
 <input type="reset" name="Reset" value="Reset">
 <br>
</form>
<hr>
```

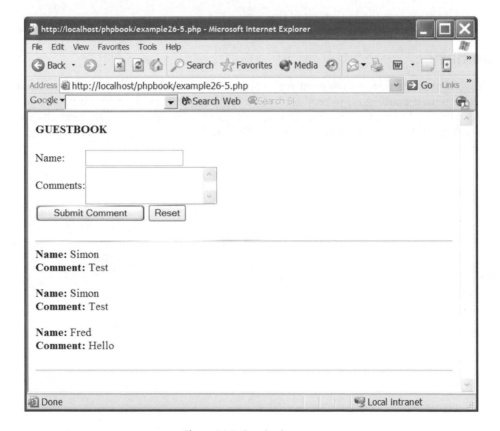

Figure 26.4 Guestbook output.

The final part checks whether the file exists and outputs the contents of the guestbook:

```
if (file_exists($datafile)) {
    $read_data = file($datafile);
    $num_comments = count($read_data);
```

```
        for($c=0;$c<$num_comments-1;$c++){

                $content = explode("::", $read_data[$c]);

                echo "<b>Name:</b> $content[0]";
                echo "<br>";
                echo "<b>Comment:</b> $content[1]";
                echo "<br><br>";
        }
}
?>
```

Figure 26.4 illustrates the output from this script.

Summary

In this chapter we have introduced some simple file handling. We have introduced the functions which enable you to read and write to files which exist or require creation. The chapter culminated in the creation of a simple guestbook script. In the next chapter we shall look a little more closely at some other file-handling facilities provided by PHP.

More File Handling 27

Introduction

In the previous chapter we introduced the concept of files and illustrated how they can be created and how data can be written to them. However, there is much more to file handling than simple creation and data writing. PHP has quite a number of functions which allow us to use and manipulate existing files. In this chapter we shall introduce some of these functions and illustrate their usefulness.

Getting File Types

We have already shown that PHP can open a file using the simple function fopen(). Sometimes it is useful to know if a file is a regular file or a directory. PHP provides two functions to help us determine this:

Function prototypes:

```
bool is_file (string filename);
bool is_dir (string filename);
```

Function arguments and return details:

Name	Type	Description
filename	String	The name of the file and its full system path
is_file() returns	Boolean	"TRUE" if the given file name exists and is a regular file
is_dir() returns	Boolean	"TRUE" if the given file name exists and is a regular directory

Function examples:

```
$checkFile = is_file ("/home/book/file.txt");
$checkDir = is_dir ("/home/book/");
```

These functions do not work on remote files, so the file name to be examined must be accessible via the server's file system. The following script illustrates the use of these functions:

```php
<?php

// More File Handling - Example 27-1
//-------------------------------

$datafile = "files/data.txt";

if(isset($_POST['submit'])){

     $filename = $_POST['filename'];

if (is_file($filename))
     echo "$filename is a file";
elseif (is_dir($filename))
     echo "$filename is a directory";
else
     echo "Don't know what $filename is!";
}

?>

<html>
<body bgcolor="#FFFFFF" text="#000000">
<h2>File Check</h2>
<form name="form1" method="post" action="<?php echo
$_SERVER['PHP_SELF'];
?>">

File Name:<input type="text" name="filename">

<input type="submit" name="submit" value="Submit Filename">
<input type="reset" name="Reset" value="Reset">
</form>
</body>
</html>
```

The script consists of two main parts – the first determines whether the form has been submitted and then accesses the file name:

```php
$datafile = "files/data.txt";

if(isset($_POST['submit'])){

     $filename = $_POST['filename'];
```

It then invokes the is_file() and is_dir() functions to determine if the file name is a file or directory or failing that something else:

```
if (is_file($filename))
      echo "$filename is a file";
elseif (is_dir($filename))
      echo "$filename is a directory";
else
      echo "Don't know what $filename is!";
}
```

The last part of the script outputs the form which the user uses to enter the file name:

```
<html>
<body bgcolor="#FFFFFF" text="#000000">
<h2>File Check</h2>
<form name="form1" method="post" action="<?php echo
$_SERVER['PHP_SELF'];
?> ">

File Name:<input type="text" name="filename">

<input type="submit" name="submit" value="Submit Filename">
<input type="reset" name="Reset" value="Reset">
</form>
</body>
</html>
```

The output from this script is illustrated in Figure 27.1.

File Size

Some files can be very large. It is important that we can see the size of a file before we start using it. In the previous chapter we saw that we could use the filesize() function to determine a file's size. Here is a rewrite of the previous script to display the size of the file entered in bytes:

```
<?php

// More File Handling - Example 27-2
//-------------------------------

$datafile = "files/data.txt";

if(isset($_POST['submit'])){
```

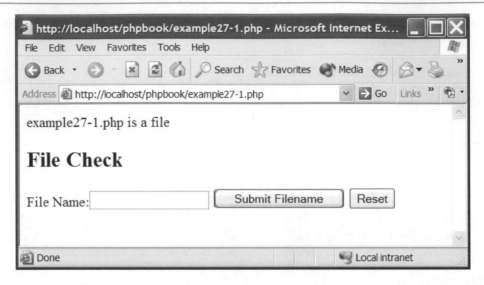

Figure 27.1 Files and directories.

```
        $filename = $_POST['filename'];

if (is_file($filename)) {
        $bytes = filesize($filename);
        echo "$filename is $bytes bytes in size.";
}
else
{
        echo "Don't know what $filename is!";
}

?>

<html>
<body bgcolor="#FFFFFF" text="#000000">
<h2>File Check</h2>
<form name="form1" method="post" action="<?php echo
$_SERVER['PHP_SELF'];
?> ">

File Name:<input type="text" name="filename">

<input type="submit" name="submit" value="Submit Filename">
<input type="reset" name="Reset" value="Reset">
</form>
</body>
</html>
```

The output from this script is illustrated in Figure 27.2.

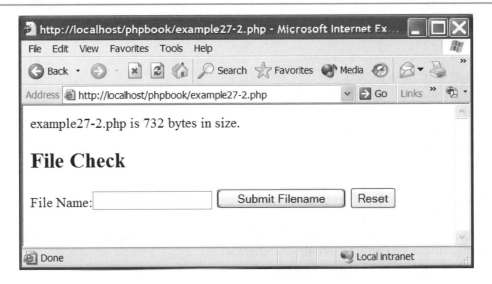

Figure 27.2 File size in bytes.

File Stats

More information about a file can be gained using the functions stat() and lstat(). The difference between these two functions is that lstat() can also return information about symbolic links as well as files. These functions will not work on remote files or local folders and the file to be examined must be accessible via the server's file system:

Function prototypes:

```
array stat (string filename);
array lstat (string filename);
```

Function arguments and return details:

Name	Type	Description
filename	String	File to be used and its full system path
stat() returns	Array	Returns an array with the statistics of the file (see later)
lstat() returns	Array	Returns an array with the statistics of the file or symbolic link

Function example:

```
$statistics = stat ($filename);
```

These functions gather the statistics of the file named by filename and returns an array with the statistics of the file/symbolic link with the following elements:

0. device [dev]
1. inode [ino]
2. inode protection mode [mode]
3. number of links [nlink]
4. user id of owner [uid]
5. group id owner [gid]
6. device type if inode device [rdev] (only valid on systems supporting the st_blksize type – other systems (i.e. Windows) return –1)
7. size in bytes [size]
8. time of last access [atime]
9. time of last modification [mtime]
10. time of last change [ctime]
11. blocksize for filesystem I/O [blksize] (only valid on systems supporting the st_blksize type – other systems (i.e. Windows) return –1)
12. number of blocks allocated [blocks]

The following script illustrates the use of the stat() function:

```php
<?php

// More File Handling - Example 27-3
//-------------------------------

$datafile = "files/data.txt";

if(isset($_POST['submit'])){

    $filename = $_POST['filename'];
if (is_file($filename)) {
    $stats = stat($filename);
    echo "The statistics of $filename are:";
    echo "<br>Device " . $stats['dev'];
    echo "<br>Inode " . $stats['ino'];
    echo "<br>inode protection mode " . $stats['mode'];
    echo "<br>number of links " . $stats['nlink'];
    echo "<br>user id of owner " . $stats['uid'];
    echo "<br>group id owner " . $stats['gid'];
    echo "<br>device type if inode device " . $stats['rdev'];
    echo "<br>size in bytes " . $stats['size'];
    echo "<br>time of last access " . $stats['atime'];
    echo "<br>time of last modification " . $stats['mtime'];
    echo "<br>time of last change " . $stats['ctime'];
    echo "<br>blocksize for filesystem I/O " . $stats['blksize'];
    echo "<br>number of blocks allocated " . $stats['blocks'];

}
```

```
else
        echo "Don't know what $filename is!";
}

?>

<html>
<body bgcolor="#FFFFFF" text="#000000">
<h2>File Statistics</h2>
<form name="form1" method="post" action="<?php echo
$_SERVER['PHP_SELF'];
?> ">

File Name:<input type="text" name="filename">

<input type="submit" name="submit" value="Submit Filename">
<input type="reset" name="Reset" value="Reset">
</form>
</body>
</html>
```

The output from this script is illustrated in Figure 27.3.

Checking File Attributes

File attribute properties can be examined using the following four functions. With these we can easily check whether a file is readable, writable, executable or uploaded:

Function prototypes:

```
bool is_readable (string filename);

bool is_writable (string filename);

bool is_executable (string filename);

bool is_uploaded_file (string filename);
```

Function arguments and return details:

Name	Type	Description
filename	String	The name of the file and its full system path
is_readable() returns	Boolean	"TRUE" if the given file name exists and is readable
is_writable() returns	Boolean	"TRUE" if the given file name exists and is writeable
is_executable() returns	Boolean	"TRUE" if the given file name exists and is executable
is_uploaded_file() returns	Boolean	"TRUE" if the file named by filename was uploaded via HTTP POST

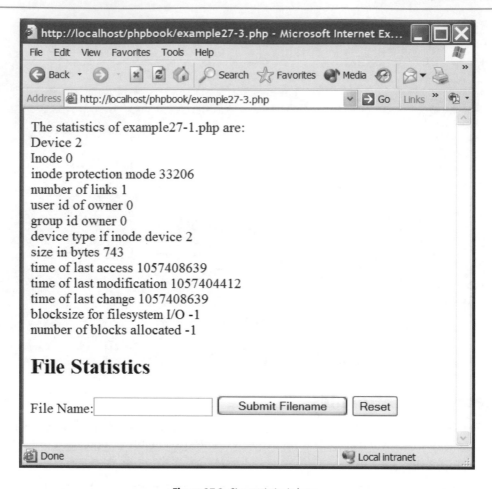

Figure 27.3 Size statistics in bytes.

Function examples:

```
$checkReadable = is_readable ("/home/book/file.txt");

$checkFileWriteable = is_writable ("/home/book/file.txt");

$checkDirWriteable = is_writable ("/home/book/ ");

$checkExecutable = is_executable ("/usr/sbin/ping");

$checkUploadedFile = is_uploaded_file ("/home/book/upload.txt");
```

These functions will not work on remote files and the file to be examined must be accessible via the server's file system. The function is_writeable() is an alias for function is_writable()

and the filename argument may be a directory name allowing us to check whether a directory is writeable. Function is_executable() is not available on Win32 platforms.

Modifying a File

The following functions can be used to apply the major file system activities to a file. These activities enable you to copy a file, rename a file, delete a file, create a symbolic link and change the permissions of a file.

Function prototypes:

```
int copy (string source, string destination);

bool rename (string oldname, string newname);

int unlink (string filename);

int delete (string filename);

int symlink (string target, string link);

int chmod ( string filename, int mode);
```

Function arguments and return details:

Name	Type	Description
filename	String	The name of the file and its full system path
source	Boolean	The source file name
destination	Boolean	The new file name, a raw copy of source
oldname	String	Current name of file
newname	String	New name of file
target	String	The target file name of the link
link	String	The link name
copy() returns	Integer	"TRUE" if copy was successful
rename() returns	Boolean	"TRUE" if rename was successful
unlink() returns	Integer	"TRUE" if unlink (delete) was successful
delete() returns		
symlink() returns	Integer	"TRUE" if the symbolic link creation was successful
mode	Integer	Permission modes of file (e.g. 0755)

Function examples:

```
$copyFile = copy ("/home/book/test.txt", "/home/book/test2.txt");

$renameFile = rename ("/home/book/test.txt", "/home/book/test.php");

$deleteFile = unlink ("/home/book/test.txt");
```

```
$deleteFile = delete ("/home/book/test.txt");

$createLink = symlink ("/home/book/test.txt",
"/home/book/test.link");

$changeMode = chmod ("/home/book/test.txt", 0755);
```

The function unlink() is used to delete files, symbolic links and directories and the function delete() is an alias to unlink(). These functions will not work on remote files and the file to be used must be accessible via the server's file system.

Directory Handling

In much the same way as the previous functions enabled us to manipulate files, PHP provides a number of functions which enable us to manipulate directories. These are:

Function prototypes:

```
int mkdir (string pathname, int mode);

bool rmdir (string dirname);

bool rename (string oldname, string newname);
```

Function arguments and return details:

Name	Type	Description
pathname	String	Real pathname where the directory will be created
mode	Integer	Permission modes of file (e.g. 755)
dirname	String	Directory to be deleted
oldname	String	Current name of file
newname	String	New name of file
mkdir() returns	Integer	Returns "1" on success or "0" on failure
rmdir() returns	Boolean	Returns "TRUE" on success or "FALSE" on failure
rename() returns	Boolean	Returns "TRUE" on success or "FALSE" on failure

Function examples:

```
$createDir = mkdir ("/home/book/new", "0755");

$rmDir = rmdir ("/home/book/new");

$renameDir = rename ("/home/book/old", "/home/book/new);
```

When creating a new directory with mkdir(), mode permissions can be given using the mode parameter. The original pathname should also be specified and the place where the new directory is to be created should have write permissions enabled. When using rmdir() the specified directory should be empty and the relevant permissions must permit this.

Opening and Reading a Directory

Three very powerful functions enable us to open a directory on your file system and read its contents before closing it. This enables us to see (and display if we wish) the contents of the directory. The functions are:

Function prototypes:

```
resource opendir (string path);

string readdir (resource dirHandle)

void closedir (resource dirHandle)
```

Function arguments and return details:

Name	Type	Description
path	String	Directory to be used with full system path
dirHandle	Resource	Directory handle by opendir()
opendir() returns	Resource	Directory handle
readdir() returns	String	File name(s) of the next file from the directory
closedir() returns	Void	Returns nothing

Function examples:

```
$openDirectory = opendir ("/home/book/new");

$readDirectory = readdir ($openDir);

$closeDirectory = closedir ($openDir);
```

If "path" is not a valid directory or the directory cannot be opened due to permission restrictions or file system errors, opendir() returns "FALSE" and generates a PHP error. To prevent these types of errors, use a "@" in front of each function to block error reporting (e.g. $open = @opendir(..);). This was first mentioned in Chapter 24. The following script provides an example of the use of these functions:

```php
<?php

// More File Handling - Example 27-4
//-------------------------------

$datafile = "files/data.txt";

if(isset($_POST['submit'])){
```

```
        $dirname = $_POST['dirname'];

        if (is_dir($dirname)) {

            echo "<h2>Contents of Directory $dirname :</h2>";

            $dir = opendir($dirname);
            while($file = readdir($dir)) {
                echo "$file<br />";
            }
            closedir($dir);
        }
        else
            echo "$dirname is not a directory.";
}
?>

<html>
<body bgcolor="#FFFFFF" text="#000000">
<h2>Directory Contents</h2>
<form name="form1" method="post" action="<?php echo
$_SERVER['PHP_SELF'];
?> ">

Directory Name:<input type="text" name="dirname">

<input type="submit" name="submit" value="Submit Filename">
<input type="reset" name="Reset" value="Reset">
</form>
</body>
</html>
```

The script is a rewrite of the previous examples in this chapter. The most interesting part is the section where the directory name is checked to determine that it is a directory and then, using a while loop, the contents of the directory are read and displayed:

```
        $dirname = $_POST['dirname'];

        if (is_dir($dirname)) {

            echo "<h2>Contents of Directory $dirname :</h2>";

            $dir = opendir($dirname);
            while($file = readdir($dir)) {
                echo "$file<br />";
            }
            closedir($dir);
```

The output from this script is illustrated in Figure 27.4.

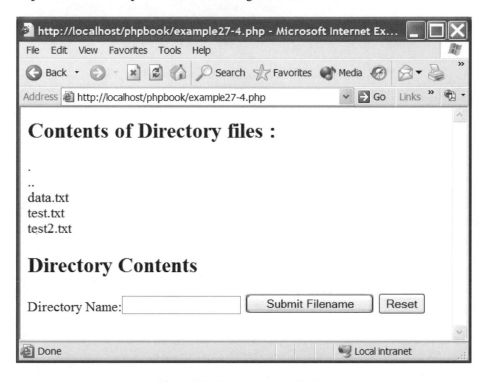

Figure 27.4 Directory contents display.

Summary

This chapter has introduced a number of additional functions which can be used to modify and create files and directories. We have illustrated how functions can be employed to determine a file's statistics, delete and move files and directories and even view the entire contents of a directory. In the following chapter we shall introduce the concept of file uploading.

File Uploading Using Forms

28

Introduction

Forms allow users to enter data via form fields such as the text and password fields. We introduced forms in Chapter 18. One thing that we omitted from that chapter was a field type to allow a user to submit an entire file along with the form. The form input type "file" enables users to browse your local computer directory and select a file to upload to the Web server.

Once uploaded, a PHP script can be written to access this file, move it, store it and, as we shall see, use it for the user's benefit.

Form Input Type File

To create a form which allows us to upload a file we must insert the attribute "enctype" into the form element with the value "multipart/form-data". This informs the server that the form may contain an uploaded file:

```
<form enctype='multipart/form-data' action='form.php'
method='post'>
```

The form input element can be assigned the attribute type="file" to create a form input field in which we can browse for and select a file on the local machine to upload to the server. The format of this element is as follows:

```
<input name='myFileName' type='file'>
```

In addition, the maximum file size in bytes can be limited using a hidden field in which the system variable MAX_FILE_SIZE is set to a certain value. An example of this is:

```
<input type='hidden' name='MAX_FILE_SIZE' value='100000'>
```

An example of a form with a file upload field is:

```php
<?php

// File Upload - Example 28-1
//--------------------

?>

<form enctype='multipart/form-data' action='<?php echo
$_SERVER["PHP_SELF"];
?>' method='post'>

<input type='hidden' name='MAX_FILE_SIZE' value='100000'>
Document File: <input name='myfile' type='file'
value='$file'><br><br>
<input type='submit' value='Submit the Document' name='send'>
</form>
```

Figure 28.1 illustrates what this form looks like when viewed in a browser.

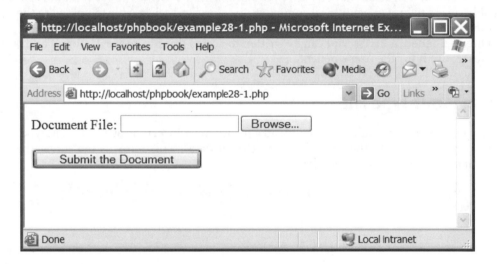

Figure 28.1 Simple file upload form.

You can enter the name and location of the file to upload in the form field or you can click the Browse button to open a "choose a file window" and locate and select the file to upload. This window is shown in Figure 28.2.

Unfortunately, while we have created our form, we have not yet written any PHP code with which to access it.

Accessing an Uploaded File with PHP

There are a number of steps, which need to be followed in writing a PHP script to access an uploaded file. We need to be careful to do this correctly as there are many security risks

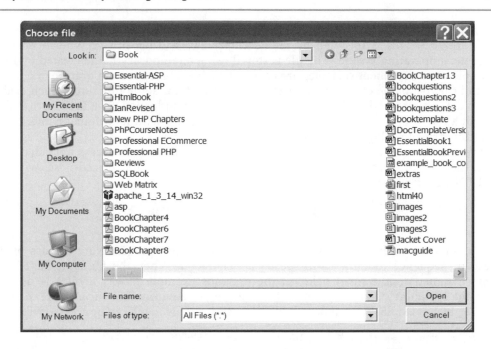

Figure 28.2 Choose a file window.

if you do not. Before we introduce these steps let's examine how file upload in PHP works. This is illustrated in Figure 28.3.

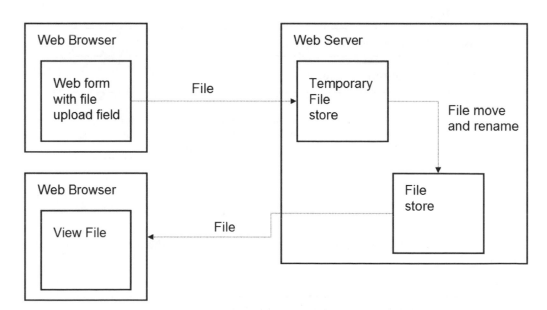

Figure 28.3 How file upload in PHP works.

When a file is uploaded via a form the file is stored in a temporary directory as shown in Figure 28.3. This is specified by the developer and will depend very much on your computer's operating system. The file is stored using a temporary name created by PHP. A couple of environment variables are created which enables the temporary name of the file and the real name of the file to be stored. PHP contains some functions which enable you to determine whether the temporary file was indeed uploaded via a PHP form and, if so, will allow you to move the file to its final resting place with its original name. These functions provide a degree of security from would-be invaders.

Let's examine the different PHP instructions which allow us to access uploaded files. First, the temporary directory into which uploaded files are first placed is set with the $TMPDIR environment variable, for example:

```
$TMPDIR = "c:\\Temp\\uploads";
```

This example sets the temporary directory to a c:\temp\uploads. Note the use of the \\ escape sequence to allow us to specify a \ character. When the file is uploaded, the name assigned to the form field (in the previous example it was myfile) is used to store the temporary and real names of the files in an environment variable array called $HTTP_POST_FILES. The temporary file name and real file name can be accessed like this:

```
$filename = $HTTP_POST_FILES['myfile']['tmp_name'];
$realname =$HTTP_POST_FILES['myfile']['name'];
```

It is important to access this information as we need to use it to check whether this is a genuine file, which was uploaded correctly. To do this we use the is_uploaded_file() function:

Function prototype:

```
bool is_uploaded_file(string filename);
```

Function arguments and return details:

Name	Type	Description
filename	String	The name of the file to check has been uploaded
is_uploaded_file() returns	Bool	A value of "TRUE" if the file is a valid uploaded file, otherwise it returns "FALSE"

Function example:

```
$res = Is-Iploaded_file($filename);
```

If the file is genuine, then it can be moved and renamed using the move_uploaded_file() function:

Function prototype:

```
bool move_uploaded_file(string filename, string destination);
```

Function arguments and return details:

Name	Type	Description
filename	String	The temporary name of the uploaded file
destination	String	The name and location to which to move the file
move_uploaded_file() returns	Bool	A value of "TRUE" if the file is moved successfully, otherwise it returns "FALSE"

Function example:

```
move_uploaded_file($filename,("c:\\Program
Files\\httpd\\HtDocs\\bigbook\\uploads\\".$newname));
```

We now have enough information to create a simple file upload program.

A Simple File Upload

For this example we began by creating four images which we stored in c:\temp\pics. These pictures were saved as rope.jpg, bluedots.jpg, dandelions.jpg and grass.jpg and are shown in Table 28.1.

Table 28.1 Our file images and names.

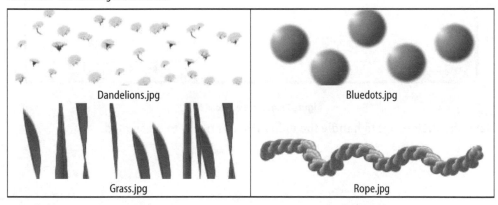

| Dandelions.jpg | Bluedots.jpg |
| Grass.jpg | Rope.jpg |

Next, a simple file upload form was created allowing two files to be uploaded. These were given the names picture1 and picture2; the script is:

```
<?php

// File Upload - Example 28-2
//---------------------

?>
```

```
<form enctype='multipart/form-data' action='example28-3.php'
method='post'>
<input type='hidden' name='MAX_FILE_SIZE' value='1000000'>
First Picture: <input name='picture1' type='file'><br>
Second Picture: <input name='picture2' type='file'><br><br>
<input type='submit' value='Submit the Pictures' name='send'>
</form>
```

This form is shown in Figure 28.4. The form was designed to upload two of the four images created previously, although no error checking is made to ensure that the uploaded files are, in fact, images.

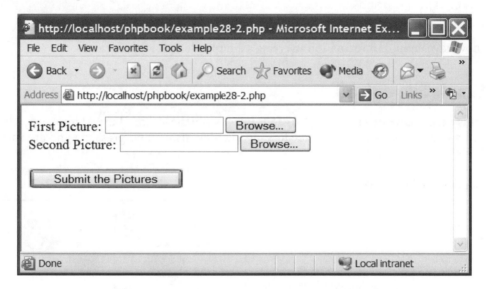

Figure 28.4 Picture upload form.

Next, the PHP script to handle the uploaded files needs to be created:

```
<?php

// File Upload - Example 28-3
//---------------------

$TMPDIR = "c:\\Temp\\uploads";
$filename = $HTTP_POST_FILES['picture1']['tmp_name'];
if (is_uploaded_file($filename))
    move_uploaded_file($filename,
    "c:\\Inetpub\\wwwroot\\phpbook\\graphics\\picture1.jpg");
$filename = $HTTP_POST_FILES['picture2']['tmp_name'];
if (is_uploaded_file($filename))
    move_uploaded_file($filename,
    "c:\\Inetpub\\wwwroot\\phpbook\\graphics\\picture2.jpg");
```

```
?>
<img src="graphics\picture1.jpg">
<br>
<img src="graphics\picture2.jpg">
<br>
<br>
<a href="example28-2.php">Back</a> to form upload.
```

This script checks that the first file (picture1) is a valid file and moves this to

```
"c:\\Inetpub\\wwwroot\\phpbook\\graphics\\picture1.jpg");
```

Then the second file (picture2) is checked and moved to

```
"c:\\Inetpub\\wwwroot\\phpbook\\graphics\\picture2.jpg");
```

Finally, the script displays the two images using the <IMG SRC> element and provides a hyperlink back to the file upload form. An example output from the script is shown in Figure 28.5. Note that the images displayed will depend on which images you choose to upload.

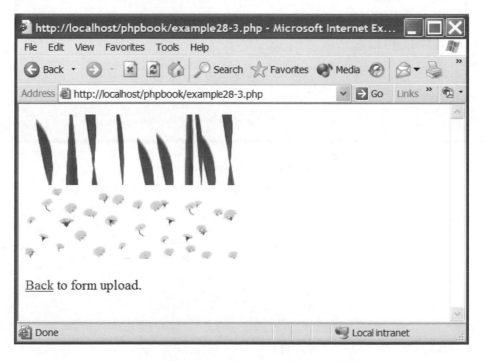

Figure 28.5 Picture upload display.

Securing File Uploads

While our previous file upload example illustrates how the concept of file uploading and manipulation works, it also highlights a major issue of file uploading – that of security. In our example no check is made on who is uploading images and thus anyone who knows the address of the upload form page can upload an image and replace those previously installed. While in this example this would be nothing more than an annoyance, if you were uploading documents that you only wanted certain people to be able to upload then a more secure environment is required. Let's begin to investigate how we would do this.

The first thing we need to consider is that we need to create a mechanism which will allow us to identify who is trying to upload a document and determine if you wish them to be allowed to do so. A simple username and password system would suffice. To create a system we first create a simple username and password file where each username and password is listed on separate lines of the file using the Notepad text editor. Each username and password is separated with a space character. An example of such a file is illustrated in Figure 28.6 and can be saved as a file called password.txt. Make sure you don't save this in your Web-server directory or potential hackers will be able to access this and view your list of passwords and usernames.

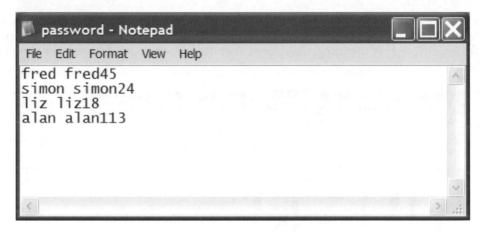

Figure 28.6 Username and password file.

We are now ready to create the file submit application and here it is:

```php
<?php

// File Upload - Example 28-4
//---------------------

if (isset($_POST['username']))
  $username = $_POST['username'];
else
  $username = "";
if (isset($_POST['password']))
  $password = $_POST['password'];
```

```php
else
  $password = "";
if (isset($_POST['file']))
  $file = $_POST['file'];
else
  $file = "";

$passwordOkay = 0;

if (isset($_POST['send'])) {
  $okay =
checkUsernamePassword("c:\\Temp\\password.txt",$username,$password);
  if($okay) {
    $passwordOkay = 1;
    $TMPDIR = "c:\\Temp\\uploads";
    $filename = $HTTP_POST_FILES['myfile']['tmp_name'];
    $realname = $HTTP_POST_FILES['myfile']['name'];
    if (is_uploaded_file($filename)) {
      $date = fDate();
      $time = fTime();
      $newname = ($realname . "-" . $date . "-" . $time);

  move_uploaded_file($filename,
  ("c:\\Inetpub\\wwwroot\\phpbook\\uploads\\".
$newname));
      appendToFile("uploads\\uploads.txt", $date . " "
. $time . " " . $username . " " . $realname);
      echo("Thank you document submitted. Click <a
href='example28-5.php'>here</a> to see a list of submitted
documents.");
    }
  }
  else
    echo("Incorrect Password and/or Username.");
}

$phpself = $_SERVER['PHP_SELF'];

if(!isset($_POST['send']) || $passwordOkay == 0) {
  echo("<h2>Welcome to the Documents Submission Page</h2>");
  echo("Please complete the form and press the send file
button.<P>");
  echo("<form enctype='multipart/form-data' action='$phpself'
method='post'>");
  echo("<input type='hidden' name='MAX_FILE_SIZE' value='100000'>");
  echo("Username: <input type='text' name='username'
value='$username'><br>");
  echo("Password: <input type='password' name='password'
value='$password'><br>");
```

```
   echo("Document File: <input name='myfile' type='file'
value='$file'><br><br>");
   echo("<input type='submit' value='Submit the Document'
name='send'>");
   echo("</form>");
}

function fDate() {
  $date = getdate();
  $monthText = $date["month"];
  $year = $date["year"];
  $mday = $date["mday"];
  return $mday . "-" . $monthText . "-" . $year;
}

function fTime() {
  $time = localtime();
  return $time[2] . "-" . $time[1] . "-" . $time[0];
}

function appendToFile($file,$data) {
  $out = fopen($file,"a");
  fputs($out,$data."\n");
  fclose($out);
}

function checkUsernamePassword($file,$username,$password) {
  $found=0;
  $in = fopen($file,"r");
  $line = fgets($in,4096);
  while(!feof($in) && !$found) {
    $splitLine = explode (" ", $line);
    $splitLine[1] = substr($splitLine[1],0,strlen($splitLine[1])-2);
    if($splitLine[0] == $username && $splitLine[1] == $password)
      $found=1;
    $line = fgets($in,4096);
  }
  fclose($in);
return $found;
}
?>
```

It is a little longer than our first example – but don't worry we shall examine this a little at a time explaining what is going on. The first part of the script obtains the form variables:

```
if (isset($_POST['username']))
     $username = $_POST['username'];
```

```
    else
        $username = "";
    if (isset($_POST['password']))
        $password = $_POST['password'];
    else
        $password = "";
    if (isset($_POST['file']))
        $file = $_POST['file'];
    else
        $file = "";

    $passwordOkay = 0;
```

The next part of the script checks that the form data have been sent and, if so, invokes the function checkUsernamePassword(), passing it the parameters password text file location, username and password:

```
if (isset($_POST['send'])) {
        $okay =
checkUsernamePassword("c:\\Temp\\password.txt",$username,$password);
```

The checkUsernamePassword() function returns a "0" if the username/password does not exist or "1" if all is okay. We shall return to this function later when we encounter its definition further down the listing. If the password and username are okay, then the next part of the script sets the temporary directory and acccsses the temporary and real names of the uploaded file. It then checks that the file is a valid file upload by calling the is_uploaded_file() function:

```
        if($okay) {
                $passwordOkay = 1;
                $TMPDIR = "c:\\Temp\\uploads";
                $filename = $HTTP_POST_FILES['myfile']['tmp_name'];
                $realname = $HTTP_POST_FILES['myfile']['name'];
                if (is_uploaded_file($filename)) {
```

If the file is a valid upload, then the date and time are obtained by invoking the functions fDate() and fTime(). The date and time returned from these functions are used to create a new file name which encorporates the real file name along with the date and time:

```
                $date = fDate();
                $time = fTime();
                $newname = ($realname . "-" . $date . "-" . $time);
```

The file is then moved to a directory that we have created called uploads. You can change the location of this directory if you wish.

```
    move_uploaded_file($filename,
("c:$\\Inetpub\\wwwroot\\phpbook\\uploads\\".
$newname));
```

The function appendToFile() is invoked, passing the parameters of the file name to write to and the date, time, username and realname of the file as a single string. Finally, a message confirming the submission of the document and asking the user if they wish to view the submitted documents is displayed:

```
appendToFile("uploads\\uploads.txt", $date . " " . $time . " " .
$username . " " . $realname);
                echo("Thank you document submitted. Click <a
href='example28-5.php'>here</a> to see a list of
submitted documents.");
    }
```

If the username or password is incorrect, a message is displayed to that effect:

```
    else
        echo("Incorrect Password and/or Username.");
```

If the form was not submitted or the password/username was incorrect, then the form is displayed. This consists of fields which allow the user to enter the username, password and the document to upload:

```
$phpself = $_SERVER['PHP_SELF'];

if(!isset($_POST['send']) || $passwordOkay == 0) {
    echo("<h2>Welcome to the Documents Submission Page</h2>");
    echo("Please complete the form and press the send
file button.<P>");
    echo("<form enctype='multipart/form-data' action='$phpself'
method='post'>");
    echo("<input type='hidden' name='MAX_FILE_SIZE' value='100000'>");
    echo("Username: <input type='text' name='username'
value='$username'><br>");
    echo("Password: <input type='password' name='password'
value='$password'><br>");
    echo("Document File: <input name='myfile' type='file'
value='$file'><br><br>");
    echo("<input type='submit' value='Submit the Document'
name='send'>");
    echo("</form>");
}
```

The remainder of the program consists of the user-defined functions, which we have invoked previously. The first two of these are the fDate() and fTime() functions which return the date and time as strings:

```
function fDate() {
    $date = getdate();
    $monthText = $date["month"];
    $year = $date["year"];
    $mday = $date["mday"];
    return $mday . "-" . $monthText . "-" . $year;
}

function fTime() {
    $time = localtime();
    return $time[2] . "-" . $time[1] . "-" . $time[0];
}
```

The appendToFile() function writes a record of the document, which was just uploaded to the uploads.txt file. This text file is used by our second PHP program to display the documents which have been uploaded:

```
function appendToFile($file,$data) {
    $out = fopen($file,"a");
    fputs($out,$data."\n");
    fclose($out);
}
```

The final part of the program is the checkUsernamePassword() function. This function opens the passwords.txt file and reads each line of the file:

```
function checkUsernamePassword($file,$username,$password) {
    $found=0;
    $in = fopen($file,"r");
    $line = fgets($in,4096);
    while(!feof($in) && !$found) {
```

Each line of the file is split apart using the explode function to obtain the stored username and password:

```
    $splitLine = explode (" ", $line);
```

As a text file often has some line-feed characters inserted at the end of each line, these are removed using the substr() function which deletes the last two hidden characters from the string:

```
$splitLine[1] = substr($splitLine[1],0,strlen($splitLine[1])-2);
```

The username and passwords passed to the function are compared with those read from the file and, if they match, the variable $found is set to "1" and this is returned by the function:

```
        if($splitLine[0] == $username && $splitLine[1] == $password)
            $found=1;
        $line = fgets($in,4096);
    }
    fclose($in);
return $found;
}
```

The output produced by this program is shown in Figure 28.7.

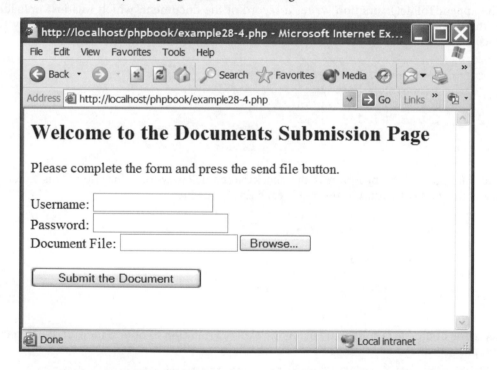

Figure 28.7 Secure file upload screen.

If a correct username and password are entered and a file successfully uploaded then the message illustrated in Figure 28.8 is shown.

The next stage is to create the program, which will display the documents uploaded when the user selects the <u>here</u> hyperlink. The program simply opens the uploads.txt file and reads each line of the file. The details of each uploaded file is displayed within a table:

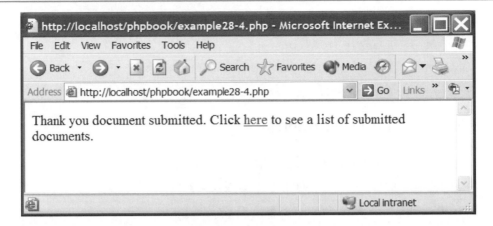

Figure 28.8 Successful upload.

```
<h2>Submitted Documents</h2>
<table border=1>
<tr bgcolor='cyan'><td width=130>Date</td><td width=80>Time</td><td
width=100>Username</td><td>Document</td></tr>

<?php

// File Upload - Example 28-5
//--------------------

$in = fopen("uploads//uploads.txt","r");
$line = fgets($in,4096);
while(!feof($in)) {
   $splitLine = explode (" ", $line);
   echo("<tr bgcolor='lightgreen'><td>" . $splitLine[0] .
    "</td><td>" .
$splitLine[1] . "</td><td>" . $splitLine[2] .
   "</td><td><a href='uploads\\" . $splitLine[3] . "-" .
$splitLine[0] . "-" . $splitLine[1] . "'>" . $splitLine[3] .
"</a></td></tr>");
   $line = fgets($in,4096);
}
fclose($in);
?>
</table>
<a href='example28-4.php'>Return</a> to submit document page.
```

An example output from this program is shown in Figure 28.9.

The user can access the uploaded files by clicking on the name of the document. Depending on the type of document this will either, as in the case of an image file, be

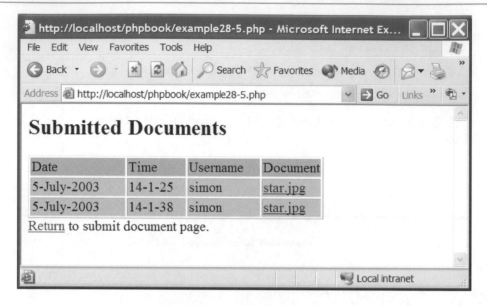

Figure 28.9 Uploaded documents.

displayed or, if a document, the user may be prompted as to whether they wish to download a copy of the document to their local computer.

Summary

This chapter has introduced the concept of file upload via a form. We have shown how this can be achieved and the use to which such a facility can be put. We have explained that there are security issues in allowing file upload and have discussed how PHP ensures that the uploaded files are genuine, in addition to what you, the programmer, must do to restrict user access. In the next chapter we shall examine what PHP can accomplish by manipulating simple images.

Part 8

Graphics

Simple Image Manipulation 29

Introduction

This chapter examines how PHP can be used to perform some simple manipulations of graphical images. Being able to perform such changes can enable you to develop Web sites that are more dynamic, appear to be very sophisticated and have increased accessibility. The types of image manipulation that we will examine are simple things such as choosing which graphic to display or resizing and stretching images. Even confining ourselves to just these activities enables us to obtain some quite effective results.

Replacing an Image

One of the simplest things that PHP can do is to control what images appear on your Web site. Quite often Web designers want their Web sites to appear to be under constant change without the need for high maintenance. One thing that many sites choose to do is

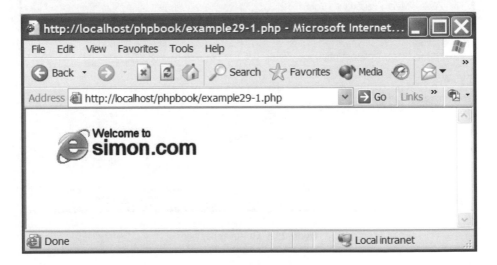

Figure 29.1 Boring Web graphic.

to have some graphics on their site which change depending on the time of year. Consider Figure 29.1 which illustrates a typical company Web logo.

What we would like is for the logo to change depending on the date that the Web page is viewed. Therefore, if it is Christmas Eve then the logo in Figure 29.2 is displayed and, on Christmas day, the logo shown in Figure 29.3 is displayed.

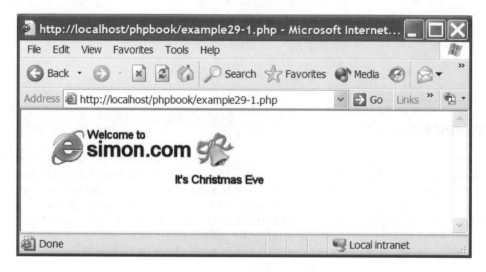

Figure 29.2   Christmas Eve logo.

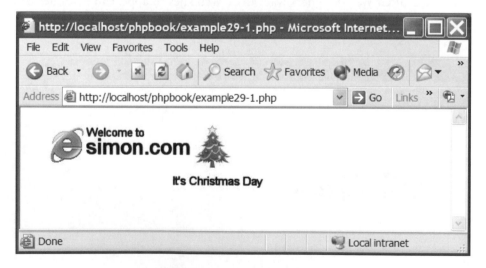

Figure 29.3   Christmas Day logo.

Luckily, the code required to implement this is very simple:

```php
<?php

// Simple Images - Example 29-1
//---------------------

$date = getdate();
$day = $date["mday"];
$month = $date["mon"];
if($day == 25 && $month== 12)
      echo("<img src='graphics/simoncomcd.jpg'>");
elseif($day == 24 && $month== 12)
      echo("<img src='graphics/simoncomce.jpg'>");
else
      echo("<img src='graphics/simoncom.jpg'>");
?>
```

In order for this program to work, we need to have three separate images from which to choose. Our images are simoncomcd.jpg, simoncomce.jpg and simoncom.jpg. Table 29.1 illustrates these images and their file names.

Table 29.1 Script images.

The program begins by obtaining the system date and storing the day and month in two variables $day and $month. For this example, the year is not required:

```php
$date = getdate();
$day = $date["mday"];
$month = $date["mon"];
```

Then an if, elseif – else construct is used to check the dates to determine which image to display:

```
if($day == 25 && $month== 12)
       echo("<img src='graphics/simoncomcd.jpg'>");
elseif($day == 24 && $month== 12)
       echo("<img src='graphics/simoncomce.jpg'>");
else
       echo("<img src='graphics/simoncom.jpg'>");
```

Thus, if it is Christmas Day, the image simoncomcd.jpg is displayed, if it is Christmas Eve then the image 'simoncomce.jpg' is displayed and, on all other days, the logo simoncom.jpg is displayed. If you want to test this and don't wish to wait until the date is actually Christmas Eve or Day, then insert the following two lines of code before the if statement to set the month and day:

```
$month = 12;
$day = 24;
```

Resizing an Image

The images used on Web pages have a fixed size in terms of the number of pixels in them. Normally these images are displayed at their default size using the <img src="imagename"> element. However, this element has two attributes – height and width – that allow you to specify the exact size that the image should be displayed, regardless of the physical size of the graphic.

It is possible to alter the values of the width and height of an image dynamically allowing an image to appear to be resized. The quality of the image that is displayed will depend on the original size of the image. For example an image of 10×10 pixels enlarged to 100×100 pixels will look very "blocky" as each original pixel has been multiplied tenfold. Figure 29.4 illustrates an example of image resizing. The Web page consists of a palm tree image and a simple form consisting of two buttons. One button is marked with a "+" and the other with a "−" symbol. Clicking on the "+" button will enlarge the image, while clicking on the "−" button will shrink the image.

Figure 29.5 illustrates the same image after it has been shrunk slightly by clicking on the "−" button. Some controls have been built into the program to limit the minimum and maximum size that an image can be enlarged or reduced.

The program code required to implement this Web page is:

```
<?php

// Simple Images - Example 29-2
//---------------------

if(!isset($_POST['x']))
       $x=150;
else
       $x=$_POST['x'];
```

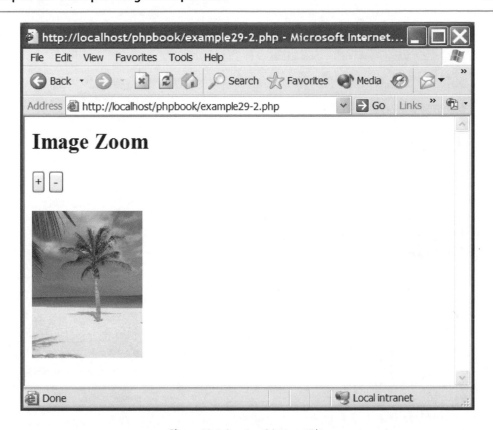

Figure 29.4 Image resizing example.

```
if(!isset($_POST['y']))
      $y=200;
else
      $y=$_POST['y'];

if (isset($_POST['bigger'])) {
      if($_POST['bigger']) {
            if($x < 300){
                  $x=$x*2;
                  $y=$y*2;
            }
      }
}
if (isset($_POST['smaller'])) {
      if($_POST['smaller']) {
            if($x > 38){
                  $x=$x/2;
                  $y=$y/2;
```

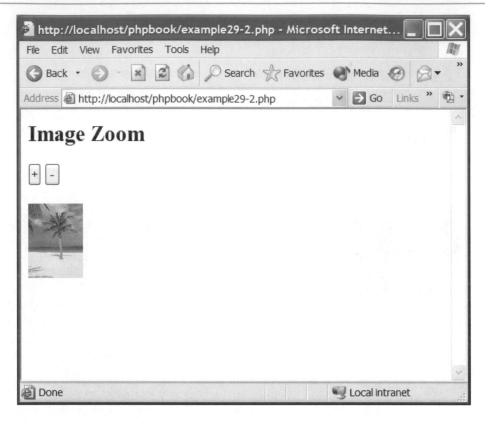

Figure 29.5 A shrunken image.

```
            }
        }
    }
?>
<h2>Image Zoom</h2>
<form action="<?php echo $_SERVER["PHP_SELF"]; ?>" method='post'>
<input type='hidden' name='x' value='<?php echo($x); ?>'>
<input type='hidden' name='y' value='<?php echo($y); ?>'>
<input type='submit' name='bigger' value='+'>
<input type='submit' name='smaller' value='-'>
</form>
<img src='graphics/palm.jpeg' width='<?php echo($x); ?>'
height='<?php echo($y); ?>'>
```

The program begins by determining the values of variables $x and $y:

```
if(!isset($_POST['x']))
    $x=150;
```

```
else
     $x=$_POST['x'];

if(!isset($_POST['y']))
     $y=200;
else
     $y=$_POST['y'];
```

Next, if the "+" button is pressed then the values of $x and $y are doubled so long as the value of $x is less than 300:

```
if (isset($_POST['bigger'])) {
     if($_POST['bigger']) {
          if($x < 300){
               $x=$x*2;
               $y=$y*2;
          }
     }
}
```

Next, if the "–" button is pressed then the values of $x and $y are halved so long at the value of $x is greater than 38:

```
if (isset($_POST['smaller'])) {
     if($_POST['smaller']) {
          if($x > 38){
               $x=$x/2;
               $y=$y/2;
          }
     }
}
```

The next section of code displays the Web form, which includes the hidden values of the $x and $y variables:

```
<h2>Image Zoom</h2>
<form action="<?php echo $_SERVER["PHP_SELF"]; ?>" method='post'>
<input type='hidden' name='x' value='<?php echo($x); ?>'>
<input type='hidden' name='y' value='<?php echo($y); ?>'>
<input type='submit' name='bigger' value='+'>
<input type='submit' name='smaller' value='-'>
</form>
```

Finally, the image is displayed, using the values of $x and $y to set the size of the image:

```
<img src='graphics/palm.jpeg' width='<?php echo($x); ?>'
height='<?php echo($y); ?>'>
```

Stretching an Image

Instead of resizing an image by keeping the aspect ratio of the image the same, it is possible to resize an image by changing either its width or height and, thus, in effect to stretch the image. This will distort a normal image and, thus, would appear not to be that useful. However, you would be wrong. Consider the example illustrated in Figure 29.6. The figure shows a simple form and a percentage scale.

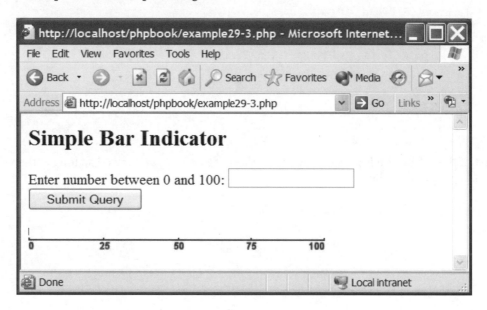

Figure 29.6 Simple bar indicator.

When the user enters a value between 0 and 100 on the form and clicks the submit button the value is illustrated on the bar scale, as shown in Figure 29.7.

Being able to create bar scales like this is very useful as it provides a graphical means to represent data on your Web page without having to create a new image from scratch. So how is it done? Consider the following source code:

```
<h2>Simple Bar Indicator</h2>
<form action='<?php echo($_SERVER['PHP_SELF']); ?>' method='post'>
Enter number between 0 and 100: <input type='text' name='scale'>
<input type='submit'>
</form>

<?php
```

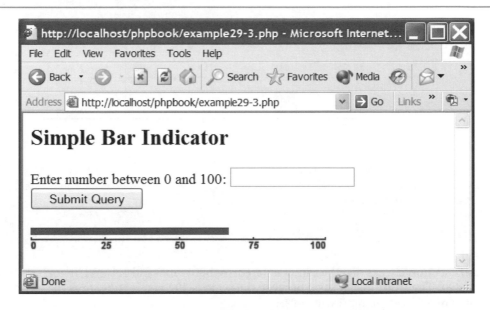

Figure 29.7 Bar set at 75%.

```
// Simple Images - Example 29-3
//---------------------

if(!isset($_POST['scale']))
     $scale = 0;
else
     $scale = $_POST['scale'];
if ($scale < 0)
     $scale=0;
elseif($scale >= 100)
     $scale=400;
else
     $scale=$scale*4;
echo("<img src='graphics/bluesquare.jpg' width='$scale'
height='10'>");
?>
<BR><img src='graphics/barscale.jpg'>
```

The program works by first requiring the creation of two images. The first is the barscale.jpg image and is a simple numerical scale. The second image is a simple 10×10 pixel Blue Square. These are illustrated in Table 29.2.

It is this image that we use to create the bar on the scale. Examining the script we see that the first section displays the form into which the user enters the value to be displayed:

Table 29.2 Bar images.

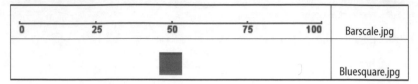

	Barscale.jpg
	Bluesquare.jpg

```
<h2>Simple Bar Indicator</h2>
<form action='<?php echo($_SERVER['PHP_SELF']); ?>' method='post'>
Enter number between 0 and 100: <input type='text' name='scale'>
<input type='submit'>
</form>
```

The next section checks that the values entered are between 0 and 100 and, if not, sets them to 0 or 400. The value of 400 is set because the scale is 400 pixels wide, thus the bar needs to be 400 pixels wide to represent 100%:

```
if(!isset($_POST['scale']))
        $scale = 0;
else
        $scale = $_POST['scale'];
if ($scale < 0)
        $scale=0;
elseif($scale >= 100)
        $scale=400;
```

If the value entered on the form is between 0 and 100, then the value is multiplied by four to scale up the entered value:

```
else
      $scale=$scale*4;
```

Next, the blue square image is displayed with its width adjusted to the value of $scale:

```
echo("<img src='graphics/bluesquare.jpg' width='$scale'
height='10'>");
?>
```

Finally, the bar scale graphic is displayed.

```
<BR><img src='graphics/barscale.jpg'>
```

Bar scales such as this are often used on Web pages to denote data in a graphical form obtained from databases or files. The dynamic nature of the graph enables the image to represent an up-to-date picture of the data.

Summary

This chapter has illustrated what PHP can accomplish by manipulating existing images. Although these are quite trivial examples, they can be really very effective. In the following chapter we shall continue examining the subject of image manipulation and introduce the PHP GD library which enables you to create your own images from scratch.

SUMMARY

GD Library 30

Introduction

The majority of Web pages contain images that are used to enhance the Web page appearance and usability. In the previous chapter we saw how PHP can be used to manipulate existing images. However, Web designers have to be careful when using images as to not to annoy the Web page user by overusing images and thus reducing accessibility.

PHP has a library of functions that allow us to create and manipulate images. Using PHP, images can be created and displayed using a very small number of lines of code. In this chapter we shall introduce some of the library of functions that are available. However, remember what we said about being careful with over using images. Just because PHP provides you with the facility to create and manipulate images doesn't mean that you have to!

Obtaining the GD Library

PHPs image manipulation library is provided by the GD library. This now comes as standard with the PHP installation for MS Windows (assuming that you download the binaries zip package and not the smaller installer file). However, you will need to edit your php.ini file to activate it. The php.ini file can be found in the c:\windows\ directory on a windows system. To activate the GD library you will need to open the php.ini file in an editor such as Notepad. You then need to find the following line in the file:

```
;extension=php_gd2.dll
```

To activate the library you simply need to remove the ; from start of the line and save the file. Figure 30.1 illustrates the php.ini file displayed in Notepad. You will also need to ensure that the extensions directory points to where your gd2.dll file resides on your computer. In our case:

```
extension_dir = "c:\Program Files\php\extensions\"
```

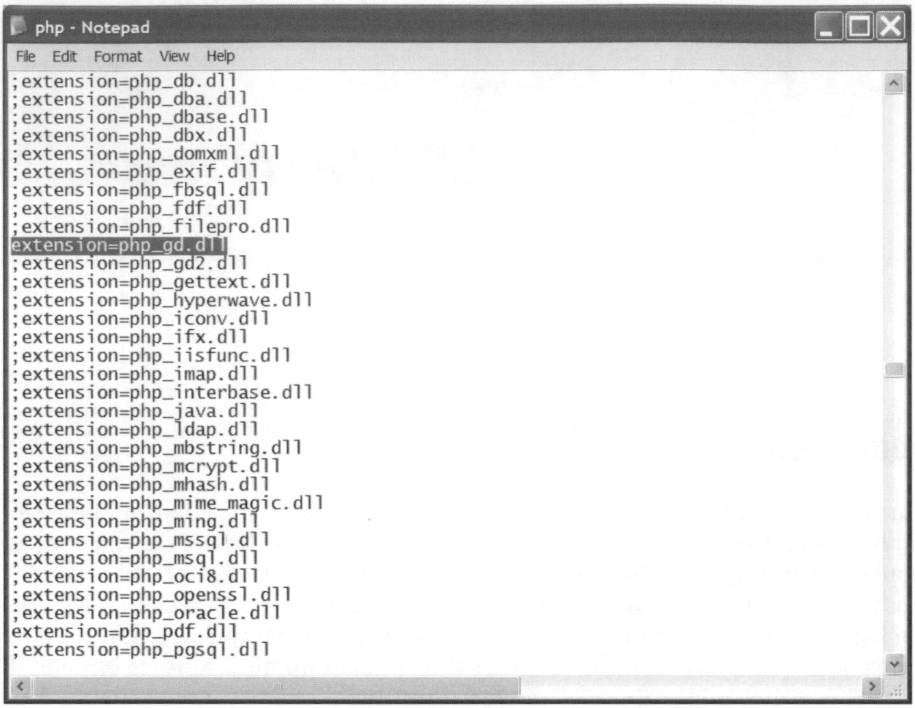


```
;extension=php_db.dll
;extension=php_dba.dll
;extension=php_dbase.dll
;extension=php_dbx.dll
;extension=php_domxml.dll
;extension=php_exif.dll
;extension=php_fbsql.dll
;extension=php_fdf.dll
;extension=php_filepro.dll
extension=php_gd.dll
;extension=php_gd2.dll
;extension=php_gettext.dll
;extension=php_hyperwave.dll
;extension=php_iconv.dll
;extension=php_ifx.dll
;extension=php_iisfunc.dll
;extension=php_imap.dll
;extension=php_interbase.dll
;extension=php_java.dll
;extension=php_ldap.dll
;extension=php_mbstring.dll
;extension=php_mcrypt.dll
;extension=php_mhash.dll
;extension=php_mime_magic.dll
;extension=php_ming.dll
;extension=php_mssql.dll
;extension=php_msql.dll
;extension=php_oci8.dll
;extension=php_openssl.dll
;extension=php_oracle.dll
extension=php_pdf.dll
;extension=php_pgsql.dll
```

Figure 30.1 The php.ini file.

GD Library Versions

Early versions of the GD library provided support for the creation of JPEG (Joint Photographics Experts Group) and GIF (Graphic Interchange Format) image formats. However, with the legal battle concerning the ownership of the GIF format, later versions of the GD library removed the support for GIF image creation and introduced support for the PNG (Portable Network Graphics), a file format designed for Web graphics. In this chapter we shall focus on the creation of JPEG and PNG images.

Creating a Basic JPEG Image

We shall begin by illustrating how to create a very simple JPEG image. In order to do this we need to introduce a number of GD library functions. The first of these is the ImageCreate() function:

Function prototype:

```
int ImageCreate(int x_size, int y_size);
```

Function arguments and return details:

Name	Type	Description
x	Int	Width of image in pixels
y	Int	Height of image in pixels
imageCreate() returns	Int	The ImageCreate() function returns an integer value, which is used to store the handle of the image

Function example:

```
$image = ImageCreate(100,100);
```

This will create a image 100×100 pixels in size. The next function is the ImageColorAllocate(), the format of which is:

Function prototype:

```
int ImageColorAllocate(int image, int red, int green, int blue);
```

Function arguments and return details:

Name	Type	Description
image	Int	Image handle obtained from function imageCreate
red	Int	Value specifying the amount of red used to form the colour. Values are between 0 and 255
green	Int	Value specifying the amount of green used to form the colour. Values are between 0 and 255
blue	Int	Value specifying the amount of blue used to form the colour. Values are between 0 and 255
imageColorAllocate() returns	Int	Returns a colour identifier to the colour we have specified

Function example:

```
$red = ImageColorAllocate($image,255,0,0);
```

This example creates the colour red which is stored in the variable $red.

Next, the ImageFill() function can be used to "flood-fill" the image with a particular colour:

Function prototype:

```
Int ImageFill(int image, int x, int y, int colour);
```

Function arguments and return details:

Name	Type	Description
image	Int	Image handle obtained from function imageCreate
x	Int	The X coordinate to begin floodfill
y	Int	The Y coordinate to begin floodfill
colour	Int	The colour to be used. This is received from the ImageColorAllocate function
imageFill() returns	Int	Returns "TRUE" if okay or "FALSE" if an error occurs

Function example:

```
ImageFill($image,0,0,$red);
```

This example will flood-fill our image $image, beginning at the top left-hand corner of the image with the colour specified with the variable $red.

Next we are ready to create and store the image. To do this we use the ImageJPEG() function:

Function prototype:

```
Int ImageJPEG(int image, string filename);
```

Function arguments and return details:

Name	Type	Description
image	Int	Image handle obtained from function imageCreate
filename	String	The file name of the image
imageJPEG() returns	Int	Returns "TRUE" or "FALSE" depending on whether the function was successful

Function example:

```
ImageJPEG($image,'redsquare.jpeg');
```

This example will create an image called redsquare.jpeg. Finally, the function ImageDestroy() is used to free up any memory used in the generation of the image. The format of this function is:

Function prototype:

```
Int ImageDestroy(int image);
```

Function arguments and return details:

Name	Type	Description
image	Int	Image handle obtained from function imageCreate
imageDestroy() returns	Int	Returns "TRUE" or "FALSE" depending on whether the function was successful

Function example:

```
ImageDestroy($image);
```

The following script lists all of these functions together to produce a simple image:

```
<?php

// GD Images - Example 30-1
//--------------------

$image = ImageCreate(100,100);
$red =ImageColorAllocate($image,255,0,0);
ImageFill ($image,0,0,$red);
ImageJPEG($image, 'graphics/redsquare.jpeg');
ImageDestroy($image);
?>
<img src='graphics/redsquare.jpeg'>
```

The output from the script is illustrated in something similar to that shown in Figure 30.2.

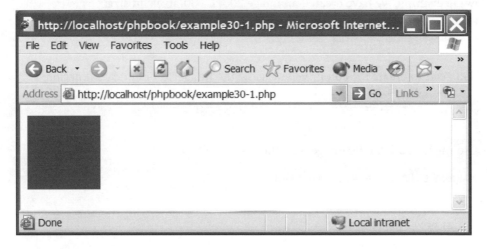

Figure 30.2 Simple JPEG image.

Checking the Web server directory where your .PHP files are stored will reveal that an image called redsquare.jpeg is present. This image is displayed on our Web page using the HTML element <img src="redsquare.jpeg">. The generated image can be viewed and edited using any graphics manipulation software you may have.

Creating a Basic PNG Image

The previous PHP program resulted in the creation of a JPEG image. If we want to create a PNG image then the program is very similar. In fact only one line of code changes as we need to use the ImagePNG() function:

Function prototypes:

```
Int ImagePNG(int image, string name);
```

Function arguments and return details:

Name	Type	Description
image	Int	Image handle obtained from function imageCreate
filename	String	The file name of the image
imagePNG() returns	Int	Returns "TRUE" or "FALSE" depending on whether the function was successful

Function example:

```
ImagePNG($image, 'yellowrectangle.png');
```

This example will create an image called yellowrectangle.png. To create a yellow rectangle we need to change the ImageCreate() function so that it does not create a square. In the following example we have created an image 200 × 100 pixels in size:

```
$image = ImageCreate(200,100);
```

We also need to create the colour yellow using the ImageColorAllocate function:

```
$yellow = ImageColorAllocate($image,255,255,0);
```

We also must flood-fill the image with the colour yellow:

```
ImageFill($image,0,0,$yellow);
```

Our script now looks like this:

```
<?php

// GD Images - Example 30-2
//---------------------

$image = ImageCreate(200,100);
$yellow = ImageColorAllocate($image,255,255,0);
ImageFill($image,0,0,$yellow);
ImagePNG($image, 'graphics/yellowrectangle.png');
ImageDestroy($image);
?>
<img src='graphics/yellowrectangle.png'>
```

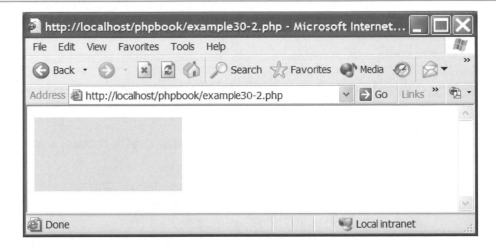

Figure 30.3 Simple PNG image.

Viewing the output from this script in a browser window should result in something similar to that shown in Figure 30.3.

An examination of the Web directory will result in the location of an image file labelled yellowrectangle.png.

Drawing Rectangles and Squares

The GD library contains two functions which allow you to create rectangles and squares on your image. These are ImageFilledRectangle() and ImageRectangle() which allow the creation of a solid rectangle or square and an outline rectangle or square. The format of these functions is:

Function prototypes:

```
Int ImageFilledRectangle(int image, int x1, int y1, int x2, int y2, int colour);
Int ImageRectangle(int image, int x1, int y1, int x2, int y2, int colour);
```

Function arguments and return details:

Name	Type	Description
image	Int	Image handle obtained from function imageCreate
x1	Int	The X coordinate of the top left-hand corner of the rectangle
y1	Int	The Y coordinate of the top left-hand corner of the rectangle
x2	Int	The X coordinate of the bottom right-hand corner of the rectangle
y2	Int	The Y coordinate of the bottom right-hand corner of the rectangle
colour	Int	Colour of the rectangle
imageFilledRectangle() returns imageRectangle() returns	Int	Returns "TRUE" or "FALSE" depending on whether the function was successful

Function example:

```
ImageFilledRectangle($image, 20, 20, 50, 50, $red);

ImageRectangle($image, 100, 20, 150, 150, $blue);
```

The following script uses these functions to create an image, which contains a rectangle and a square:

```php
<?php

// GD Images - Example 30-3
//---------------------

$image = ImageCreate(200,200);
$yellow = ImageColorAllocate($image,255,255,0);
$red = ImageColorAllocate($image,255,0,0);
$blue = ImageColorAllocate($image,0,0,255);
ImageFill($image,0,0,$yellow);
ImageFilledRectangle($image, 20, 20, 50, 50, $red);
ImageRectangle($image, 100, 20, 150, 150, $blue);
ImagePNG($image, 'graphics/rectangles.png');
ImageDestroy($image);
?>
<img src='graphics/rectangles.png'>
```

Viewing the output from this script should result in something similar to that illustrated in Figure 30.4.

Drawing Solid Lines

The function ImageLine() provides a means for drawing straight lines on our image. The format of the function is as follows:

Function prototype:

```
Int ImageLine(int image, int x1, int y1, int x2, int y2, int colour);
```

Function arguments and return details:

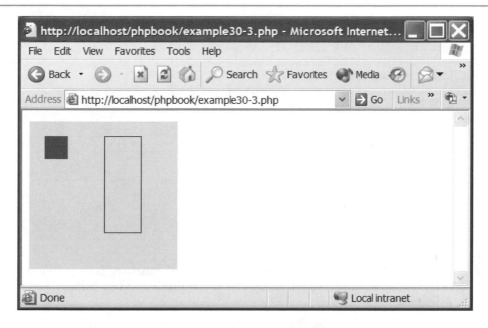

Figure 30.4 Rectangles and squares.

Name	Type	Description
image	Int	Image handle obtained from function imageCreate
x1	Int	The X coordinate of the top left-hand corner of the line
y1	Int	The Y coordinate of the top left-hand corner of the line
x2	Int	The X coordinate of the bottom right-hand corner of the line
y2	Int	The Y coordinate of the bottom right-hand corner of the line
colour	Int	Colour of the line
imageLine() returns	Int	Returns "TRUE" or "FALSE" depending on whether the function was successful

Function example:

```
ImageLine($image, 10,10,50,50,$red);
```

Consider the following script:

```
<?php

// GD Images - Example 30-4
//---------------------
```

```
$image = imagecreate(101,101);
$yellow = ImageColorAllocate($image,255,255,0);
$black = ImageColorAllocate($image,0,0,0);
ImageFill($image,0,0,$yellow);
for($x=0;$x<=100;$x+=10) {
      ImageLine($image,$x,0,$x,100,$black);
}
for($y=0;$y<=100;$y+=10) {
      ImageLine($image,0,$y,100,$y,$black);
}
ImagePNG($image, 'graphics/yellowgrid.png');
ImageDestroy($image);
?>
<img src='graphics/yellowgrid.png'>
```

This script illustrates an example of using the ImageLine() function. Let's examine this in more detail. First, an image is created using 101 × 101 pixels and two colours, yellow and black, are defined:

```
$image = imagecreate(101,101);
$yellow = ImageColorAllocate($image,255,255,0);
$black = ImageColorAllocate($image,0,0,0);
```

Next, the image is then filled with the colour yellow:

```
ImageFill($image,0,0,$yellow);
```

The next few lines of code use a for loop to create 11 lines which appear from top to bottom on the image, 10 pixels apart:

```
for($x=0;$x<=100;$x+=10) {
      ImageLine($image,$x,0,$x,100,$black);
}
```

The next few lines create 11 lines, which appear from left to right on the image, 10 pixels apart:

```
for($y=0;$y<=100;$y+=10) {
      ImageLine($image,0,$y,100,$y,$black);
}
```

Finally, the image is saved and the memory used to create the image released and the image is displayed:

```
ImagePNG($image, 'graphics/yellowgrid.png');
ImageDestroy($image);
?>
<img src='graphics/yellowgrid.png'>
```

The output produced from this program is shown in Figure 30.5.

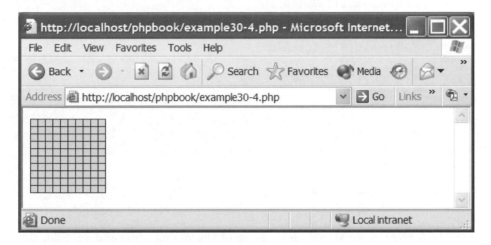

Figure 30.5 Drawing solid lines.

Drawing Dashed Lines

The ImageSetStyle() function is used in conjunction with the ImageLine() function to describe the format of the line. The format of the function is as follows.

Function prototype:

```
Int ImageSetStyle(int image, array style);
```

Function arguments and return details:

Name	Type	Description
image	Int	Image handle obtained from function imageCreate
style	Array	Array of pixels describing the line
imageSetStyle() returns	Int	Returns "TRUE" or "FALSE" depending on whether the function was successful

Function example:

```
ImageSetStyle ($image, $style);
```

The following script provides as example of the use of this function:

```php
<?php

// GD Images - Example 30-5
//--------------------

$image = imagecreate(100,100);
$lightblue = ImageColorAllocate($image,64,64,255);
$white = ImageColorAllocate($image,255,255,255);
ImageFill($image,0,0,$lightblue);

$style = array ($white, $lightblue);

ImageSetStyle($image,$style);
ImageLine($image,10,50,90,50,IMG_COLOR_STYLED);
ImageLine($image,50,10,50,90,IMG_COLOR_STYLED);
ImagePNG($image, 'graphics/bluedashed.png');
ImageDestroy($image);
?>
<img src='graphics/bluedashed.png'>
```

Note that the $style is defined as a simple array of alternating white and lightblue dots:

```php
$style = array ($white, $lightblue);
```

This is then defined as a style:

```php
ImageSetStyle($image,$style);
```

Finally, the imageLine function is called. This function knows to use the defined style through the IMG_COLOR_STYLED constant:

```php
ImageLine($image,10,50,90,50,IMG_COLOR_STYLED);
ImageLine($image,50,10,50,90,IMG_COLOR_STYLED);
```

Figure 30.6 illustrates the output produced by this script.

Inserting Text

The GD library supports functions that allow text to be inserted into an image. These are the ImageString() function that allows text to be inserted from left to right and the ImageStringUp() function that allows text to be inserted from top to bottom. The format of these functions is as follows:

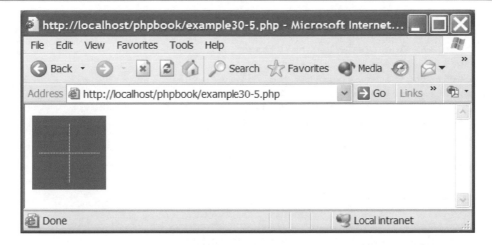

Figure 30.6 Drawing dashed lines.

Function prototypes:

Int ImageString(int image, int size, int x, int y, string text, int colour);

Int ImageStringUp(int image, int size, int x, int y, string text, int colour);

Function arguments and return details:

Name	Type	Description
image	Int	Image handle obtained from function imageCreate()
size	Int	The size of the text to be displayed
x	Int	The X coordinate of the top left-hand corner of the text
y	Int	The Y coordinate of the top left-hand corner of the text
text	String	The text to be displayed
colour	Int	Colour of the rectangle
imageString() and imageStringUp() returns	Int	Returns "TRUE" or "FALSE" depending on whether the function was successful

Function example:

```
ImageString($image,4,10,10,"Hello", $white);
```

The following script illustrates an example of the use of this function:

```php
<?php

// GD Images - Example 30-6
//---------------------
```

```
$image = imagecreate(100,100);
$darkred = ImageColorAllocate($image,192,0,0);
$white = ImageColorAllocate($image,255,255,255);
ImageFill($image,0,0,$darkred);
ImageString($image,4,10,10,"Hello", $white);
ImageString($image,3,10,25,"My", $white);
ImageString($image,2,10,40,"Name", $white);
ImageString($image,1,10,55,"is", $white);
ImageString($image,5,10,65,"Simon", $white);
ImagePNG($image, 'graphics/redtext.png');
ImageDestroy($image);
?>
<img src='graphics/redtext.png'>
```

Figure 30.7 illustrates the output produced by this script.

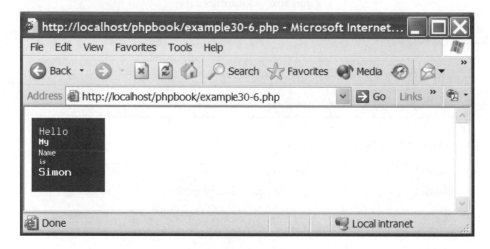

Figure 30.7 Image text.

As mentioned before, the ImageStringUp() function is similar to the ImageString() function. In fact, the parameters required are exactly the same. The following script illustrates an example of the use of this function:

```
<?php

// GD Images - Example 30-7
//--------------------

$image = imagecreate(100,100);
$darkred = ImageColorAllocate($image,192,0,0);
```

```
$white = ImageColorAllocate($image,255,255,255);
ImageFill($image,0,0,$darkred);
ImageStringUp($image,4,20,90,"Hello", $white);
ImageStringUp($image,4,40,70,"Simon", $white);
ImagePNG($image, 'graphics/redtextup.png');
ImageDestroy($image);
?>
<img src='graphics/redtextup.png'>
```

Figure 30.8 illustrates the output produced by this script.

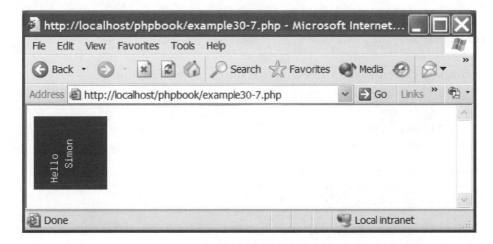

Figure 30.8 Image up text.

Displaying Individual Characters

In addition to being able to display strings of characters, two functions exist to display individual characters. These are the ImageChar() and ImageCharUp() functions and they operate in exactly the same way as the ImageString() and ImageStringUp() functions. The format of the functions is as follows:

Function prototypes:

Int ImageChar(int image, int size, int x, int y, char character, int colour);

Int ImageCharUp(int image, int size, int x, int y, char character, int colour);

Function arguments and return details:

Name	Type	Description
image	Int	Image handle obtained from function imageCreate()
size	Int	The size of the character to be displayed
x	Int	The X coordinate of the top left-hand corner of the character
y	Int	The Y coordinate of the top left-hand corner of the character
character	char	The character to be displayed
colour	Int	Colour of the rectangle
imageChar() and imageCharUp() returns	Int	Returns "TRUE" or "FALSE" depending on whether the function was successful

Function example:

```
ImageChar($image,4,20,70,"H", $white);

ImageCharUp($image,4,40,40,"S", $white);
```

The following script illustrates an example of the use of this function:

```php
<?php

// GD Images - Example 30-8
//---------------------

$image = imagecreate(100,100);
$black = ImageColorAllocate($image,0,0,0);
$white = ImageColorAllocate($image,255,255,255);
ImageFill($image,0,0,$black);
ImageChar($image,4,20,70,"H", $white);
ImageCharUp($image,4,40,40,"S", $white);
ImagePNG($image, 'graphics/blackchar.png');
ImageDestroy($image);
?>
<img src='graphics/blackchar.png'>
```

Figure 30.9 illustrates the output produced by this script.

Font Heights and Widths

Difference size fonts obviously have different size widths and heights and the fonts used in the GD library are no exception to this rule. The GD library has two functions, which you can use to determine the width and height of the font you are using. These functions are ImageFontWidth() and ImageFontHeight(). The format of the functions is as follows:

Function prototype:

```
int ImageFontWidth(int font);

int ImageFontHeight(int font);
```

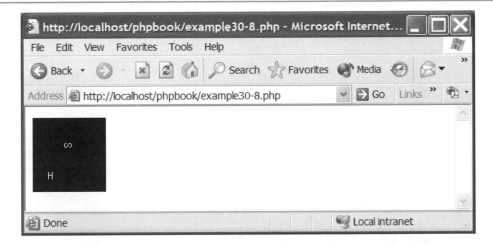

Figure 30.9 Outputting single characters.

Function arguments and return details:

Name	Type	Description
font	Int	The font size you check determine its pixel size
imageFontWidth() and imageFontHeight() return		Both functions return an integer value that is either the width or the height of the font in pixels

Function example:

```
$height = ImageFontHeight(4);
$width - ImageFontWidth( 4);
```

The following script illustrates an example of the use of this function:

```php
<?php

// GD Images - Example 30-9
//--------------------

$image = imagecreate(300,100);
$lightgrey = ImageColorAllocate($image,192,192,255);
$darkgreen = ImageColorAllocate($image,0,192,0);
ImageFill($image,0,0,$lightgrey);
$height = ImageFontHeight(4);
$width = ImageFontWidth(4);
$text = "The Height of this text is " . $width;
$text2 = "The Width of this text is " . $height;
ImageString($image,4,10,20,$text, $darkgreen);
```

```
ImageString($image,4,10,50,$text2, $darkgreen);
ImagePNG($image, 'graphics/fontheight.png');
ImageDestroy($image);
?>
<img src='graphics/fontheight.png'>
```

Figure 30.10 illustrates the output produced by this script.

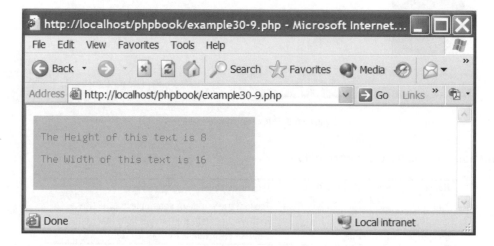

Figure 30.10 Obtaining the width and height of text.

Why would you want to know the height or width of the text you are displaying? Well, it allows you to place the text exactly on the image. A good example of this is shown next.

Centring Text

One of the uses of the ImageFontWidth() function is to allow us to centre text on the image. Consider the following script that illustrates the centring of text:

```
<?php

// GD Images - Example 30-10
//---------------------

$image = imagecreate(300,100);
$blue = ImageColorAllocate($image,0,0,255);
$yellow = ImageColorAllocate($image,255,255,0);
ImageFill($image,0,0,$blue);
$text = "This text is centered";
$width = ImageFontWidth(4) * strlen($text);
$x = (300 - $width)/2;
```

```
ImageString($image,4,$x,40,$text, $yellow);
ImagePNG($image, 'graphics/fontcentre.png');
ImageDestroy($image);
?>
<img src='graphics/fontcentre.png'>
```

Let's examine the important parts of this script, which enable us to centre our text. First, the text which is going to be displayed is stored in the variable string $text:

```
$text = "This text is centered";
```

You can change the text in this string to anything you wish. The next line calculates the width of the font using the ImageFontWidth() function and multiplies this value by the number of characters in the string obtained using the strlen() function. This is stored in the variable $width:

```
$width = ImageFontWidth(4) * strlen($text);
```

Variable $width now knows the exact length in pixels of the whole string. We now need to determine where to place this on our image in order to centre the text. To do this we need to know the width of the image which, in our example, is 300 pixels. We already know the width of the text. The only thing we need to do is to divide the difference between the two values by two to ensure that the text is placed in the centre of the image. This is illustrated in Figure 30.11.

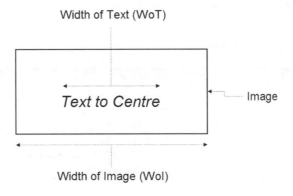

Figure 30.11 Centring text.

To calculate the centre position we subtract the width of the Image (WoI) from the width of Text (WoT) and then divide by two. The code to calculate the position of our X coordinate is:

```
$x = (300 - $width)/2;
```

Figure 30.12 illustrates the output produced by this program.

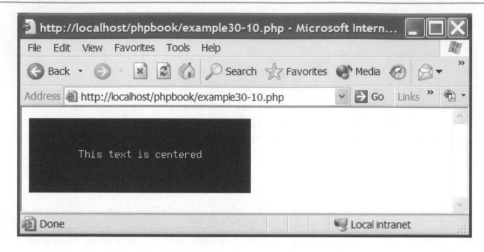

Figure 30.12 Centring text.

Creating Polygons

In addition to simple rectangles and squares, the GD library provides support for the creation of more complex polygons. The function ImagePolygon() is used to create these and the format of this function is as follows:

Function prototye:

```
int ImagePolygon(int image, array points, int number, int colour);
```

Function arguments and return details:

Name	Type	Description
image	Int	Image handle obtained from function imageCreate()
points	Array	The array which stores the image points
number	Int	The number of points making up the polygon
colour	Int	The colour of the polygon
imagePolygon() returns	Int	Returns "TRUE" or "FALSE" depending on whether the function was successful

Function example:

```
$coords =array(0,50,35,35,50,0,65,35,100,50,65,65,50,100,35,65);
ImagePolygon($image,$coords,8,$yellow);
```

Note, that in this example the polygon consists of eight points which are stored in the array $coords as eight X–Y pairs. The following script illustrates an example of the use of this function:

```
<?php

// GD Images - Example 30-11
//---------------------

$image = imagecreate(100,100);
$blue = ImageColorAllocate($image,0,0,255);
$yellow = ImageColorAllocate($image,255,255,0);
ImageFill($image,0,0,$blue);

$coords = array(0,50,35,35,50,0,65,35,100,50,65,65,50,100,35,65);
ImagePolygon($image,$coords,8,$yellow);
ImagePNG($image, 'graphics/star.png');
ImageDestroy($image);
?>
<img src='graphics/star.png'>
```

Figure 30.13 illustrates the output produced by this script.

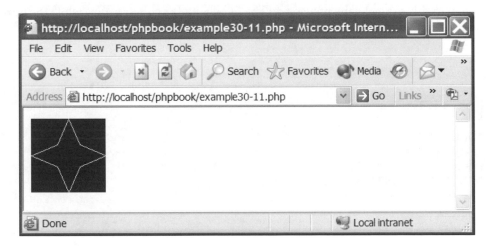

Figure 30.13 Creating a polygon.

Filling in Shapes

What if we wanted to create a polygon like the one shown previously which was not a simple outline but a solid colour? Unfortunately, there is no ImagePolygonFilled() function. However, there is something almost as good – the ImageFillToBorder() function. This function allows part of an image to be "flood-filled" with colour. A change in the background colour of the image signifies the extent to which the flood of colour will occur. The format of this function is as follows:

Function prototype:

```
Int ImageFilledToBorder(int Image, int x, int y, int borderColour, int colour);
```

Function arguments and return details:

Name	Type	Description
image	Int	Image handle obtained from function imageCreate
x	Int	The X coordinate of the start of the fill
y	Int	The Y coordinate of the start of the fill
borderColor	Int	The border colour at which to stop filling
colour	Int	Colour of the fill
imageFilledToBorder() returns	Int	Returns "TRUE" or "FALSE" depending on whether the function was successful

Function example:

```
ImageFillToBorder($image,50,50,$yellow,$red);
```

Note that, in this example, the polygon will be filled with the colour yellow while the border of the polygon will be red. The following script illustrates an example of the use of this function:

```php
<?php

// GD Images - Example 30-12
//---------------------

$image = imagecreate(100,100);
$blue = ImageColorAllocate($image,0,0,255);
$yellow = ImageColorAllocate($image,255,255,0);
$red = ImageColorAllocate($image,255,0,0);
ImageFill($image,0,0,$blue);

$coords = array(0,50,35,35,50,0,65,35,100,50,65,65,50,100,35,65);
ImagePolygon($image,$coords,8,$yellow);
ImageFillToBorder($image,50,50,$yellow,$red);
ImagePNG($image, 'graphics/filledstar.png');
ImageDestroy($image);
?>
<img src='graphics/filledstar.png'>
```

Figure 30.14 illustrates the output produced by this script.

Creating New Images from Existing Ones

When using the GD library you don't have to begin creating your image from scratch. You can load an existing image and modify it. Support is provided for three different

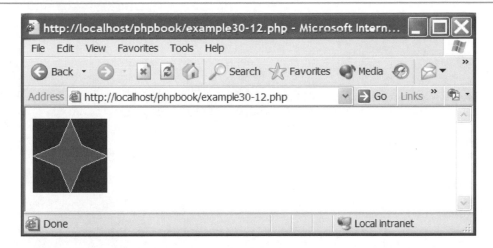

Figure 30.14 Flood-filled polygon.

image formats: JPEG, GIF and PNG with the functions: ImageCreateFromJPEG(), ImageCreateFromGIF() and ImageCreateFromPNG(). The format of these functions are the same and are:

Function prototypes:

```
int ImageCreateFromJPEG(string filename);

int ImageCreateFromGIF(string filename);

int ImageCreateFromPNG(string filename);
```

Function arguments and return details:

Name	Type	Description
filename	String	The file name of the image as the basis of your new image
imageCreateFromGIF()	Int	The function returns an integer value, which is used to
imageCreateFromPNG()		store the handle of the image, in the same way as the
imageCreateFromJPEG()		ImageCreate() function
returns		

Function example:

```
$image = ImageCreateFromJPEG("palm.jpeg");$image =
ImageCreateFromJPEG("palm.jpeg");
```

The following script illustrates an example of the use of the ImageCreateFromJPEG function:

```php
<?php

// GD Images - Example 30-13
//---------------------

$image = ImageCreateFromJPEG("graphics/palm.jpeg");
$blue = ImageColorAllocate($image,0,0,255);

$text = "Welcome to Aruba!";
$width = ImageFontWidth(4) * strlen($text);
$x = (300 - $width)/2;
ImageString($image,4,$x,330,$text, $blue);
ImagePNG($image, 'graphics/palm.png');
ImageDestroy($image);
?>
<img src='graphics/palm.png'>
```

Figure 30.15 illustrates the output produced by this script.

Okay, so we can modify an existing image but what real use could be made of being able to do this? Well, one example is illustrated in the following section.

Creating "Magic" Buttons

In this example we illustrate how using an existing image we can create new images which may be of use. The basic concept here is that if you imagine that you have a Web page, which has a number of buttons already on it that the user can click on to jump to further pages of information. Consider, however, if you wanted to give your users the ability to modify the text on the buttons so that they could customize their view of your Web page. To do this we start by creating a blank button graphic, see Figure 30.16.

We then created a script that uses a simple form to demonstrate the creation of these buttons dynamically. The script allows the user to type some text into a form field that is then centred on a button. The more times they enter text and click the form submit button the more text buttons they create. Here is the script:

```php
<?php

// GD Images - Example 30-14
//---------------------

if(isset($_POST['text']))
        $text = $_POST['text'];
else
        $text = "";

if(!isset($_POST['count']))
        $count=1;
else
```

Figure 30.15 Modifying an existing image.

Figure 30.16 Blank button.

```
        $count = $_POST['count'];

if($text == "reset")
        $count=1;
else {
        $image = ImageCreateFromJPEG("graphics/button.jpg");
        $blue = ImageColorAllocate($image,0,0,255);
        $width = ImageFontWidth(4) * strlen($text);
        $x = (200 - $width)/2;
        ImageString($image,4,$x,15,$text, $blue);
        $name = "graphics/button" . $count . ".png";
        ImagePNG($image, $name);
        ImageDestroy($image);
}
echo("<form method='post' action='" . $_SERVER['PHP_SELF'] . "'>");
echo("Enter Text: <input type='text' name='text'>");
echo("<input type='hidden' name='count' value='" . ++$count . "'>");
echo("<input type='submit'>");
echo("</form>");
for($a=2;$a<$count;$a++)
echo("<img src='graphics/button" . $a . ".png'>");
?>
```

Let's examine the script in a little more detail. The first few lines check the value of text which is used to store the text for the button:

```
if(isset($_POST['text']))
        $text = $_POST['text'];
else
        $text = "";
```

The next few lines of code check to see if the variable $count exists and, if not, sets this to one. Variable $count is used to store how many buttons have been created:

```
if(!isset($_POST['count']))
        $count=1;
else
        $count = $_POST['count'];
```

The next couple of lines check to see if the value of $text is equal to "reset". The variable $text is used to hold the text entered via the form and is used to create the text placed on the button. If the user types "reset", then the number of buttons created is set back to one allowing the user to begin again:

```
if($text == "reset")
     $count=1;
else {
```

If the value of the variable $text was anything other than "reset", then the button image is created:

```
$image = ImageCreateFromJPEG("graphics/button.jpg");
$blue = ImageColorAllocate($image,0,0,255);
$width = ImageFontWidth(4) * strlen($text);
$x = (200 - $width)/2;
ImageString($image,4,$x,15,$text, $blue);
$name = "graphics/button" . $count . ".png";
ImagePNG($image, $name);
ImageDestroy($image);
```

Next the input form is output allowing interaction with the user:

```
echo("<form method='post' action='" . $_SERVER['PHP_SELF'] .
"'>");
echo("Enter Text: <input type='text' name='text'>");
echo("<input type='hidden' name='count' value='" . ++$count .
"'>");
echo("<input type='submit'>");
echo("</form>");
```

Finally, a for loop is used to display all the buttons which have been created:

```
for($a=2;$a<$count;$a++)
     echo("<img src='graphics/button" . $a . ".png'>");
?>
```

Figure 30.17 illustrates some example output produced by this script. In this screen shot three buttons have already been created by the user.

Using Circles, Ellipses and Arcs

The ImageArc function can be used to produce circles, ellipses, semi-circles and arcs. The format of this function is as follows.

Function prototype:

```
Int ImageArc(int $image, int centreX, int centreY, int width, int height, int startDegree, int
endDegree, int colour);
```

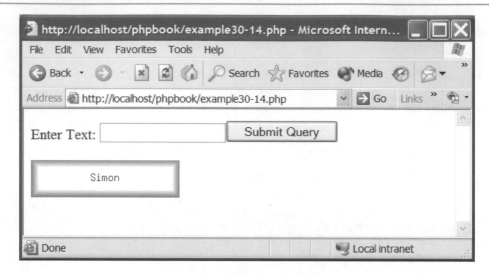

Figure 30.17 Output from magic buttons.

Function arguments and return details:

Name	Type	Description
image	Int	Image handle obtained from function imageCreate
centreX	Int	The X coordinate of the centre of the circle or ellipse
centreY	Int	The Y coordinate of the centre of the circle or ellipse
width	Int	Width of the circle or ellipse
height	Int	Height of the circle or ellipse
startDegree	Int	Start drawing from this degree
endDegree	Int	End drawing at this degree
colour	Int	The colour of the circle or ellipse
imageArc() returns	Int	Returns "TRUE" or "FALSE" depending on whether the function was successful

Function example:

```
ImageArc($image,150,150,100,100,0,360,$darkblue);
```

When drawing a circle, ellipse or an arc, you need to specify the starting degree and finishing degree. Imagine you wished to create a complete circle. Well, the start degree would be zero and the finishing degree would be 360 as you want a complete circle. If, however, you wanted to draw a half circle then you may specify that the start degree is 90 and the finishing degree would be 270. The following script illustrates an example of the use of the ImageArc function:

```php
<?php

// GD Images - Example 30-15
//---------------------

$image = ImageCreate(300,300);
$darkblue = ImageColorAllocate($image,0,0,192);
$white = ImageColorAllocate($image,255,255,255);
ImageFill($image,0,0,$white);
ImageArc($image,150,150,100,100,0,360,$darkblue);
ImageArc($image,50,50,100,50,0,360,$darkblue);
ImageArc($image,50,150,50,100,90,270,$darkblue);
ImagePNG($image, 'graphics/circle.png');
ImageDestroy($image);
?>
<img src='graphics/circle.png'>
```

Figure 30.18 illustrates some example output produced by this script.

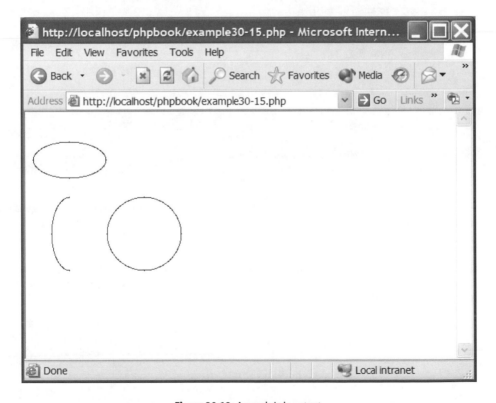

Figure 30.18 Arc and circle output.

Producing Random "Bubbles"

The ImageArc() function can be used to produce some very interesting effects. One simple example of its use is shown in the following script:

```php
<?php

// GD Images - Example 30-16
//---------------------

$image = ImageCreate(300,300);
$lightblue = ImageColorAllocate($image,64,64,255);
$blue = ImageColorAllocate($image,0,50,255);
$darkblue = ImageColorAllocate($image,0,0,192);
$cols = array($lightblue,$blue,$darkblue);
$white = ImageColorAllocate($image,255,255,255);
ImageFill($image,0,0,$white);
srand((double)microtime() * 1000000);

for ($dots=1;$dots<100;$dots++){
      $posx = rand(0,300);
      $posy = rand(0,300);
      $size = rand(10,30);
      $col = rand(0,2);
      ImageArc($image,$posx,$posy,$size,$size,0,360,$cols[$col]);

}
ImagePNG($image, 'graphics/bubbles.png');
ImageDestroy($image);
?>
<img src='graphics/bubbles.png'>
```

This script produces an image which consists of randomly placed circles. The image could be used (if it were improved a little) as a random backdrop to a Web page for example. For now though, we have chosen simply to generate the image and display this on the Web. The output from the script is shown in Figure 30.19.

Let's have a closer look at how this program works. The first few lines of code should be very familiar to you and they simply create an image 300 × 300 pixels in size, define a few colours to use and fill the image with the colour white:

```php
$image = ImageCreate(300,300);
$lightblue = ImageColorAllocate($image,64,64,255);
$blue = ImageColorAllocate($image,0,50,255);
$darkblue = ImageColorAllocate($image,0,0,192);
$cols = array($lightblue,$blue,$darkblue);
$white = ImageColorAllocate($image,255,255,255);
ImageFill($image,0,0,$white);
```

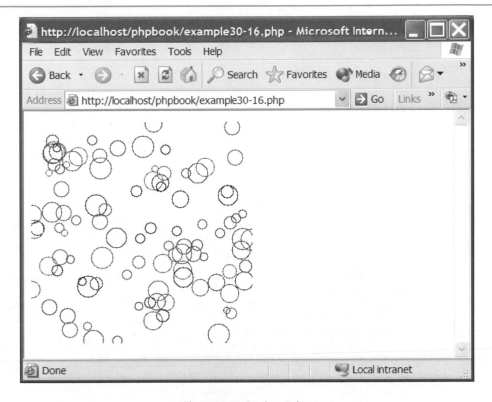

Figure 30.19 Random circles.

The next line of code is used to "seed" the random number generator:

```
srand((double)microtime() * 1000000);
```

The next few lines of code use a for loop to generate 100 circles. Each circle has random *X* and *Y* coordinates on the image together with a random size and colour. The rand() function is used to produce the random numbers. It requires two parameters – the minimum and maximum random numbers it should produce:

```
for ($dots=1;$dots<100;$dots++){
    $posx = rand(0,300);
    $posy = rand(0,300);
    $size = rand(10,30);
    $col = rand(0,2);
    ImageArc($image,$posx,$posy,$size,$size,0,360,$cols[$col]);

}
```

Finally, the image is stored and all memory used in its creation is released:

```
ImagePNG($image, 'graphics/bubbles.png');
ImageDestroy($image);
```

Repetitive Patterns

In this section we illustrate what can be produced with a simple program, a random number and a basic set of rules. The following script doesn't introduce any new functions or concepts – it is simply an illustration of what can be produced:

```php
<?php

// GD Images - Example 30-17
//--------------------

$image = ImageCreate(251,251);
$blue = ImageColorAllocate($image,0,50,255);
$white = ImageColorAllocate($image,255,255,255);
ImageFill($image,0,0,$white);
srand((double)microtime() * 1000000);

$x = array(125,250,0);
$y = array(0,250,250);

ImageLine($image,$x[0],$y[0],$x[1],$y[1],$blue);
ImageLine($image,$x[1],$y[1],$x[2],$y[2],$blue);
ImageLine($image,$x[2],$y[2],$x[0],$y[0],$blue);

$lx=0;
$ly=0;
$count=0;
while ($count < 10000) {
      $count++;
      $rand = rand(0,2);
      $nx = ($x[$rand] - $lx) / 2;
      $ny = ($y[$rand] - $ly) / 2;
      ImageLine($image,$lx+$nx,$ly+$ny,$lx+$nx,$ly+$ny,$blue);
      $lx = $lx+$nx;
      $ly = $ly+$ny;
}

ImagePNG($image, 'graphics/triangle.png');
ImageDestroy($image);
?>
<img src='graphics/triangle.png'>
```

This program produces output similar to that shown in Figure 30.20.

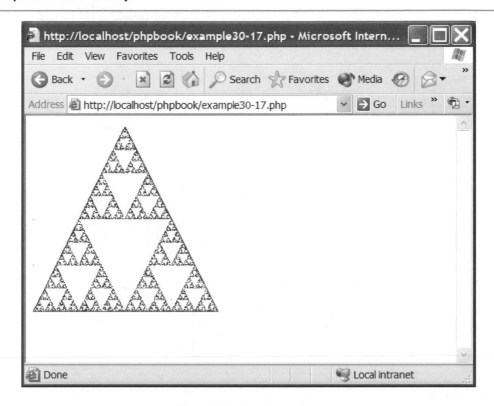

Figure 30.20 Repetitive patterns.

Let's examine this script a little more closely and see how the image shown in Figure 30.20 was formed. The first few lines of code define a image of 251×251 pixels and create some colours to use. The image is filled with white and the random number generator is seeded:

```
$image = ImageCreate(251,251);
$blue = ImageColorAllocate($image,0,50,255);
$white = ImageColorAllocate($image,255,255,255);
ImageFill($image,0,0,$white);
srand((double)microtime() * 1000000);
```

Next, two arrays of X and Y coordinates are created and their contents are used by three ImageLine functions to create the outline triangle on our image:

```
$x = array(125,250,0);
$y = array(0,250,250);

ImageLine($image,$x[0],$y[0],$x[1],$y[1],$blue);
ImageLine($image,$x[1],$y[1],$x[2],$y[2],$blue);
ImageLine($image,$x[2],$y[2],$x[0],$y[0],$blue);
```

Next, a while loop is used to generate a line (which is actually only one pixel long) on the image. This results in the geometric pattern being produced:

```
$lx=0;
$ly=0;
$count=0;
while ($count < 10000) {
        $count++;
        $rand = rand(0,2);
        $nx = ($x[$rand] - $lx) / 2;
        $ny = ($y[$rand] - $ly) / 2;
        ImageLine($image,$lx+$nx,$ly+$ny,$lx+$nx,$ly+$ny,$blue);
        $lx = $lx+$nx;
        $ly = $ly+$ny;
}
```

Finally, the image is stored and the memory released:

```
ImagePNG($image, 'graphics/triangle.png');
ImageDestroy($image);
```

Summary

This chapter has introduced the GD library and shown how images can be created from scratch and how images that already exist can be modified. Once you have grasped the basics of the function library you should be able to produce some very complex images should you so wish. We have provided some examples of what effects can be produced using the library and, in the following chapter, we shall explain how the techniques and functions learnt in this chapter can be used to create a useful dynamic graphical image.

A Useful Dynamic Image 31

Introduction

In the previous chapter we introduced the GD library and illustrated some of the many functions available for graphic creation and manipulation. We also provided some examples of the use of the library in terms of how the functions could be put to use for dynamic Web-page development. In this chapter, however, we present a complete application that makes use of many of the library functions introduced in the previous chapter.

We shall begin by introducing our application, providing some examples of what it can do and then walk you through the script explaining how the application was developed.

An Introduction to the Image

So what does this script do? Well, the script is capable of generating simple bar graphs. An example of what can be produced is illustrated in Figure 31.1. The image is generated by invoking a function called graph. The graph function is configurable enabling the user to determine the actual size of the bar graph produced, the colours used, titles and labelling text as well as the data values it displays. This versatile function can, therefore, be used to display a variety of different types of data dynamically on your Web site.

Why would you want to do this? Well, you may wish to present graphically the number of new users accessing the site month by month or it could be Web site users' responses to a series of questions from a questionnaire.

While the data displayed on this graph are static, you will learn in later chapters how to interface PHP to databases. This will allow you to obtain data via a Web form, store this in a database and then retrieve these data and display them using our graph function.

But for now let's examine the example screen shot in Figure 31.1. This example illustrates a graph displaying 12 monthly values. The graph is 300×200 pixels in size. The scale of the graph is automatically calculated and has the range 0–100.

Figure 31.2 illustrates another graph produced using the same graph function. This example illustrates five values representing quality of service. The size of this graph is 250×200 pixels and once again the scale of the graph is automatically created, producing a scale of 0–1456.

Finally, Figure 31.3 illustrates another bar-graph example, consisting of two data values. These represent responses to a yes–no style question.

All three examples illustrate the fact that the developer has control over the size of the graph image, the colours used, the labels displayed and the data values used to create the bars.

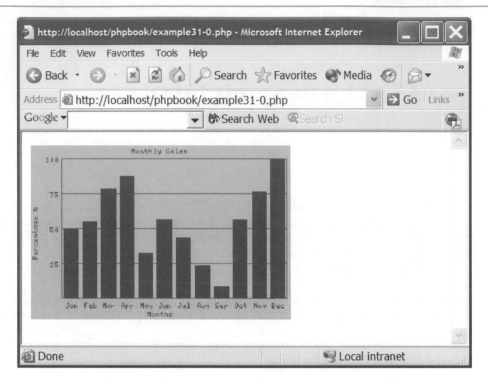

Figure 31.1 Monthly bar graph – Example 1.

We shall continue this chapter by examining how the graph function was created. We have broken the final design down into smaller easier-to-understand pieces and we shall examine each of these in turn, resulting in the creation of the complete application.

Creating a Scalable Coloured Background

We shall begin the development of our graph by designing the parts of our function that allow us to create the graph image and colour it. Our graph function initially looks like this:

```php
<?php

function graph($name,$w,$h,$bgc) {
    $image = ImageCreate($w,$h);
    $cols = colours($image);
    ImageFill($image,0,0,$cols[$bgc]);
    ImageJPEG($image, $name);
    ImageDestroy($image);
}
```

The function has been written to receive four parameters: the name of the image to be created, its width, its height and the colour of the background:

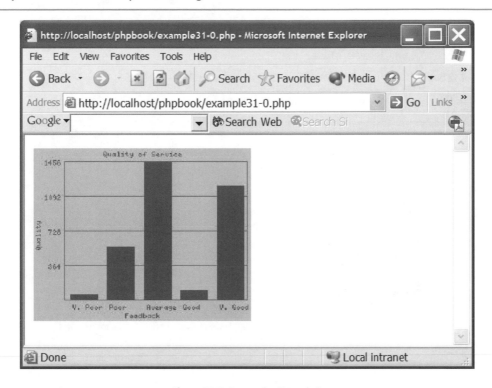

Figure 31.2 Bar graph – Example 2.

```
function graph($name,$w,$h,$bgc) {
```

Next, the ImageCreate() function is invoked to create the image using the width and height values stored in $w and $h:

```
$image = ImageCreate($w,$h);
```

A function called colours() is invoked. This returns an array of colours, which have been defined for use with the image. The defined colours are stored in the array $cols:

```
$cols = colours($image);
```

The image background is created using the ImageFill() function. Note that the cols array used is subscripted using the $bgc variable which stores the background colour of the image:

```
ImageFill($image,0,0,$cols[$bgc]);
```

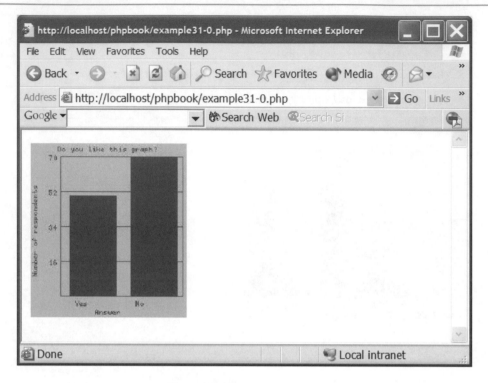

Figure 31.3 Bar graph – Example 3.

Finally, the graph function is completed by creating the image using the value stored in $name and the memory freed:

```
ImageJPEG($image, $name);
ImageDestroy($image);
```

The function colours is used to create an array of colour definitions for use with the image. By providing a value from 0 to 14 the user can refer to a particular colour stored in the array:

```
function colours($image) {
    $white = ImageColorAllocate($image,255,255,255);
    $black = ImageColorAllocate($image,0,0,0);
    $lightblue = ImageColorAllocate($image,64,64,255);
    $blue = ImageColorAllocate($image,0,0,255);
    $darkblue = ImageColorAllocate($image,0,0,192);
    $red = ImageColorAllocate($image,255,0,0);
    $lightred = ImageColorAllocate($image,255,64,64);
    $darkred = ImageColorAllocate($image,192,0,0);
    $green = ImageColorAllocate($image,0,255,0);
    $lightgreen = ImageColorAllocate($image,64,255,64);
```

```
    $darkgreen = ImageColorAllocate($image,0,192,0);
    $yellow = ImageColorAllocate($image,255,255,0);
    $grey = ImageColorAllocate($image,192,192,192);
    $darkgrey = ImageColorAllocate($image,128,128,128);
    $lightgrey = ImageColorAllocate($image,192,192,255);
    $cols =
array($white,$black,$lightblue,$blue,$darkblue,$red,$lightred,
$darkred,$green,$lightgreen,$darkgreen,$yellow,$grey,
$darkgrey,$lightgrey);
    return $cols;
}
```

The graph function is invoked with a simple function call. The values passed to the function are "graph.jpeg" which is the name of our image, 200 and 150 which are the width and heights and 14 which is the background colour which corresponds to lightgrey:

```
graph("graphics/graph.jpeg", 200, 150, 14);


?>
<img src='graphics/graph.jpeg'>
```

So, far our completed graph script is as follows:

```
<?php

// GD Graph - Example 31-1
//---------------------

function graph($name,$w,$h,$bgc) {
        $image = ImageCreate($w,$h);
        $cols = colours($image);
        ImageFill($image,0,0,$cols[$bgc]);
        ImageJPEG($image, $name);
        ImageDestroy($image);
}

function colours($image) {
        $white = ImageColorAllocate($image,255,255,255);
        $black = ImageColorAllocate($image,0,0,0);
        $lightblue = ImageColorAllocate($image,64,64,255);
        $blue = ImageColorAllocate($image,0,0,255);
        $darkblue = ImageColorAllocate($image,0,0,192);
        $red = ImageColorAllocate($image,255,0,0);
        $lightred = ImageColorAllocate($image,255,64,64);
        $darkred = ImageColorAllocate($image,192,0,0);
```

```
        $green = ImageColorAllocate($image,0,255,0);
        $lightgreen = ImageColorAllocate($image,64,255,64);
        $darkgreen = ImageColorAllocate($image,0,192,0);
        $yellow = ImageColorAllocate($image,255,255,0);
        $grey = ImageColorAllocate($image,192,192,192);
        $darkgrey = ImageColorAllocate($image,128,128,128);
        $lightgrey = ImageColorAllocate($image,192,192,255);
        $cols =
array($white,$black,$lightblue,$blue,$darkblue,$red,$lightred,
$darkred,$green,$lightgreen,$darkgreen,$yellow,$grey,$darkgrey,
$lightgrey);
        return $cols;
}

graph("graphics/graph.jpeg", 200, 150, 14);

?>
<img src='graphics/graph.jpeg'>
```

The output produced from this program is shown in Figure 31.4.

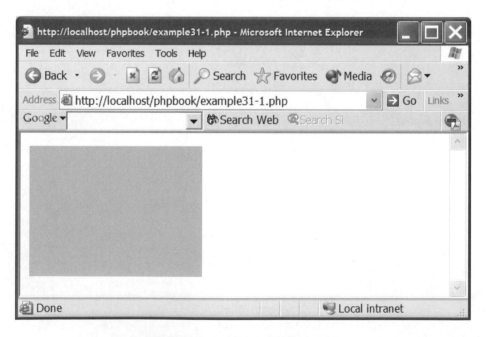

Figure 31.4 Graph Part 1 – scalable image.

Creating the Graph Axis and Horizontal Rules

The next stage of our graph script involves the creation of a border marking the axis of the bar graph and some horizontal rules. The first modifications to our script are to the graph function where the number of parameters is increased to allow the user to specify the foreground colour:

```
function graph($name,$w,$h,$bgc,$fgc) {
```

Next, four variables are added to the beginning of the graph function to define the top, right, left and bottom boarders of our graph:

```
$top=15;
$right=5;
$left=35;
$bottom=25;
```

Next, following the ImageFill() function call within the graph function, two new function calls are inserted:

```
drawAxis($image,$w,$h,$cols[$fgc],$top,$right,$left,$bottom);
drawLines($image,$w,$h,$cols[$fgc],$top,$right,$left,$bottom);
```

These two functions will produce the graph axis and the horizontal dashed lines on our graph. Both functions are passed the image handle, width, height, foreground colour and border variables. That's all the changes we need to make to the graph function. However, we still need to create the two functions drawAxis() and drawDashedLines(). Function drawAxis() is the most simple and uses its parameters to draw the axis of the graph as a simple rectangle:

```
function drawAxis($image, $w, $h, $col, $top,$right,$left,$bottom) {
    ImageRectangle($image,$left,$top,$w-$right,$h-$bottom,$col);
}
```

Function drawDashedLines() is a little more complex. It first calculates the height of the graph itself taking into account the top and bottom borders. It then calculates the spacing between the dashed lines, the value of which is stored in the variable $space. Finally, it uses a for loop to display the four lines on the graph:

```
function drawLines($image, $w, $h, $col, $top,$right,$left,$bottom) {
    $gHeight = $h - ($top + $bottom);
    $space = $gHeight / 4;
    $y = $top;
```

```
    for($a=1;$a<5;$a++) {
        ImageLine($image,$left,$y,$w-$right,$y,$col);
        $y=$y+$space;
    }
}
```

The graph function invocation needs to have an additional parameter to specify the foreground colour which, in this case, is lightblue:

```
graph("graphics/graph.jpeg", 200, 150, 14, 2);
```

The script so far now follows:

```php
<?php

// GD Graph - Example 31-2
//---------------------

function graph($name,$w,$h,$bgc,$fgc) {
    $top=15;
    $right=5;
    $left=35;
    $bottom=25;
    $image = ImageCreate($w,$h);
    $cols = colours($image);
    ImageFill($image,0,0,$cols[$bgc]);
    drawAxis($image,$w,$h,$cols[$fgc],$top,$right,$left,$bottom);
    drawLines($image,$w,$h,$cols[$fgc],$top,$right,$left,$bottom);
    ImageJPEG($image, $name);
    ImageDestroy($image);
}

function colours($image) {
    $white = ImageColorAllocate($image,255,255,255);
    $black = ImageColorAllocate($image,0,0,0);
    $lightblue = ImageColorAllocate($image,64,64,255);
    $blue = ImageColorAllocate($image,0,0,255);
    $darkblue = ImageColorAllocate($image,0,0,192);
    $red = ImageColorAllocate($image,255,0,0);
    $lightred = ImageColorAllocate($image,255,64,64);
    $darkred = ImageColorAllocate($image,192,0,0);
    $green = ImageColorAllocate($image,0,255,0);
    $lightgreen = ImageColorAllocate($image,64,255,64);
    $darkgreen = ImageColorAllocate($image,0,192,0);
    $yellow = ImageColorAllocate($image,255,255,0);
```

```
    $grey = ImageColorAllocate($image,192,192,192);
    $darkgrey = ImageColorAllocate($image,128,128,128);
    $lightgrey = ImageColorAllocate($image,192,192,255);
    $cols =
array($white,$black,$lightblue,$blue,$darkblue,$red,$lightred,
$darkred,$green,$lightgreen,$darkgreen,$yellow,$grey,$darkgrey,
$lightgrey);
    return $cols;
}


function drawAxis($image, $w, $h, $col, $top,$right,$left,$bottom) {
    ImageRectangle($image,$left,$top,$w-$right,$h-$bottom,$col);
}


function drawLines($image, $w, $h, $col, $top,$right,$left,$bottom) {
    $gHeight = $h - ($top + $bottom);
    $space = $gHeight / 4;
    $y = $top;
    for($a=1;$a<5;$a++) {
        ImageLine($image,$left,$y,$w-$right,$y,$col);
        $y=$y+$space;
    }
}


graph("graphics/graph.jpeg", 200, 150, 14, 2);

?>
<img src='graphics/graph.jpeg'>
```

The output from the graph function is shown in Figure 31.5.

Creating the Title and Axis Labels

The next stage is to include the title and X- and Y-axis labels. The graph function is modified to include three additional parameters: the title and the two labels:

```
function graph($name,$w,$h,$bgc,$fgc,$title,$xtitle,$ytitle) {
```

Next, a function call in included below the invocation of the drawLines() function which will display these labels:

```
drawTitles($image,$w,$h,$cols[$fgc],$title,$xtitle,$ytitle);
```

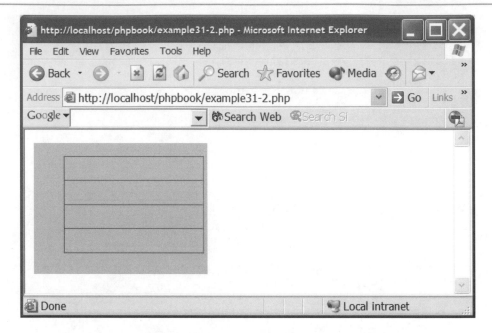

Figure 31.5 Graph Part 2 – border and horizontal rules.

The drawTitles() function must be included. This function calculates the length of the title and two labels and displays them centrally in set positions on the image. No check is made to ensure that the text will fit. It is assumed that the developer will make sure that the graph is large enough to display the titles and labels:

```
function drawTitles($image,$w,$h,$col,$title,$xtitle,$ytitle){
    $width = ImageFontWidth(1) * strlen($title);
    $x = ($w - $width)/2;
    ImageString($image,1,$x,3,$title,$col);
    $width = ImageFontWidth(1) * strlen($ytitle);
    $x = ($w - $width)/2;
    ImageString($image,1,$x,$h-10,$ytitle,$col);
    $height = ImageFontWidth(1) * strlen($xtitle);
    $y = ($h - $height)/2;
    ImageStringUp($image,1,1,$y+$height,$xtitle,$col);
}
```

Finally, the invocation of the graph function is modified to include the three extra parameters:

```
graph("graphics/graph.jpeg", 200, 150, 14,2,"Total Number of
Sales","Sales
£","Weekdays");
```

The output from the graph function is shown in Figure 31.6.

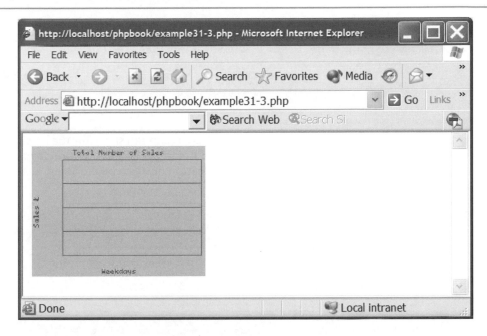

Figure 31.6 Graph Part 3 – title and labels.

Creating the *X*-axis Data Labels

To create the *X*-axis labels we need to add two new parameters to the graph function. These are the number of data labels (and forthcoming data items) and an array containing the labels themselves:

```
function graph($name,$w,$h,$bgc,$fgc,$title,$xtitle,$ytitle,$numX,
$xTitles) {
```

A function call is included below the invocation of the drawTitles() function which will display these labels:

```
drawXLables($image,$w,$h,$right,$left,$cols[$fgc],$numX,$xTitles);
```

The function drawXLables() needs to be included. This function calculates the spacing between each of the labels and then using a for loop outputs them on the graph:

```
function drawXLables($image,$w,$h,$right,$left,$col,$numX,$xTitles) {
    $graphWidth = $w - ($right+$left);
    $spacing = $graphWidth/$numX;
    $x = $left + ($spacing/4);
```

```
    for($a=0;$a<$numX;$a++) {
        ImageString($image,1,$x,$h-20,$xTitles[$a],$col);
        $x=$x+$spacing;
    }
}
```

Once again it is the developer who must check that there is enough space for the labels to fit across the graph. Finally, an array needs to be defined before the graph function invocation to contain the *X*-axis labels. The graph function invocation needs to be modified to include the number of labels and the array:

```
$xTitles = array("Mon","Tue","Wed","Thu","Fri");
graph("graph.jpeg", 200, 150, 14,2,"Total Number of Sales","Sales
£","Weekdays",5,$xTitles);
```

The output from the graph function is shown in Figure 31.7.

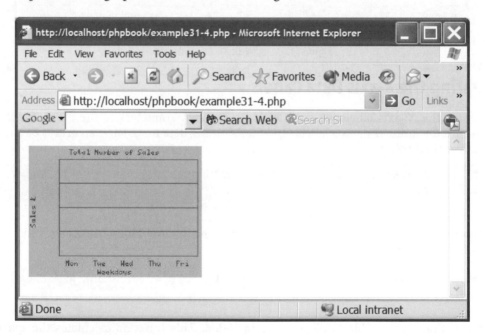

Figure 31.7 Graph Part 4 – *X*-axis labels.

Creating the *Y*-axis Numerical Scale

In order to display the *Y*-axis numerical scale we need to know what data values are to be displayed. Therefore, we need to modify the graph function so that the data values can be passed as an array and stored in variable $xValues:

```
function graph($name,$w,$h,$bgc,$fgc,$title,$xtitle,$ytitle,$numX,
$xTitles,$xValues) {
```

Next, a call to function calcMaxDataItem() is used to determine the largest data item value and thus allow us to calculate the Y-axis scale. This is inserted below the call to function drawXLables():

```
$max = calcMaxDataItem($xValues,$numX);
```

After this a function call to drawYLables() will enable us to display the numerical values:

```
drawYLables($image,$w,$h,$cols[$fgc],$top,$right,$left,$bottom,$max);
```

The function calcmaxDataItem() uses a simple for loop to examine each of the data items and determine which is the largest:

```
function calcMaxDataItem($xValues, $numX) {
    $temp=0;
    for($a=0;$a<$numX;$a++) {
        if($xValues[$a] > $temp)
            $temp = $xValues[$a];
    }
    return $temp;
}
```

Having determined the largest value of our Y-axis' scale function drawYLables() is able to calculate the values of the four numbers to display on the Y-axis by subtracting a quarter of the maximum number four times. The function determines the number of characters in each Y-axis scale number in order to place it correctly against the Y-axis:

```
function drawYLables($image,$w,$h,$col,$top,$right,$left,$bottom,
$max) {
    $gHeight = $h - ($top + $bottom);
    $space = $gHeight / 4;
    $y = $top;
    $quater = round($max/4,0);
    for($a=1;$a<5;$a++) {
        $len = strlen($max);
        $width = ImageFontWidth(1) * $len;
        ImageString($image,0,32.$width,$y-2,$max,$col);
        $y=$y+$space;
        $max=$max-$quater;
    }
}
```

Finally, an array to store the values must be created and the graph function invocation modified to pass this to the graph function:

```
$xValues = array(50,55,78,87,32);
graph("graph.jpeg", 200, 150, 14,2,"Total Number of Sales","Sales
£","Weekdays",5,$xTitles,$xValues);
```

The output from the graph function is shown in Figure 31.8.

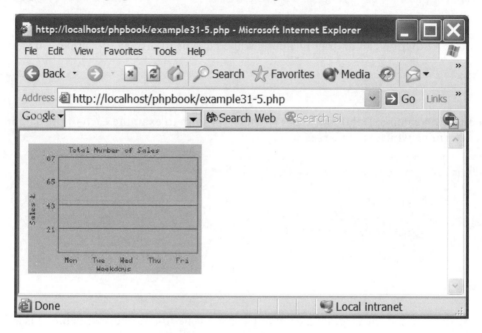

Figure 31.8 Graph Part 5 – Y-axis numbers.

Displaying the Data

We are almost finished! The last task we need to accomplish is to display the data on the graph. We begin by including a final parameter in our graph function to hold the colour value of the graph bars:

```
function
graph($name,$w,$h,$bgc,$fgc,$title,$xtitle,$ytitle,$numX,$xTitles,
$xValues,$bc) {
```

Next we insert a function call to the drawData() function below the drawYLabels() function to process our graph data:

```
drawData($image,$w,$h,$cols[$bc],$top,$right,$left,$bottom,$numX,
$xValues,$max);
```

Next, the drawData() function is implemented. This calculates the size of each graph bar depending on the overall size of the image and the value of the data item. Each bar is displayed using the ImageFilledRectangle() function:

```php
function
drawData($image,$w,$h,$col,$top,$right,$left,$bottom,$numX,$xValues,
$max) {
    $graphHeight = $h - ($top+$bottom);
    $pixelValue = $graphHeight / $max;
    $graphWidth = $w - ($right+$left);
    $spacing = $graphWidth/$numX;
    $gap = $spacing/4;
    $x = $left + ($spacing/6);
    for($a=0;$a<$numX;$a++) {
        $rectSize = ($graphHeight + $top) - $xValues[$a]*$pixelValue;
        ImageFilledRectangle($image,$x,$rectSize,$x+($spacing-$gap),$h-
$bottom,$col);
        $x=$x+$spacing;
    }
}
```

Finally, the invocation of the graph function is modified to include a parameter representing the colour of the bars, in this case red:

```php
graph("graph.jpeg", 200, 150, 14,2,"Total Number of Sales","Sales
£","Weekdays",5,$xTitles,$xValues,5);
```

The finished script is as follows:

```php
<?php

// GD Graph - Example 31-6
//--------------------

function
graph($name,$w,$h,$bgc,$fgc,$title,$xtitle,$ytitle,$numX,$xTitles,
$xValues,$bc) {
    $top=15;
    $right=5;
    $left=35;
    $bottom=25;
    $image = ImageCreate($w,$h);
    $cols = colours($image);
    ImageFill($image,0,0,$cols[$bgc]);
    drawAxis($image,$w,$h,$cols[$fgc],$top,$right,$left,$bottom);
    drawLines($image,$w,$h,$cols[$fgc],$top,$right,$left,$bottom);
```

```
    drawTitles($image,$w,$h,$cols[$fgc],$title,$xtitle,$ytitle);
    drawXLables($image,$w,$h,$right,$left,$cols[$fgc],$numX,$xTitles);
    $max = calcMaxDataItem($xValues,$numX);
    drawYLables($image,$w,$h,$cols[$fgc],$top,$right,$left,$bottom,
$max);
    drawData($image,$w,$h,$cols[$bc],$top,$right,$left,$bottom,$numX,
$xValues,$max);
    ImageJPEG($image, $name);
    ImageDestroy($image);
}

function colours($image) {
    $white = ImageColorAllocate($image,255,255,255);
    $black = ImageColorAllocate($image,0,0,0);
    $lightblue = ImageColorAllocate($image,64,64,255);
    $blue = ImageColorAllocate($image,0,0,255);
    $darkblue = ImageColorAllocate($image,0,0,192);
    $red = ImageColorAllocate($image,255,0,0);
    $lightred = ImageColorAllocate($image,255,64,64);
    $darkred = ImageColorAllocate($image,192,0,0);
    $green = ImageColorAllocate($image,0,255,0);
    $lightgreen = ImageColorAllocate($image,64,255,64);
    $darkgreen = ImageColorAllocate($image,0,192,0);
    $yellow = ImageColorAllocate($image,255,255,0);
    $grey = ImageColorAllocate($image,192,192,192);
    $darkgrey = ImageColorAllocate($image,128,128,128);
    $lightgrey = ImageColorAllocate($image,192,192,255);
    $cols =
array($white,$black,$lightblue,$blue,$darkblue,$red,$lightred,
$darkred,$green,$lightgreen,$darkgreen,$yellow,$grey,
$darkgrey,$lightgrey);
    return $cols;
}

function drawAxis($image, $w, $h, $col, $top,$right,$left,$bottom) {
    ImageRectangle($image,$left,$top,$w-$right,$h-$bottom,$col);
}

function drawLines($image, $w, $h, $col, $top,$right,$left,$bottom) {
    $gHeight = $h - ($top + $bottom);
    $space = $gHeight / 4;
    $y = $top;
    for($a=1;$a<5;$a++) {
        ImageLine($image,$left,$y,$w-$right,$y,$col);
        $y=$y+$space;
    }
}
```

```php
function drawTitles($image,$w,$h,$col,$title,$xtitle,$ytitle) {
    $width = ImageFontWidth(1) * strlen($title);
    $x = ($w - $width)/2;
    ImageString($image,1,$x,3,$title,$col);
    $width = ImageFontWidth(1) * strlen($ytitle);
    $x = ($w - $width)/2;
    ImageString($image,1,$x,$h-10,$ytitle,$col);
    $height = ImageFontWidth(1) * strlen($xtitle);
    $y = ($h - $height)/2;
    ImageStringUp($image,1,1,$y+$height,$xtitle,$col);
}

function drawXLables($image,$w,$h,$right,$left,$col,$numX,$xTitles) {
    $graphWidth = $w - ($right+$left);
    $spacing = $graphWidth/$numX;
    $x = $left + ($spacing/4);
    for($a=0;$a<$numX;$a++) {
        ImageString($image,1,$x,$h-20,$xTitles[$a],$col);
        $x=$x+$spacing;
    }
}

function calcMaxDataItem($xValues, $numX) {
    $temp=0;
    for($a=0;$a<$numX;$a++) {
        if($xValues[$a] > $temp)
            $temp = $xValues[$a];
    }
    return $temp;
}

function drawYLables($image,$w,$h,$col,$top,$right,$left,$bottom,
$max) {
    $gHeight = $h - ($top + $bottom);
    $space = $gHeight / 4;
    $y = $top;
    $quater = round($max/4,0);
    for($a=1;$a<5;$a++) {
        $len = strlen($max);
        $width = ImageFontWidth(1) * $len;
        ImageString($image,0,32.$width,$y-2,$max,$col);
        $y=$y+$space;
        $max=$max-$quater;
    }
}

function drawData($image,$w,$h,$col,$top,$right,$left,$bottom,$numX,
$xValues,$max) {
```

```
    $graphHeight = $h - ($top+$bottom);
    $pixelValue = $graphHeight / $max;
    $graphWidth = $w - ($right+$left);
    $spacing = $graphWidth/$numX;
    $gap = $spacing/4;
    $x = $left + ($spacing/6);
    for($a=0;$a<$numX;$a++) {
        $rectSize = ($graphHeight + $top) - $xValues[$a]*$pixelValue;
        ImageFilledRectangle($image,$x,$rectSize,$x+($spacing-$gap),
$h-$bottom,$col);
        $x=$x+$spacing;
    }
}

$xTitles = array("Mon","Tue","Wed","Thu","Fri");
$xValues = array(50,55,78,87,32);
graph("graphics/graph.jpeg", 200, 150, 14,2,"Total Number of Sales",
"Sales £","Weekdays",5,$xTitles,$xValues,5);

?>
<img src='graphics/graph.jpeg'>
```

The output from the graph function is shown in Figure 31.9.

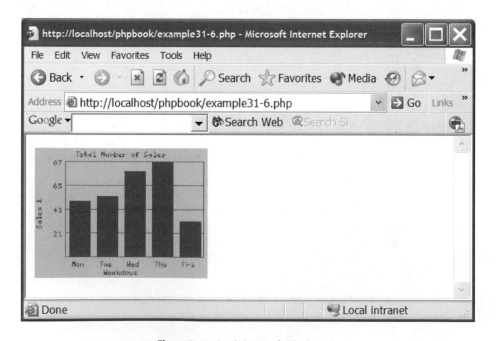

Figure 31.9 Graph Part 6 – finished graph.

That's it. Six steps towards completing a useful image which can be used for many different Web pages.

Summary

This chapter has illustrated how the GD library can be used to create a useful graphical image that is flexible enough to be used for a variety of different uses. The following chapter introduces the PDF function library and illustrates how these functions can be used to create your own PDF documents.

Part 9

PDF Library Extension

Creating PDF Documents 32

Introduction

PDFlib is a library of functions which have been created to allow you to generate documents in Adobe's Portable Document Format (PDF). PDF has become a standard for document storage on the Web. The PDFlib library is now available for use with PHP; in fact, the latest version of PHP comes with the PDFlib already included. All you need to do to activate it and then you can begin creating your own dynamic PDF documents. In this chapter we shall introduce the PDFlib library and examine some of the functions available to the developer.

Activating the PDFlib

The PDFlib library of functions is supplied along with your PHP installation. However, you need to edit your php.ini file in order to activate it. The php.ini file can be found in the c:\windows\directory on a Windows system. To activate the PDFlib you will need to open the php.ini file in an editor such as Notepad. You then need to find the following line in the file:

```
;extension=php_pdf.dll
```

To activate the library you simply need to remove the ; from start of the line and save the file. Figure 32.1 illustrates the php.ini file displayed in Notepad.

We are now ready to begin PDFlib development. In order to view the output created by the scripts in this chapter you will need to obtain a copy of Adobe® Acrobat® Reader, which is available from www.adobe.com.

Why use PDFlib?

PDFlib was developed to enable the creation of dynamic PDF documents via the World Wide Web. A PDF document which includes data received from a Web user and/or obtained from a Web-enabled database can be created, hence allowing dynamically customized PDF documents to be created.

PDFlib integrates seamlessly with PHP removing the need to invoke the traditional creation path of postscript to Acrobat Distiller to PDF. It is very fast and, thus, ideal for

```
php - Notepad
File  Edit  Format  View  Help
;extension=php_hyperwave.dll
;extension=php_iconv.dll
;extension=php_ifx.dll
;extension=php_iisfunc.dll
;extension=php_imap.dll
;extension=php_interbase.dll
;extension=php_java.dll
;extension=php_ldap.dll
;extension=php_mbstring.dll
;extension=php_mcrypt.dll
;extension=php_mhash.dll
;extension=php_mime_magic.dll
;extension=php_ming.dll
;extension=php_mssql.dll
;extension=php_msql.dll
;extension=php_oci8.dll
;extension=php_openssl.dll
;extension=php_oracle.dll
extension=php_pdf.dll
;extension=php_pgsql.dll
;extension=php_printer.dll
;extension=php_shmop.dll
;extension=php_snmp.dll
;extension=php_sockets.dll
;extension=php_sybase_ct.dll
;extension=php_w32api.dll
;extension=php_xmlrpc.dll
;extension=php_xslt.dll
;extension=php_yaz.dll
;extension=php_zip.dll
```

Figure 32.1 The php.ini file.

dynamic document generation and is available for a number of platforms as well as other programming languages in addition to PHP. Full documentation on PDFlib can be found at: www.pdflib.com.

Creating our First PDF Document

To create a PDF document (even the most simple), we need to undertake five main steps and introduce a number of new functions. The first thing we need to do is to state that we wish to begin to create a PDF document – we do this with the pdf_new() function:

Function prototype:

> Int pdf_new(void);

Function arguments and return details:

Name	Type	Description
pdf_new() returns	Int	The function returns a handle to a PDF document. This handle will be used in all subsequent functions that relate to this particular PDF document

Function example:

```
$myPDF = pdf_new();
```

Having obtained a handle to a PDF document, we now need to give it a file name that will be used to store the PDF file on the server. The function pdf_open_file() is used to accomplish this – its format is:

Function prototype:

```
int Pdf_open_file(int PdfHandle, string filename)
```

Function arguments and return details:

Name	Type	Description
pdfHandle	Int	Handle to PDF document being created.
filename	String	Filename of the PDF document we are to create
pdf_open() returns	Int	Returns "TRUE" if the function is successful or "FALSE" if it is not

Function example:

```
pdf_open_file($myPDF,"first.pdf");
```

So far we have created a PDF document but it currently contains nothing. The next step is to insert a page into the document using the pdf_begin_page() function:

Function prototype:

```
Void Pdf_begin_page(int handle, double width, double height);
```

Function arguments and return details:

Name	Type	Description
pdfHandle	Int	Handle to PDF document being created
width	Double	Width of the page specified in points
height	Double	Width of the page specified in points
pdf_begin_page() returns	Void	Returns nothing

Function example:

```
pdf_begin_page($myPDF,595,842);
```

The width and height of a page are specified in points, where 1 point is equal to 1/72 of an inch. Luckily, we normally only want to create pages of set sizes, for example A4. Table 32.1 provides the width and heights of common paper sizes in points:

Table 32.1 Paper sizes.

Paper size	Width	Height
A0	2380	3368
A1	1684	2380
A2	1190	1684
A3	842	1190
A4	595	842
A5	421	595
A6	297	421
B5	501	709
Letter	612	792
Legal	612	1008

Having created the page we can close it (a signal that we have finished with it) with the pdf_end_page() function:

Function prototype:

```
Void Pdf_end_page(int PdfHandle)
```

Function arguments and return details:

Name	Type	Description
pdfHandle	Int	Handle to PDF document being created
pdf_end_page() returns	Void	Returns nothing

Function example:

```
pdf_end_page($myPDF);
```

Repeated calls to pdf_begin_page() and pdf_end_page() enable more than one page to be created. The final step in the document creation is the invocation of function pdf_close():

Function prototype:

```
Void Pdf_close(int PdfHandle)
```

Function arguments and return details:

Name	Type	Description
pdfHandle	Int	Handle to PDF document being created
pdf_close() returns	Void	Returns nothing

Combining these functions into a PHP script results in the following:

```php
<?php

// PDF Documents - Example 32-1
//---------------------

$pageWidth=595;
$pageHeight=842;

$myPDF = pdf_new();
pdf_open_file($myPDF,"pdf/first.pdf");
pdf_begin_page($myPDF,$pageWidth,$pageHeight);

pdf_end_page($myPDF);
pdf_close($myPDF);
?>
<a href="pdf/first.pdf">View generated PDF document.</a>
```

Note that this script includes a hyperlink, which enables you to view the PDF file within your Web browser. If you click the link, the Adobe Acrobat Reader will be launched and you will be able to view your generated document. Unfortunately, all you will find is a PDF document consisting of a blank page. We will need to introduce a few more functions to ensure our document is a little more interesting.

Inserting Some Text

In order to enhance our PDF document, we shall add some text to the document. To accomplish this, we need to use three functions: pdf_findfont(), pdf_setfont() and pdf_show_xy(). The first of these, pdf_findfont(), has the following syntax:

Function prototype:

Int Pdf_findfont(int PdfHandle, string fontName, string encoding, int embedded);

Function arguments and return details:

Name	Type	Description
pdfHandle	Int	Handle to PDF document being created
fontname	String	The name of the font to be used. Common fonts include "Times New Roman", "Arial" and "Courier"
encoding	String	Encoding selects the particular character encoding for the font selected. The encoding is an 8-bit numerical code mapped to a particular character in the font set. Normally a value of "host" is used for the encoding string as this selects the encoding system appropriate to the server operating system
embedded	Int	A binary switch, where 1 indicates that the font will be embedded within the PDF document and 0 indicates that it will not
pdf_findfont() returns	Int	Returns a handle to the selected font. An example of the use of this function follows

Function example:

```
$arial = pdf_findfont($myPDF, "Arial", "host", 1);
```

This will create an Arial font which is embedded within the PDF document. Once a font has been defined, we can choose to use the font using the pdf_setfont() function:

Function prototype:

```
void pdf_setfont(int handle, int font, double fontSize)
```

Function arguments and return details:

Name	Type	Description
pdfHandle	Int	Handle to PDF document being created
font	Int	The font handle returned from function pdf_find_font
fontSize	Double	The size of the font supplied in points
pdf_setfont() returns	Void	Returns nothing

Function example:

```
pdf_setfont($myPDF, $arial, 12);
```

This sets the font as the Arial font specified previously, at a size of 12 points. We are now ready to write some text to a position on the page. To do this, we use the pdf_show_xy function, the syntax of which is:

Function prototype:

```
Void Pdf_show_xy(int PdfHandle, string text, double x, double y)
```

Function arguments and return details:

Name	Type	Description
pdfHandle	Int	Handle to PDF document being created
text	String	The text to be displayed
x	Double	The X coordinate on the page
y	Double	The Y coordinate on the page
pdf_show_xy() returns	Void	Returns nothing

Function example:

```
pdf_show_xy($myPDF, "Hello and welcome to the world of PDF",
70,700);
```

If we incorporate these functions into our previous script, we arrive at the following:

```php
<?php

// PDF Documents - Example 32-2
//--------------------

$pageWidth=595;
$pageHeight=842;

$myPDF = pdf_new();
pdf_open_file($myPDF,"pdf/second.pdf");
pdf_begin_page($myPDF,$pageWidth,$pageHeight);

$arial = pdf_findfont($myPDF, "Arial", "host", 1);
pdf_setfont($myPDF, $arial, 12);
pdf_show_xy($myPDF, "Hello and welcome to the world of PDF",
70,700);

pdf_end_page($myPDF);
pdf_close($myPDF);
?>
<a href="pdf/second.pdf">View generated PDF document.</a>
```

The output from this script is shown in Figure 32.2.

Figure 32.2 illustrates that the text "Hello and welcome to the world of PDF" has been displayed at position 70 by 700 on the page.

Lines of Text Spilling off the Page

So far things seem to be going well. In our previous example we managed to create a PDF document which contained some text. Unfortunately, things are not that simple. The following script modifies the previous example by moving the start position of the text we wish to print on the page:

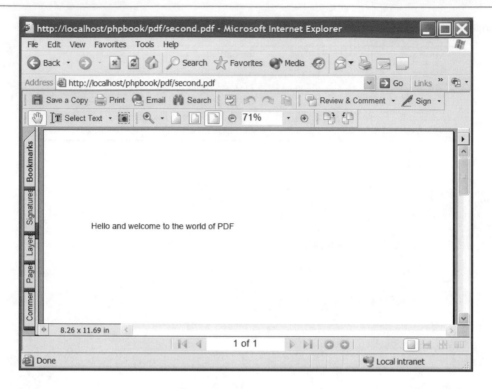

Figure 32.2 Text output in PDF.

```php
<?php

// PDF Documents - Example 32-3
//---------------------

$pageWidth=595;
$pageHeight=842;

$myPDF = pdf_new();
pdf_open_file($myPDF,"pdf/third.pdf");
pdf_begin_page($myPDF,$pageWidth,$pageHeight);

$arial = pdf_findfont($myPDF, "Arial", "host", 1);
pdf_setfont($myPDF, $arial, 12);
pdf_show_xy($myPDF, "Hello and welcome to the world of PDF",
400,700);

pdf_end_page($myPDF);
pdf_close($myPDF);
?>
<a href="pdf/third.pdf">View generated PDF document.</a>
```

The output from this script is shown in Figure 32.3. You will note that the X position of the text was moved across the page to position 400. Instead of automatically looping the text to the next line the text simply falls off the side of the page. This is how PDF documents work – we must control the positioning of anything and everything on the page as there is no automatic formatting as in a word processor. If you want to ensure that the text you write to the page doesn't fall off the edge then you need to write the code to ensure that this does not happen.

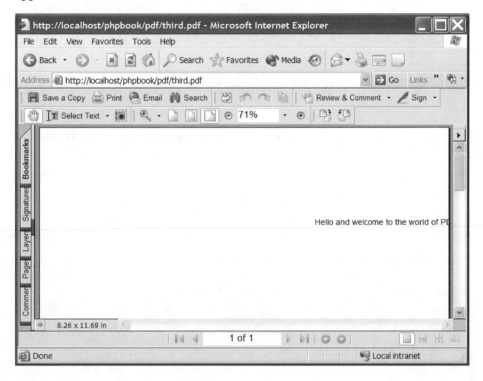

Figure 32.3 Text falling off the page.

Formatting Paragraphs of Text

It would be an excellent idea if we were able to control the output of text to the page to ensure that it all fitted nicely and that none of the text disappeared off the edge of the page. In order to do this we would need to build up a line of text word by word checking that each word we added to the sentence will fit on the line. If not, then the line of words should be added to the page and a new line started. This would need to be repeated until all the words had been output. Of course, in order to do this, we would need to be able to calculate the exact width of a word in points. Luckily for us there is a function called pdf_stringwidth() that does this for us, the format of which is:

Function prototype:

```
double pdf_stringwidth(int PdfHandle, string theString);
```

Function arguments and return details:

Name	Type	Description
pdfHandle	Int	Handle to PDF document being created
theString	String	The string of characters to measure to obtain their exact width
pdf_stringwidth() returns	Double	The function returns the width of the string as a float in points

Function example:

```
pdf_stringwidth($pdf,$line);
```

Using this function we can ensure that our text fits the page. The following script illustrates a method of formatting a paragraph of text:

```php
<?php

// PDF Documents - Example 32-4
//--------------------

$text="The quick brown fox jumped over the lazy dog. The quick
brown fox jumped over the lazy dog. The quick brown fox jumped over
the lazy dog. The quick brown fox jumped over the lazy dog.
The quick brown fox jumped over the lazy dog. The quick brown fox
jumped over the lazy dog. The quick brown fox jumped over the
lazy dog. The quick brown fox jumped over the lazy dog. The quick
brown fox jumped over the lazy dog. ";

$pointSize=16;
$pageWidth=595;
$pageHeight=842;
$lrMargin=80;
$tbMargin=80;
$lineWidth=$pageWidth-($lrMargin*2);
$textPos=$pageHeight-$tbMargin;

$words = explode(" ",$text);

$pdf = pdf_new();
pdf_open_file($pdf,"pdf/singlePara.pdf");
pdf_begin_page($pdf,$pageWidth,$pageHeight);
$arial = pdf_findfont($pdf,"Arial","host",1);
pdf_setfont($pdf,$arial,$pointSize);
```

```
$lines = array("");
$line=0;
foreach($words as $word){
    if(pdf_stringwidth($pdf,$lines[$line] . " " . $word) <
$lineWidth){
        $lines[$line] = $lines[$line] . $word . " ";
    }
    else {
        $line++;
        $lines[$line] = $word . " ";
    }
}

pdf_set_text_pos($pdf,$lrMargin,$pageHeight-$tbMargin);

foreach($lines as $aline) {
        pdf_show_xy($pdf,$aline,$lrMargin,$textPos);
        $textPos=$textPos-($pointSize+2);
}

pdf_end_page($pdf);
pdf_close($pdf);
?>
<a href="pdf/SinglePara.pdf">View generated PDF document.</a>
```

The script begins by declaring a text string, which we shall output to the PDF page:

```
<?php

// PDF Documents - Example 32-4
//---------------------

$text="The quick brown fox jumped over the lazy dog. The quick
brown fox
jumped over the lazy dog. The quick brown fox jumped over the
lazy dog. The quick brown fox jumped over the lazy dog. The quick
brown fox jumped over the lazy dog. The quick brown fox jumped
over the lazy dog. The quick brown fox jumped over the lazy dog.
The quick brown fox jumped over the lazy dog. The quick brown
fox jumped over the lazy dog. ";
```

Variables are declared to represent the point size of the font, page height and width, paper margin sizes, maximum width of a line of text (taking into account the margins) and finally the starting text position:

```
$pointSize=16;
$pageWidth=595;
$pageHeight=842;
$lrMargin=80;
$tbMargin=80;
$lineWidth=$pageWidth-($lrMargin*2);
$textPos=$pageHeight-$tbMargin;
```

The text string is then exploded into an array in order to access all the individual words in the sentence. The space character is used to separate each word:

```
$words = explode(" ",$text);
```

The next part of the script declares a new PDF document, gives it a file name, inserts a page and selects and assigns a font to use:

```
$pdf = pdf_new();
pdf_open_file($pdf,"pdf/singlePara.pdf");
pdf_begin_page($pdf,$pageWidth,$pageHeight);
$arial = pdf_findfont($pdf,"Arial","host",1);
pdf_setfont($pdf,$arial,$pointSize);
```

Using a foreach loop, each word held in the $words array is measured and added to the end of a sentence. When the sentence is going to be longer than the width of the page the sentence is stored in an array called lines and a new sentence started. The result of which is that the individual words from the $words array are combined together to form an array of lines. Each sentence is shorter than the maximum line width of the page:

```
$lines = array("");
$line=0;
foreach($words as $word){
  if(pdf_stringwidth($pdf,$lines[$line] . " " . $word) < $lineWidth){
     $lines[$line] = $lines[$line] . $word . " ";
  }
  else {
     $line++;
     $lines[$line] = $word . " ";
  }
}
```

Finally, beginning at the top of the page, all of the lines of text held in the $lines array are output onto the page. The page is then closed and saved:

```
pdf_set_text_pos($pdf,$lrMargin,$pageHeight-$tbMargin);

foreach($lines as $aline) {
        pdf_show_xy($pdf,$aline,$lrMargin,$textPos);
        $textPos=$textPos-($pointSize+2);
}

pdf_end_page($pdf);
pdf_close($pdf);
?>
<a href="pdf/SinglePara.pdf">View generated PDF document.</a>
```

The output from this script is illustrated in Figure 32.4. The script appears to work very well, although it does have some drawbacks. For instance, the script can only handle a single paragraph of text; it has no means yet of separating paragraphs. Also, if the paragraph were to be very large, then there is the potential for the text to disappear off the bottom of the page as the script has no means of adding new pages. Let's consider a script which can correct these problems.

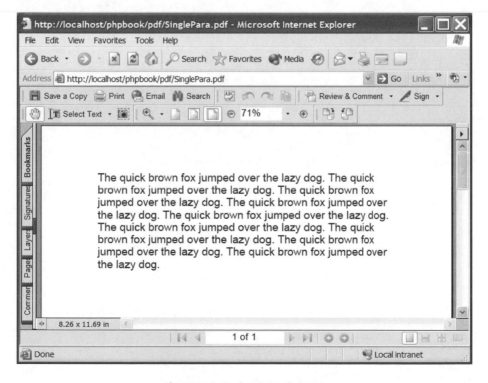

Figure 32.4 Single-paragraph output.

Paging a Text Document

The following script is a modification of the previous one and improves upon it by adding functionality to handle paragraphs and paging. The script begins by declaring two text strings. Note the "\n" character which we will use as a means of detecting the start of a new paragraph. The two strings are concatenated together a number of times to form a large string called $text:

```php
<?php

// PDF Documents - Example 32-5
//--------------------

$text1="The quick brown fox jumped over the lazy dog. The quick
brown fox jumped over the lazy dog. The quick brown fox jumped
over the lazy dog. The quick brown fox jumped over the lazy
dog. The quick brown fox jumped over the lazy dog. The quick
brown fox jumped over the lazy dog. The quick brown fox jumped
over the lazy dog. The quick brown fox jumped over the lazy dog.
The quick brown fox jumped over the lazy dog. ";

$text2="\n The quick brown fox jumped over the lazy
dog. The quick brown fox jumped over the lazy dog. The quick
brown fox jumped over the lazy dog. The quick brown fox jumped
over the lazy dog. The quick brown fox jumped over the lazy dog.
The quick brown fox jumped over the lazy dog. The quick brown fox
jumped over the lazy dog. The quick brown fox jumped over the
lazy dog. The quick brown fox jumped over the lazy dog. ";

$text = $text1 . $text2 . $text2 . $text2 . $text2 . $text2 .
$text2 . $text2;
```

The following section of the script is unchanged from the previous example:

```php
$pointSize=16;
$pageWidth=595;
$pageHeight=842;
$lrMargin=80;
$tbMargin=80;
$lineWidth=$pageWidth-($lrMargin*2);
$textPos=$pageHeight-$tbMargin;

$words = explode(" ",$text);

$pdf = pdf_new();
pdf_open_file($pdf,"pdf/paragraphs.pdf");
pdf_begin_page($pdf,$pageWidth,$pageHeight);
$arial = pdf_findfont($pdf,"Arial","host",1);
pdf_setfont($pdf,$arial,$pointSize);
```

This section of the script builds the lines of text to be output to the page. It is very similar to the previous script but it now contains an additional if statement within the foreach loop to check for the presences of a "\n" character. If this is found then the "\n" is inserted into the lines array on its own, to indicate a blank line should be outputted:

```
$lines = array("");
$line=0;
foreach($words as $word){
    if($word == "\n"){
        $line++;
        $lines[$line] = $word;
        $line++;
        $lines[$line] = "";
    }
    elseif(pdf_stringwidth($pdf,$lines[$line] . " " .
$word) < $lineWidth){
        $lines[$line] = $lines[$line] . $word . " ";
    }
    else {
        $line++;
        $lines[$line] = $word . " ";
    }
}

pdf_set_text_pos($pdf,$lrMargin,$pageHeight-$tbMargin);
```

Two modifications have been made to the following foreach loop, which outputs the lines of text to the page. First, a check is made for a line consisting of "\n". If one is found then the $textPos variable which is used to store the horizontal position of the text on the page is reduced by one line of text. This has the effect of forming a space between the paragraphs:

```
foreach($lines as $aline) {
    if($aline == "\n"){
        $textPos=$textPos-($pointSize+2);
    }
    else {
        pdf_show_xy($pdf,$aline,$lrMargin,$textPos);
        $textPos=$textPos-($pointSize+2);
    }
}
```

In addition, a check is made to see if the $textPos variable has fallen below the minimum position on the page that we wish to output text. If this happens, then the existing page is ended and a new page begun to allow the text to be output on the following page:

```
    if($textPos <= $tbMargin){
        $textPos=$pageHeight-$tbMargin;
        pdf_end_page($pdf);
        pdf_begin_page($pdf,$pageWidth,$pageHeight);
        $arial = pdf_findfont($pdf,"Arial","host",1);
        pdf_setfont($pdf,$arial,$pointSize);
        pdf_set_text_pos($pdf,$lrMargin,$pageHeight-$tbMargin);
    }
}
pdf_end_page($pdf);
pdf_close($pdf);
?>
<a href="paragraphs.pdf">View generated PDF document.</a>
```

The output produced from this script is illustrated in Figure 32.5.

Note that the text appear on two pages. Feel free to adjust the size of the font and to see if the text appears on the pages correctly. Figure 32.6 illustrates the output produced from the same script with the font size reduced to 12 points.

Inserting Graphics

In addition to text, we can also incorporate images into PDF documents. To do this we must first introduce a number of new functions. The first of these is pdf_open_image_file() which allows us to specify an image we are going to incorporate into our PDF document:

Function prototype:

Int ImageHandle pdf_open_image_file(int pdfHandle, string imageType, string imageName)

Function arguments and return details:

Name	Type	Description
pdfHandle	Int	Handle to PDF document being created
imageType	String	Type of image file: can be png, gif, jpeg or tiff
imageName	String	File name of image
imageHandle() returns	Int	The function returns a handle to the image

Function example:

```
$image = pdf_open_image_file($pdf,"jpeg","palm.jpeg");
```

Having selected an image we wish to use, the next thing we need to do is to determine the size of the image. Function pdf_get_value() is a multi-role function which returns values on a whole number of things depending on the parameters supplied to it. In this instance, the format of the function is:

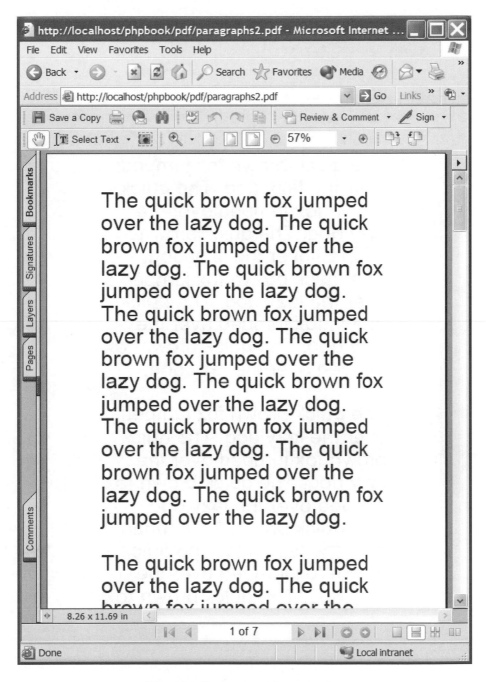

Figure 32.5 Graph paging with a 16-point font.

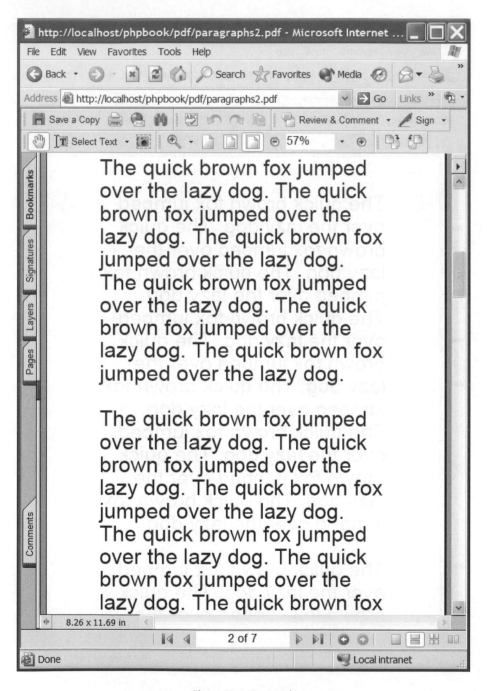

Figure 32.5 Continued.

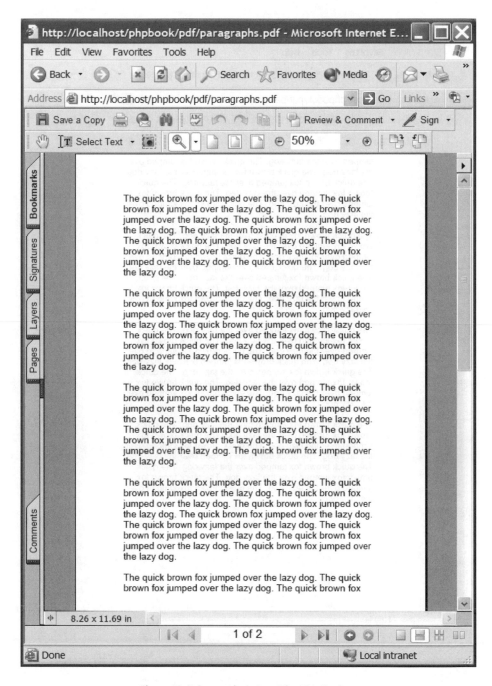

Figure 32.6 Paragraph paging with a 12-point font.

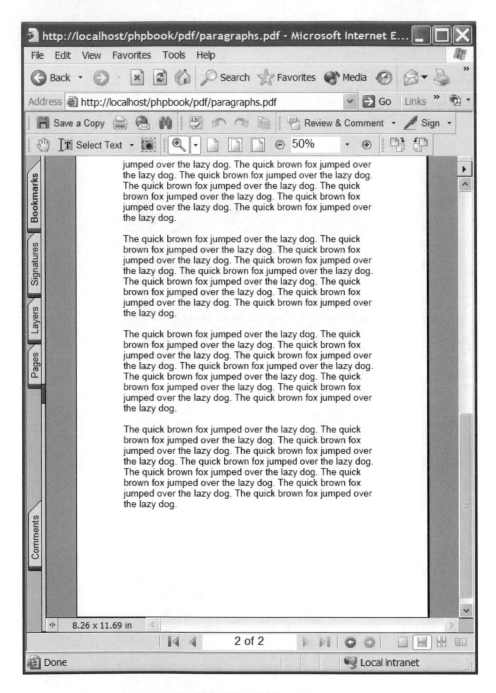

Figure 32.6 Continued.

Function prototype:

```
Float value pdf_get_value(int pdfHandle, string Para, int Image)
```

Function arguments and return details:

Name	Type	Description
pdfHandle	Int	Handle to PDF document being created
para	String	Either "imageheight" or "imagewidth"
image	Int	Image handle returned from function pdf_open_image_file
pdf_get_value() returns	Float	Will return the width or height of the image in points

Function example:

```
$height = pdf_get_value($pdf,"imageheight",$image);
```

Knowing the size of the image enables us to place the image where we would like on the page. The function used to place the image on the page is pdf_place_image():

Function prototype:

```
Void pdf_place_image(int pdfHandle, int Image, float X, float Y, float scale)
```

Function arguments and return details:

Name	Type	Description
pdfHandle	Int	Handle to PDF document being created
image	Int	Image handle returned from function pdf_open_image_file
x	Float	The X coordinate on the page where the bottom left-hand corner of the image will be placed
y	Float	The Y coordinate on the page where the bottom left-hand corner of the image will be placed
scale	Float	The scaling factor. A value of 1 will display the image at full size, 0.5 will display it at half size
pdf_place_image() returns	Void	Returns nothing

Function example:

```
pdf_place_image($pdf,$image,100,100,1);
```

The following script illustrates the use of these functions to include an image in a PDF document. In order for us to include an image in our document we need one. We have used an image called palm.jpeg:

```php
<?php

// PDF Documents - Example 32-6
//---------------------

$pageWidth=595;
$pageHeight=842;
$lrMargin=80;
$tbMargin=80;
$pos=$pageHeight-$tbMargin;

$pdf = pdf_new();
pdf_open_file($pdf,"pdf/picture.pdf");
pdf_begin_page($pdf,$pageWidth,$pageHeight);

$image = pdf_open_image_file($pdf,"jpeg","graphics/palm.jpeg");
$height = pdf_get_value($pdf,"imageheight",$image);
pdf_place_image($pdf,$image,$lrMargin,$pos-$height,1);

pdf_end_page($pdf);
pdf_close($pdf);
?>
<a href="pdf/picture.pdf">View generated PDF document.</a>
```

The output produced by this script is illustrated in Figure 32.7. Figure 32.7 illustrates that our palm.jpeg image is displayed at the top left-hand corner of our page.

Creating Your Own Graphics

The PDFlib has a large number of functions that enable you to create your own graphics within a PDF document including various shapes and lines. However, once you understand how to create one type, then creating the others is very similar and just requires looking up the appropriate function. We shall examine how to create lines and rectangles. In PDF, creating shapes involves three main tasks: defining a colour to use, defining the shape to display and then displaying it. Function pdf_setcolor() is used to define a colour:

Function prototype:

Void Pdf_setcolor(int PdfHandle, string type, string colourSpace, float r, float g float b)

Figure 32.7 Image in a PDF document.

Function arguments and return details:

Name	Type	Description
pdfHandle	Int	Handle to PDF document being created
type	String	Is the colour we are defining to be used as the outline to the shape "stroke", to fill the contents of the shape "fill" or both "both"
colourSpace	String	This specifies how we are going to define the colour. We would recommend using "rgb"
r	Float	Intensity of the colour red
g	Float	Intensity of the colour green
b	Float	Intensity of the colour blue
pdf_setcolor() returns	Void	Returns nothing

Function example:

```
pdf_setcolor($pdf,"stroke","rgb",0,0,255/255);
```

The last three parameters allow us to specify the intensity of the colours – red, green and blue. HTML programmers will be used to specifying colours with an RGB triplet with values ranging from 0 to 255 for each red, green and blue colour combination. Unfortunately, pdf_setcolour() requires that the red, green and blue values are specified in an intensity between 0 (none) and 1 (100%). Don't worry – there is an easy solution. Suppose you wanted to specify a lime green colour which you would normally specify with the values: r,64;g,255.b,64. The easy solution is simply to divide them each by 255.

To specify a line involves two function: pdf_moveto() and pdf_lineto(). The first specifies the start of the line and the second the end of the line. The functions have the form:

Function prototypes:

```
Void Pdf_moveto(int PdfHandle, float X, float Y)
Void Pdf_lineto(int PdfHandle, float X, float Y)
```

Function arguments and return details:

Name	Type	Description
pdfHandle	Int	Handle to PDF document being created
x	Float	The X coordinate on the page
y	Float	The Y coordinate on the page
pdf_moveto() pdf_lineto() returns	Void	Returns nothing

Function example:

```
pdf_moveto($pdf,$lrMargin,100);
pdf_lineto($pdf,$pageWidth-$lrMargin,100);
```

Finally, to draw the line we use the function pdf_stroke():

Function prototype:

> Void Pdf_stroke(int PdfHandle)

Function arguments and return details:

Name	Type	Description
pdfHandle	Int	Handle to PDF document being created
pdf_stroke() returns	Void	Returns nothing

Function example:

```
Pdf_stroke($pdf);
```

Rectangles are specified and displayed in a similar way. The function pdf_rect() is used to specify the rectangle:

Function prototype:

> Void Pdf_rect(int PdfHandle, float X, float Y, float width, float height)

Function arguments and return details:

Name	Type	Description
pdfHandle	Int	Handle to PDF document being created
x	Float	The X coordinate on the page
y	Float	The Y coordinate on the page
width	Float	Width of the rectangle
height	Float	Height of the rectangle
pdf_rect() returns	Void	Returns nothing

Function example:

```
pdf_rect($pdf,$lrMargin+10,110,$pageWidth-($lrMargin*2)-
20,$pageHeight-220);
```

To display the rectangle we use the pdf_fill_stroke() function to display the shape on the page:

Function prototype:

> Void Pdf_fill_stroke(int PdfHandle)

Function arguments and return details:

Name	Type	Description
pdfHandle	Int	Handle to PDF document being created
pdf_fill_stroke() returns	Void	Returns nothing

Function example:

```
pdf_fill_stroke($pdf);
```

The following script illustrates the use of these functions in a simple example. The script produces a document consisting of a page with two lines at the top and bottom and a large pink rectangle:

```php
<?php

// PDF Documents - Example 32-7
//---------------------

$pageWidth=595;
$pageHeight=842;
$lrMargin=80;
$tbMargin=80;
$pos=$pageHeight-$tbMargin;

$pdf = pdf_new();
pdf_open_file($pdf,"pdf/linerect.pdf");
pdf_begin_page($pdf,$pageWidth,$pageHeight);

pdf_setcolor($pdf,"stroke","rgb",0,0,255/255);
pdf_moveto($pdf,$lrMargin,100);
pdf_lineto($pdf,$pageWidth-$lrMargin,100);
pdf_stroke($pdf);

pdf_moveto($pdf,$lrMargin,$pageHeight-100);
pdf_lineto($pdf,$pageWidth-$lrMargin,$pageHeight-100);
pdf_stroke($pdf);

pdf_setcolor($pdf,"both","rgb",233/255,157/255,157/255);
pdf_rect($pdf,$lrMargin+10,110,$pageWidth-($lrMargin*2)-
20,$pageHeight-220);
pdf_fill_stroke($pdf);

pdf_end_page($pdf);
pdf_close($pdf);
?>
<a href="pdf/linerect.pdf">View generated PDF document.</a>
```

The output from this script is illustrated in Figure 32.8.

Figure 32.8 Rectangle and lines.

Summary

This chapter has introduced some of the functions which are part of the PDF library. We have shown how you can create some simple PDF documents and how to overcome some of the difficulties that can be encountered in formatting such documents. In the next chapter we shall relational and database table design.

Part 10

MySQL Database Management

Databases and Table Design 33

Introduction

In this chapter we shall explain relational database management systems, databases, tables and column fields and records. Where appropriate, reference will be made to the MySQL database management system as this is the database system which we will use later in this book to manage our databases.

What is a Database?

A database is a structured collection of data. Databases occurred in the real world before computers were invented. Examples of real-world databases include:

- a TV times guide,
- a filing cabinet of documents,
- a telephone book.

A computer-based database is used to store, in a structured form, information which can be retrieved and examined quickly and easily. Examples of computer-based databases are:

- DVLA (Driver and Vehicle Licensing Agency) which stores information of all vehicles registered within the UK;
- HOLMES (Home Office Large Major Enquiry System) which stores data on offenders and suspects involved with current and previous police investigations; and
- Amazon.com, an e-commerce-linked database of books to sell.

Of course, all these databases are very large but whether large or small the concept of a database remains the same.

What is a Database Management System (DBMS)?

A Database Management System (DBMS) is the software that facilitates the creation and maintenance of a computerized database. In general, a DBMS

- manages large amounts of data;
- provides access to the data using a query language;
- provides some form of security to the data; and

- Enables multiple database access.

MySQL is a relational DBMS. A relational database stores data in separate tables instead of one single store. In theory, this provides a faster, more flexible database system.

What is a Database Table?

A database table is very similar to a table inserted into a word processed document as it has both rows and columns. Columns are often referred to as "fields" and are used to delimit the data structure into the correct order. The rows in a database table are where the records are stored. A database table also has a unique name assigned to it within a specific database. A simple database table is illustrated in Figure 33.1.

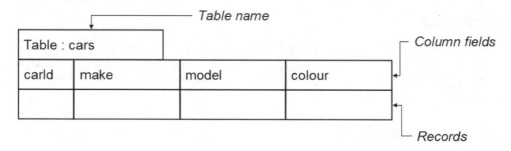

Figure 33.1 Database table.

In Figure 33.1 we can see that the database table is called cars and that it consists of four fields: carId, make, model and colour. There are no data records in this table.

What are Database Fields?

Database fields define the structure of the data within a table. Like variables, database fields can be defined as being of different types. To make things a little more complex, the types by which the database fields can be defined are not always the same as the programming language being used to access the database. In the MySQL database management system there are quite a few different field types which can be defined. These are listed in Tables 33.1–33.3.

Figure 33.2 illustrates our database table modified so that it specifies the type of each of the fields.

Note that the field carId has been specified as type integer, which can store numbers up to 11 digits in size. Fields, make, model and colour have all been specified as type varchar, with a maximum size of 40 characters.

Field Special Attributes and Keys

In addition to their type you can also specify certain special attributes for a field. These are listed in Table 33.4. These attributes describe certain special properties about the field.

Table 33.1 Text field types.

Type	Max. length	Description
Varchar	255 characters	Variable-length text field type
Char	255 characters	Fixed-length text field type
Tinytext	255 characters	Variable-length text field type
Text	65 535 characters	Variable-length text field type
Mediumtext	16 777 215 characters	Variable-length text field type
Longtext	4 294 967 295 characters	Variable-length text field type
Enum	65 535 characters	Potential values of a text field

Table 33.2 Numeric field types.

Type	Numeric size	Description
Int	4 294 967 295	Signed or unsigned numeric field type
TinyInt	255	Signed or unsigned numeric field type
MediumInt	16 777 215	Signed or unsigned numeric field type
BigInt	18 446 744 073 709	Signed or unsigned numeric field type
Float	-	Signed floating-point numeric field type
Double	-	Signed floating-point numeric field type
Decimal	-	Signed numeric field type (numbers stored as characters)

Table 33.3 Date and time field types.

Type	Values	Description
Date	1001–01–01 to 9999–12–31	Stores data values in a date format: YYYY–MM–DD
Time	−838:59:59 to 838:59:59	Stores data values in a time format
Datetime	1001–01–01 00:00:00 to 9999–12–31 23:59:59	Stores data values in a date–time format: YYYY–MM–DD HH:MM:SS
Timestamp	2–14	Stores numeric values to present different types of UNIX time stamp
Year	1901 to 2155	Stores four digits (or two digits) to present year.

Table 33.4 Special attributes.

Attribute	Description
Auto-increment	The field value is automatically generated when a new record is created. This is not supplied by the user. This is used mainly to ensure that a unique field value is created as the value produced is one larger than the last one produced.
Not null	The database field cannot be blank. If it is, then a error is generated.
Default	This specifies a value to which the field will be set if no value is supplied

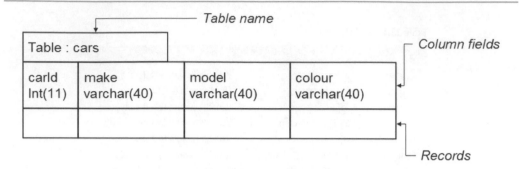

Figure 33.2 Database table with field types.

Unique Fields

Fields can be specified as being unique. This means that no two records in a table can have the same value in the field. An example of this would be a table holding a list of people's names and national insurance numbers. While it is possible that two people can have the same name, they cannot have the same national insurance number.

Keys

Fields within a table can be specified as being primary keys. A primary key is used to form an index of database records within a table. The primary key also has to be unique but, in addition, an index is formed of the table allowing much faster searching and retrieval of records.

Database records

Database records (also known as rows) form the rows of the database table. The records have to correspond to the type and special attributes of each field. Figure 33.3 illustrates our database table with three records.

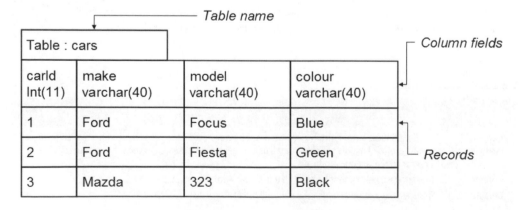

Figure 33.3 Database table records.

Summary

In this chapter we have described what a database and database management system are. We have also explained the concept of a database table and described the various field types which are available with MySQL. In the next chapter we shall explain how to install the MySQL database management system and PHPMyAdmin software.

MySQL Database and PHPMyAdmin Installation 34

Introduction

This chapter describes how to obtain, install and set up the MySQL database management system. According to the MySQL Web site, "MySQL is the most popular open source database server in the world with more than 4 million installations powering Websites, datawarehouses, business applications, logging systems and more. Customers such as Yahoo! Finance, MP3.com, Motorola, NASA, Silicon Graphics, and Texas Instruments use the MySQL server in mission-critical applications". The great thing about MySQL is that you can download and use it for free.

While MySQL is a very powerful database with many features (normally only found in commercial products costing a great deal of money), it does suffer from not having a simple graphical user interface. However, all is not lost as the PHPMyAdmin project provides us a very sophisticated, but easy to use tool written in PHP. This product is designed to handle the administration of MySQL over the World Wide Web. We are going to use both MySQL and PHPMyAdmin to design and create our database applications. We shall begin by explaining how to obtain MySQL.

MySQL Download

MySQL is available to download free from www.mysql.com. We recommend that you download the latest stable release from http://www.mysql.com/downloads/mysql-4.0.html. There are many different versions available for different operating systems and you should ensure that you select the correct one.

If you wish to download MySQL for use on a Windows platform, you may elect to obtain a complete PHP application bundle from AppServ Open Project available at: http://appserv.sourceforge.net/. This includes the latest stable version of MySQL and PHPMyAdmin. More details on this application bundle were described previously in Chapter 3.

MySQL Server Installation (on Linux/UNIX Servers)

If you are installing MySQL on a Windows platform, or if your service provider or systems administration has already installed and configured MySQL, then you can ignore this section.

You can install the MySQL database on a UNIX server by following these instructions:

1. Login to your server under username "root"
2. Unpack all source files:
   [root@server root]# tar -xzf mysql-4.0.13.tar.gz
3. Change current working directory to mysql-4.0.13:
   [root@server root]# cd mysql-4.0.13
4. Configure the MySQL Server:
   [root@server root]# ./configure --prefix=/usr/local/mysql
5. Make and install the MySQL Server:
   [root@server root]# make
   [root@server root]# make install
6. Install main MySQL database:
   [root@server root]# ./scripts/mysql_install_db
7. Create a symbolic link to mysqld executable:
   [root@server root]# ln -s /usr/local/mysql/share/mysql/mysql.server /sbin/mysqld
8. Create a mysql group:
   [root@server root]# groupadd mysql
9. Create a mysql user:
   [root@server root]# useradd -g mysql mysql
10. Create appropriate ownerships:
    [root@server root]# chown -R mysql:mysql /usr/local/mysql

You can start, stop and restart MySQL by typing:

[root@server root]# mysqld start
[root@server root]# mysqld stop
[root@server root]# mysqld restart

You can uninstall MySQL with these instructions:

[root@server root]# rm -rf /usr/local/mysql
[root@server root]# rm -rf /data/mysql
[root@server root]# rm -rf /sbin/mysqld

MySQL Server Installation (on Windows Servers)

If you downloaded MySQL as part of the AppServ Open Project or if your service provider or systems administration has already installed and configured MySQL, then you can ignore this section.

You can install the MySQL database on a Windows system by following these instructions:

1. Unzip the MySQL zipped file into a temporary directory.
2. Run the setup.exe file and following the onscreen instructions.

3. The MySQL application can be configured to launch and run in the "background" of the operating system automatically when the computer is started. We would recommend that you select this option.

PHPMyAdmin Installation

PHPMyAdmin is an application written using PHP and it is, therefore, platform independent. You don't need worry about obtaining different versions for different operating systems. To install PHPMyAdmin you need to download the full package from http://www.phpmyadmin.net/. You then need to unzip all the files into an appropriate directory and change the config.inc.php which comes with PHPMyAdmin so that it matches your database settings.

To download the latest version of PHPMyAdmin visit the following URL: http://phpmyadmin.sourceforge.net/ and select an appropriate file to download. Although the versions are the same for Linux and Windows, you should select a file which has been appropriately packed for the correct operating system. For a Linux server you should choose a .tar.gz file format and .zip for Windows systems.

To ConFigure PHPMyAdmin:

1. Unpack all files into a Web-folder (a folder that can be viewed through the Web e.g: C:\Inetpub\wwwroot\phpMyAdmin\

2. Change the following lines on config.inc.php in the C:\Inetpub\wwwroot\ phpMyAdmin\ folder:

$cfg['PmaAbsoluteUri'] = 'http://localhost/phpMyAdmin/';

$cfg['Servers'][$i]['auth_type'] = 'http';

$cfg['Servers'][$i]['user'] = 'username';

This configuration should allow you to login and provide your user name and password. However, in the event that this doesn't work, you can force a login, using the following settings:

$cfg['Servers'][$i]['auth_type'] = 'config';

$cfg['Servers'][$i]['user'] = 'root';

$cfg['Servers'][$i]['password'] = '';

Note: that the password field will include the password you will select later in setting up your root-user account. Leave it blank for now and we shall inform you of when to change this. You should be aware that inserting passwords into this ini file is a security risk.

The config.inc.php file is illustrated in Figure 34.1.

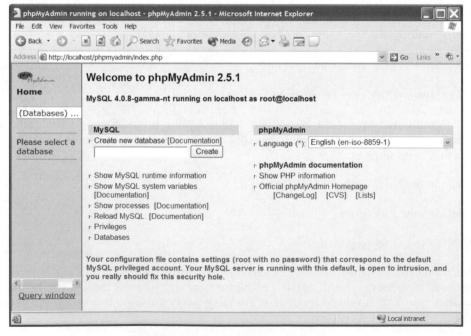

Figure 34.1 config.inc.php file editing.

Figure 34.2 The main PHPMyAdmin page.

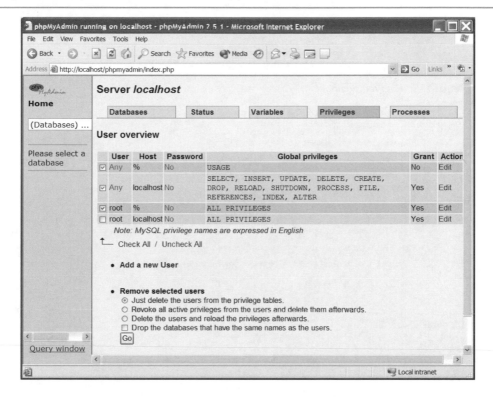

Figure 34.3 "Users" page with four default MySQL users.

To Access PHPMyAdmin:

Access PHPMyAdmin from the URL you entered into the config.inc.php file earlier: http://localhost/phpMyAdmin/index.php). You should be presented with a Web page similar to that shown in Figure 34.2.

MySQL Setting up Root User and Host

When starting MySQL Server four users are created by default. The list of users can be found by selecting the "Users" link or the "Privileges" link (depending on whether you are using Linux or Windows) from the screen shown in Figure 34.2. The list of user screens is shown in Figure 34.3. You must delete the first three users (as shown in Figure 34.3) and leave only user "root" with host set to "localhost". To delete the users, select the tick box next to the first three listed and then click the Go button below the table.

After clicking the Go button you will be presented with the screen shown in Figure 34.4.

We are now ready to add a password to the "root" user. Scroll down the currently viewed page and where you see the "User overview" table click the Edit action link next to the only user in the table, which is the root user. You should be presented with the edit privileges screen as shown in Figure 34.5. Scrolling down the screen will reveal the form fields where you need to enter a password (twice). Do this and then click the Go button.

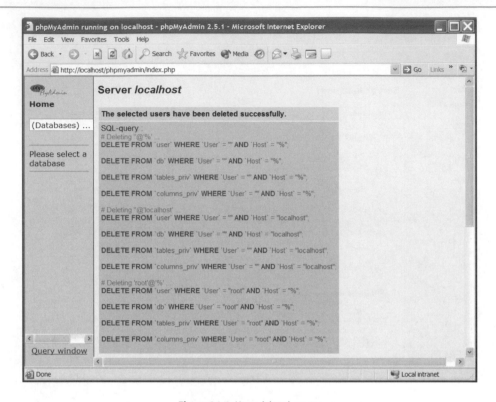

Figure 34.4 Users deleted screen.

Clicking the Privileges tab at the top of the screen will return you to the list of users (only one now) and you should now see (as shown in Figure 34.6) that a password is now set for the user. You will now need to go back and edit the config.inc.php file to include the password you have set (but only if you needed to set the "auth_type" variable to "config"):

$cfg[' Servers '][$i][' password '] = ' mypassword ';

Add or Modify MySQL Users

To connect to a single or multiple database, a username and password must be given to let PHP scripts access MySQL database servers and make appropriate queries to retrieve data from it. For security and accessibility reasons, creating a new user for databases that are to be used by the same person or site is recommended. On PHPMyAdmin this can be done very easily. First, click the reload button on the browser to return to the main screen. Then click either the "users" or "privileges" link and then scroll down to "add a new user" link and select this. Figure 34.7 illustrates the screen which should be displayed.

When a new user is to be added, four areas must be filled in:

1. **Host:** on this field a host name (which represents the host from where a MySQL database will permit access) must be given. If the option is on "Any host" a connection to MySQL can be done locally or by a remote server. If the option is on "Host: localhost" MySQL connections are limited to local users.

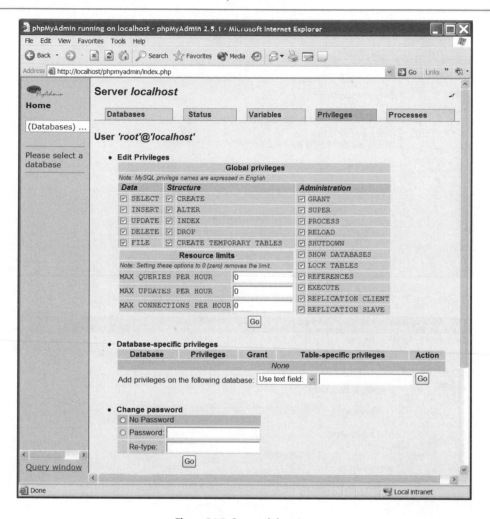

Figure 34.5 Password changing.

2. **User name:** on this field a username must be given. Do not use the "Any user" option.
3. **Password:** password associated with given username. All passwords are encrypted using the MD5 encrypting method but, for maximum safety, it must be eight or more characters long with multiple symbols and numbers.
4. **Privileges:** privileges must always left unchecked when creating a simple user. These are nothing to do with database privileges as they cover the global permissions a user has on the MySQL Database server. If creating a second root administrator, these must all be checked.

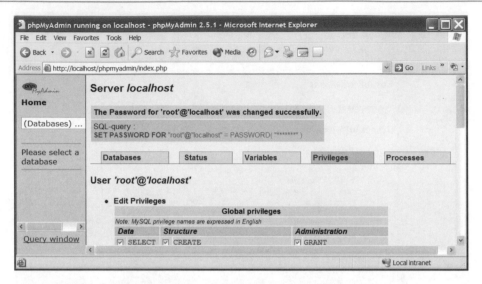

Figure 34.6 "Users" page with the appropriate root administrator.

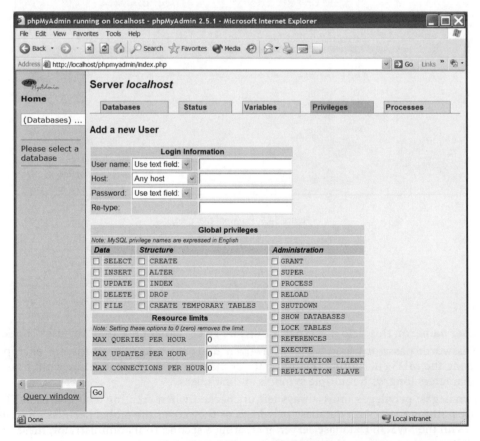

Figure 34.7 Adding a new MySQL user.

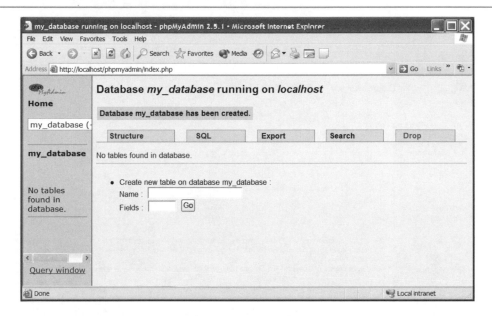

Figure 34.8 Creating a database.

Creating a Database

Creating a new database is very easy. From the main PHPMyAdmin screen you simply enter the name of the database you wish to create in the form field and click the Create button. We have created a database by the name "my_database" and clicked the Create button. If you do this, you should be presented with a screen similar to that in Figure 34.8.

The screen shown in Figure 34.8 allows us to add some tables to our database. A table is where a relational database stores its data. Other database management systems, store all the data in one large area but not in a relational database. Instead, these use tables to store information. Each table within a database is given a unique name and contains some fields which describe the individual items of data within the table. So, for example, we could create a table called Cars which could store the following items of data about our cars: make, model and colour. As there are three fields of data we wish to create we would enter "cars" in the form name field followed by 3 in the fields field and click the Go button. PHPMyAdmin will then display the table editor as shown in Figure 34.9.

The table field and their data type set need to be named on this screen. Depending on the type selected, then an appropriate field length may be required. Figure 34.10 illustrates our completed form, just before we create the table fields by clicking the Save button.

When completed the database should be like the one reproduced in Figure 34.11.

Figure 34.11 illustrates that the my_database database now has a single table called cars consisting of three data fields.

Accessing a Database Quickly

You should note that now you have created a database that this is accessible from the drop-down menu on the left of the screen. Each time you create a new database it will be added to this menu allowing you an easy method of database access.

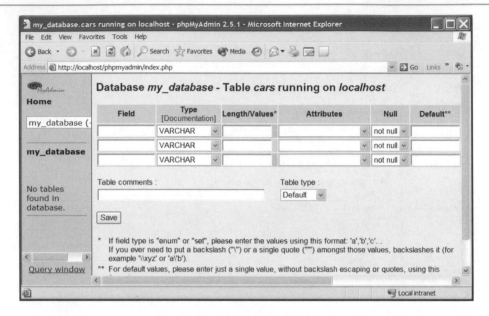

Figure 34.9 Editing table fields.

Dropping Databases and Tables

Once you have selected a database you can modify the tables that form the database. You can delete (drop) a table completely. To do this, select the database from the drop-down list on the left of the PHPMyAdmin screen. You should click on the name of the database on the left of the screen below the pull-down list. This will show the tables available within that database. This is illustrated in Figure 34.12. You can drop any of the database tables by checking the box next to the table to drop the table and then select Drop from the With selected drop-down menu. Finally clicking Go will drop the table from the database.

Backup and Restore MySQL Server or Databases

It is good practice to backup and restore your databases regularly. PHPMyAdmin provides a convenient method of doing this. First, select the database which you wish to backup from the drop-down menu on the left of the screen. Next, when the database table structure is displayed, select the Export tab at the top of the screen. You should then see the screen shown in Figure 34.13.

To create a backup of the database, ensure that all tables are selected in the Export window, then check the Save as file option and enter a file name in the form field. When the Go button is clicked, the database structure and data content will be saved using the file name you entered.

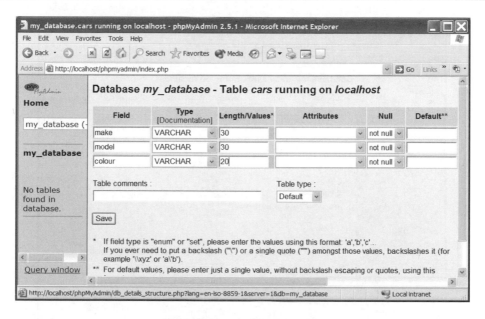

Figure 34.10 Completed table fields.

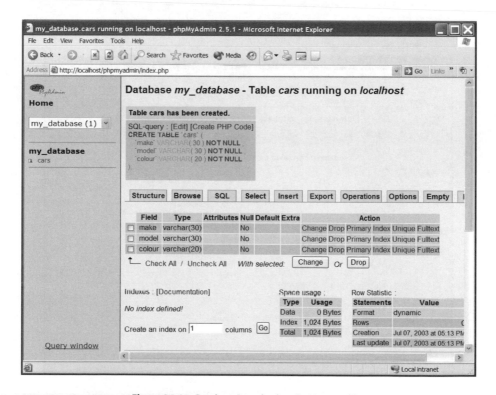

Figure 34.11 Database "my_database" with cars table.

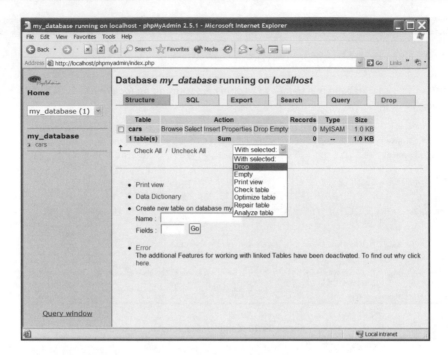

Figure 34.12 Dropping database tables or whole databases.

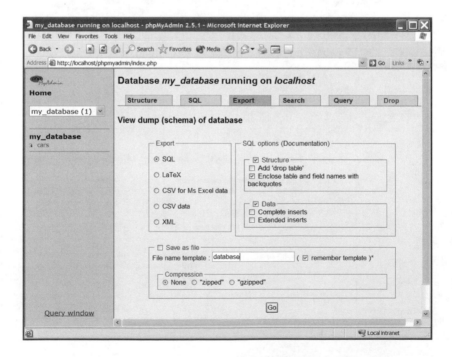

Figure 34.13 Creating a dump file for "my_database" (backup).

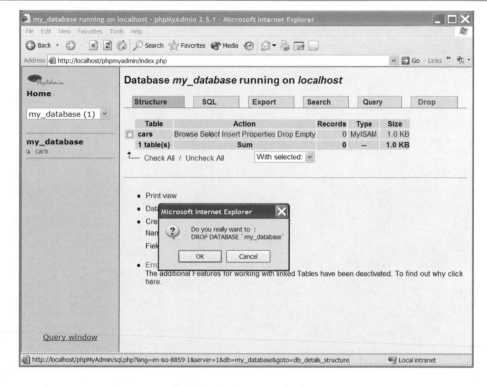

Figure 34.14 Dropping a database.

Dropping a Database

You can drop an entire database using PHPMyAdmin. To do this, select the database you wish to drop from the pull-down menu. Then click the Drop tab at the top of the screen, as shown in Figure 34.14. A pop-up window should confirm the deletion of the database.

Summary

In this chapter we have introduced the MySQL database manager, described where it can be obtained and how it can be installed. We have also described the PHPMyAdmin tool which acts as a user-friendly front-end manager to the MySQL database and shown how this can be used to create and edit your databases. In the next chapter we shall look a little bit more closely into how we can add actual data into our database tables, using the PHPMyAdmin tool.

Creating Databases Using PHPMyAdmin 35

Introduction

In this chapter we shall examine how we can use the PHPMyAdmin tool to create a simple database consisting of three tables. We shall then show how to populate these tables with data records.

Creating the Database

We are going to create a database called "friends&cars". From the main PHPMyAdmin screen, type into the form field the name of this database and click the Create button. This database is to consist of three separate tables. The design of this database is shown in Figure 35.1.

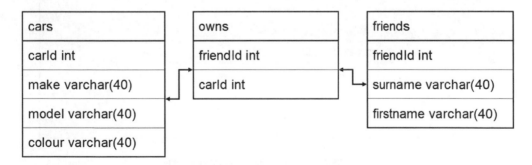

Figure 35.1 Database friends&cars table structure and fields.

Create a table called cars and insert the four fields into the table as shown in Figure 35.2. Note that cardId field is of type Int, is the Primary key and is set to auto_increment. This means that each time a new record is created MySQL will automatically generate the value for the field.

When you have clicked the Save button to store this table you will be presented with the screen shown in Figure 35.3. Note that the database name on the left of the screen now sports the table name "cars" below it.

475

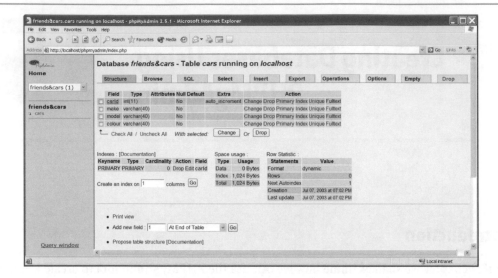

Figure 35.2 Table cars and field values.

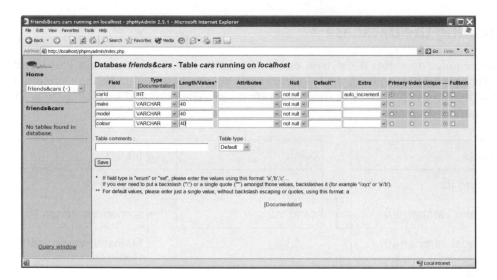

Figure 35.3 Database friends&cars with cars table.

Click the database name "friends&cars" under the pull-down menu on the left of the screen and in the form fields presented create the next table called "friends", which consists of three fields. Figure 35.4 illustrates the completed table before the Save button is clicked.

When clicked you should note that below the database name "friends&cars" on the left of the window is now listed both the table names "cars" and "friends". Finally, repeat the process to create our final database table "owns", which consist of two fields. Figure 35.5 illustrates the completed table before the Save button is clicked.

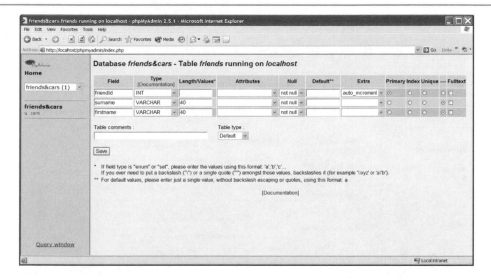

Figure 35.4 Database friends&cars with friends table.

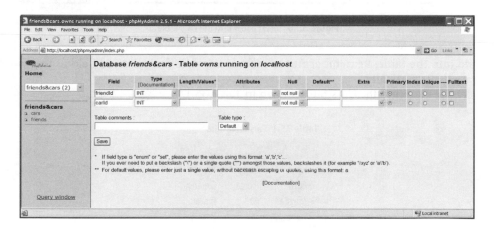

Figure 35.5 Database friends&cars with owns table.

We have now completed our database structure and are now ready to begin to add data records to our database.

Adding Data to the Database

We can use PHPMyAdmin to add data records to our database tables. To do this simply click on the table name you wish to add a record to (let's add a record to the cars table). Table names are located below the database name on the left of the screen. Then click the "insert" tab at the top of the screen, this will display the insert a row screen, as shown in Figure 35.6, where we have inserted some record data ready to click the Go button to insert

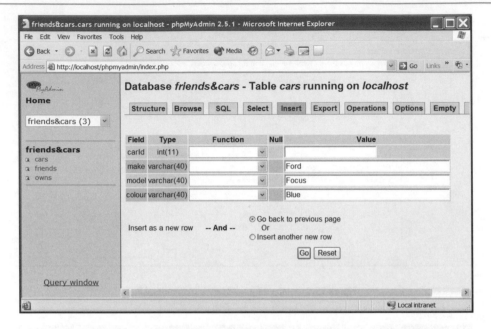

Figure 35.6 Insert a row into the Cars table.

the data into the table. Remember not to include any data for the carId field as this will be generated automatically.

Insert the data into the Cars table shown in Table 35.1.

Table 35.1 Cars table data.

Make	Model	Colour
Ford	Focus	Blue
Ford	Fiesta	Green
Mazda	323	Black
Renault	Clio	Blue
Toyota	Celica	Silver

You can view the data which you have entered into the table by clicking on the little icon to the left of the table name below the database name on the left of the screen. Clicking on the icon next to the cars table name should result in the screen displaying the data records within the table, as illustrated in Figure 35.7.

Add the data shown in Tables 35.2 and 35.3 to the Friends and Owns database tables respectively.

Figure 35.8 illustrates the data in Table 35.2 inserted in the database.

Figure 35.9 illustrates the data in Table 35.3 inserted in the database.

Note that the Owns table allows us to specify that an individual friend owns more than one car, for example friend number 1 and 4. Likewise we can specify that a particular car can be owned by more than one friend, for example car 3 is owned by three different people.

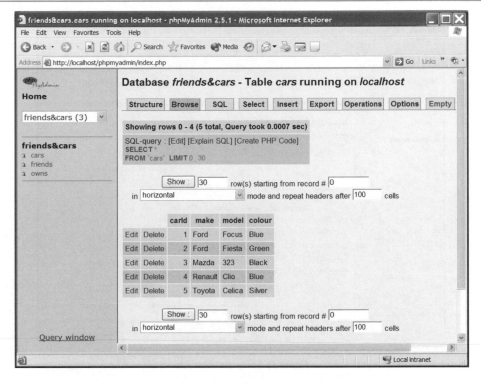

Figure 35.7 Cars table data.

Table 35.2 Friends table data.

Surname	Firstname
Smith	Mike
Jones	Simon
Brown	Alan
Parrington	David
Walker	Ian

Table 35.3 Owns table data.

friendId	carId
1	1
1	3
2	2
3	3
4	3
4	4
5	5

Editing and Deleting Data

If during the course of adding your records to the database you have found that you have made an error and need to make a correction, then this can easily be done. When you wish to delete a data record, simply click the icon next to the table name to display the table of data records. Note that next to each record there are Edit and Delete buttons. Clicking the Delete button will result in a popup window appearing asking you to confirm the delete. This is illustrated in Figure 35.10.

Clicking the edit link will display an edit window, like that shown in Figure 35.11.

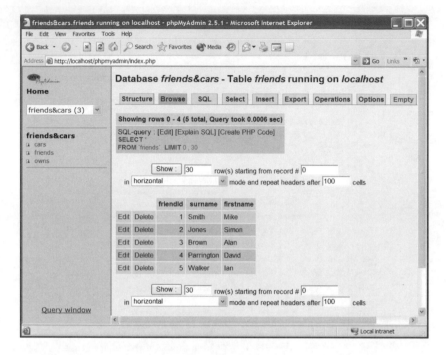

Figure 35.8 Friends table data.

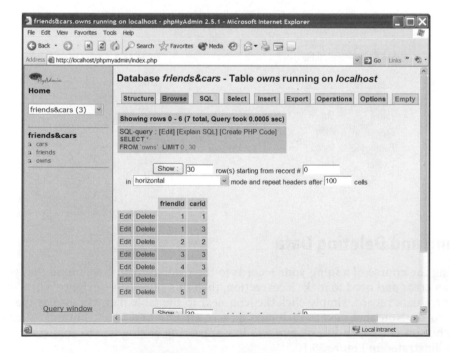

Figure 35.9 Owns table data.

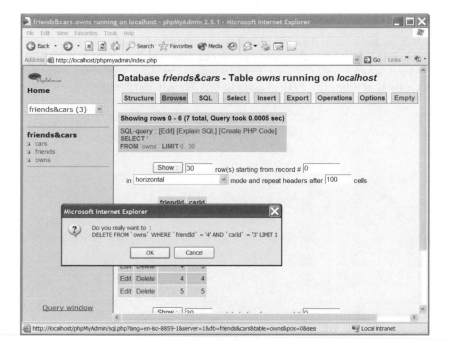

Figure 35.10 Deleting data.

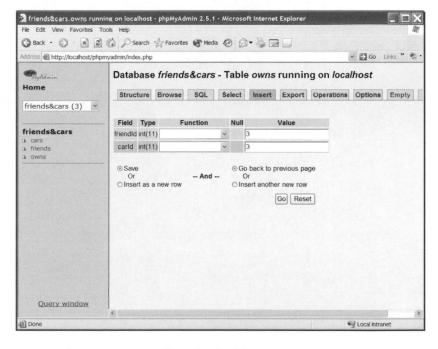

Figure 35.11 Editing data.

Summary

In this chapter we illustrated how PHPMySQL can be used to populate a database with data and how that data can be manipulated. However, the real power of the MySQL database can only be seen when we start to use PHP to access the data. In the following chapter we illustrate exactly that – linking PHP scripts to our MySQL database.

Accessing MySQL Using PHP **36**

Introduction

In previous chapters we have described how to create databases, create table structures within them and insert data records into these fields. While this is useful it does not fully illustrate the power of the database. In this chapter we explore how PHP can be used to access, display and modify database records via a Web page. This technology is the building block for the majority of dynamic Web applications, in particular e-commerce systems.

Connecting to Database

To connect a PHP script to a MySQL database we need to introduce four functions. The first is mysql_connect and forms a connection from the script to the location of a specific database.

Function prototype:

```
resource mysql_connect(string server, string username, string password);
```

Function arguments and return details:

Name	Type	Description
server	String	Name of the server
username	String	User name
password	String	Password
mysql_connect() returns	Resource identifier	A resource identifier pointing to the server

The mysql_connect() function returns a resource identifier type. This type of variable was first mentioned way back in Chapter 6. We will need this resource identifier as we shall use it in all related database functions from now on.

The next function is mysql_select_db() which allows us to specify which database at the location defined in the mysql_connect() function we wish to use.

Function prototype:

```
bool mysql_select_db(string databasename resource identifier);
```

Function arguments and return details:

Name	Type	Description
databasename	String	Name of the database
identifier	Resource	The resource identifier returned from the mysql_connect() function
mysql_select_db() returns	Bool	Returns "TRUE" if successful otherwise "FALSE"

Next we need to mention the function die() which is an alias of exit(). This function was first mentioned in Chapter 24. The die() function is combined with an or operator in order to stop execution of the script if the previous database connection could not be formed. Finally function mysql_error() returns the text of the error message from the previous MYSQL operation:

Function prototype:

```
string mysql_error()
```

Function arguments and return details:

Name	Type	Description
mysql_error() returns	String	Error message

The following provides an example of how these functions are used together:

```
$db = mysql_connect("localhost", "root", "stobbie")
    or die("Could not connect: " . mysql_error());

mysql_select_db("friends&cars",$db);
```

Note that in this example mysql_connect() the specified host is "localhost" but if the MySQL server is not located on the same machine on which you are developing the site this would have the Web address of that computer. The second parameter is the user name, in this case "root". The user name must be specified if the database has been created with security restrictions. The final parameter is the password you have selected for your user name.

The mysql_select_db() selects the friends@cars database which we created in the previous chapter.

For the ease of use we will create a MySQL script example36-db.php where the connection to the database is performed:

```
<?php

//Accessing MySQL - Example 36-db
//-------------------------------

$db = mysql_connect("localhost", "root", "stobbie")
    or die("Could not connect: " . mysql_error());

mysql_select_db("friends&cars",$db);

?>
```

This file will be included on every example in the remainder of this chapter.

Selecting Data

The mysql_query function is used to select data from a database using a Structured Query Language (SQL) query. The function has the following structure:

Function prototype:

```
resource mysql_query (string query, resource identifier);
```

Function arguments and return details:

Name	Type	Description
query	String	SQL query
identifier	Resource	The resource identifier returned from the mysql_connect() function
mysql_query() returns	Resource	Resource identifier to the records returned

Function example:

```
$result = mysql_query("SELECT * FROM users",$db);
```

Having obtained a set of results we need a function which will return the contents of one record cell from the record set. This function is called mysql_result:

Function prototype:

```
mixed mysql_result (resource result, int row, mixed field);
```

Function arguments and return details:

Name	Type	Description
result	Resource	Resource identifier returned from the mysql_result function
identifier	Int	Cell number to return, 0 is the first cell
field	Mixed	The field name to return
mysql_query() returns	Mixed	Database field cell

Function example:

```
$rec= mysql_result($result,0, "surname");
```

We shall begin by creating a script to extract a single record from the "friends" table in the "friends&cars" database. Consider the following PHP script:

```php
<?php

//Accessing MySQL - Example 36-1
//-------------------------------

require ("example36-db.php");
?>

<html>
<body>

<?php

$result = mysql_query("SELECT * FROM friends",$db);

echo "first name: ". mysql_result($result,0,"firstname") .
"<br />";
echo "surname: ". mysql_result($result,0,"surname") . "<br />";
?>

</body>
<html>
```

This example displays the contents of the first row (row 0) of the database record field.

Of course this is still not all that useful an example as only one record is displayed. Let's create a new example that includes a loop which will allow us to display all the database records. In order to do this we need to introduce a new function mysql_fetch_row():

Function prototype:

```
Array mysql_fetch_row(resource result);
```

Function arguments and return details:

Name	Type	Description
result	Resource	Resource identifier returned from the mysql_result function
mysql_fetch_row() returns	Array	Array of the fetched database record

Function example:

```
$records = mysql_fetch_row($result);
```

Because the function returns an array of the fields for the record we access the fields by subscripting the array. For example, the following will return the second field of a record:

```
$records[1];
```

The following script illustrates a modified version of our previous example that will display all of our records in the database:

```php
<?php

//Accessing MySQL - Example 36-2
//------------------------------

require ("example36-db.php");
?>

<html>
<body>

<?php

$result = mysql_query("SELECT * FROM friends",$db);

while ($records = mysql_fetch_row($result)) {
    echo "first name: ". $records[2] . "<br />";
    echo "surname: ". $records[1] . "<br />";
}

?>

</body>
<html>
```

This script is similar to the previous example but introduces a loop instruction:

```
while ($rec = mysql_fetch_row($result)) { }
```

Note that within the loop there is a new function, mysql_fetch_row(). This function returns a single record, stored in the $result variable. The record is stored in an array called $rec. Note that the echo statements display each of the elements of the $rec[] array. The array contains the value of each of the records fields. The array element [0] contains the record id, while [1] contains the friend's first name and [2] their surname. Each interaction around the while loop will cause function mysql_fetch_row() to be invoked. Each time it will return the next record from the database. When no more records can be found, it will return "FALSE" and the loop will be terminated.

The output from this script is illustrated in Figure 36.1.

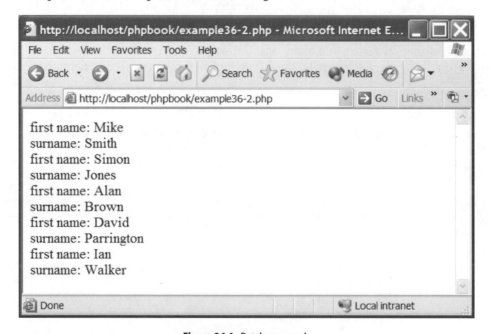

Figure 36.1 Database records.

In the previous example the mysql_fetch_row() function was used to access and display the database records. While this works okay the programmer writing the script has to refer to the separate fields using array numbers. This does not make the code very easy to read and mistakes can be introduced. The function mysql_fetch_array() is an extended version of the function mysql_fetch_row():

Function prototype:

```
Array mysql_fetch_array(resource result);
```

Function arguments and return details:

Name	Type	Description
result	Resource	Resource identifier returned from the mysql_result function
mysql_fetch_array() returns	Array	Array of the fetched database record

Function example:

```
$records = mysql_fetch_array($result);
```

This function is the same as the mysql_fetch_row() function, except that it allows us to refer to the database fields by their name. The following script illustrates the use of this function:

```php
<?php

//Accessing MySQL - Example 36-3
//-------------------------------

require ("example36-db.php");
?>

<html>
<body>

<?php

$result = mysql_query("SELECT * FROM friends",$db);

while ($records = mysql_fetch_array($result)) {
    echo "first name: ". $records['firstname'] . "<br />";
    echo "surname: ". $records['surname'] . "<br />";
}

?>

</body>
<html>
```

Advanced Data Selection

The SQL query statements which are sent to the database using the mysql_query() function are capable of much more powerful things than the examples we have illustrated so far in this chapter. Let's take a moment to look at some of its abilities to help us select the data we want from the database.

Selecting a Certain Number of Records:

Our SQL queries can use the option LIMIT to select a certain number of records from a table. The option limit has two parameters: the first one (x) represents the starting row and the second one (y) represents the number of records to be selected after "x", for example:

```
$query = mysql_query ("SELECT field(s) FROM table
LIMIT 1, 3", $db);
```

This example will begin selecting records from row 1 but only return four records. The following script illustrates this:

```php
<?php

//Accessing MySQL - Example 36-4
//--------------------------------

require ("example36-db.php");
?>

<html>
<body>

<?php

$result = mysql_query("SELECT * FROM friends LIMIT 1,3",$db);

while ($records = mysql_fetch_array($result)) {
    echo "first name: ". $records['firstname'] . "<br />";
    echo "surname: ". $records['surname'] . "<br />";
}

?>

</body>
<html>
```

Note that the output from this script is the same as the previous script, except that only three records are output.

Sort Records

Our SQL queries can use the option ORDER BY to sort our selected data. The SORT BY option should be followed by the name of the column (field) and an extra option which defines whether the ordering is to be ascending (asc) or descending (desc):

```
$query = mysql_query ("SELECT field(s) FROM table ORDER
BY surname desc", $db);
```

The following script shows our results ordered by surname in a descending order:

```php
<?php

//Accessing MySQL - Example 36-5
//-------------------------------

require ("example36-db.php");
?>

<html>
<body>

<?php

$result = mysql_query("SELECT * FROM friends ORDER BY surname
desc",$db);

while ($records = mysql_fetch_array($result)) {
    echo "first name: ". $records['firstname'] . "<br />";
    echo "surname: ". $records['surname'] . "<br />";
}

?>

</body>
<html>
```

The output from this script is illustrated in Figure 36.2.

Inserting Data

So far we have seen how we can extract data from the database but it would be useful if we could also add new data. The mysql_query() function using the "INSERT INTO" query can do just this:

```php
$insert = mysql_query("INSERT INTO table (column1,
column2, ..., column-x) VALUES ('value', 'value', ...,
'value')" ,$db);
```

With an INSERT INTO query the table column field names must be specified and values of these should be specified in the same order. Note that there is no restriction on how many columns we can use to insert data but it is recommended to specify all columns on an INSERT query with empty values for those that we want to be left empty.

However, we can use no columns at all and have an alternative structure for the insert query as in the following example. Note that the first value will now be inserted into the first column, the second value into the second column, etc.

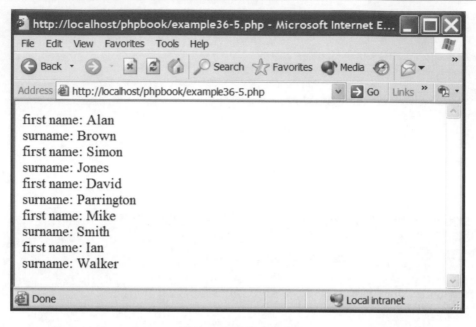

Figure 36.2 Sorted output.

```
$insert = mysql_query("INSERT INTO table VALUES
('value', 'value', ..., 'value')" ,$db);
```

The following example uses the INSERT query to add a new record on table "friends":

```php
<?php

<?php

//Accessing MySQL - Example 36-6
//-------------------------------

require ("example36-db.php");
?>

<html>
<body>

<?php

$insert = mysql_query("INSERT INTO friends VALUES (", 'Hinds',
'Kevin')" ,$db);

$result = mysql_query("SELECT * FROM friends ORDER BY surname desc",
$db);
```

```
while ($records = mysql_fetch_array($result)) {
    echo "Id: ". $records['friendId'] . "<br />";
    echo "first name: ". $records['firstname'] . "<br />";
    echo "surname: ". $records['surname'] . "<br /><br />";
}

?>

</body>
<html>
```

The output from this script is shown in Figure 36.3 and shows the newly added record.

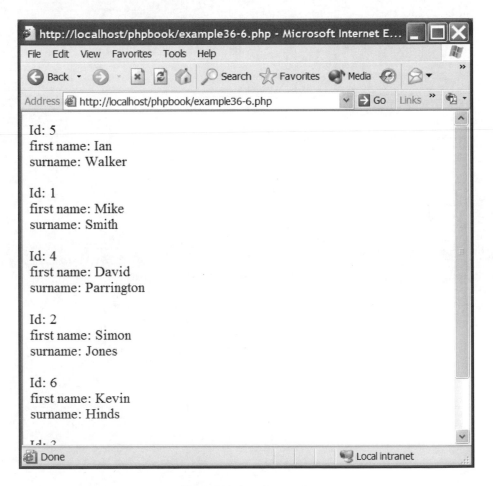

Figure 36.3 Inserting records.

Deleting Data

We can delete records from tables using the mysql_query() function using the DELETE FROM query:

```
$DELETE = mysql_query ("DELETE FROM table WHERE
column='$value'", $db);
```

The following illustrates a script that will allow us to delete any record which we have inserted into our database. All you need to enter is the id number:

```php
<?php

//Accessing MySQL - Example 36-7
//-------------------------------

require ("example36-db.php");
?>

<html>
<body>

<?php

if (isset($_POST['id'])) {
    $delete = mysql_query("DELETE FROM friends WHERE
friendId=$_POST[id]",$db);
        echo ("<br>Record Deleted<br>");
}


$result = mysql_query("SELECT * FROM friends",$db);

while ($records = mysql_fetch_array($result)) {
    echo "Id: ". $records['friendId'] . "<br />";
    echo "first name: ". $records['firstname'] . "<br />";
    echo "surname: ". $records['surname'] . "<br /><br />";
}

?>
<form action="<?php echo $_SERVER['PHP_SELF'] ?>" method="post">
    Id: <input type="text" name="id"><br>
    <input type="submit" value="Delete Record">
</form>

</body>
<html>
```

The output from this script is illustrated in Figure 36.4, where record id 6 has just been deleted.

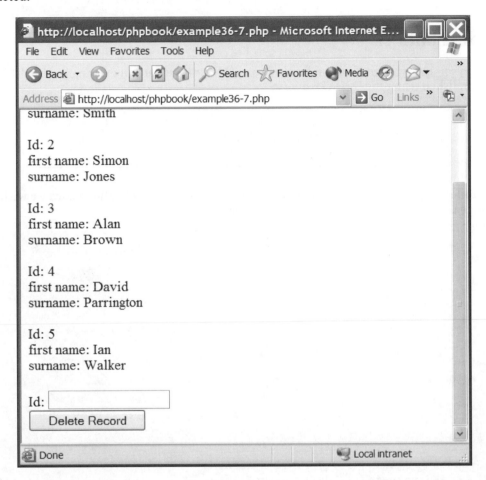

Figure 36.4 Deleted record id 6.

This script contains an if statement which checks the value of $id, indicating whether the form has been submitted. $id is used to select the record to be deleted:

```
if (isset($_POST['id'])) {
```

If the variable $id contains a value, the mysql_query() function is invoked:

```
    $delete = mysql_query("DELETE FROM friends WHERE
friendId=$_POST[id]",$db);
        echo ("<br>Record Deleted<br>");
    }
```

This deletes the record in the database with an id equal to $id. Note that there is no error checking in this script and the user is free to type in any id number.

Update Data

The mysql_query() function can be used to enable us to update an existing record. This is accomplished using the UPDATE query:

```
$update = mysql_query ("UPDATE table SET
column1='value', column2='value' ... columnX='value'
WHERE column='value'",$db);
```

The following script uses a form to update existing records. The id of the record we wish to change is used to ensure that we modify the correct record:

```php
<?php

//Accessing MySQL - Example 36-8
//-------------------------------

require ("example36-db.php");
?>

<html>
<body>

<?php

if (isset($_POST['id'])) {

$result = mysql_query("UPDATE friends
     SET surname='$_POST[surname]',
     firstname='$_POST[firstname]'
     WHERE friendId='$_POST[id]'",$db);

}

$result = mysql_query("SELECT * FROM friends",$db);

while ($records = mysql_fetch_array($result)) {
     echo "Id: ". $records['friendId'] . "<br />";
     echo "first name: ". $records['firstname'] . "<br />";
     echo "surname: ". $records['surname'] . "<br /><br />";
}

?>
```

```
<form action="<?php echo $_SERVER['PHP_SELF'] ?>" method="post">
    Id: <input type="text" name="id"><br />
    Firstname: <input type="text" name="firstname"><br />
    Surname: <input type="text" name="surname"><br />
    <input type="submit" value="Update Record">
</form>

</body>
<html>
```

Count Rows and Check Existence of Records

The mysql_num_rows() function can be used to count the number of records in a table and also whether a record exists:

Function prototype:

```
int mysql_num_rows(resource result);
```

Function arguments and return details:

Name	Type	Description
result	Resource	Resource identifier returned from the mysql_result function
Mysql_fetch_array() returns	Int	Number of record rows

Function example:

```
$records = mysql_num_rows($result);
```

Consider the following example where the function mysql_num_rows() is used to count current records (rows) on the table "friends".

```
<?php

//Accessing MySQL - Example 36-9
//-------------------------------

require ("example36-db.php");
?>
```

```
<html>
<body>

<?php


$result = mysql_query("SELECT * FROM friends",$db);

$rows = mysql_num_rows($result);

if($rows) {
    echo "$rows records found";
}
else {
    echo "No records found";
}

?>

</body>
<html>
```

This script will display the message "5 records found".

Summary

This chapter has illustrated how a PHP script can be used to extract data from a MySQL database. In addition we have shown that PHP can also delete and amend existing records. In the next chapter we shall examine the object-oriented concept of classes and objects.

Part 11

Classes and Objects Concepts

Classes and Objects 37

Introduction

Many modern programming languages now support the object-oriented paradigm. Object orientation is an alternative way of designing and implementing programs. Within the object-oriented paradigm, programmers model things known as classes and then use these within a program by creating instances of these classes known as objects. PHP supports the creation of classes and the implementation of objects and enables the programmer to develop object-oriented programs. In this chapter we shall describe the concept of object orientation and provide some examples of what aspects of the paradigm PHP supports.

What are Classes and Objects

Object orientation is a paradigm which encourages and helps to enable code reuse effectively. It also aims to minimize the impact of any programming change through the technique known as encapsulation. Object orientation is a different way of thinking about solving a programming problem. Traditional structured programming techniques solve problems by breaking the solution down into simple easy-to-program functions. These functions are grouped together within the program to perform the task required of the program, see Figure 37.1. This is the technique we have employed to solve the problems within this book.

While this technique has proven successful over the years, it doesn't help programmers to reuse their code effectively nor does it help protect data from accidental change. You see, with a functional approach local data may be declared within a function but this may be required as a parameter for another function to enable further processing. If the data structures being passed from function to function are large and complex, then it is easy for programming bugs to creep into the design resulting in data being altered when it shouldn't.

Object orientation takes a different approach to the design of data. In an object-oriented design, data and methods (also known as functions) are wrapped up together in what is known as a class. The data cannot be accessed from outside the class and so it is protected from the rest of the program. This is known as encapsulation. Only the methods associated with the class can access and alter these data and form an "interface" with the data. Invoking class methods in this way is known as sending a message to the class. This is illustrated in Figure 37.2.

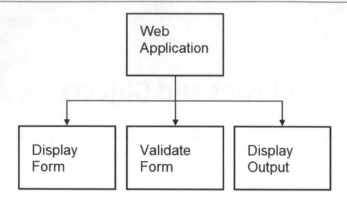

Figure 37.1 Functional programming design.

Object orientation encourages software reuse by allowing the programmer to define new classes which are similar to existing one. Effectively the programmer is able to say: "This class is the same as that one, except that it has these small differences". The great thing is that the programmer only needs to say what the differences are and all the stuff, which has already been programmed for the original class, is automatically accessible by the new one. This is known as inheritance.

Class Car

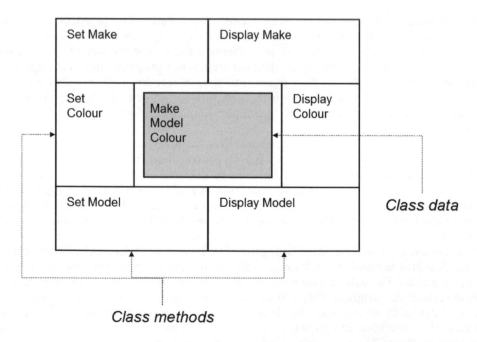

Figure 37.2 Object orientation – classes.

Object orientation also supports the concept of polymorphism. Polymorphism is a concept where a number of related classes all have a method which shares the same name. For example, we could have created a number of classes, which draw different shapes on the screen. All of the shapes have a method called draw which allows them to display themselves. The programmer can invoke the draw method in any of the classes knowing that it will result in the shape being displayed. However, the resulting image will be different depending on which shape class the message is sent.

Creating classes is not the end of the story. Classes are, in effect, templates which define what data can be held and what things it can do. Classes are essentially a sophisticated version of a variable. Variables are designed to hold data of a specific type and you can do certain things with a particular variable. However, before a variable can be used, we need to create an instance of one. The same is true with classes. The class is the template and to use it we must create an instance of the class with some specific data. An instance of a class is known as an object.

Classes and Objects in PHP

While most object-oriented programming languages will implement the features described previously, this is about as similar as many programming languages get. In fact, depending on what programming language you are using, the terminology will differ. For example, class methods, functions and procedures are all used to describe the same thing. Likewise data members and class variables are terms used to mean the same thing.

PHP keeps things simple and consistent with other aspects of the PHP language. In defining a class, the programmer specifies class variables and functions which are encompassed within the class. We shall not use any new names for these as this would be confusing. Instances of classes will be referred to as objects. Let's now create a simple class to show how easy it is.

Creating a Simple Class

The keyword used to define a class is class. Each class must be given a unique name and uses { } to denote the start and end of the class definition. For example, creating a class called vehicle we would use the following syntax:

```php
<?php
class vehicle {
}
?>
```

Classes can have variables encapsulated within them. Class variables are defined in the same way as other variables within PHP except that they must have the keyword var placed in front of them, for example:

```php
var $description;
```

Class variables must be placed inside the class definition, i.e. between the start and end braces, for example:

```php
<?php
class vehicle {
     var $description;
}
?>
```

Classes can also have functions associated with them. The functions provide an interface to the class data. All class variables are accessible by all functions within the class. Each class function is defined in exactly the same way as a standard function defined outside of the class, for example:

```php
function display() {
}
```

Class functions can be created to receive parameters and/or return a value, for example:

```php
function set($d) {
}
```

The functions should also be embedded within the class start and end braces:

```php
<?php
class vehicle {
     var $description;

     function set($d) {
     }

     function display() {
     }
}
?>
```

These functions don't do anything at the moment as they contain no code. What we would like them to do is for the set function to assign the variable parameter $d to the class variable $description. This will implement a function which allows the value of $description to be set when an object of the class is created. You are probably thinking that the statement:

```php
$description = $d;
```

would assign the value of $d to $description. However, you would be wrong. Because $description is a class variable and not declared or passed to function set() we need a special syntax to refer to it. To do this we use the variable $this which means "this class" and then the operator -> followed by the variable name, for example:

```
$this->description
```

Note that you don't place a $ on the front of the variable name. To assign a variable $d to this variable we use the statement:

```
this->description = $d;
```

In the case of function display() all we want this to do is to echo the value of $description. To do this we use the statement:

```
echo($this->description);
```

The following class includes these completed functions.

```php
<?php
class vehicle {
    var $description;

    function set($d) {
        $this->description = $d;
    }

    function display() {
        echo($this->description);
    }
}
?>
```

We now have a class which contains a variable and has two functions which allow us to set and view the value of the variable. If you were to view the output from the previous script in a browser you would be very disappointed as nothing would appear. This is because while we have correctly created a class we have not used it. What we need to do now is to create an instance of this class, known as an object.

Using the Simple Vehicle Class

To make use of our vehicle class we need to create an object (a variable if you like) of that class. To do this we need to use the keyword new with the following syntax:

```
$ObjectName = new className;
```

Therefore, to create a object called $veh which is an instance of class vehicle we would write:

```
$veh = new vehicle;
```

This is essentially the same as declaring a variable $veh. While this is perfectly fine we haven't yet assigned a value to it. Our class has been designed to hold a single item of data in the variable called $description. We cannot simply say something like:

```
$description = "A blue car";
```

It wouldn't work as we cannot assign values to classes only to objects. Okay, you say, why can't I write something like

```
$veh->description = "A blue car";
```

Well, you are getting closer as this tries to assign a value to a specific variable belonging to an object you have created. However, one of the "rules" of object orientation is the concept of encapsulation. This hides data within an object from the outside world and does not permit you to view or change it. So how do we assign a value to this variable? Well, through the class functions we have created – that's how.

To assign a value to our object we need to invoke the set function as this has been designed to receive a parameter and to store this in our $description class variable. To invoke an objects function we use the syntax:

```
$ObjectName->functionName()
```

Therefore, to invoke our $veh objects set() function, passing it the data "My big shiny new car." We would write:

```
$veh->set("My big shiny new car.");
```

This statement passes the string "My big shiny new car" to the function set() belonging to object veh. The function stores this string in class variable $description. To view the value stored in the string we need to invoke function display(), like so:

```
$veh->display();
```

This statement reads as follows: invoke function display of the object $veh. The following script adds these statements to our script which contains the vehicle class:

```php
<?php

// Classes - Example 37-1
//----------------------

class vehicle {
    var $description;

    function set($d) {
        $this->description = $d;
    }

    function display() {
        echo($this->description);
    }
}

$veh = new vehicle;
$veh->set("My big shiny new car.");
$veh->display();
?>
```

The output from this script is shown in Figure 37.3. Not very exciting we know but it is a start!

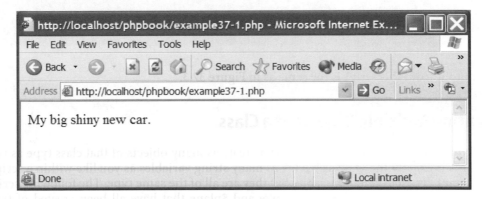

Figure 37.3 Really exciting output from a class.

Invoking Class Functions from Within a Class

Class functions can be invoked from within a class itself. The syntax for doing this is as follows:

```
$this->functionName();
```

This facility is useful as it enables you to invoke functions automatically. Consider the following class example which is a modification of the previous example. Here you will note that the function set() now has a call to function display() within it. This enables the value of description to be automatically displayed when the function set() is invoked and thus removes the need to invoke the function display() outside of the object when the object is created.

```php
<?php

// Classes - Example 37-2
//----------------------

class vehicle {
     var $description;

     function set($d) {
          $this->description = $d;
          $this->display();
     }

     function display() {
          echo($this->description);
     }
}

$veh = new vehicle;
$veh->set("My big shiny new car.");
?>
```

The output from this script is the same as in Figure 37.3.

Creating Multiple Objects of a Class

Once you have created your class, you can create as many objects of that class type as you like. This is exactly the same as having as many string variables as you like within a script. The strings are all different variables but they are all of the same type. The following script illustrates three objects called $car, $bike and $plane that have all been created of type vehicle:

```php
<?php

// Classes - Example 37-3
//----------------------

class vehicle {
     var $description;
```

```
        function set($d) {
            $this->description = $d;
            $this->display();
        }

        function display() {
            echo($this->description . "<br>");
        }
}

$car = new vehicle;
$car->set("Sports Car");
$bike = new vehicle;
$bike->set("Mountain Bike");
$plane = new vehicle;
$plane->set("Jet Fighter");
?>
```

The output from this script is shown in Figure 37.4.

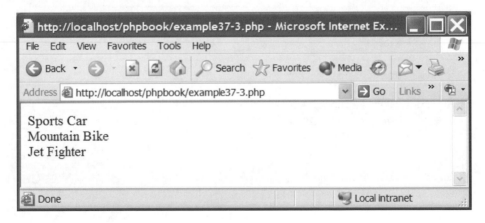

Figure 37.4 Multiple objects of the same type.

Constructors

You will have noticed by now that creating an object is a two-stage process. First we create a new object, then we call a function that populates that object with data, for example:

```
$car = new vehicle;
$car->set("Sports Car");
```

There is, however, a way to perform these two operations in one. In order to do so, we need to create a constructor. A constructor is a function which is automatically called when a new object is created. A function becomes a constructor when it has the same name as the class. For example, a constructor function for our vehicle class would look like this:

```php
function vehicle($d) {
    $this->description = $d;
    $this->display();
}
```

The constructor assigns the value of variable $d to variable $description and then invokes function display(). Having created a constructor, we can now combine the creation of the object and the population of data with the syntax:

```php
$car = new vehicle("Sports Car");
```

This will create a new object called $car of class vehicle and pass the string "Sports Car" to the constructor function. The complete script is as follows:

```php
<?php

// Classes - Example 37-4
//----------------------

class vehicle {
        var $description;

        function vehicle($d) {
            $this->description = $d;
            $this->display();
        }

        function display() {
            echo($this->description . "<br>");
        }
}

$car = new vehicle("Sports Car");
$bike = new vehicle("Mountain Bike");
$plane = new vehicle("Jet Fighter");
?>
```

The output from this script is the same as that shown in Figure 37.4.

Arrays of Objects

Objects that have been created can be treated in the same way as variables. Therefore, you can easily create an array of objects for example:

```php
<?php

// Classes - Example 37-5
//---------------------

class vehicle {
        var $description;

        function vehicle($d) {
            $this->description = $d;
            $this->display();
        }

        function display() {
            echo($this->description . "<br>");
        }
}

$car = new vehicle("Sports Car");
$bike = new vehicle("Mountain Bike");
$plane = new vehicle("Jet Fighter");
$array = array($car,$bike,$plane);
foreach($array as $theVehicle)
        echo($theVehicle->display());
?>
```

This script illustrates that the three vehicle objects we have created can be placed inside an array (called $array) and then accessed using a foreach loop. The output from this script is illustrated in Figure 37.5.

Functions and Objects

Objects can be passed to functions in the same way as variables. The following script, however, illustrates a problem to be wary of:

```php
<?php

// Classes - Example 37-6
//---------------------

class vehicle {
    var $description;

    function vehicle($d) {
            $this->description = $d;
            $this->display();
    }
```

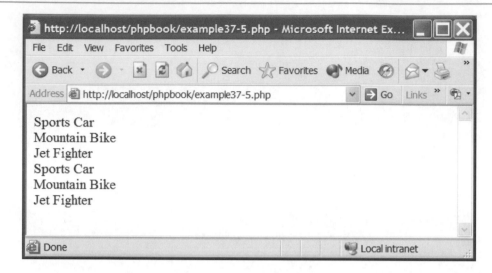

Figure 37.5 Using objects in an array.

```
        function set($d) {
                $this->description = $d;
                $this->display();
        }

        function display() {
                echo($this->description . "<br>");
        }
}

function change($veh){
        $veh->set("Red Sports Car");
}



$car = new vehicle("Sports Car");
change($car);
$car->display();
?>
```

The script contains a modified vehicle class. Note that the modification involves the addition of the set() function which will allow us to modify the vehicle description once an object has been created. A non-class function called change() has also been included. This receives a vehicle object as a parameter and then invokes the objects set() function.

The script creates the $car object, invokes the change() function and passes it the $car object and, finally, it invokes the $car display function. As the change function alters the description, you may expect to see the output "Sports Car" (when the object was created), then "Red Sports Car", when the description was changed in function change(), and, finally, "Red Sports Car" when the display() function was called after the function is complete. The actual output produced is illustrated in Figure 37.6. Note that the output is as expected until the last call to the object function display(). The object appears to have returned to its original description. In fact, all that has happened is that a copy of the object was sent to function change() and the function changed the copy! If you want the function to alter the copy, then you will need to modify the function call as follows:

```
change(&$car);
```

Passing a variable by reference was explained in Chapter 13.

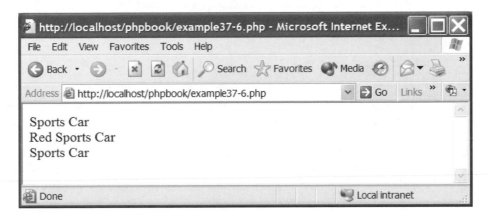

Figure 37.6 Output from function example.

Function Overloading and Default Arguments

Class functions, like their non-class counterparts, can include default argument values. This allows a function to be called with an argument or without, if it is known that the missing default value will be set. The constructor function in the following script illustrates this by setting the vehicle description to "Unknown Constructor". Classes do not support function overloading. Overloading is where a class can have a number of functions with the same name. In the following script you will note that we have had to implement two functions set() and setu(): one which receives a parameter and one which does not. In the case of the second function, the value of the description is set to "unknown set function":

```php
<?php

// Classes - Example 37-7
//---------------------

class vehicle {
    var $description;
```

```
     function vehicle($d='Unknown Constructor') {
         $this->description = $d;
         $this->display();
     }

     function set($d) {
         $this->description = $d;
         $this->display();
     }

     function setu() {
         $this->description = 'Unknown set function';
         $this->display();
     }

     function display() {
         echo($this->description . "<br>");
     }
}


$car = new vehicle("Sports Car");
$car2 = new vehicle();
$car2->setu();
?>
```

The output from this script is shown in Figure 37.7

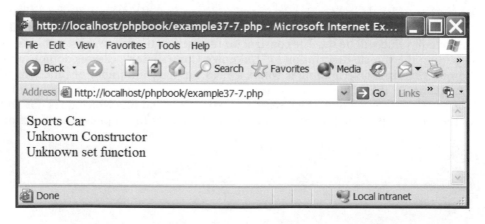

Figure 37.7 Function overloading output.

Creating a More Complex Class

We have, up to now, produced very simple class examples to illustrate the object-oriented features that PHP supports. The following example illustrates a slightly more complex class and some object interaction. In this example we are going to create a jug class which allows us to model the operation of a jug. Each jug object can store a specified amount of liquid. But the example does not stop there. We are going to create two jugs and any jug can pour some or all of its liquid into any other jug. Let's see how we would do this.

```php
<?php

// Classes - Example 37-8
//---------------------

class jug {
    var $maxVol;
    var $currentVol;
    var $name;

    function jug($n,$m,$c) {
        $this->name = $n;
        $this->maxVol = $m;
        $this->currentVol = $c;
        $this->display();
    }

    function addLiquid($v){
        $this->currentVol = $this->currentVol + $v;
    }

    function name(){
        return $this->name;
    }

    function isThereLiquid($vol) {
        if($this->currentVol >= $vol)
            return 1;
        else
            return 0;
    }
    function isThereSpace($vol) {
        if(($this->maxVol - $this->currentVol) >= $vol)
            return 1;
        else
            return 0;
    }
```

```
        function display() {
                echo("<br>" . $this->name . " had a max volume of " .
$this->maxVol . " and currently contains " . $this->currentVol);
        }

        function pourInTo($otherJug,$vol) {
                echo("<br>Pouring $vol units from " . $this->name() .
" into " . $otherJug->name());
                if($this->isThereLiquid($vol)) {
                    if($otherJug->isThereSpace($vol)) {
                        $otherJug->addLiquid($vol);
                        $this->currentVol = $this->currentVol - $vol;
                        $this->display();
                        $otherJug->display();
                    }
                    else {
                        echo("<br>Attempt failed - Not enough space.");
                        return 0;
                    }
                }
                else {
                    echo("<br>Attempt failed - Not enough liquid.");
                    return 0;
                }
        return 1;
        }
}

$myJug = new jug("Jug 1",100,50);
$anotherJug = new jug("Jug 2",50,25);
$myJug->pourInTo(&$anotherJug,10);
$anotherJug->pourInTo(&$myJug,34);
?>
```

The script begins by creating a class called jug. The class consists of three variables which are used to store the maximum volume of liquid the jug can hold, the current amount of liquid in the jug and the name of the jug (just used to identify it):

```
<?php
class jug {
     var $maxVol;
     var $currentVol;
     var $name;
```

The constructor constructs the object with the three variables it receives and invokes the display() function to output the status of the jug:

```
function jug($n,$m,$c) {
    $this->name = $n;
    $this->maxVol = $m;
    $this->currentVol = $c;
    $this->display();
}
```

The addLiquid() function enables additional liquid to be added to the jug. The name() function returns the name of the jug:

```
function addLiquid($v){
    $this->currentVol = $this->currentVol + $v;
}

function name(){
    return $this->name;
}
```

The function isThereLiquid() checks to see if the liquid in the jug is equal to or more than the volume passed to the function in $vol. If there is enough liquid then the value 1 is returned, else 0:

```
function isThereLiquid($vol) {
    if($this->currentVol >= $vol)
        return 1;
    else
        return 0;
}
```

The function isThereSpace() checks to see if the volume of liquid passed to the function in $vol would fit into the jug. If it will, the value 1 is returned, else the value 0:

```
function isThereSpace($vol) {
    if(($this->maxVol - $this->currentVol) >= $vol)
        return 1;
    else
        return 0;
}
```

The function display() displays the amount of liquid the jug can hold and the amount it currently holds:

```
    function display() {
        echo("<br>" . $this->name . " had a max volume of " .
$this->maxVol . " and currently contains " . $this->currentVol);
    }
```

The function pourInTo() is the most complex function yet, so we shall break this down examining it little by little. First, the function accepts two arguments $otherJug and $vol. These represent the jug object that we will be pouring into and the number of units to pour:

```
    function pourInTo($otherJug,$vol) {
```

Next, the function displays the amount of units it will be pouring from this jug into the other. Note that the name of the other jug is obtained through calling the function $otherJug->name():

```
        echo("<br>Pouring $vol units from " . $this->name() .
    " into " . $otherJug->name());
```

Next, a call to function isThereLiquid() determines if there is enough liquid in this jug to pour into the other one:

```
    if($this->isThereLiquid($vol)) {
```

If there is enough liquid, the otherJug function isThereSpace() is invoked to see if the other jug can accept the liquid. If so, the addLiquid() function of the otherJug is invoked to add the liquid and the current volume of liquid in this jug is reduced. The contents of both jugs are then displayed:

```
        if($otherJug->isThereSpace($vol)) {
            $otherJug->addLiquid($vol);
            $this->currentVol = $this->currentVol - $vol;
            $this->display();
            $otherJug->display();
        }
```

If there is not enough space, an error message is generated:

```
        else {
            echo("<br>Attempt failed - Not enough space.");
            return 0;
        }
    }
```

If there is not enough liquid, an error message is generated:

```
        else {
                echo("<br>Attempt failed - Not enough liquid.");
                return 0;
            }
        return 1;
        }
}
```

Two jugs are created: the first, Jug 1, has a maximum volume of 100 units and is currently half full. Jug 2 has a maximum capacity of 50 units and is also half full:

```
$myJug = new jug("Jug 1",100,50);
$anotherJug = new jug("Jug 2",50,25);
```

The function pourInTo() of object myJug is invoked, passing it the values of $anotherJug and 10. This will result in myJug trying to pour 10 units from it into anotherJug:

```
$myJug->pourInTo(&$anotherJug,10);
```

Finally, the function pourInTo() of object anotherJug is invoked, passing it the values of $myJug and 34. This will result in anotherJug trying to pour 34 units from it into myJug:

```
$anotherJug->pourInTo(&$myJug,34);
?>
```

The output from this script is illustrated in Figure 37.8.

Note that Figure 37.8 illustrates the creation of both jugs and the interactions between them. After some liquid has been poured from Jug 1 to Jug 2 and back from Jug 2 to Jug 1, we see that the volume of liquid in the two jugs has changed from 50 and 25 to 1 and 74.

Objects within Classes

We have shown that objects can invoke their own functions and those of other objects. What we have not seen yet is that objects can be created which contain other objects. Such objects are sometimes referred to as composite objects. In our example we are going to create a class called lock and a composite class called door that will contain a lock. You can create objects of type lock separately (and you might wish to) but when you create a door, the door and a lock are both created together. Let's see how we would do this. Let's begin with the lock class which contains a single variable to store whether the lock is locked or not, a constructor to set up the lock and a display() function to display the state of the lock:

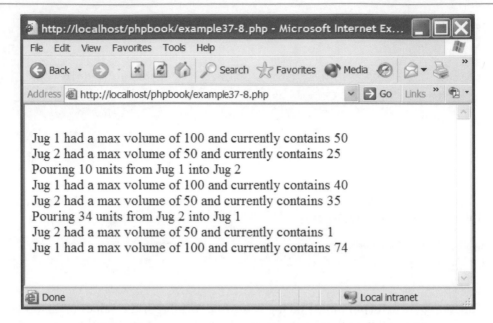

Figure 37.8 Jug object output.

```php
<?php

// Classes - Example 37-9
//----------------------

class lock {
    var $lockUnlock;

    function lock($lu) {
        $this->lockUnlock = $lu;
    }

    function display() {
        echo("<br>The Lock is " . $this->lockUnlock);
    }
}
```

The door class is a little more complex (but not much). It contains two variables: the first $openClosed which is used to store if the door is open or closed; the second, $lock, is used to store the lock object we shall create:

```php
class door {
    var $openClosed;
    var $lock;
```

The constructor receives two parameters. The first of these, $oc, is used to set the value of variable $openClosed. The second, $lu, is passed to the constructor of the lock class when we create the lock object:

```
function door($oc,$lu){
    $this->openClosed = $oc;
    $this->lock = new lock($lu);
    $this->display();
}
```

Note that when the $lock variable within class door is assigned a value, it is, in fact, an instance of a new lock object. The display() function outputs the value of the $openClosed variable within the door class. It then invokes the display function of the lock object which belongs to the lock class. Note that this call requires two -> operators:

```
function display(){
    echo("<br>The Door is " . $this->openClosed);
    $this->lock->display();
}
}

$myDoor = new door("Closed","Locked");
?>
```

The output from this script is shown in Figure 37.9.

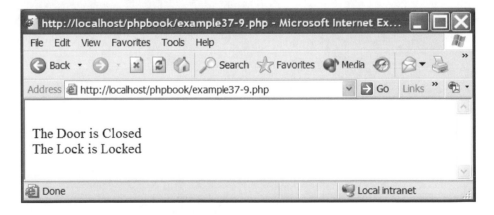

Figure 37.9 Objects within objects output.

We can see that we have created a composite object door as when the door was created a lock object was also formed.

Summary

This chapter has introduced the concept of object orientation. We have explained the difference between classes and objects and illustrated how these can be used within PHP. We have created some simple classes and shown how class variables and functions are built. We have explained the concept of encapsulation and shown that interactions between variables should be with through class functions. We concluded with an explanation of the concept of a composite object. However, this is not the end of the object-oriented story. Object orientation provides a key feature in software reuse. This is known as inheritance and it is this which we shall examine in the following chapter.

Class Inheritance **38**

Introduction

In the previous chapter we have introduced the concepts of object orientation, classes and objects. We have shown how PHP can be used to create classes and how instances of these classes can be used to create objects. At the start of the previous chapter we mentioned that one of the benefits of object orientation was its support for software reuse. The main feature of object orientation which supports reuse is that of class inheritance. We shall introduce inheritance within this chapter, illustrating how and why it is useful. We shall also introduce the concept of polymorphism which is related to inheritance and illustrate why this is also extremely useful.

What is Class Inheritance?

One of the strengths of object orientation is its ability to inherit properties from other classes that exist. This saves the programmer time, reduces the complexity of the solution and helps raise quality by reducing code duplication and thus error introduction. The programmer is able to access all the variables and functions of the class from which they are inheriting and add variables and functions to the new class. An example of inheritance is shown in Figure 38.1. In the example there are two classes writingImplement and pencil. The arrow from pencil to writingImplement indicates that pencil inherits from writingImplement.

The arrow can be read as "is a", so the diagram illustrates that a pencil "is a" writingImplement. The arrow also indicates that all the variables and functions of the writingImplement class are available to the pencil class. Let's examine how we would implement this using PHP.

The Extends Keyword

The extends keyword is used to indicate that a class inherits from another and the syntax is as follows:

```
Class className extends otherClassName
```

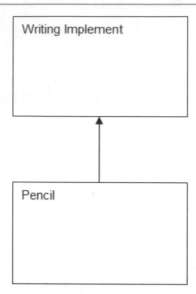

Figure 38.1 Inheritance.

To implement the two classes in Figure 38.1, we would write the following:

```
class writingImplement {
}

class pencil extends writingImplement {
}
```

Of course, these are simply the class templates without any variables or functions. What we need to do now is to provide some class content so, for example, the writingImplement class could be implemented as follows:

```
class writingImplement {
    var $textColour;

    function writingImplement($t) {
        $this->textColour = $t;
    }

    function display() {
        echo("the colour is " . $this->textColour . "<br>");
    }
}
```

The writingImplement class contains a single variable $textColour. This will be used to store the colour of text the writing implement produces. The class also contains a constructor to construct the object's text colour and a display() function to display the value of the text colour.

We are now ready to implement the pencil class. We shall keep this as simple as possible initially:

```
class pencil extends writingImplement {

    function pencil ($t) {
        $this->writingImplement($t);
    }
}
```

Note that the pencil class is very simple. It contains no variables of its own and its only function is that of a constructor. Classes that inherit from other classes normally need a constructor because if an instance of the class is created we need to be able to construct the value of the variables in the inherited class. In this example the constructor class simply invokes the constructor of the writingImplement class, passing it the value of the pencil lead colour. Note that the constructor of the writingImplement class is invoked as though it were a member of the pencil class, using the syntax:

```
$this->writingImplement($t);
```

This is because all functions, including the constructor from the inherited class, form part of the pencil class.

Taking a look at our pencil class we can see that the class as it stands is a rather pointless inheritance (no pun intended) as the pencil class does nothing different from the writingImplement class. What we need to do is to extend the functionality of the pencil class so that it operates differently from the writingImplement class and thus becomes useful.

Adding New Functions and Variables

In the previous section we had created a pencil class which inherits from the class writingImplement. Unfortunately, the pencil class did not include any variables or functions of its own to make it any different from the inherited class. Let's change this:

```
class pencil extends writingImplement {
    var $sharp;

    function pencil($t,$s) {
        $this->sharp = $s;
        $this->writingImplement($t);
        $this->display2();
    }
```

```
    function display2() {
        echo("<br>The pencil is " . $this->sharp . " and ");
        $this->display();
    }
}
```

Note that the pencil class now has a variable $sharp, which will be used to store whether the pencil is sharpened or blunt. The constructor has been modified to construct the variable $sharp and to invoke the writingImplement class constructor where the text colour will be constructed. Finally, a display2() function has been included to display the value of the variable sharp and to invoke the writingImplement display() function.

We can now create objects of type writingImplement and pencil:

```
$thing = new writingImplement("blue");
$thing->display();
$myGreyPencil = new pencil("grey","sharp");
```

The complete listing is:

```
<?php

// Class Inheritance - Example 38-1
//----------------------

class writingImplement {
    var $textColour;

    function writingImplement($t) {
        $this->textColour = $t;
    }

    function display() {
        echo("the colour is " . $this->textColour . "<br>");
    }
}

class pencil extends writingImplement {
    var $sharp;

    function pencil($t,$s) {
        $this->sharp = $s;
        $this->writingImplement($t);
        $this->display2();
    }
```

```
        function display2() {
            echo("<br>The pencil is " . $this->sharp . " and ");
            $this->display();
        }
}

$thing = new writingImplement("blue");
$thing->display();
$myGreyPencil = new pencil("grey","sharp");
```

Combining this into a script will produce the output shown in Figure 38.2.

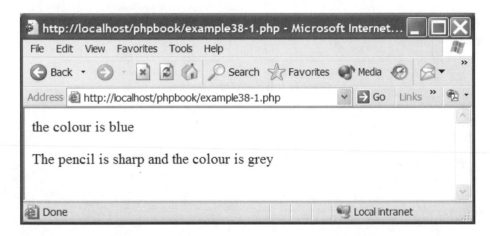

Figure 38.2 Inheritance output.

Note that Figure 38.2 illustrates that the output is different from the two objects. Using inheritance we have managed to create a new class pencil, which reuses some of the code from the class writingImplement. In doing this we did not alter the class writingImplement in any way and have only stated what the differences between the pencil and the writingImplement classes are.

Extending the Inheritance Again

Once we have created an inheritance structure we can continue to extend this as much as we like. Figure 38.3 illustrates an additional class called pen. This class also inherits from the writingImplement. We could have added a class which inherited from the pencil class – maybe a class called "Magic Never go blunt pencils". This would then inherit all of the pencil class attributes and those of writingImplement class but, for now, let's build our pen class.

The following script illustrates the implementation of Figure 38.3. The classes writingImplement and pencil remain unchanged, but there is now a new class called pen. The class pen contains a constructor and a display2() function:

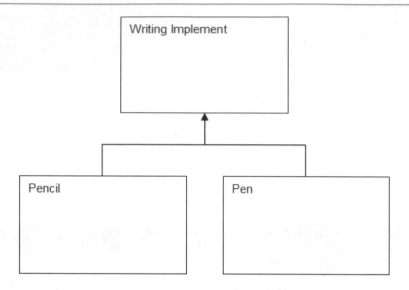

Figure 38.3 Extending the inheritance.

```php
<?php

// Class Inheritance - Example 38-2
//----------------------

class writingImplement {
    var $textColour;

    function writingImplement($t) {
        $this->textColour = $t;
    }

    function display() {
        echo("the colour is " . $this->textColour . "<br>");
    }
}

class pencil extends writingImplement {
    var $sharp;

    function pencil($t,$s) {
        $this->sharp = $s;
        $this->writingImplement($t);
        $this->display2();
    }
}
```

```
        function display2() {
            echo("<br>The pencil is " . $this->sharp . " and ");
            $this->display();
        }
    }

class pen extends writingImplement {
    var $inkPresent;

    function pen($t,$i) {
        $this->inkPresent = $i;
        $this->writingImplement($t);
        $this->display2();
    }

    function display2() {
        echo("<br>The pen has " . $this->inkPresent . " and ");
        $this->display();
    }
}

$thing = new writingImplement("blue");
$thing->display();
$myGreyPencil = new pencil("grey","sharp");
$myRedPen = new pen("red","ink")
?>
```

Three different objects are constructed and displayed and their output is illustrated in Figure 38.4.

A More Complex Inheritance Example

Let's now create an inheritance example consisting of a larger number of classes. Consider the example inheritance tree in Figure 38.5 which consists of six classes.

The inheritance tree in Figure 38.5 is more complex than before and illustrates a little more clearly the concept of classification, the subdividing of classes, in this way. At the bottom of the tree we have bicycles which are non-motor vehicles which are, in turn, vehicles. We have cars and speed boats which are motor vehicles and are, in turn, vehicles. In our example, we shall be only producing objects of type bicycle, car and speed boat, and not of vehicle, non-motor vehicle and motor vehicle. The reason for this is that vehicle, non-motor vehicle and motor vehicle have been created simply to allow us to form an inheritance structure – we never intended to have objects of these types. However, they were required in order for us to structure our inheritances correctly. Such classes are often referred to as abstract classes.

Let's begin by creating the outline classes which we need in order to create the structure in Figure 38.5:

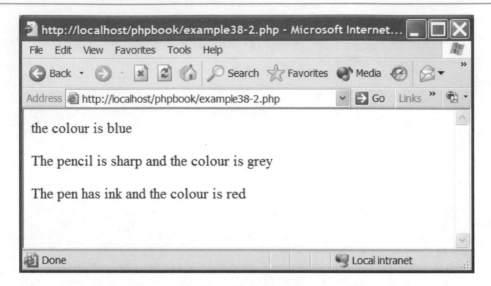

Figure 38.4 More inheritance.

```php
<?php
class vehicle {
}

class motorVehicle extends vehicle {
}

class nonMotorVehicle extends vehicle {
}

class bicycle extends nonMotorVehicle {
}

class powerboat extends motorVehicle {
}

class car extends motorVehicle {
}

?>
```

This provides us with the outline templates of the classes which we are going to create. What we need to do now is to determine the functions and variables each of these classes will contain. Figure 38.6 enhances the structure shown in Figure 38.5 and provides some details on the variables and functions each class will contain.

To keep things simple each class contains a constructor and a display function which will output the values of its variables. Each class contains between one and three variables. The

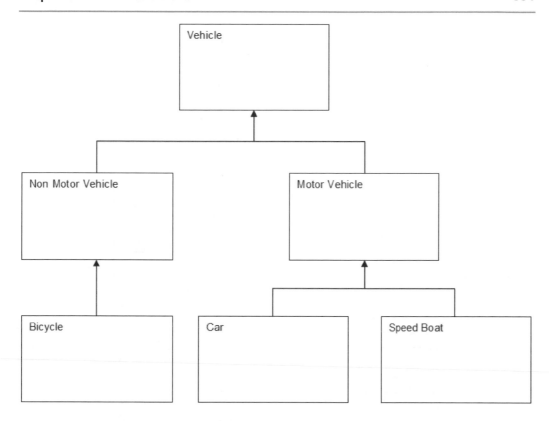

Figure 38.5 Vehicle inheritance tree.

vehicle class contains three variables to store a description of the vehicle, its colour and the name of the image file to be displayed to represent the vehicle. The non-motor vehicle class has a variable powerSource, which will store the power source of the vehicle, such as wind, human etc. The motor vehicle class contains two variables to store the fuel type (unleaded, diesel) and the BHP value of the vehicle. The bicycle class contains two variables to hold the frame size and number of gears of the bike. The car class contains a variable to store the size of the wheels on the vehicle. Finally, the speed boat class contains a variable engine type which will store whether the engine is an inboard or outboard type.

The following script implements Figure 38.6:

```php
<?php

// Class Inheritance - Example 38-3
//----------------------

class vehicle {
    var $description;
    var $colour;
    var $pic;
```

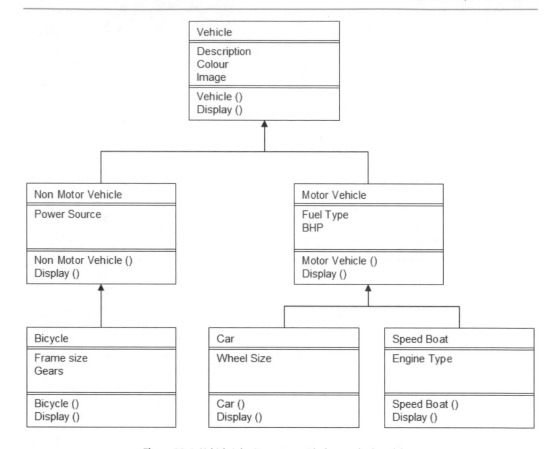

Figure 38.6 Vehicle inheritance tree with class methods and data.

```
function vehicle($d,$c,$p) {
     $this->description = $d;
     $this->colour = $c;
     $this->pic = $p;
}

function display() {
     echo("<table border='1'>");
     echo("<tr><td colspan='2'><img src='graphics/" .
$this->pic . "'></td></tr>");
     echo("<tr><td><font size='2'>Description:</font></td><td>
<font size='2'>" . $this->description . "</font></td></tr>");
     echo("<tr><td><font size='2'>Colour:</font></td><td><font
size='2'>" . $this->colour . "</font></td></tr>");
     }
}
```

```php
class motorVehicle extends vehicle {
    var $fuelType;
    var $bhp;

    function motorVehicle($ft,$b,$d,$c,$p) {
        $this->fuelType = $ft;
        $this->bhp = $b;
        $this->vehicle($d,$c,$p);
    }

    function display2() {
        $this->display();
        echo("<tr><td><font size='2'>Fuel Type:</font></td><td>
<font size='2'>" . $this->fuelType . "</font></td></tr>");
        echo("<tr><td><font size='2'>Bhp:</font></td><td><font
size='2'>" . $this->bhp . "</font></td></tr>");
    }
}

class nonMotorVehicle extends vehicle {
    var $powerSource;

    function nonMotorVehicle($ps,$d,$c,$p) {
        $this->powerSource = $ps;
        $this->vehicle($d,$c,$p);
    }

    function display2() {
        $this->display();
        echo("<tr><td><font size='2'>Power:</font></td><td><font
size='2'>" .
$this->powerSource . "</font></td></tr>");
    }
}

class bicycle extends nonMotorVehicle {
    var $frameSize;
    var $gears;

    function bicycle($ps,$fs,$g,$d,$c,$p) {
        $this->frameSize = $fs;
        $this->gears = $g;
        $this->nonMotorVehicle($ps,$d,$c,$p);
    }

    function display3() {
        $this->display2();
        echo("<tr><td><font size='2'>Frame size:</font></td><td>
<font size='2'>" . $this->frameSize . "</font></td></tr>");
```

```
        echo("<tr><td><font size='2'>Gears:</font></td><td><font
size='2'>" . $this->gears . "</font></td></tr>");
        echo("</table>");
    }
}

class powerboat extends motorVehicle {
    var $engineType;

    function powerboat($et,$ft,$b,$d,$c,$p) {
        $this->engineType = $et;
        $this->motorVehicle($ft,$b,$d,$c,$p);
    }

    function display3() {
        $this->display2();
        echo("<tr><td><font size='2'>Engine:</font></td><td><font
size='2'>" . $this->engineType . "</font></td></tr>");
        echo("</table>");
    }
}

class car extends motorVehicle {
    var $wheelSize;

    function car($ws,$ft,$b,$d,$c,$p) {
        $this->wheelSize = $ws;
        $this->motorVehicle($ft,$b,$d,$c,$p);
    }

    function display3() {
        $this->display2();
        echo("<tr><td><font size='2'>Wheel Size:</font></td><td>
<font size='2'>" . $this->wheelSize . "</font></td></tr>");
        echo("</table>");
    }
}


$veh = new powerboat("Outboard","Diesel",60,"Boat","Yellow",
"speedboat.jpg");
$veh2 = new bicycle("Human",18,21,"Bike","Green","bicycle.jpg");
$veh3 = new car(17,"Unleaded",147,"Car","Red","car.jpg");
$vehicles = array ($veh,$veh2,$veh3);
foreach ($vehicles as $vehicle){
    $vehicle->display3();
}
?>
```

This script declares three objects – a powerboat, a bicycle and car. These are copied into an array and a foreach loop used to display each object by invoking the display3() function. The script uses three images, which will be displayed along with the vehicle data to make the output from the script more interesting. Table 38.1 lists these images and their filenames.

Table 38.1 Vehicle images.

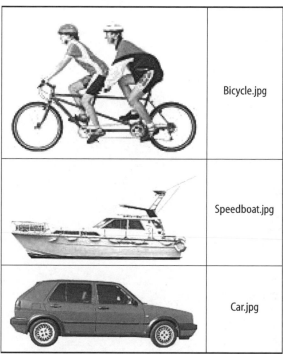

	Bicycle.jpg
	Speedboat.jpg
	Car.jpg

The output produced from the script is illustrated in Figure 38.7. Note that the foreach loop accesses each of the objects in the array and outputs them by calling a single function. It all works very well indeed but there is a problem, something which we will need to solve if we are going to be able to use the full power of inheritance to our advantage. This problem is discussed in the next section named polymorphism.

Polymorphism

We mentioned earlier that there is a problem. What problem I hear you cry, the previous example works very well indeed. Well, it does but only because of the way it has been used. You may have noticed that each of the classes within a branch of the inheritance tree has a display() function. Each display function is given a different name at each level: display(), display2() and display3(). This allows us to invoke the display function in the next class up the structure. This does not cause us any problem in the current design but what if we wanted to add a new class as shown in Figure 38.8.

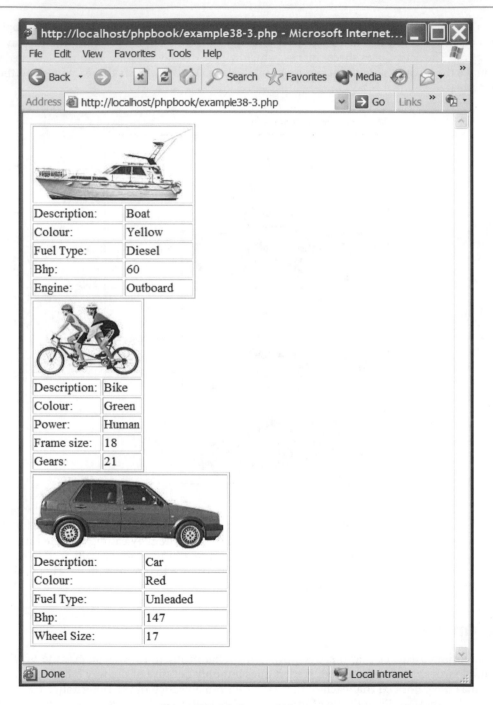

Figure 38.7 Inheritance vehicle output.

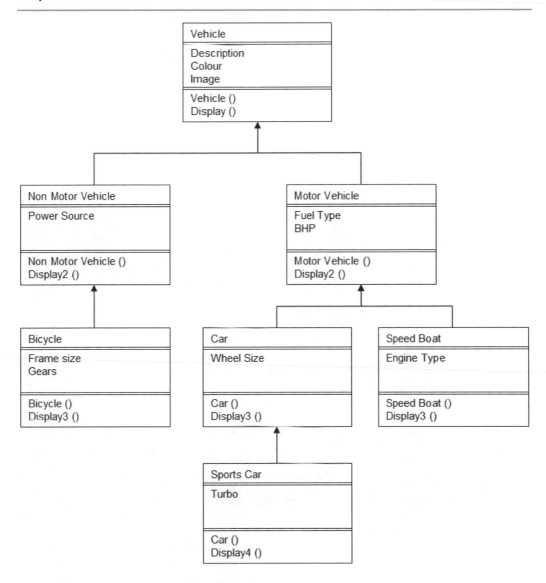

Figure 38.8 Sports car class.

Figure 38.8 illustrates that we now have a new class called sports car. The class has a variable turbo which is used to store the bar pressure of the turbo (we have assumed that all sports cars have a turbo charger). The class has a display function called Display4(). We can implement the class quite easily:

```php
<?php

// Class Inheritance - Example 38-4
//----------------------
```

```php
class vehicle {
     var $description;
     var $colour;
     var $pic;

     function vehicle($d,$c,$p) {
          $this->description = $d;
          $this->colour = $c;
          $this->pic = $p;
     }

     function display() {
          echo("<table border='1'>");
          echo("<tr><td colspan='2'><img src='graphics/" .
$this->pic . "'></td></tr>");
          echo("<tr><td><font size='2'>Description:</font></td><td>
<font size='2'>" . $this->description . "</font></td></tr>");
          echo("<tr><td><font size='2'>Colour:</font></td><td><font
size='2'>" .
$this->colour . "</font></td></tr>");
     }
}

class motorVehicle extends vehicle {
     var $fuelType;
     var $bhp;

     function motorVehicle($ft,$b,$d,$c,$p) {
          $this->fuelType = $ft;
          $this->bhp = $b;
          $this->vehicle($d,$c,$p);
     }

     function display2() {
          $this->display();
          echo("<tr><td><font size='2'>Fuel Type:</font></td><td>
<font size='2'>" . $this->fuelType . "</font></td></tr>");
          echo("<tr><td><font size='2'>Bhp:</font></td><td><font
size='2'>" .
$this->bhp . "</font></td></tr>");
     }
}

class nonMotorVehicle extends vehicle {
     var $powerSource;

     function nonMotorVehicle($ps,$d,$c,$p) {
          $this->powerSource = $ps;
          $this->vehicle($d,$c,$p);
```

```
        }

    function display2() {
        $this->display();
        echo("<tr><td><font size='2'>Power:</font></td><td>
<font size='2'>" .
$this->powerSource . "</font></td></tr>");
    }
}

class bicycle extends nonMotorVehicle {
    var $frameSize;
    var $gears;

    function bicycle($ps,$fs,$g,$d,$c,$p) {
        $this->frameSize = $fs;
        $this->gears = $g;
        $this->nonMotorVehicle($ps,$d,$c,$p);
    }

    function display3() {
        $this->display2();
        echo("<tr><td><font size='2'>Frame size:</font></td><td>
<font size='2'>" . $this->frameSize . "</font></td></tr>");
        echo("<tr><td><font size='2'>Gears:</font></td><td>
<font size='2'>" .
$this->gears . "</font></td></tr>");
    }
}

class powerboat extends motorVehicle {
    var $engineType;

    function powerboat($et,$ft,$b,$d,$c,$p) {
        $this->engineType = $et;
        $this->motorVehicle($ft,$b,$d,$c,$p);
    }

    function display3() {
        $this->display2();
        echo("<tr><td><font size='2'>Engine:</font></td><td>
<font size='2'>" .
$this->engineType . "</font></td></tr>");
    }
}

class car extends motorVehicle {
    var $wheelSize;
```

```php
    function car($ws,$ft,$b,$d,$c,$p) {
        $this->wheelSize = $ws;
        $this->motorVehicle($ft,$b,$d,$c,$p);
    }

    function display3() {
        $this->display2();
        echo("<tr><td><font size='2'>Wheel Size:</font></td><td>
<font size='2'>" . $this->wheelSize . "</font></td></tr>");
    }
}

class sportsCar extends car {
    var $turbo;

    function sportsCar($t,$ws,$ft,$b,$d,$c,$p) {
        $this->turbo = $t;
        $this->car($ws,$ft,$b,$d,$c,$p);
    }

    function display4() {
        $this->display3();
        echo("<tr><td><font size='2'>Turbo Pressure:</font>
</td><td> <font size='2'>" . $this->turbo . "</font></td></tr>");
    }
}

$veh4 = new sportsCar(2,18,"Unleaded",289,"sportsCar","Yellow",
"sportsCar.jpg");
$veh4->display4();
echo("</table>");
?>
```

This script used an additional image to represent the sports car. This is illustrated in Table 38.2.

Table 38.2 Additional vehicle image.

	sportsCar.jpg

Note that the output of a </table> element has been removed from within the base classes of the tree as we now do not know when to output the closing </table> element. Instead this is now displayed after the objects display function is called. The output from this script is illustrated in Figure 38.9.

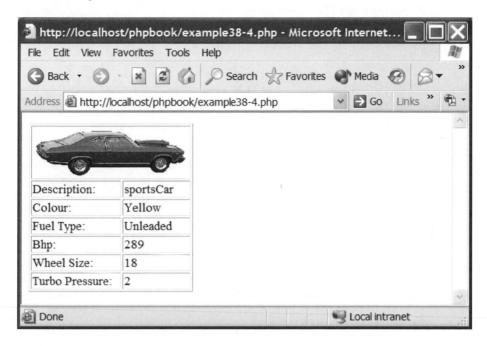

Figure 38.9 Sports car.

The problem comes when we try to create a number of objects for each of our different classes. While we can create them and place them in an array, when we try and output them using a foreach loop we encounter the problem (at last!) – we don't know which display function to call – display3() or display4() that is we don't know which object in the array is of which type:

```
$veh = new powerboat("Outboard","Diesel",60,"Boat","Yellow",
"speedboat.jpg");
$veh2 = new bicycle("Human",18,21,"Bike","Green","bicycle.jpg");
$veh3 = new car(17,"Unleaded",147,"Car","Red","car.jpg");
$veh4 = new sportsCar(2,18,"Unleaded",289,"sportsCar","Yellow",
"sportsCar.jpg");
$vehicles = array ($veh,$veh2,$veh3,$veh4);
foreach ($vehicles as $vehicle){
    $vehicle->display3(); // problem occurs here!
    echo("</table>");
}
```

The solution comes in the form of polymorphism (which means many forms). What we need to create are inherited classes each of which contains functions with the same name. In our example all display functions should be called display(), this is illustrated in

Figure 38.10. Here, every class in the inheritance tree has a function called display(). With all the functions having the same name we remove the problem illustrated earlier as we can now invoke the objects display() function like this:

```
$vehicle->display();
```

It now doesn't matter which object we refer to as all of them have a display function with the same name. However, this brings with it a new problem. Consider the following display function from the sportsCar class:

```
function display() {
    $this->display();
    echo("<tr><td><font size='2'>Turbo Pressure:</font></td><td>
<font size='2'>" .
$this->turbo . "</font></td></tr>");
}
```

The display() function wants to invoke the display() function of the next class up the inheritance tree, namely the car class. It attempts to do this with the statement:

```
$this->display();
```

Unfortunately this will not work as it will attempt to call the display() function within the sportsCar class itself. What we need to do is to be able to specify which display() function to invoke. We can do this with the :: operator, for example:

```
car::display();
```

will invoke the display() function of class car.

Amending our script to use the :: operator function results in the following:

```
<?php

// Class Inheritance - Example 38-5
//----------------------

class vehicle {
    var $description;
    var $colour;
    var $pic;

    function vehicle($d,$c,$p) {
```

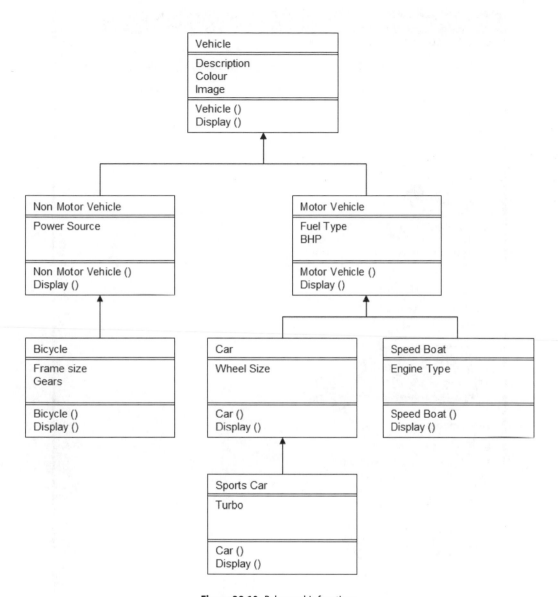

Figure 38.10 Polymorphic functions.

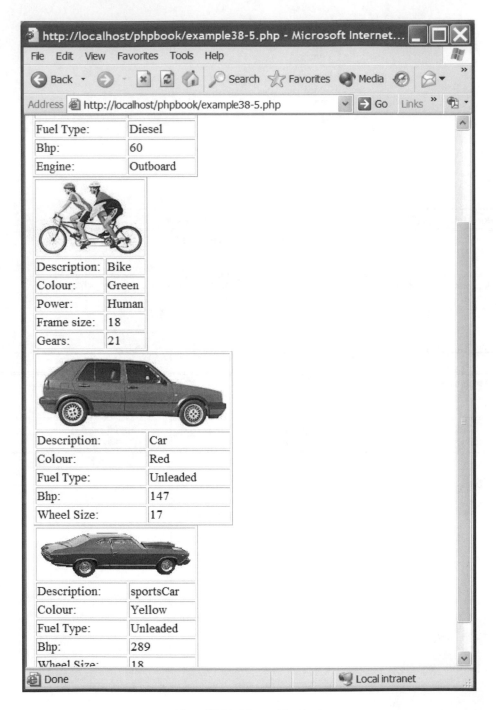

Figure 38.11 Polymorphic output.

```php
            $this->description = $d;
            $this->colour = $c;
            $this->pic = $p;
        }

    function display() {
            echo("<table border='1'>");
            echo("<tr><td colspan='2'><img src='graphics/" .
$this->pic . "'></td></tr>");
        echo("<tr><td><font size='2'>Description:</font></td><td>
<font size='2'>" . $this->description . "</font></td></tr>");
            echo("<tr><td><font size='2'>Colour:</font></td><td>
<font size='2'>" .
$this->colour . "</font></td></tr>");
        }
}

class motorVehicle extends vehicle {
    var $fuelType;
    var $bhp;

    function motorVehicle($ft,$b,$d,$c,$p) {
            $this->fuelType = $ft;
            $this->bhp = $b;
            $this->vehicle($d,$c,$p);
        }

    function display() {
            vehicle::display();
            echo("<tr><td><font size='2'>Fuel Type:</font></td><td>
<font size='2'>" . $this->fuelType . "</font></td></tr>");
            echo("<tr><td><font size='2'>Bhp:</font></td><td>
<font size='2'>" .
$this->bhp . "</font></td></tr>");

        }
}

class nonMotorVehicle extends vehicle {
    var $powerSource;

    function nonMotorVehicle($ps,$d,$c,$p) {
            $this->powerSource = $ps;
            $this->vehicle($d,$c,$p);
        }

    function display() {
            vehicle::display();
```

```
            echo("<tr><td><font size='2'>Power:</font></td><td>
<font size='2'>" .
$this->powerSource . "</font></td></tr>");
    }
}

class bicycle extends nonMotorVehicle {
    var $frameSize;
    var $gears;

    function bicycle($ps,$fs,$g,$d,$c,$p) {
        $this->frameSize = $fs;
        $this->gears = $g;
        $this->nonMotorVehicle($ps,$d,$c,$p);
    }

    function display() {
        nonMotorVehicle::display();
        echo("<tr><td><font size='2'>Frame size:</font></td><td>
<font size='2'>" . $this->frameSize . "</font></td></tr>");
        echo("<tr><td><font size='2'>Gears:</font></td><td>
<font size='2'>" .
$this->gears . "</font></td></tr>");
    }
}

class powerboat extends motorVehicle {
    var $engineType;

    function powerboat($et,$ft,$b,$d,$c,$p) {
        $this->engineType = $et;
        $this->motorVehicle($ft,$b,$d,$c,$p);
    }

    function display() {
        motorVehicle::display();
        echo("<tr><td><font size='2'>Engine:</font></td><td>
<font size='2'>" .
$this->engineType . "</font></td></tr>");
    }
}

class car extends motorVehicle {
    var $wheelSize;

    function car($ws,$ft,$b,$d,$c,$p) {
        $this->wheelSize = $ws;
        $this->motorVehicle($ft,$b,$d,$c,$p);
    }
```

```
        function display() {
            motorVehicle::display();
            echo("<tr><td><font size='2'>Wheel Size:</font></td><td>
<font size='2'>" . $this->wheelSize . "</font></td></tr>");
        }
}

class sportsCar extends car {
    var $turbo;

    function sportsCar($t,$ws,$ft,$b,$d,$c,$p) {
        $this->turbo = $t;
        $this->car($ws,$ft,$b,$d,$c,$p);
    }

    function display() {
        car::display();
        echo("<tr><td><font size='2'>Turbo Pressure:</font>
</td><td> <font size='2'>" . $this->turbo . "</font></td></tr>");
    }
}

$veh = new powerboat("Outboard","Diesel",60,"Boat","Yellow",
"speedboat.jpg");
$veh2 = new bicycle("Human",18,21,"Bike","Green","bicycle.jpg");
$veh3 = new car(17,"Unleaded",147,"Car","Red","car.jpg");
$veh4 = new sportsCar(2,18,"Unleaded",289,"sportsCar","Yellow",
"sportsCar.jpg");
$vehicles = array ($veh,$veh2,$veh3,$veh4);
foreach ($vehicles as $vehicle){
    $vehicle->display();
    echo("</table>");
}
?>
```

The output from this script is shown in Figure 38.11. Here we can see that the polymorphic functions enable us to output all four different objects from our array.

Summary

This chapter has introduced the concept of class inheritance. We have shown how inheritance can be used to create new classes which are based on existing classes. We have also introduced the concept of polymorphism and shown how this can help us manipulate and use classes in an inheritance structure. In the following chapter we shall examine the role of e-commerce and how PHP can be employed to create an e-commerce Web application.

Part **12**

An E-Commerce Application

3:Phase E-Commerce System 39

Introduction

In this chapter we shall introduce an e-commerce system we have created in PHP using many of the features of the language we have described previously in this book. The PHP code for this system is both large and, in some places, complex and thus we have decided not to include the listings. We will, however, make these scripts available from our Web site. In this chapter we shall describe some of the design features of the system and explain how the database which is used to store details of the transactions operates. We shall begin by examining the main welcome page of the system.

The E-Commerce System

The e-commerce system has been created for a company known as 3:Phase. This company sells computer software. We have written both the front- and back-end e-commerce system. The front-end system is described in this chapter and enables customers to select and purchase software. The back-end system is described in the next chapter and enables the 3:Phase company to maintain and perform its electronic trading.

3:Phase Welcome Page

Figure 39.1 illustrates the main index page for our e-commerce system.

The Main Index page consists of four main parts. The first is the company logo at the top left of the page, under which is the main control menu for the system. The main part of the screen is taken up with the products which have been chosen to be displayed on this page. To the right of the screen is a product category index which enables us to view different software which have been categorized by the company which produces it. Below this list is a small form which allows us to change the currency from pounds sterling to euros which is the currency in which all products are sold and calculations are made.

A database table called products is used to store details of the various products (software) for sale. It is this table which is used to determine which products to display on the main page. The field structure, descriptions and example data values for this table are shown in Table 39.1.

Figure 39.1 Main Index screen.

The main screen is able to read this table to determine which products should be displayed on the main page, their name, description, price and image.

The Products table to the right of the main page is created by reading a database table called groups. The details for this table are shown in Table 39.2.

Product Info Window

If you were to click on the "info" icon next to one of the main products shown, you would launch a pop-up window which provides more details about the product. This window is shown in Figure 39.2.

In this window further details from the products table are displayed. These include the manufacturers Web page and a full description of the product.

Table 39.1 Products table.

Field	Description	Example value
id int(10) NOT NULL auto_increment,	Key	17
Pgroup varchar(20) NOT NULL default '',	Product group	macromedia
Pid varchar(10) NOT NULL default ' 0 ',	Unique key	MC004
Name varchar(30) NOT NULL default '',	Software name	Macromedia Freehand 10
Description text NOT NULL,	Description	Design once and publish across multiple mediums. Use FreeHand 10 to create extraordinary illustrations, design and organize Web site storyboards, and layout graphics-rich documents in a unique multi-page workspace
Price varchar(20) NOT NULL default ' 0 ',	Price	78.99
Items int(10) NOT NULL default ' 1 ',	Number of items in stock	197
Details text NOT NULL,	Full description	Design once and publish across multiple mediums. Use FreeHand 10 to create extraordinary illustrations, design and organize Web site storyboards, and layout graphics-rich documents in a unique multi-page workspace. Easily produce superior Macromedia Flash movies, and test them right inside of FreeHand with the new Flash Navigation Panel.\r\n\r\nDo more with your designs. Macromedia Studio MX brings the power of FreeHand, Macromedia Flash, Dreamweaver, and Fireworks together, combining all four products in one tightly integrated, highly approachable solution. Learn more about Macromedia Studio MX
Url varchar(40) NOT NULL default '',	Home URL	http://www.macromedia.com
Image varchar(40) NOT NULL default '',	Image	boxshot_freehand10.jpeg
Active tinyint(1) NOT NULL default ' 1 ',	Product available for sale	1
Onindex tinyint(2) NOT NULL default ' 0 ',	Display on main index page	0
Lastupdated varchar(10) NOT NULL default '',	Last updated	21-5-2002

Manufacturer's Products

If you click on one of the product groups on the right of the window a list of products for that manufacturer will be displayed. This is illustrated in Figure 39.3.

Table 39.2 Groups table.

Field	Description	Example value
id int(10) NOT NULL auto_increment,	Key	7
Name varchar(20) NOT NULL default ",	Unique key	Macromedia
Title varchar(40) NOT NULL default ",	Group title	Macromedia
Description text NOT NULL,	Description	Web development tools, animation application
Active tinyint(1) NOT NULL default ' 1 ',	Group active?	1

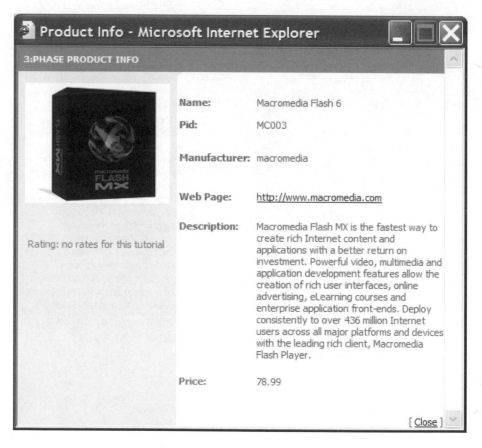

Figure 39.2 Product information window.

While these pages look different to the main products page they provide the same information from the same table. To return to the main screen the Products option from the control menu at the top of the screen should be used.

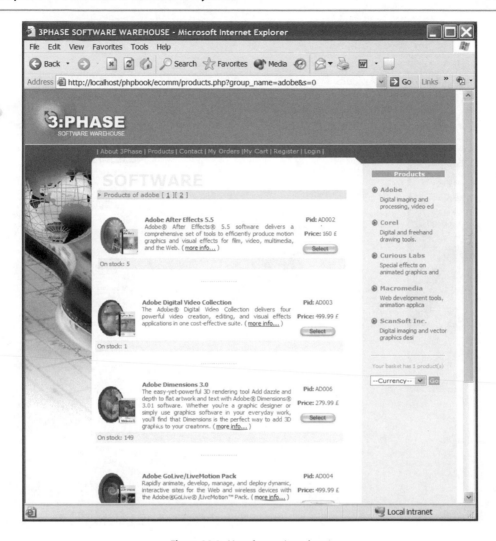

Figure 39.3 Manufacturer's products.

About Details

Clicking the About menu option will display details about the 3:Phase company. This is illustrated in Figure 39.4.

The information on this page is not stored in the database.

Contact Details

Clicking the Contact menu option will display details about how to contact the 3:Phase company. This is illustrated in Figure 39.5.

The information on this page is not stored in the database.

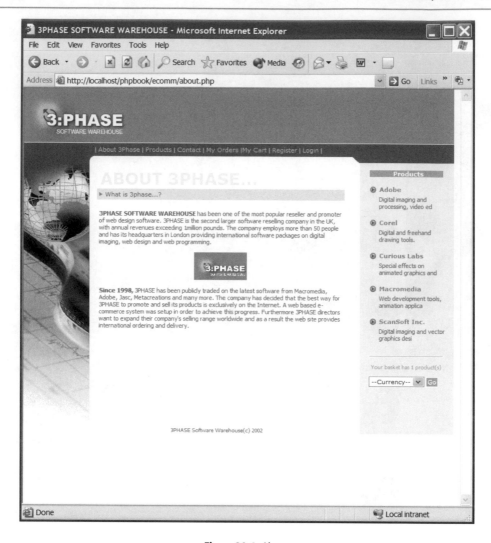

Figure 39.4 About.

Adding Items to the Shopping Cart

The 3:Phase e-commerce system is designed to allow potential customers to select products they wish to purchase without the need to first register or login. To add products to the shopping cart click the Buy button next to the product you wish to purchase. A small pop-up window confirming that a particular product has been added to the shopping cart is displayed. This is illustrated in Figure 39.6.

When an anonymous user selects a item to place in their shopping cart an entry is made in the users_anonymous table which is given in Table 39.3.

In addition an entry is made in the cart table. This is illustrated in Table 39.4.

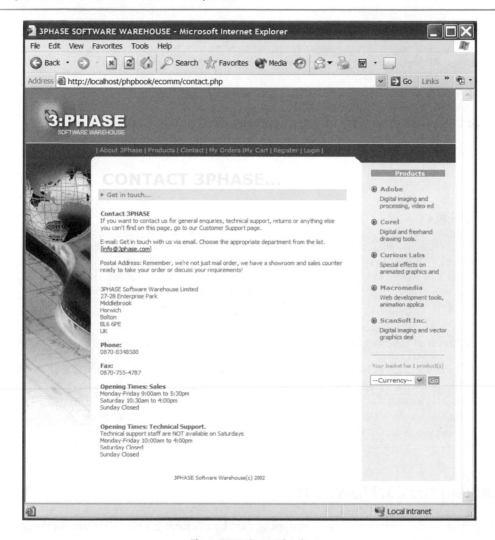

Figure 39.5 Contact details.

Figure 39.6 Added to shopping cart window.

Table 39.3 Users_anonymous table.

Field	Description	Example value
id int(10) NOT NULL auto_increment,	Key	14
IDName varchar(40) NOT NULL default ",	Unique key	d827db4a157.228.22.42
Address varchar(30) NOT NULL default ",	URL of the users computer	157.228.22.42
Currency varchar(30) NOT NULL default ' pounds ',	Currency	pounds
Timestamp int(20) NOT NULL default ' 0 ',	Time stamp	0

Table 39.4 Cart table.

Field	Description	Example value
id int(10) NOT NULL auto_increment,	Key	14
Username varchar(30) NOT NULL default ",	Generated user name. This is the same as the IDName field in the users_anonymous table and provides a link to that table	d827db4a157.228.22.42
Pid varchar(10) NOT NULL default ",	Product id, linking to the product table	MC003
Pname varchar(60) NOT NULL default ",	Product name	Macromedia Flash 6
Price varchar(20) NOT NULL default ",	Price	79.99
Quantity int(10) NOT NULL default ' 1 ',	Quantity	1
Date varchar(30) NOT NULL default ",	Date	14-07-2003
Timestamp int(20) NOT NULL default ' 0 ',	Time stamp	0

Viewing the Cart Contents

You can view the contents of your shopping cart by clicking on the My Cart menu option. An example of doing this is illustrated in Figure 39.7

You can remove items from the shopping cart, adjust the quantity of each item you wish to purchase, return to shopping in order to add more items to the shopping basket or you can proceed to the checkout and purchase your chosen items.

Registering with the System

Before you can purchase any products from 3:Phase you must first register with the system. Once you have registered you can then login and identify yourself and not have to register again. To register you can click the Register menu option and complete the Register form as shown in Figure 39.8.

Once registered a welcome message on the main page will identify who you are and that you are logged in. In our Case the message reads "Hello stobbie". When registered, a

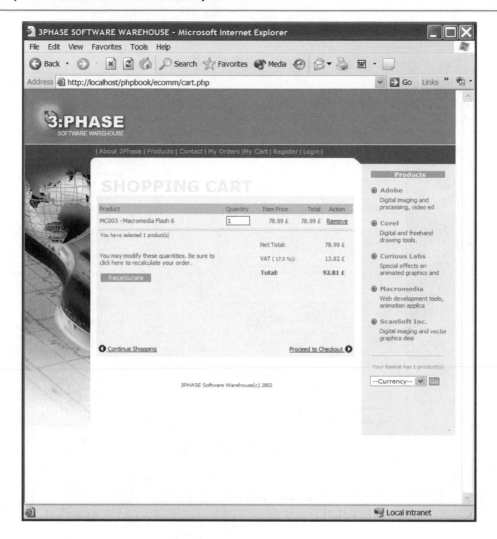

Figure 39.7 Viewing your shopping cart.

record in the users database table is created and the entry in the users_anonymous table is removed as the system now knows who you are. Table 39.5 shows the users table.

Once registered your shopping cart items in the cart table are amended so that the username field is the same as your registered username. Note that you can log out of the system by clicking the Logout menu option which has replaced the Login menu item.

Logging In

Once you have registered you only need to login when you return to the system. The login screen can be accessed by clicking the Login menu item and is shown in Figure 39.9.

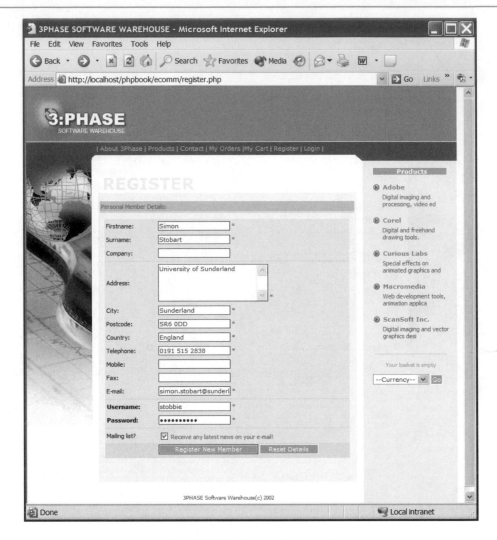

Figure 39.8 Viewing your shopping cart.

Once logged in any items that you placed in the shopping basket on a previous visit will be recovered. Items in the shopping basket will not be removed unless the user deletes them or they are purchased.

Making a Purchase

When the user is ready to purchase their products, they can click the Proceed to checkout link from the shopping cart. If they have not already logged in or registered then the system will provide the necessary forms in order for the user to do so. If the user has already logged in, they will be prompted for their password once more as a final security feature. This is illustrated in Figure 39.10.

Table 39.5 Users table.

Field	Description	Example value
id int(10) NOT NULL auto_increment,	Key	1
Username varchar(20) NOT NULL default ",	Username – unique key	stobbie
Password varchar(32) NOT NULL default ",	Password (encrypted)	3b59fb8a38f8c1694d1576c62bde0bae
Firstname varchar(30) NOT NULL default ",	Firstname	Simon
Surname varchar(30) NOT NULL default ",	Surname	Stobart
Company varchar(30) NOT NULL default ",	Company	University of Sunderland
Address varchar(50) NOT NULL default ",	Address	University of Sunderland
City varchar(30) NOT NULL default ",	City	Sunderland
County varchar(30) NOT NULL default ",	County	Tyne and Wear
Postcode varchar(20) NOT NULL default ",	Postcode	SR6 0DD
Country varchar(20) NOT NULL default ",	Country	England
Telephone bigint(20) NOT NULL default '0',	Telephone	01915142838
Mobile bigint(20) NOT NULL default '0',	Mobile	094623838940
Fax bigint(20) NOT NULL default '0',	Fax	094623838940
Email varchar(30) NOT NULL default ",	E-mail – unique key	Simon.stobart@sunderland.ac.uk
Currency varchar(30) NOT NULL default 'pounds',	Currency	Pounds
Regdate varchar(30) NOT NULL default ",	Registration date	
Purchases int(20) NOT NULL default '0',	Number of purchases	0
Logins int(20) NOT NULL default '0',	Number of logins	0

Having successfully confirmed their password (or logged in or registered), the user will be presented with a screen which outlines the terms and conditions of purchase and clearly lists the products to be purchased and the total price to be paid. This screen is illustrated in Figure 39.11.

If the user is happy with the terms and conditions and the total amount to pay they simply check the "I have read the terms and conditions" box and click the Proceed button. The next and final step in the purchasing of products is presented to the user. This screen displays the details of the user purchasing the products, the items to be purchased and the delivery address of where items should be sent. By default this address is the same as those supplied by the user when they registered but can be changed now if required. The user simply enters their card type and number and expiry date into the form and clicks the purchase items button. This is illustrated in Figure 39.12.

The process of checking whether a credit card is valid is not part of this example e-commerce system. When completed a thank you page is displayed, thanking the user for purchasing from 3:Phase, before they are automatically returned to the main welcome screen. The thank you page is illustrated in Figure 39.13.

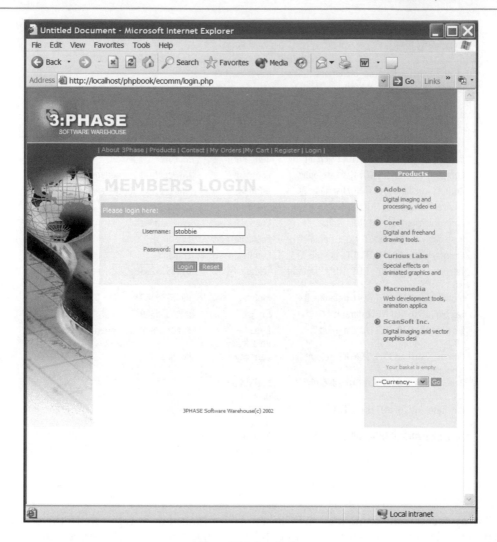

Figure 39.9 Logging in.

During this process a number of database table entries are created. An entry is made in the cardholders table. This stores the information provided by the purchaser for future records, see Table 39.6.

An entry in the shipping table is made to note the address of where the orders are to be shipped. The shipping table is illustrated in Table 39.7.

Finally, entries are made in the orders table for each item on the shopping cart. The orders table is illustrated in Table 39.8.

The orders that have been purchased are also removed from the shopping cart. This completes the customer's purchase and there is nothing more to do other than to sit back and wait for the products to arrive.

Table 39.6 Cardholders table.

Field	Description	Example value
id int(10) NOT NULL auto_increment,	Key	14
Username varchar(20) NOT NULL default ",	User name – unique key	stobbie
Firstname varchar(30) NOT NULL default ",	First name	Simon
Surname varchar(30) NOT NULL default ",	Surname	Stobart
Company varchar(30) NOT NULL default ",	Company	University of Sunderland
Address varchar(50) NOT NULL default ",	Address	University of Sunderland
City varchar(30) NOT NULL default ",	City	Sunderland
Postcode varchar(20) NOT NULL default ",	Postcode	SR6 0DD
Country varchar(20) NOT NULL default ",	Country	England
Telephone int(20) NOT NULL default ' 0 ',	Telephone	01915142838
Mobile int(20) NOT NULL default ' 0 ',	Mobile	094623838940
Fax int(20) NOT NULL default ' 0 ',	Fax	094623838940
E-mail varchar(30) NOT NULL default ",	E-mail – unique key	Simon.stobart@sunderland.ac.uk
Cardtype varchar(10) NOT NULL default ",	Card type	visa
Cardname varchar(40) NOT NULL default ",	Card name	stobbie
Cardnumber varchar(30) NOT NULL default ' 0 ',	Card number	12345678
Cardexpire varchar(10) NOT NULL default ",	Card expiry date	23/05/06

Table 39.7 Shipping table.

Field	Description	Example value
id int(10) NOT NULL auto_increment,	Key	0
Username varchar(20) NOT NULL default ",	User name	stobbie
Firstname varchar(30) NOT NULL default ",	First name	Simon
Surname varchar(30) NOT NULL default ",	Surname	Stobart
Address varchar(100) NOT NULL default ",	Address	University of Sunderland
City varchar(30) NOT NULL default ",	City	Sunderland
Postcode varchar(10) NOT NULL default ",	Postcode	SR6 0DD
Country varchar(20) NOT NULL default ",	Country	England
Telephone int(20) NOT NULL default ' 0 ',	Telephone	01915142838

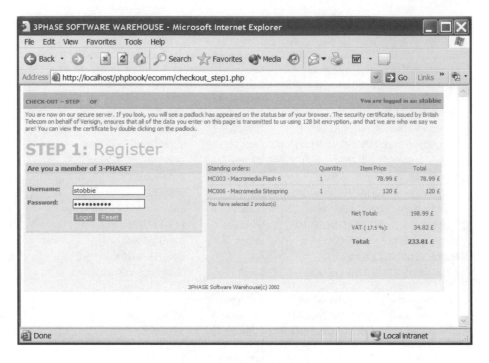

Figure 39.10 Purchasing step 1.

Table 39.8 Orders table.

Field	Description	Example value
id int(10) NOT NULL auto_increment,	Key	0
Username varchar(20) NOT NULL default ",	User name	stobbie
Pid varchar(20) NOT NULL default ' 0 ',	Product Id, linking to the product table.	MC003
Pname varchar(30) NOT NULL default ",	Product name	Macromedia Flash 6
Price varchar(10) NOT NULL default ",	Price	79.99
Quantity int(20) NOT NULL default ' 0 ',	Quantity	1
Currency varchar(40) NOT NULL default ",	Currency	Pounds
Date varchar(10) NOT NULL default ",	Date	14-07-2003
PTid int(20) NOT NULL default ' 0 ',	Product transaction ID	1
Status varchar(10) NOT NULL default ",		Pending

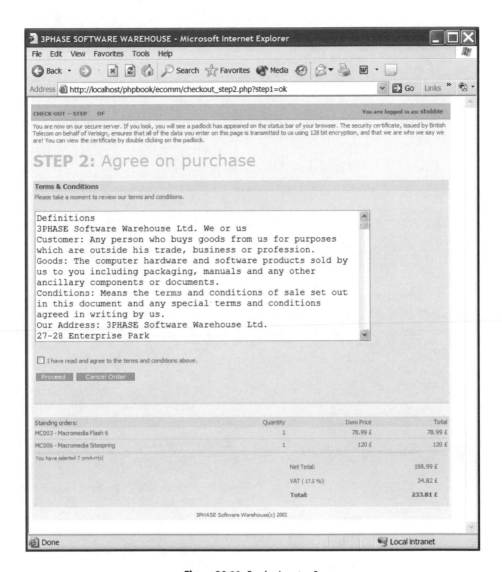

Figure 39.11 Purchasing step 2.

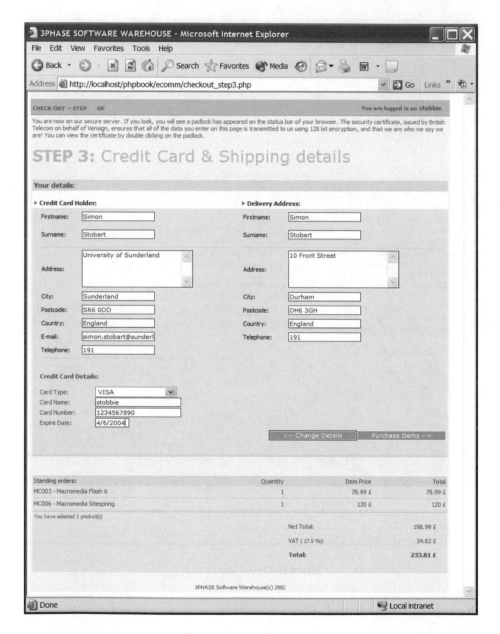

Figure 39.12 Purchasing step 3.

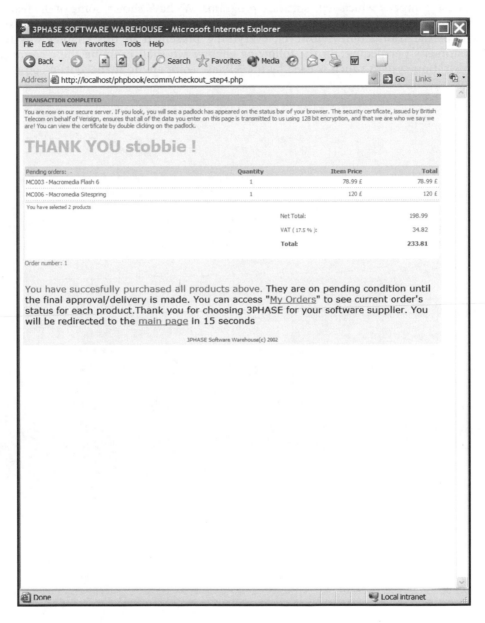

Figure 39.13 Thank you screen.

Summary

In this chapter we have described the front-end to the e-commerce system we have created for 3:Phase company which sells software programs. We have shown some of the features the system provides and described some of the database tables we have created to store records of the transactions. However, everything presented in this chapter was from the customer's perspective. In the following chapter we shall examine the e-commerce administration system which is used by the 3:Phase company to manage its e-commerce activities.

3:Phase E-Commerce System – Administration 40

Introduction

In this chapter we shall introduce the administration part of the e-commerce system which is hidden from the users and purchases of software from the 3:Phase company. Although most Web users never see the administration parts of the e-commerce systems they may use on a daily basis these back-end systems are just as important to the effective running of an e-commerce site as the front-end part of the system.

The E-Commerce Administration System

E-commerce administration systems typically enable the management of the products for sale, enabling the adding of new products, removing of obsolete products, updating stock levels and product descriptions etc. They also let us manage the orders placed by our customers and adjust member details if required. The following system implements only the most basic of facilities which would be required in a professional system.

Any changes to the group fields are stored in the groups table, illustrated in Table 40.1.

Table 40.1 Groups table.

Field	Description	Example value
id int(10) NOT NULL auto_increment,	Key	7
Name varchar(20) NOT NULL default ",	Unique key	Macromedia
Title varchar(40) NOT NULL default ",	Group title	Macromedia
Description text NOT NULL,	Description	Web development tools, animation application
Active tinyint(1) NOT NULL default ' 1 ',	Group active?	1

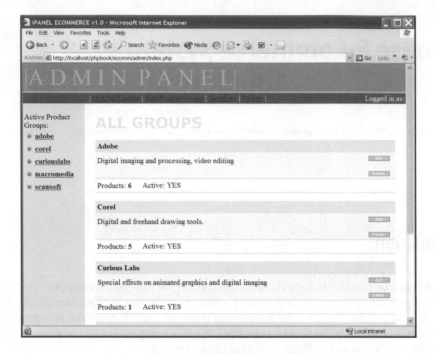

Figure 40.1 Administration main screen.

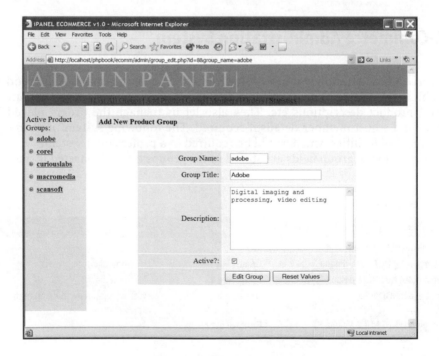

Figure 40.2 Edit a group screen.

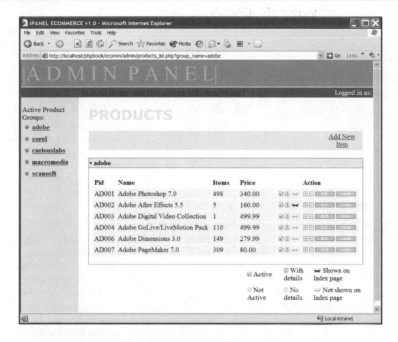

Figure 40.3 Products within a group list.

Figure 40.4 Edit Products screen.

Table 40.2 Products table. *TABLE REPEAT*

Field	Description	Example value
id int(10) NOT NULL auto_increment,	Key	17
Pgroup varchar(20) NOT NULL default ",	Product group	Macromedia
Pid varchar(10) NOT NULL default ' 0 ',	Unique key	MC004
Name varchar(30) NOT NULL default ",	Software name	Macromedia Freehand 10
Description text NOT NULL,	Description	Design once and publish across multiple mediums. Use FreeHand 10 to create extraordinary illustrations, design and organize Web site storyboards, and layout graphics-rich documents in a unique multi-page workspace
Price varchar(20) NOT NULL default ' 0 ',	Price	78.99
Items int(10) NOT NULL default ' 1 ',	Number of items in stock	197
Details text NOT NULL,	Full description.	Design once and publish across multiple mediums. Use FreeHand 10 to create extraordinary illustrations, design and organize Web site storyboards, and layout graphics-rich documents in a unique multi-page workspace. Easily produce superior Macromedia Flash movies, and test them right inside of FreeHand with the new Flash Navigation Panel.\r\n\r\nDo more with your designs. Macromedia Studio MX brings the power of FreeHand, Macromedia Flash, Dreamweaver, and Fireworks together, combining all four products in one tightly integrated, highly approachable solution. Learn more about Macromedia Studio MX
Url varchar(40) NOT NULL default ",	Home URL	http://www.macromedia.com
Image varchar(40) NOT NULL default ",	Image	boxshot_freehand10.jpeg
Active tinyint(1) NOT NULL default ' 1 ',	Product available for sale	1
Onindex tinyint(2) NOT NULL default ' 0 ',	Display on main index page	0
Lastupdated varchar(10) NOT NULL default ",	Last updated	21-5-2002

The Administration Main Screen

Figure 40.1 illustrates the main screen which welcomes the user to the administration system. You will note that its design is far more basic compared to the front-end system as there is no need to invest time and effort in the design of fancy graphics etc.

The main screen consists of a simple menu at the top of the screen. A list of all the product groups which have been created are displayed on the left and the main part of the screen is taken up with details of each group. Here, the group name, description, number of products within the group and whether the group is active is displayed. For each group two buttons enable the editing or deletion of the group. Clicking the edit button displays a form with the current values of the group inserted into the form fields. The user can alter

TABLE REPEAT

Table 40.3 User's table.

Field	Description	Example value
id int(10) NOT NULL auto_increment,	Key	1
Username varchar(20) NOT NULL default ",	Username - unique key	stobbie
Password varchar(32) NOT NULL default ",	Password (encrypted)	3b59fb8a38f8c1694d1576c62bde0bae
Firstname varchar(30) NOT NULL default ",	Firstname	Simon
Surname varchar(30) NOT NULL default ",	Surname	Stobart
Company varchar(30) NOT NULL default ",	Company	University of Sunderland
Address varchar(50) NOT NULL default ",	Address	University of Sunderland
City varchar(30) NOT NULL default ",	City	Sunderland
County varchar(30) NOT NULL default ",	County	Tyne and Wear
Postcode varchar(20) NOT NULL default ",	Postcode	SR6 0DD
Country varchar(20) NOT NULL default ",	Country	England
Telephone bigint(20) NOT NULL default ' 0 ',	Telephone	01915142838
Mobile bigint(20) NOT NULL default ' 0 ',	Mobile	094623838940
Fax bigint(20) NOT NULL default ' 0 ',	Fax	094623838940
E-mail varchar(30) NOT NULL default ",	E-mail – unique key	Simon.stobart@sunderland.ac.uk
Currency varchar(30) NOT NULL default ' pounds ',	Currency	Pounds
Regdate varchar(30) NOT NULL default ",	Registration date	
Purchases int(20) NOT NULL default ' 0 ',	Number of purchases	0
Logins int(20) NOT NULL default ' 0 ',	Number of logins	0

Table 40.4 Orders table.

Field	Description	Example value
id int(10) NOT NULL auto_increment,	Key	0
Username varchar(20) NOT NULL default ",	Username	stobbie
Pid varchar(20) NOT NULL default ' 0 ',	Product Id, linking to the product table.	MC003
Pname varchar(30) NOT NULL default ",	Product name	Macromedia Flash 6
Price varchar(10) NOT NULL default ",	Price	79.99
Quantity int(20) NOT NULL default ' 0 ',	Quantity	1
Currency varchar(40) NOT NULL default ",	Currency	Pounds
Date varchar(10) NOT NULL default ",	Date	14-07-2003
PTid int(20) NOT NULL default ' 0 ',	Product transaction ID	1
Status varchar(10) NOT NULL default ",		Pending

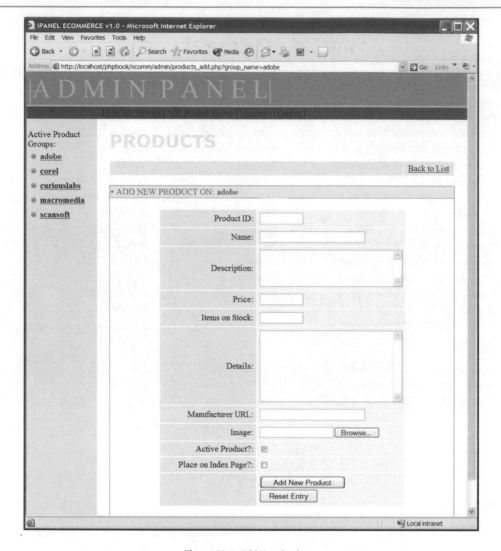

Figure 40.5 Add New Products.

these values and resave the group information. The edit a group screen is illustrated in Figure 40.2.

Add New Products Group

Clicking the Add Products Group menu option will display the same screen shown in Figure 40.2 but without the form fields completed. This allows the user to enter a new product group.

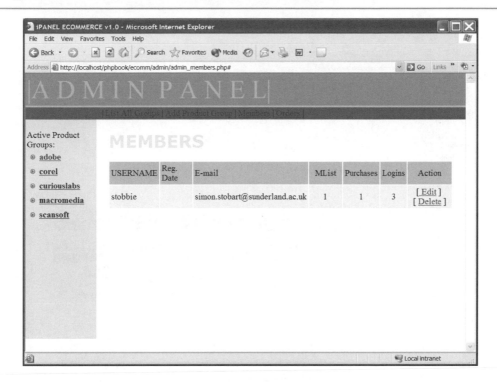

Figure 40.6 Edit Members.

Editing Products

If you return to the main screen which lists all product groups, by clicking the list all groups menu item you can edit the products that reside within a specific group. Select one of the groups from the active group list on the left of the screen. This will result in the products within that group being displayed on the screen, as shown in Figure 40.3.

For each product the product id, name, number of items in stock and price is displayed. Next to each product are three icons which indicate whether the product is active, whether they have a detailed description and whether they are to be displayed on the main index page. Next to these icons are four buttons. The first button is represented by a "+" character and clicking this will increase the amount of stock held for that product. The next button represented by a "-" character enables the amount of stock to be reduced. Finally, two buttons enable the product details to be edited or deleted from the system.

Clicking the edit button will display the Edit Products screen. This screen consists of a form with the current product details already inserted into the form fields, as shown in Figure 40.4.

The user is free to make any changes that are wanted and these are stored in the products table as shown in Table 40.2.

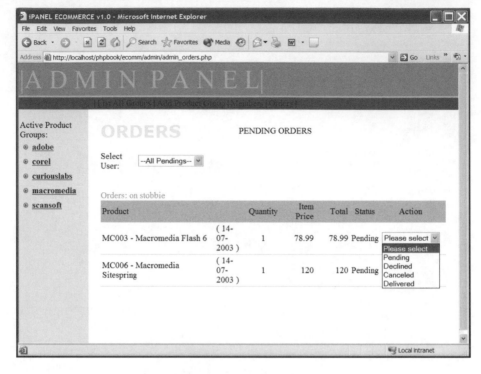

Figure 40.7 Process Orders screen.

Add New Products

You can also add new products to those in a group. Returning to the list of products screen, as shown in Figure 40.3, and clicking the Add New Item link at the top right of the screen will display the Add New Products screen, shown in Figure 40.5.

Edit Member Details

Clicking the members menu option allows you to adjust the member details or even delete a member. This screen is shown in Figure 40.6.

Changes to the member details will be reflected in the users table, given in Table 40.3.

Processing Orders

Clicking the Orders option from the menu will display the Process Orders screen. This screen is shown in Figure 40.7.

This screen displays all outstanding orders and enables the user to adjust the status of each order when it is completed and delivered to the customer. As an order's status is changed, this is reflected in the Orders table, shown in Table 10.4.

Note that in a real e-commerce system the tracking of orders would be much more sophisticated than shown here.

Summary

In this chapter we have described the e-commerce administration system. We have shown some of the features the system provides and described some of the database tables we have created to manage the purchasing of products and tracking of order transactions.

Summary

In this chapter, we have described the ... of ... ... system. We have shown some of the ... of the system-provisioning guide, which covers the database, ... should enhance the purchasing ... Purchasing, Inventory, and Reservation.

Index